YALE

HISTORICAL PUBLICATIONS

MISCELLANY

IV

ISSUED UNDER THE DIRECTION OF THE
DEPARTMENT OF HISTORY
FROM THE INCOME OF
THE FREDERICK JOHN KINGSBURY
MEMORIAL FUND

THE READJUSTER MOVEMENT
IN VIRGINIA

BY

CHARLES CHILTON PEARSON, Ph.D.

Professor of Political Science in Wake Forest College

GLOUCESTER, MASS.

PETER SMITH

1969

PREFACE

The half century just ended is the "Dark Age" of the South. Beginning with the attempt of Radicals to build upon the ruins of the old a foreign and ultra-democratic system, this period is probably now coming to its end in the educational and economic renaissance. And the overlapping of the two ages may be studied today, throughout the older South, in farm and factory, state debt and schools, in poor white and aristocrat and "substantial citizen," and in the still uncertain status of the negro citizen and voter.

After the brief reign of Radicalism, during the "Dark Age," came a time of reaction, when "Confederate Brigadiers" ruled, and the South was "solid." This was good. Times were exceedingly "hard," however, and heavy depression lay upon the spirit of the people. The excesses of Radicalism had disgusted many. So the gradual democratic advance discernible under the old system, to which war should have imparted a stimulus, was sharply checked.

During this time of reaction there occurred in most, if not all, of the Southern states a series of independent movements, some of which are still manifesting themselves. The earlier of these movements were aided by the vote of the negro; the later, by the prejudice against him. In all, however, the leaders professed themselves inspired with zeal for the interests of the common white man. And it is not improbable that, studied closely and together, these movements may prove to have been, in origin and effects, democratic—an outworking of forces strengthened by war but restrained by reaction, and, however crude and sordid, harbingers of the renaissance.

One of the earliest and most far-reaching of these movements occurred in Virginia. It gathered about a state debt of long and interesting history. Eventually it produced a leader of national importance. This study, however, is not primarily an account either of the debt or of Mahone and his machine. It is, rather, a chapter in the history of Virginia, from the Civil War to the first administration of Grover Cleveland, in which some of the forces that moulded the present state are shown in their operation; and in the showing the "Readjuster" claim to liberalism, democracy, and progress is tested and due record made of the achievements and solid worth of those who stood for conservatism, aristocracy, and scrupulous honesty.

Hearty thanks are due to many who have aided me. Some have loaned materials or given information, specific acknowledgment of which is made below. The Virginia State Library staff have been untiringly helpful and courteous. Under the encouragement of Professor William A. Dunning the task had its beginning; if its completion proves worth while, the credit is due primarily to the sympathetic interest and practical assistance of Professor Max Farrand. In preparing the manuscript for the press Professor C. M. Andrews has placed me under lasting obligations.

C. C. Pearson.

Wake Forest, N. C.,
   January 1, 1917.

CONTENTS

CHAPTER I

THE STATE DEBT AND THE OLD RÉGIME,
1784-1867

From the Revolution to the Civil War one of the most important economic and social activities of the state of Virginia was the furtherance of a system of "Public Works."[1]

There were four main stages in the legislation under which this system was developed. It was inaugurated in 1784 when the state became, through purchase, a minority stockholder in corporations created for the improvement of the James and Potomac rivers. Among the sponsors for this beginning were a Newton, a Taylor, an Ambler, and a Southall, names still honored in Virginia; and a peculiar but characteristic mingling of business and sentiment appeared in the gift by the commonwealth of shares to "George Washington, esquire," in appreciation of his "unexampled merits" and his interest in enterprises which, the legislature thought, would be "the durable monuments of his glory."[2] To the policy thus begun a decided impetus was imparted in 1816 when all the state's holdings in

[1] There is no adequate study of the social and economic aspects of this system. Sydenstricker and Burger's *School History of Virginia* (1914) gives a brief but correct account based on the work of Mr. Sydenstricker which is still in manuscript. C. H. Ambler, in his *Sectionalism in Virginia from 1776 to 1861*, has described its political bearings in elaborate and scholarly fashion.

[2] W. W. Hening, *Statutes at Large*, XI, pp. 450, 510, 525. *Cf.* G. S. Callender, *Economic History of the United States*, p. 335 (quoting).

such companies were converted into one fund pledged
for fifty years to the sole purpose of improving traffic
and communication and managed by a special "Board
of Public Works."[3] As the demands on this fund were
greater than could be met by it, the legislature in 1838
directed the board to obtain money for all authorized
improvements by selling state bonds.[4] This was an
important step; for it meant that the state was entering,
on credit, a business that was necessarily speculative.
Here, practically, began the state debt. Twelve years
later the fully developed policy was embodied in an act,
still in force when the Civil War began, under which the
board might borrow "from time to time, on the credit
of the state of Virginia, such sums of money as may be
needed to redeem the engagements of the state," which,
of course, included not only new investments but also
unearned interest.[5] In the development of this policy
the western counties were most insistent.[6]

Behind this policy lay one great purpose, clearly
indicated by the act of 1816 and adhered to with reasonable fidelity throughout the period. It was to knit
together and develop the commonwealth as an economic
unit. Such unity· was demanded by the state's geographic divisions, the rivalry of outside markets, and
the untouched wealth of the trans-Alleghany region.

[3] *Revised Code of the Laws of Virginia, 1819*, II, p. 201. The state's
holdings in banks were placed in the same fund.

[4] *Code of Virginia, 1849*, p. 342; *Journal of the Senate of the Commonwealth of Virginia*, 1877-1878, Doc. XXIV, being a report of the committee
on finance, prepared by Bradley T. Johnson. This journal will be cited
hereafter as Sen. *Jour.*, the corresponding one of the House as House *Jour.*
Documents are to be found (unless otherwise indicated) in the appendix
of each.

[5] *Code of Virginia, 1860*, p. 386.

[6] Brief of Attorney-General William A. Anderson, in *Virginia vs. West
Virginia, Supreme Court of the U. S., October term, 1909. Original Record*,
p. 5.

Railroads, canals, turnpikes, were thought the best instrumentalities; so for these the state borrowed and spent. Powerful business interests, antagonistic sections, political parties all tried to shape the system in their own behalf, but none seriously opposed it as a whole. And when, in 1861, the policy was abruptly terminated, it had pre-empted the natural lines of commerce.[7]

The prevailing method of investment was determined in part by this dominant purpose and in part by the tendency of local capital to lock itself up in lands and labor. Instead of building and owning outright, the state endeavored to entice capital into transportation ventures by chartering stock companies therefor and itself becoming a partner in them. Terms too strict would have defeated the end; and so the state was generally less well secured than private undertakers; and often very poorly secured.[8] But the results obtained were distinctly creditable. For the thirty-five millions[9] which the state had invested down to 1861, it had secured, besides smaller improvements, a canal from Richmond to the Valley and a railroad system which cost nearly seventy millions and which was nearly half as long in miles as that of all New England.[10]

[7] *Cf.* Anderson, *op. cit.*, and Ambler, *Sectionalism, passim;* Charles Bruce, *Speech in the Senate of Virginia on the Internal Improvement Policy of the State, February 16, 1858* (1858).

[8] See terms of act of 1816, *op. cit.; Messages and Documents*, 1861-1862, No. 8; Bruce, *op. cit.;* Governor, *Message*, March 8, 1870. The governor's messages will be found in both Sen. *Jour.* and House *Jour.* under date of messages; they will be cited by date only.

[9] Round numbers will be used wherever exactness is not necessary to clearness.

[10] Expenditure figures are taken from *Messages and Documents*, 1861-1862, No. 8, table J; railroad figures from *American Railroad Journal*, January 5, 1861. $1,784,000 was spent by the state without the aid of a stock company. The total length of the railroad system was 2,483 miles;

The extent to which this policy dominated all other social and economic activities of the state finds striking illustration in its attitude toward education.[11] A "Literary Fund," nominally created in 1810 by the segregation of certain small revenues, was firmly established in 1816 by turning into it the proceeds of a large war debt which the federal government had paid, the whole being solemnly pledged to educational purposes. This fund appears to have been honestly handled and was gradually increased until in 1860 it amounted to over a million and three-quarters of dollars invested mainly in state bonds. Most of the income from it and all the poll tax receipts after 1851 were regularly apportioned to the counties and towns. But the education offered was intended only for confessed indigents selected in aristocratic fashion by a board of local officials. The schools used were private with but nominal public supervision. Only in rare cases was assistance extended beyond the most elementary stages. Not unfittingly was the system often called the "pauper system,"[12] a name which expressed the fundamental idea of the ruling class that a man's children should be educated by himself, in proportion to his social status. Any considerable education of the masses, they believed,

in operation, 1,805 miles. The amount invested in railroads by the state was some twenty millions. The estimates of B. T. Johnson (*op. cit.*) are somewhat larger.

[11] State Superintendent of Public Instruction, *Reports*, especially for 1871 and 1878, printed separately and in *Annual Reports of Officers, Boards and Institutions of the Commonwealth of Virginia*. Reports in the latter collection will be cited (as above) under name of the reporting official or official board. See also House *Jour.*, 1838, Doc. 4; *Documents and Messages*, 1861-1862, No. 7; A. D. Mayo, *Education in Southwest Virginia;* Ambler, *Sectionalism*, ch. IX; G. W. Dyer, *Democracy in the South before the Civil War*. No account is taken here of appropriations to professional or collegiate institutions.

[12] This term was used in other states at similar stages of public school development.

must lead to unrest which could result only in disappointment or in "levelling." Only when charity absolutely demanded it should the state intervene.[13] Yet, despite the tremendous power of such opinion, the annual amount thus spent increased from $44,000 in 1836 to $214,000 in 1860, and the number thus "educated," from 18,000 to 62,000—which meant that by 1860 the state was paying the tuition of one-half of those at school within the limits of the present Virginia. Moreover, in some western counties and in parts of the older section open to outside influences, the desire for state aid had prompted experiments in schools supported jointly by state and local governments and free, or nearly free, to all. These facts, together with the reports sent in to Richmond by local officials, irregular and imperfect though they were, seem to demonstrate clearly that the old aristocratic idea was giving way before the new and democratic impulse.[14] Could a direct issue have been forced, the latter must have triumphed. But eastern Virginia had now become politically and financially committed to the policy of internal improvements, while the western part of the state, always the leader in democratic movements, was too much absorbed in its desire for more railroads and more turnpikes,[15] to put the matter to a test.

On the whole, fiscal conditions and prospects in 1860 appeared to be satisfactory. There was, indeed, a

[13] Professor Dyer thinks otherwise: "The method of Virginia may be criticised, but the motive was thoroughly democratic," *Democracy in the South*, p. 77.

[14] Another defect, inherent in the dominant theory, was the lack of co-ordination and adequate supervision. Strongly backed attempts had been made to remedy this also.

[15] Ambler, *Sectionalism, passim*. Professor Ambler attributes the unusual activity in building public works from 1850 to 1860 to the program for a united South. *Ibid.*, 311.

bonded debt of $33,000,000.[16] But offsetting this were
assets of a face value of $43,000,000, consisting chiefly
of the stocks and bonds of the railroads and canals.[17]
As yet less than one-fifth of these were yielding the state
an income; but most of the rest, as most of the debt, had
been accumulated only within the last decade, and time
was needed to make extensions and develop the western
trade, for which purpose charters had already been
issued and appropriations authorized.[18] That the debt
had trebled within the last decade and would probably
continue to increase under the operation of the act of
1850 was certainly ominous. But, on the other hand, the
constitution adopted in 1850 removed old dangers by
forbidding the state to guarantee corporate liabilities
or release the corporations from their obligations to it.
The constitution also provided for a sinking fund which
must be adequate, safe, and unimpairable in times of
peace, and into which must be converted the proceeds
of any assets sold.[19] Back of debt and speculative
assets was a settled population of over a million and a
half, two-thirds of which was white, and property worth
over a billion dollars. From dividends and from taxes
on polls, incomes, property, and business licenses the
state derived an annual revenue of over four millions,[20]
of which less than one million was needed for the ordinary purposes of government.[21] Back of all this was a
record of fiscal honor which none was disposed to tarnish

[16] Exclusive of the bonds owned by the literary and sinking funds,
Messages and Documents, 1861-1862, No. 8. There was a small sterling
debt.

[17] *Ibid.*, table T.

[18] *Ibid.*, table K. There appears to have been no ''water'' in the stock
of these ''public works.''

[19] F. N. Thorpe, *American Charters, Constitutions, and Organic Laws*,
VII, 3841-3842. This will be cited as *Thorpe*.

[20] Auditor, *Report*, 1861-1862.

[21] *Cf.* p. 54.

by questioning the honesty of the debt or the state's ability to pay it. State bonds in the first half of 1860 sold above 90.[22]

When the Civil War was over, the state's great system of public works was an utter ruin.[23] The canal lay incomplete, dismantled, profitless—"a great gash across the heart of the commonwealth." Though, bit by bit, the railroads patched up their worn-out rails and rolling-stock, rebuilt burned bridges and depots, and opened for business, yet it was all too obvious that they must have time and a great deal of money before they either paid dividends or met the needs of the people.[24] Western Virginia, for the development of which these railroads had been built so largely, and to which the worn-out eastern counties had looked for a lightening of taxes, was now gone, a full third of the old state.

Sadly reduced, too, was the people's tax-paying capacity.[25] "By the abolition of slavery and of the 'Confederate debt,'" said the *Commercial and Financial Chronicle*,[26] "nearly the whole of the accumulated and available capital of the South was practically annihilated." Of the rest, that which had been invested directly in the public works brought little return or none, and that which had been invested in state bonds, perhaps

22 For favorable opinion see *Journal of Banking, Currency and Finance*, January, 1860.

23 Contemporary newspapers; "Personal Recollections."

24 *American Railroad Journal*, July 1, 15, 29; September 9, 23; October 14; November 4, 1865; also, 1866, 1867, 1868, *passim*.

25 An interesting report on the losses of war, made by a committee consisting of ex-Governor William Smith, W. T. Taliaferro, and T. J. Armstrong, and adopted by the House, January 13, 1877, was as follows: personal property, $116,000,000; realty, $121,000,000; internal improvements, $26,000,000; banking capital, $15,000,000; circulation, $12,000,000; state's interest in banks, $4,000,000; slaves and other property, $163,-000,000.

26 January 18, 1868.

the greater part of the whole debt,[27] was shrunk two-thirds in market value. Farm lands, long deteriorating, now through the necessary change in labor system had become less desirable from a social point of view, and less productive, too, even where the ex-slave settled down on a wage or crop-sharing basis.[28] As offsets there were, indeed, high prices for tobacco, corn, and wheat, and a rise of land values in and about the towns, which was caused by the shifting of the native population and the incoming of outsiders.[29] But, despite the excellent credit of Virginia farmers abroad, to borrow on lands divorced from slaves was difficult.[30] Yet borrow one must for fences, for farming implements and livestock, for houses, for mills—for almost everything which four years of business stagnation and ruthless devastation could destroy. With state assets and the tax-paying power of the people fully two-thirds reduced, what hope was there for the payment of the public debt now increased by war time interest to $38,000,000?[31]

The legislature which faced this almost hopeless

[27] Governor, *Message*, December 4, 1865. In 1887 ex-Governor Peirpoint stated that 80 per cent was supposed to be owned in Virginia just after the war, E. H. Hancock, *Autobiography of John E. Massey*, p. 120 (cited hereafter as Massey, *Autobiography*). Wm. L. Royall, *History of the Virginia State Debt Controversy*, p. 6, and John P. McConnell, in *The South in the Building of the Nation*, I, p. 133, appear to hold a contrary opinion. The sale to outsiders was rapid. In 1874 it was estimated that only one-fourth was owned in Virginia, Second Auditor, *Report*, 1874.

[28] B. B. Munford, *Virginia's Attitude toward Slavery and Secession*, ch. 19; B. W. Arnold, *History of the Tobacco Industry in Virginia*, ch. 2.

[29] The increase in the number of whites at work was at least offset by the waste in the general transition; nor should the increase be estimated too highly, Callender, *Economic History*, p. 783, and Dyer, in *The South in the Building of the Nation*, X, ch. 9.

[30] See Ruffin in Richmond *Whig*, Sept. 25, 1874. *Cf.* below pp. 25-27, 44.

[31] Governor, *Message*, December 4, 1865. The literary and sinking funds are not included, and will not be in future statements of the amount of the debt.

situation in December, 1865, was the last one thoroughly characteristic of *ante-bellum* Virginia.[32] Its acts, therefore, are important not only as immediately affecting fiscal affairs but also as disclosing mental and moral attitudes, the stubborn yielding of which to changed conditions forms a large part of the history of the next generation.

Foremost among the important matters to which Governor Peirpoint called the attention of this legislature was the state debt, for the payment of the interest on which bondholders were "pressing." Several honorable courses lay open. The legislature might delay action pending a settlement with West Virginia, for which the organic laws of both states provided.[33] By so doing it would secure the aid of powerful private interests in compelling a settlement, and thus definitely limit the state's obligations. It might frankly recognize that the state was bankrupt and seek a compromise with creditors, for men afterwards said that fifty per cent in new bonds would have been

[32] Richmond *Enquirer*, March 3, 1866. Under Lincoln's plan of reconstruction as amended by Johnson the hitherto shadowy government of "loyal" Virginia, administered from Alexandria for the most part, was extended to all Virginia. Peirpoint was governor. The legislature was chosen on practically the same basis as before the war, Eckenrode, *Political Reconstruction of Virginia*, ch. 3. John B. Baldwin was speaker of the House.

[33] The constitution of West Virginia and the act of the "loyal" Virginia legislature assenting to the division of the state clearly created a contract between the two states under which their legislatures were to adjust the debt. The act of Congress admitting the new state ratified this contract. The secession convention at Wheeling, August 3, 1861, had specified terms of adjustment, but these were not mentioned in any of the above documents and were expressly repudiated by the constitution of "loyal" Virginia (*Thorpe*, VII, 3862). The United States Supreme Court decided in 1870 (11 *Wall.*, 39) that a contract had been created as above, and, in 1911, that the Wheeling terms were only a "preliminary suggestion" (220 *U. S.*, 1).

accepted.[34] Instead, by act of March 2, 1866, the legislature not only assumed full responsibility for the entire
ante-bellum principal but also authorized the funding of
the entire war-time interest into bonds bearing the same
rate of interest as the principal, payment of interest on
the whole to begin the following year. This action was
the utmost that any creditor asked. It was taken without
a hint of improper influences and without recorded
opposition.[35]

Chief among the reasons for this policy was a scrupulous regard for the state's unblemished fiscal record.[36]
Another was the attitude toward West Virginia. Ignoring the tendency of fifty years[37] and the events of the
last four years, the members of the legislature issued
a confident "appeal to their brethren of West Virginia"
for the "restoration of the ancient commonwealth of
Virginia, with all her people, and up to her former
boundaries," and appointed a commission to effect it.
Only after the commission had failed in this effort was
it to treat for a division of the public debt and assets.[38]

At the second session of the legislature the debt question was re-opened. West Virginia had taken no action.
Crops had been poor. Private debts were pressing and
there was talk of scaling them. Why, men asked here

[34] A very interesting suggestion was offered by J. Willcox Brown, later
a banker of Virginia and Baltimore, that after assuming the debt and
levying taxes therefor the state should invite some English bankers to act
as trustees, take over her assets and make the best possible terms. Such
a course might have changed the entire *post-bellum* history, *Brown Papers*.

[35] *Acts of the General Assembly of the State of Virginia, passed in 1865-
1866*, p. 79; House and Senate *Journals*, 1865-1866, index; Governor, *Message*, December 4, 1865; contemporary *Whig, Enquirer*.

[36] This record was mentioned by foreign creditors time and again. The
faith of English business concerns in Virginia farmers was similarly
strong. See "Financial Relief That Might Have Been," *Brown Papers*.

[37] Ambler, *Sectionalism, passim*.

[38] *Acts*, 1865-1866, p. 453 (being joint resolution of February 28, 1866).

and there, should not the public debt be scaled in proportion to losses? In this "wild talk" lay the germ of
repudiation.[39] But the legislature formally reprobated
such sentiments, discussed nothing more dangerous than
declining responsibility for West Virginia's share—a
suggestion endorsed by some creditors—and, finally,
regretting its inability to do more, authorized the payment of four instead of six per cent interest for the
current year, "that being the amount which this state
feels obliged to pay until there is a settlement of
accounts between this state and West Virginia."[40]
Holders of coupon bonds could, of course, receive full
interest by presenting their coupons for taxes or other
state dues, and the same privilege was accorded holders
of registered bonds.[41] To meet the interest voted and
the expenses of government, the relatively high tax of
thirty cents was imposed on personalty and on realty
as valued in 1856.[42] No pressure appears to have been

[39] Governor, *Message*, December 3, 1866; Auditor, *Report*, 1866; *American Annual Cyclopedia*, 1866, article "Virginia." The last (which became
Appleton's with 1876) will be cited as *Annual Cyc.*, and all references not
otherwise indicated will be to "Virginia." The *Whig*, however, declared
that it had heard of no desire to scale the public debt prior to the governor's
message.

[40] *Acts*, 1866-1867, December 20, March 21; editorial résumé of daily
debates in *Whig* and *Enquirer*. For positions of these papers on the debt
see *Enquirer*, December 5, 1866, and *Whig*, March 19, 20, 22, 1867. The
vote on the act appropriating four per cent was: House, 58 to 18; Senate,
17 to 2. James Branch, of Thomas Branch & Co., bankers and brokers of
Richmond, suggested a compromise with creditors on the basis of 6 per
cent bonds for seventy per cent of the debt and certificates of West
Virginia's indebtedness for the rest, *Enquirer*, February 4, 1867. The best
people of West Virginia, in the opinion of Mr. Septimus Hall who has given
this phase much study, desired at this time to make a settlement.

[41] Act of April 25, 1867.

[42] Thirty cents on each $100, the customary statement of the tax rate in
this state. Valuation for taxation was called "assessing"; this was made
annually for personalty, every five years for realty. There were other
taxes.

used to obtain these results. Yet by this time it was certain that the state would be degraded, as no state had ever been degraded under the Congressional reconstruction measures. Moreover, bonds were rapidly passing out of the hands of native owners. Hints were, indeed, thrown out to the North by the *Whig*[43] that repudiation of private and public debts might be invited. But the legislature appeared blind alike to economic conditions and to the possibilities of compromise, sensitive only to the old ideas of honor.

Viewed from the debt standpoint only, the question of the state's assets[44] was quite simple: Should they be sold at once to reduce the immediate burden or should they be retained as a source of future revenue? Past policy and the prevailing confidence in the future suggested the latter; the burden of the interest and the cheapness of state bonds urged the former. But as these assets consisted chiefly of the stocks and bonds of railroads within the state, the transportation problem must also be considered.

Under the old policy the natural routes for great railroads had been pre-empted.[45] From north to south connecting short lines crossed the state at two points. One could go from Norfolk on the coast to Bristol in the far west by using three roads—the Norfolk and Petersburg, the Southside, and the Virginia and Tennessee. From Richmond to Covington in Alleghany County ran the Virginia Central. Charters had been issued and appropriations authorized to continue these westward lines, the one through Cumberland Gap, the other through the undeveloped Greenbrier county to the

[43] December 5, 12, 1866; March 20, 1867.

[44] For condition, see Governor, *Message*, December 4, 1865.

[45] With the exception of that of the Virginian Railroad, recently constructed.

Ohio, both seeking the Mississippi. Among these and the other numerous short lines a fair degree of unity had been attained, because through the Board of Public Works, as a kind of holding company, the state subscriptions had been made and the state stock voted.[46] But all of these roads now needed money,[47] and this the state could no longer supply directly, or indirectly.[48] The needs of commerce, therefore, seemed to demand, as the governor kept insisting, that the old policy should give way to private ownership and consolidated management.[49]

To this problem of the state's assets the legislature addressed itself at greater length and with more heat than to any other. Advocates of immediate reduction of the debt principal, supported by private interests, urged a general sale to the highest bidder.[50] But it was too much, so frankly to declare Virginia bankrupt and so completely to reverse the policy of the past. Most of the roads were, indeed, permitted to buy out the state's interests in them. They were permitted also to combine their managements. But each permission was carefully hedged about with restrictions and guarantees

[46] F. A. Magruder, *Recent Administration in Virginia*, p. 147.

[47] *Cf. American Railroad Journal*, October 23; November 4; December 16, 1865.

[48] *Thorpe*, VII, 3861-3862.

[49] There is nowhere a full description of the situation, see Governor, *Message*, December, 1865 and 1866; *Enquirer*, January 30, 31; March 7; Richmond *Dispatch*, January 23, 31, February 6, 23; *Whig*, March 6, April 19, 1867.

[50] A bill to this effect attached as a rider to the act of March 21, 1867, for payment of interest on the public debt passed the House, *Jour.*, 1866-1867, extra sess., pp. 63-64. For the long fight against outside control, see Ambler, *Sectionalism*, index, under "Baltimore and Ohio." Objections are succinctly given in *Whig*, December 8, 1866; see also *Enquirer*, March 21, 22; *Dispatch*, March 21, 1867. Motives appear in various resolutions, *e.g.*, House *Jour.*, 1865-1866, pp. 65, 377; *ibid.*, 1866-1867, pp. 12, 132, 208.

intended to prevent monopoly and to secure long-desired extensions, quite in conformity with the state's former policy.[51]

Similarly, other acts of this legislature showed it to be following old prevailing tendencies, often failing to grasp or deliberately ignoring new conditions. No attempt was made to compel an equitable compromise of old private debts, the security for which was gone in whole or in part. Instead, acts merely staying their collection until 1869 were passed.[52] With loanable funds commanding from ten to fifty per cent, pleas for a relaxation of the six per cent legal rate were refused.[53] As slavery had been patriarchal, so now equally patriarchal was the legislation directly affecting the freedman: if the latter stayed at home and attended to his work, he was better protected than the ignorant white; if he insisted upon being idle, he was practically remanded to servitude; if he committed crime, his own race could testify for or against him, but only before white judges and juries.[54] Though old appropriations to collegiate and professional schools were revived, elementary education was neglected.[55]

Outside the legislature, also, old forces reasserted themselves. The ex-planter paid his negroes a share of

[51] Out of such acts, when supplemented by further concessions, were to grow the Atlantic, Mississippi and Ohio, the Virginia Midland, and the Chesapeake and Ohio, Acts of April 18, February 14, March 1, 1867.

[52] Acts of March 2, 1866; March 2, 1867.

[53] Governor, *Message*, December, 1866; *Whig*, January 29; February 3, 1866. J. Willcox Brown gives details of an English scheme to lend five million dollars at six and one-half per cent on security of Virginia farm lands which was blocked by this refusal, *Brown Papers*.

[54] *Acts*, 1865-1867, pp. 83, 84, 89, 91; Eckenrode, *Political Reconstruction*, ch. 3; McConnell, *Negroes and their Treatment*, chs. 6, 7, 8.

[55] An argument advanced against the levying of taxes for debt interest at this time was that the proceeds might be used by the federal government to support public schools, *Whig*, March 20, 1867.

the crop instead of board and clothes. Grown men
studied law as they would have been doing three or four
years before had there been no war. Among the newspapers, the *Enquirer* and the *Whig* again dictated public
opinion, seldom agreeing. Far behind, the *Dispatch*
gathered news and talked business. Men wanted to
revive their old party lines.[56] When a party convention met, there was the old oligarchical dominance.[57]
Nowhere do we meet with new ideas, nowhere with an
adequate appreciation of what had happened; but everywhere we find infinite patience with the ex-slave, a stubborn clinging to what was deemed honor, and a strange
capacity for silent, cheerful suffering.

Thus before the Civil War Virginia concentrated her
economic activities upon a system of public works, with
the result that in 1861 she possessed assets in railroads
and canals of great potential value but offset by a very
large public debt. There was an increasing demand for
state participation in public education and the like. But
this demand was met only partially because it conflicted
at once with the policy of internal improvements and
with the individualistic and aristocratic ideas of the
ruling class. Consequently, state expenditures were
small and taxes light, and the credit of the state was
excellent. The first legislature after the war was representative of the old régime. Though the balance
between debt and assets had been fearfully upset, this
legislature recognized the debt as absolutely binding and
tried to provide for interest payment. Most of the railroad assets, it permitted to pass into private hands but
under careful restrictions. It made no provision whatever for schools or charities. In these and most other

[56] Below, p. 20.
[57] Below, p. 20.

respects the old ruling class showed itself to be adhering to past policies and standards. New ideas appearing were the consolidation of railroads, which was grudgingly and partially accepted, and the scaling of public and private debts, which was not seriously considered.

CHAPTER II

RADICALISM, 1867-1869

Hard upon this conservative legislature came the "Radical" constitutional convention of 1867-1869.[1] Called to "reconstruct" the state according to Congressional mandate, this convention in both its membership and its acts savored much of outside influences, and was characterized by ignorance and self-seeking. None the less, both its acts and its membership indicated, in however absurdly exaggerated form, social forces released or newly created that would have to be dealt with in the future.

Negroes, "scalawags," and "carpet-baggers" predominated, with only a few scions of the old régime to hector and oppose them. Unmindful of economic conditions, they struck "frugality" from the ancient Bill of Rights; but mindful of the freedmen to whom they owed their unwonted prominence, they inserted the "equal civil and political rights and public privileges" of all citizens.[2] These two alterations give the key to their plan of government.

[1] "Radical" and "Republican" were ordinarily used without distinction, and will be so used herein. This sketch, based on Eckenrode, *Political Reconstruction,* the convention journals, and the contemporary Richmond newspapers, is intended to show only the popular and expansive features of the constitution.

[2] Section 15 of the Bill of Rights as adopted in 1851 read: "That no free government, or the blessings of liberty, can be preserved to any people but by a firm adherence to justice, moderation, temperance, frugality, and virtue, and by a frequent recurrence to fundamental principles." Compare this with section 17 in the document as adopted in 1869. Section 20

Suffrage was to be based on manhood; jury service
and office-holding, on suffrage.[3]   Where before some
twenty officials had served the average county's needs,
there was now to be a minimum of forty-eight, all elected
for short terms and mostly by "townships" or smaller
territorial divisions so that power might not gravitate
into strong hands and "the people" lose their rights.
For similar reasons judicial power was transferred from
the old county board of justices to a county judge, and
above him was the circuit court, above it the supreme
court, forming a complex and costly system.   All of
these judges were dependent upon the legislature for
appointment, salary, and possibly tenure.   The legislature was also empowered to appoint all administrative
officials except three, including all school officials, the
Board of Public Works, and such other boards as it
might be pleased to establish.   Instead of the old system
of public aid doled out to indigents for education, a
uniform system of schools, free to all classes, adequately
supervised, and liberally supported by specified funds
and taxes, was to be established at once, and by 1876
extended equally and fully to all the counties and towns.
The burden of taxation should no longer fall upon the
poor; for the state might levy no poll tax above one
dollar, and the local government none above fifty cents,
and all other taxation should be *ad valorem*.[4]

Significant for the future was the attitude of the convention toward debts.   The wild talk of 1866[5] now took
the form of many resolutions offered by Radical mem-

of the latter reads: ''That all citizens of the state are hereby declared to
possess equal civil and political rights and public privileges.''

[3] For the attempted disqualification of Confederates see below.

[4] A few specified license taxes and cases where values could not be
ascertained form exceptions to the general principle.   Business capital and
incomes over $600 were taxed as other property.

[5] Above, p. 10.

bers to scale or repudiate private obligations, which
resulted in an unusual number of petty exemptions. In
close connection with these resolutions were similar,
though less vigorous, attacks upon the public debt.[6]
Efforts of conservative men, including some Radicals,
secured recognition of the latter in the constitution.[7]
But between the policy of protecting a huge public debt
and the policy of expensive and popular government
there was, under the impoverished conditions prevailing,
an incompatibility as striking as that between the old
and the new elements of the convention.

Had the Radicals been allowed to carry out the terms
of this constitution, rampant democracy would unquestionably have had full play for years to come, and one
can only conjecture the extremes to which it would
probably have gone. But by inserting clauses disfranchising many ex-Confederates,[8] the convention, alarmed
and disgusted almost the entire white population, and,
as the whites were in a decided majority, made possible
the victory of moderate men. Two steps were taken in
reaching this end.

The first to move were the extreme men of the old
school. Confronted with the probable loss not only of
their political power and their private property but also
of their highly prized civilization, and fearful of "Africanization" and "Yankeeizing,"[9] they determined to
defeat the constitution at the polls even though they

[6] The printed journals are incomplete and unindexed. See, however,
pp. 150, 442-444, 519, 705.

[7] Thorpe, VII, 3894-3895. This was contrary to the general rule in the
new constitutions of the Southern states, Dunning, Reconstruction, p. 207.

[8] Thorpe, VII, 3876. The "test oath" (ibid., 3877) would have excluded
all ex-Confederates from office.

[9] This feeling is vividly expressed in private correspondence of the time,
see Ruffner Papers; Memoirs of Gov. William Smith; T. J. Johnson, Robert
E. Dabney.

knew that this would probably mean a long continuation of military rule. Meeting in state conventions dominated by two or three *ante-bellum* leaders, they planned a complete organization under the name "Conservative," and nominated a state ticket.[10]   Their success would ultimately have meant no extravagance, no corruption, and no repudiation; no democratic local government and no concentration of power in the legislature; no common schools, no extensive public charities; no jury service or office-holding for the negroes.   An aristocratic and individualistic society, with as little governmental activity as possible and that little directed by the fittest, was the remedy for the distempers of the times thus boldly prescribed a second time by "Bourbons."[11]

To avoid the dilemma of negro rule on one side or military rule on the other, a "new movement" was begun.   Before the elections for the constitutional convention, many substantial citizens, aided by the ardent pro-Southern *Whig,* had already given strong evidence of their desire to "co-operate" with the Republican party for the restoration of the state to the Union on the basis of universal suffrage and equal civil and political rights.   The movement, however, lacked distinctive leadership and died almost still-born.[12]   After the convention and the Republican victory in the election of 1868, the idea revived in the form of an agree-

[10] *Dispatch* and *Whig,* December 12, 13, 1867; May 7, 8, 1868.   Col. R. E. Withers was nominated for governor.   Raleigh T. Daniel, John B. Baldwin, and A. H. H. Stuart were leaders.   Their dominance was, of course, due to the crisis and the trust imposed in them.   It was exercised largely through a "committee on business," named by the chairman, which shaped all matters before the convention, including party organization.   *Cf.* below, pp. 39, 49.

[11] Though the term "Bourbon" was little used until later, it will be employed here to designate the ultra-conservatives and their ideas.   We should remember that many changed their views soon after this.

[12] Eckenrode, *Political Reconstruction,* ch. 5.

ment between groups of moderate leaders in both parties, heartily supported by the *Whig,* for the adoption of the constitution without the disfranchising clause, and the election of respectable Republican state officials and a moderate legislature.[13] Having obtained permission, through the favor of President Grant, to vote for the constitution without the objectionable clause, these men next induced the "True Republican" faction[14] to endorse their plan and nominate for governor Gilbert C. Walker, a carpet-bagger Republican, but a moderate and intelligent man, strongly connected in Congressional circles. Though many Bourbons objected bitterly to this procedure, all of them yielded to its manifest advantages (some perhaps with mental reservations),[15] and withdrew their candidate.[16] Thereupon the masses of the whites rallied under the old name, "Conservative," in support of the movement. In this way originated the Conservative party of the future.

The significance of these events lay, undoubtedly, in the preference of the white masses for moderation instead of for Radicalism or Bourbonism. Pregnant

[13] For full narrative accounts see *A Narrative of the Leading Incidents,* etc., by A. H. H. Stuart, who is credited by Eckenrode (*Political Reconstruction,* ch. 7) with having initiated the move; "New Virginia," in *Whig,* February 4, 1885; and Frank G. Ruffin in *Dispatch,* October 30, 1880, emphasizing Mahone's share. For national interest and approval see New York *Herald,* January 3, 16; April 8, 29; New York *Times,* April 9, 1869.

[14] *Cf.* Rhodes, *History of the United States since 1850,* VI, 304. Mr. Rhodes's quotation cannot be applied to this faction in Virginia.

[15] *Enquirer, passim;* R. E. Withers, *Autobiography of an Octogenarian,* pp. 275 ff.; *Memoirs of Gov. William Smith,* pp. 263, 269, 276. The following ironic telegram (New York *Times,* July 8, 1869) to President Grant from R. T. Daniel excited mirth among Richmond Bourbons: "I congratulate you upon the triumph of your policy in Virginia. The gratitude of the people for your liberality is greatly enlivened by the overwhelming majority by which that policy prevails."

[16] At a meeting of the old Conservative central committee and county "superintendents," *Annual Cyc.,* 1869.

with meaning for the future, also, and of no little immediate importance, was the fact that the most efficient
of the new leaders were city men and represented large
business interests. Thus, Walker, at this time a banker
of Norfolk, was interested in Virginia bonds. Franklin
Stearns, a Republican who had been considered for the
gubernatorial nomination, appears to have been closely
associated with large railroad interests centering in
Richmond, with which the management of the *Dispatch*,
likewise a supporter of the movement, was also soon
associated. Though attracting little public notice, none
was more active than Gen. William Mahone, president
of the Atlantic, Mississippi and Ohio Railroad. To him
and to his numerous correspondents the success of
Walker meant the success of ''consolidation,'' for the
nominees of both the Radicals and the Bourbons were
bitterly hostile to his plans.[17]

Despite the concessions of the whites, the negroes
voted by a very large majority for the Radical candidate
and disfranchisement. None the less, the ''new movement'' won an easy victory. Under the deft guidance
of Walker and his advisers[18] and with pledges to abide

---

[17] Below, p. 27. Col. R. E. Withers, the Bourbon nominee, was closely
associated with the extreme Lynchburg opposition to Mahone's control of
the Va. & Tenn., Withers, *Autobiography*, pp. 242 ff. Governor Wells, the
Radical nominee, had tried to sell this road to the B. & O. Railroad (Eckenrode, *Political Reconstruction*, p. 117) and he appears to have received
B. & O. support during this campaign. Among those who assisted Mahone
were: J. F. Slaughter, of Lynchburg; Geo. W. Bolling, of Petersburg; V. D.
Groner and R. H. Glass, of Norfolk, Robert M. Hughes, of Abingdon. See
also letters of John W. Johnston, G. K. Gilmer, of Richmond; H. W.
Holliday, and ex-Governor Peirpoint, *Mahone Papers*. Walker's influence
over Grant appears to have been exercised through ''Chandler.'' James
Barbour, brother of the president of the Orange & Alexandria Railroad,
and Robert Ould, who represented Richmond's interests in the Canal, both
competitors of the A. M. & O., opposed the move.

[18] *Whig*, October 10, 12; *Dispatch*, October 2, 8, 1869; Eckenrode,
Political Reconstruction, p. 126.

by the essentially democratic features of the expurgated constitution,[19] Virginia returned finally and fully to the Union in January, 1870.

We have seen, then, that the reconstruction constitution was framed by adventurers in the interests of the "mud sills of society." It sought to create complete equality by such devices as manhood suffrage and jury service, numerous elective local offices, taxation according to wealth, and state support of common schools and charities. The sponsor for these ideas was the Radical, or Republican, party, but they were also accepted as a matter of expediency by a new party, called "Conservative," and supported by the bulk of the whites. "Bourbons," that is, advocates of the old-time policies, opposed this course. While insisting upon these democratic ideas, some Radicals of the constitutional convention endeavored to scale both public and private debts, but without success. Ratification of the new constitution was accomplished through the combination of the Conservatives with a wing of the Republican party. This combination was effected by city capitalistic leaders, and to it (and them) was entrusted the inauguration of the new régime.

[19] *Code of 1870*, preface. These included suffrage and public education. *Cf.* Dunning, *Essays on Civil War and Reconstruction*, pp. 347 ff.

CHAPTER III

"RESTORATION OF CREDIT," 1870-1871

When the first legislature of reconstructed Virginia met in January, 1870, twenty-seven negroes had seats. The absence of well-known faces was marked—acts of Congress and the exigencies of the campaign had kept them at home. Men said—some with obvious effort— that it was perhaps well; for the young men and new men could more easily forget the past and face the pressing problems which war and reconstruction had created or complicated.[1]

Chief among these problems was the serious economic and fiscal situation. The state debt now amounted to over $45,000,000[2]—$36 for each person, $62 for each white. Transition from the old to the new transportation policy awaited completion; meantime the state's assets paid little dividend and commerce was hampered. There were, however, some signs of improvement. Small farms for the landless were beginning to be created from the great estates; men unaccustomed to work were putting their hands literally to the plow; in some parts

[1] *Dispatch, Whig, Enquirer,* October 5-12, 1869. *Cf.* Mayes, *L. Q. C. Lamar,* p. 131. This legislature had in the fall of 1869 completed the reconstruction process. Its composition was: Senate, 30 Conservatives and 13 Radicals (6 negroes); House, 95 Conservatives (3 negroes) and 42 Radicals (18 negroes), *Annual Cyc.,* 1869.

[2] Under the act of March 2, 1866, "a large proportion" of interest accrued by January 1, 1867, had been funded. Under act of March 21, 1867 (above, pp. 10, 11) four per cent interest had been paid in 1867 and two per cent in 1869. Between these dates the taxes were not fully collected and government expenses were high, Governor, *Message,* March 8, 1870.

old industries were taking on new life—truck-farming, for example, in the Norfolk region, the tonging and planting of oysters in the Chesapeake's tributaries, and cattle-raising in the southwest.[3] Favored by this activity and by immigration from the north and from other parts of the state, seventeen counties and all the cities but two showed greater realty values than in 1860.[4] The masses of the people appeared cheerful, glad, for all the changes, to be back at peaceful work again.[5] But the "good times" immediately succeeding the war had already begun to pass away.[6] Protected against old debts by stay laws, men had created a fictitious prosperity by making new loans, often at usurious rates. Now stay laws were unconstitutional, but the debts remained. The Richmond *Enquirer* gravely argued that "reason and true statesmanship dictate a compulsory scale of 'ante bellum' private debt from its apparent to its true value," and public meetings endorsed the suggestion.[7] Prices of farm products were declining

[3] "Personal Recollections."

[4] The basis of these estimates is the assessed values of 1860 (being the figures of 1856 corrected in 1860) and of 1870. Petersburg and Fredericksburg showed losses. Auditor, *Report*, 1871.

[5] *Ibid.;* tone of the press; "Personal Recollections"; *Ruffner Papers; Johnson, Dabney.*

[6] Tobacco production was 123,968,000 pounds in 1860, 114,480,000 in 1866, 43,761,000 in 1870. This decrease was coincident with a heavy federal tax, Arnold, *Tobacco Industry*, ch. 2. The price of bright tobacco, very high in 1865-1867, decreased thereafter, while the corn and pork imported by the planters were high, *Whig*, March 8, December 8, 1870. In non-tobacco growing sections the high price of corn was offset by the low price of wheat, *ibid.*, March 8, 17. There had been a succession of disastrous floods in the James and Shenandoah valleys; also droughts. *Annual Cyc.*, 1865-1870; Governor, *Message*, December 7, 1870. For negro exodus see *Enquirer*, February 17; March 19 to 25; *Whig*, April 20, 1870; for transition to town, P. A. Bruce, *Rise of the New South*, ch. 30; for the optimistic view of an intelligent English tourist, Robert Somers, *The Southern States Since the War. Cf.* State Grange, *Proceedings*, 1874.

[7] *Thorpe*, VII, 3896; *Enquirer*, February 17, March 19, 1870.

and production was increasing but slowly, sometimes actually decreasing. Negro laborers were leaving or talking of leaving, and even though they remained, land in most regions had not yet become profitable. In each of seventy-four counties, not including cities, realty values were distinctly smaller than in 1860, their shrinkage totalling probably over $10,000,000.[8]

To meet this situation, Governor Walker urged[9] a "restoration of credit" policy. Let the entire $45,000,-000 of debt, he said, be funded into uniform coupon bonds bearing the same rate of interest as the old, the coupons being declared on their face receivable for taxes and other public dues. Complete the exchange of the state's interest in public works for state bonds. Curtail expenses. Tax all property at its *true* value,[10] and reach out for other sources of revenue possible under the new constitution. The honor of the state would thus be preserved and its credit restored. Then grant liberal franchises under general laws, unhamper the private interest rate and, while making concessions in the case of old debts, secure the creditor by "prompt and effective remedies for the enforcement of his rights." Private credit, as the basis of individual prosperity, would follow.

The spirit in which these recommendations were made—its extravagant optimism[11] and its sympathetic appreciation of state pride—received from the press the

[8] Assessed realty values for the entire state showed a loss of some fifteen millions, or about five per cent (currency); but the cities and favored counties showed an increase of nineteen millions.

[9] *Message*, March 8, 1870; December 6, 1871.

[10] This he assumed to be the same as the "true value" given by the census of 1860.

[11] For example: "We have a canal which, when completed, will prove as valuable an adjunct to commerce as the far-famed Suez Canal. . . . A Southern Pacific railroad has been projected with its eastern terminus at Norfolk, and I doubt not it will be built."

heartiest commendation and helped to conciliate or silence elements hitherto in opposition.[12] The legislature responded readily. It provided for the funding of the debt, adopted a liberal railroad policy, and enacted a tax law of greater reach than any heretofore passed. It took the first step toward repealing the constitutional restriction of the contractual private interest rate to twelve per cent.[13] It gave liberal interpretation to the exemption provisions of the constitution, especially as regards private debts contracted prior to the end of the war.[14] It left no room for a Radical reaction or interference of the federal government, for it set in motion the local government machinery, enacted laws for the protection of suffrage, and created an elaborate and up-to-date public school system.[15] Because of their future bearings, the first two of these acts require more extended notice.

Among the railroad acts of the legislature of 1865-1867 was one permitting Gen. William Mahone and others to merge, under careful restrictions, the managements of the three lines from Norfolk to Bristol and to build extensions with a view to connecting eventually the seaboard with the Mississippi and the Ohio. This was the Atlantic, Mississippi and Ohio Railroad. This plan, however, had met with opposition, both from those who opposed consolidation on theoretical grounds and from those with conflicting business interests. As had been expected from the alignment of forces in 1869, Mahone at first received the co-operation of Governor Walker in forcing through the legislature, with the aid of the Republican vote, an act granting the A. M. & O.

12 *Whig, Dispatch, Enquirer,* and citations in each, March 9-11, December 8, 9, 1870; above, p. 21.
13 *Acts,* 1869-1870, p. 19.
14 Act of June 27, 1870.
15 Act of July 11, 1870; below, p. 60.

valuable privileges and completely crushing the opposition within the consolidating roads.[16] Others, apparently with Mahone's assistance, received similar charters.[17] But these acts were soon seen to be only a part of the governor's "free railroad" policy. "Wherever," he said in his next annual message,[18] "a railroad, or a canal, or a transportation company, is needed, and people can be found who will invest the necessary capital, let the enterprise be organized and completed." Since this policy involved the sale of such of the state's assets as had not already been disposed of, a bill to that effect was introduced. But Mahone, deeming the policy dangerous to A. M. & O. interests, fought it. The *Enquirer*, which had recently been purchased by the Pennsylvania Central Railroad and reorganized under Richmond business men and politicians for the acknowledged purpose of advocating "Free Railroads" and the "maintenance of public and private credit of the state,"[19] urged the bill's

[16] Act of June 17, 1870; *Enquirer*, March 3, 16, 18, 20, 1871. The state's interest might be bought by the consolidated road for $4,000,000 in state bonds at par, payable in installments beginning January 1, 1885. The security for the purchase should be a mortgage on the consolidated road second to a first mortgage of $15,000,000. The proceeds of the latter were to be used for building an extension through Cumberland Gap and for certain minor purposes. To the opposition above noted (p. 22) had now been added certain Richmond men, who were interested in an air-line from Richmond to Lynchburg, and the East Tennessee, Virginia and Georgia Railroad represented by John B. Baldwin.

[17] Acts of July 11, 1870 (Richmond and Danville); March 24 (Chesapeake and Ohio); January 14, March 28, 31 (Orange and Alexandria), 1871. Mahone appears to have reached an agreement with the Baltimore and Ohio interests, which were closely connected with the Orange and Alexandria, Letter of W. W. Wood, November 16, 1871, *Mahone Papers*.

[18] December 7, 1870.

[19] *Enquirer*, March 21; *Whig*, November 10, 1871. The *Enquirer* made no denial of the *Whig's* charge, "Are not six-sevenths of the *Enquirer* stock held in Pennsylvania?" Probably Governor Walker's political interests were to be looked after by the *Enquirer* in return for his support; certainly he had some close connection with the *Enquirer's* management in

passage. So did the *Dispatch*, the owner of which was
an interested party.[20] Opposing it was the *Whig*, whose
traditional attitude was to fight outside control and the
diversion of trade from Virginia centers, and which,
through A. M. & O. patronage, was gradually passing
under Mahone's control.[21] Each side maintained an
extensive lobby—an agency scarcely known before in
Virginia, and each had legislators avowedly in its pay.[22]
In the melée Mahone lost the negro vote and the bill was
passed.[23]

Meanwhile there had come from the joint committee
on finance a bill for funding the state debt, afterwards
commonly known as "the Funding Act." It was the
governor's bill in every point[24] save that interest-bearing

1874, Walker to Ruffner, September 4, *Ruffner Papers*, December 31, 1883.
The *State* reprinted from the Chicago *Tribune* a letter of C. P. Huntington
in which he spoke of Walker as "a slippery fellow, and I rather think in
Scott's interest." See also letters of R. F. Walker (1872), in *Mahone
Papers*.

[20] Act of March 28, 1871. The short lines from Washington south
through Richmond were the main bone of contention. Some were primarily
interested in the Carolina trade (*Dispatch*, March 10, 1871); others, in a
trunk line north and south.

[21] Mahone appears to have negotiated for the purchase of the *Whig* in
1868 without success; yet from that year records of its business were regularly sent him. The *Whig's* editor asserted (March 4, 1872) that his views
were reached independently and in ignorance of Mahone's. A total of
$77,200 was paid the *Whig* by the A. M. & O., *Dispatch*, October 11, 1879.

[22] John Goode, Jr., represented Mahone (*Dispatch*, February 10, 1870;
New Virginia, in *Whig*, January 3, 1885), but the charge that he was in
the pay of Mahone is based on insufficient evidence; Walter Taylor and
A. B. Cochran, the Pennsylvania interests (*Enquirer*, November 4, 1871);
Gen. Bradley T. Johnson (who was not at this time in the legislature),
John Lyons, and John W. Jenkins, a Radical lawyer of Richmond, the
Richmond interests (*Dispatch*, February 15, 1872). The A. M. & O. paid
$13,900 apparently for lobbying in addition to sums paid the *Whig*, *op. cit.*,
1879.

[23] Act of March 28, 1871. For convenient later account of the whole
affair see *Dispatch*, June 16, 27; August 7, 8, 1877. The contemporary
papers are full of it.

[24] Above; also speech of Walker, in *Dispatch*, October 3, 1877.

coupons instead of bonds were to be issued for one-third of the debt, for which "payment . . . will be provided in accordance with such settlements as shall hereafter be made between the states of Virginia and West Virginia."[25] Obsessed by a sense of obligation to the governor, overwhelmed by other duties, and involved in the railroad war, legislators could give to this bill no adequate study. Nor did they receive light from public discussion. The *Dispatch* and General Mahone kept discreetly silent. The *Enquirer,* indeed, favored the bill, and the *Whig* opposed it; but their arguments were clouded with references to each other's railroad and political intentions, and weakened by their complete reversal of opinion within four months.[26] At the very close of the session, having previously passed the Senate, this measure was railroaded through the House, receiving the votes of just half of the Conservatives and all of the Republicans but one.[27]

Thus the "restoration of credit" policy, balanced against and protected by a careful observance of the democratic ideas of the constitution, was enacted into law. Under its operation important business connections were formed with the North in which men of all shades of political opinion participated, and before these illiberalism of all kinds was certain to give way. Almost the entire state press[28] and the outside world endorsed the policy as economically correct. Yet several consid-

[25] In the opinion of Mr. Septimus Hall (previously quoted) Walker and the railroad interests blocked a settlement with West Virginia lest the latter demand a share of Virginia's assets and so delay railroad consolidation; and the opinion became fixed in West Virginia that no settlement would ever be demanded.

[26] Compare editorials in December, 1870, with those of March, 1871.

[27] Act of March 30, 1871; contemporary *Whig, Dispatch, Enquirer;* Ruffin, *Facts,* etc.; *Journals* of both houses, March, 1871. John W. Daniel and James Stubbs protested vigorously against the procedure.

[28] *Whig,* January 9, 1873.

erations might well have given pause to the men behind this policy.

(1)   The state's most valuable fiscal assets had been contracted away upon terms that were inadequate if the grantee prospered, insecure if he did not prosper. No special privileges of the old railroads, such as exemption from taxation, proper enough under the former system, had been surrendered. No provision for control over transportation to take the place of the old method had been made. Such defects invited, if they did not compel, railroad control over the legislature.

(2)   It was questionable, at least, whether the fiscal obligations imposed by the Funding Act could be met by the state if that act were accepted by all creditors. The interest on the new debt principal would just about equal the estimated revenue under the new tax law less the minimum appropriated by the constitution for public education, leaving nothing for government expenses which the auditor estimated[29] at over one million dollars. Nor was there any obvious remedy for this situation. The debt-principal was indeed reducible by sale of the state's railroad assets; but the amount receivable in the near future from this source had been rendered almost negligible by the acts noted above.[30]   Expenses could be reduced only by undoing the democratic features of the constitution just put into effect; but at best this would require years. Any considerable increase in revenue depended upon economic improvement, which could come only gradually, or upon the always slow process of finding new subjects and new methods of taxation. Meantime the annual deficit would be accumu-

[29] *Report,* 1871.
[30] In 1874 only $3,400,000 had been received, Sen. *Jour.,* 1874-1875, Doc. 1. Walker's estimate (*op. cit.*) was $2,600,000 "immediately," and $10,000,000 more remotely, available.

lating so as to impair or destroy the efficiency of these
proposed remedies.

(3) The "restoration of credit" policy did not rest
upon a well-advised popular will. The legislature had
been elected when the main issues were not fiscal. The
true fiscal condition had not been made clear by the
governor or by the press. While some legislators had
voted from conviction for the funding and railroad acts,[31]
those acts, the very backbone of the governor's policy,
could scarcely have been passed without the combination
of interests and the skill of lobbyists. The governor
himself was known to be financially interested, directly
or indirectly, in state bonds.[32] Men said, and no one
took the trouble to deny the rumor, that the negroes had
been bought.[33] It was not at all clear that the people
would approve the funding of $13,000,000 of interest
accruing mainly during war and reconstruction days
and part of it compounded, and it would not be sufficient
to say that this was offset by the release of Virginia
from one-third of the whole debt ($16,000,000); for this
one-third was generally considered West Virginia's fair
proportion, and from this Virginia was already released
in law and in equity.[34] Nor was it clear that in the clash
bound to come between the schools and the debt, the
people would side with the latter.

(4) Factions within Conservative ranks and a ten-

[31] Among the affirmative voters were A. B. Courtney, Charles Herndon,
Daniel A. Grimsley, Meriwether Lewis, Wm. A. Anderson, George Walker,
John A. McCaul, and M. Hanger.

[32] *Enquirer*, December 22, 1871; Massey, *Autobiography*, pp. 44 ff.

[33] For evidence see House *Jour.*, 1871-1872, pp. 31, 137, 297 ff.; *Whig,
Enquirer, Dispatch*, February 14-20, 1872.

[34] C. U. Williams, *Present Financial Status of Virginia;* above, pp. 9-11
and note 38; *Enquirer*, March 28; *Whig*, March 18, 1871. It was thought
at the time that, despite the previous refusal of West Virginia to treat, her
new officials, being Democrats, would do so, Governor, *Message*, December
7, 1870, House *Docs.*, 1869-1870, Nos. 17 and 20.

dency toward demagogy were already appearing. The
men of southwestern Virginia were almost solid against
the Funding Act; and some of them were using language
which questioned the validity of the debt.[35] Mahone's
railroad supporters were strong and active men and
Mahone himself was deemed a skilful and unscrupulous
leader.[36] Against them were arrayed the governor and
the interests represented by the *Enquirer* and the
Dispatch, to which the Bourbon element was already
allying itself. Already the *Whig* was seeking to array
the masses against its enemies. "Are they not," it said,
"working for Cameron and Scott and McClure . . . the
Radical leaders of Philadelphia? . . . The demoralizing
effects of Virginia gentlemen chaffing and bargaining
with Radical adventurers are deplorable in the extreme.
Colonel this, and Major that, and Mr. Somebody else, are
seen hobnobbing with union leaguers from Pennsylvania,
and aiding them in obtaining the most valuable franchises in the state . . ." Already, too, the *Whig* was
predicting, no doubt unconsciously, its own future
course: "Suppose this . . . [the Funding bill] becomes
a law by appliances which stock-jobbers so well understand, . . . will the iniquity be patiently endured? Will
it not give a handle to demagogues to agitate for repudiation of the whole?"[37]

To sum up: The legislature, elected under the circumstances narrated in the preceding chapter, endeavored
to give effect to the democratic ideas embodied in the
new constitution. At the same time, influenced by city

[35] See resolution of Colonel Pendleton in *Whig,* December 12, 1870.

[36] The *Enquirer* (November 4, 1871) charged that John F. Lewis,
Republican, had been elected to the United States Senate through the
coalition of the A. M. & O. and the Old Dominion Steamship Company;
this appears probable, Letter of G. R. Gilmer, September 14, 1869, in
Mahone Papers.

[37] March 18; November 2, 1871.

capitalistic interests and with the expectation of restoring public, and thereby private, credit, it adopted a "free" railroad policy and enacted "the Funding Act." Under the former, control as well as ownership of the railroads passed, or would pass, almost entirely into private hands. Under the Funding Act, the annual debt interest, collectable through tax-receivable coupons, almost equalled the entire revenue of the state. Accompanying results were a bitter railroad war in the legislature and a cry that the interests of the people had been sold out.

CHAPTER IV

REACTION, AND THE COURTS, 1871-1873

The legislation described in the previous chapter came before the people for review in the summer and fall of 1871. Since the scope of the referendum was limited by peculiar political conditions which continued to dominate public policies for several years, we must note here the development of party politics since the election of 1869.

It had by no means appeared certain to party leaders in the early months of 1870 just what the lines and policies of the future would be or which party would prevail.[1] Hitherto the strength of the Radicals had been the negro vote, but now men hoped, and sometimes seemed to expect, that the negroes, won to reason by fair treatment in their homes and in the legislature, would see that their interest could be best subserved by dividing their vote.[2] Instead of assuming the Republican leadership, Governor Walker had just declared his independence of all parties.[3] The older Republican

[1] *Cf. Dispatch,* July 11 (quoting Walker in New York *World*); also, October 22, 1869.

[2] *Whig,* July 5, 6; *Dispatch,* July 2, 3; *Enquirer,* July 1, 2, November 25, 1869. For recognition of the common interests of the races see *Whig,* July 7, 12; *Dispatch,* July 9, 1869. Walker thought one-fifth had voted Conservative in 1869, and that in two years one-half would be Conservatives, *op. cit.* The *Enquirer* believed the negro was rapidly learning his political interests. Amicable relations in the legislature are shown in *Whig,* January 6, 19, 20, 23, 1871—two negroes sitting "with their political associates, the Conservatives." Ku Klux operations (at no time severe) ceased in 1868, Sen. *Reports,* 42 Cong., 2 sess., no. 41, Pt. 1, p. 92.

[3] *Message,* February 8, 1870.

leaders had been discredited by defeat and the virtual
abandonment of their policy by the federal administration. Hence, among the Republicans factions had developed, which warred with each other over the spoils and
the treatment of ex-Confederates. On the other hand,
the Conservative party, which had sprung into existence for a specific purpose, now achieved, had never
received formal and authoritative organization. The
future co-operation of ex-Whigs with ex-Democrats and
of Bourbons with liberals was not assured.[4] West of the
mountains the whites were in such overwhelming majority that they could not be expected to appreciate the
problems of the ''East''; and the reverse was also true.
Meantime, from across the northern border was coming
a call, to which some had already listened,[5] for men of
ability and good standing to align themselves with the
party which controlled national policies and distributed
the national patronage.

Such a chaotic condition of parties gave to the Congressional campaign of 1870 a state-wide interest and
importance. Early in the year the Richmond *State
Journal* began, with the approval of Washington, a
movement for a state convention which should rescue
the Republican party from factional fights and give it
leaders and policies less closely associated with events
of the last four years. The movement was successful
and the convention met in Richmond in September.[6]
Though deploring the facility with which ''our whilom
true Republicans in office have forgotten and abjured

---

[4] Above, p. 20; *Enquirer*, November 25, 26, 1869; March 14, April 15,
16, 1871; *Whig*, August 11, 1869; January 13, 17, 1871.

[5] Examples are: Gen. W. C. Wickham, vice-president of the Chesapeake
and Ohio Railway; Robert W. Hughes (below); Z. Turner, speaker of the
House; Alex. Rives, federal district judge. General Mahone and the *Whig*
were continually under suspicion.

[6] *Enquirer*, February 7, March 14, April 15, 16, 1870.

their pledges to Gen. Grant and Congress'' and though
condemning Conservatism as a ''contrivance to avoid
the issues between the two great parties,'' this convention formally abandoned the party's past policy of
''proscription and hate'' by pledging a ''conciliatory
policy'' in the selection of local officers and silence as to
the test oath; while the platform's emphasis upon public education connected the party closely with what was
best in its reconstruction work.[7]

To meet this move, leaders of *ante-bellum* Democracy
urged that the Conservatives adopt a clear-cut and
vigorous policy.[8] The non-partisan plan of 1869, they
said, was operating as a cloak for time-serving Republicans and Independents. Therefore a state convention
should be called which should draw strict party lines,
affiliate with the national Democracy, and ''fire the
hearts'' of the white people. But the outspoken suspicion of old Whigs and the widespread fear of renewed
federal interference upon the slightest provocation
counselled caution. Accordingly no convention was
called and no drawing of lines or statement of policies
was attempted. Instead, those moderate men who had
been elected to the legislature the year previous under
the name of Conservatives met in caucus and, with the
assistance of certain prominent Richmond sympathizers,
appointed a new central committee. Through this committee, effective control of which was cautiously centered
in Richmond, an address was issued. Ignoring national
matters save for a suggestion as to economic relief, this
address put forward home rule by the fittest as the para-

---

[7] *Whig, Enquirer, Dispatch,* September 27, 28, 1870; Dunning, *Essays,*
pp. 233 ff. Grant was popular in the state on account of his attitude at
Appomattox and in 1869.

[8] *E.g.,* the Lynchburg *News,* the *Tenth Legion Banner,* and the *Enquirer.*

mount issue, and on this platform invited and urged the co-operation of all.

At the ensuing elections, however, the liberal professions of neither party availed it anything. The whites voted mainly for Conservative candidates, but without enthusiasm; the negroes remained almost solidly Radical. The Radicals won eight of the eleven Congressmen, the Conservatives had a majority of 2,239 in the state as a whole.[9]

The indecisiveness of this campaign and the fact that state issues had not been directly involved left the problem of party lines and policies still an open one in the early months of 1871. Nor did the adjournment of the legislature clarify the situation, for on each of the two chief issues[10] before that body the Conservatives had divided about equally, while the Republicans had, as a whole, supported each side of both questions in turn. Hence, at the ensuing elections for local officials, men who claimed to be Conservatives ran independently in some places and received support from the negroes. Soon the Conservative central committee perceived its authority "measurably impaired" and the party itself "in the throes of distraction." Likewise, the Republicans were again divided into factions, carpet-baggers, backed by the bulk of the negroes, again insisting that Republican Congressmen should control the distribution of the federal patronage, scalawags opposing this.[11]

Again, therefore, the demand went up for a Conservative state convention. Not without misgivings, the

---

[9] *Annual Cyc.*, 1870; *Enquirer*, July 2, August 2, 5, October 7, November 11, 18; *Dispatch*, July 2, 6, August 5; *Whig*, March 8, 17, July 2, 22 (containing the address), 1870. The party plan of organization was that drawn by John B. Baldwin and adopted in 1867 (above, p. 20) slightly amended by the caucus.

[10] The railroad and the debt questions.

[11] References as in note 9.

central committee yielded, summoning the delegates to
Richmond, where its own headquarters were, and fixing
a late date for the meeting (August 30). The venture
proved a complete success. The old leaders, whom disabilities or inclination had kept in the background for six
years, now returned and were received with enthusiasm.
This was an important event, for it marked the beginning of a Confederate reaction not only against Radicalism but also against the compromising idea that had
prevailed for two years. It was, indeed, the beginning
of a "Confederate cult," the deep influence of which
was to be felt in business and social life as well as in
politics for many years to come.[12] By common consent,
issues of the Civil War period and before were laid aside
as "dead." There was no considerable expression of
Bourbon opinion on democracy and the new constitution. Despite some slight opposition on the ostensible
ground that it would give the impression of outside
dictation, an invitation to sit with the convention was
extended to Governor Walker in appreciation of his services in 1869. Six negro delegates from Richmond were
received with applause; and though bluff General Early
left in a rage, declaring that he had come thinking "this
was to be a convention of Virginia gentlemen—a white
man's convention," the Richmond press enthusiastically
described the event as "historical." As a concession to
the representative principle, a resolution offered by
H. H. Riddleberger, of the Valley, that the "consulting"
members of the central committee should be selected by
the delegates from the several Congressional districts
instead of by the convention president was adopted;
but effective party direction was left concentrated in
Richmond, and provision was made for bringing prominent local men into harmony with this management

12 *Cf.* below, pp. 48, 109, 133.

through local reorganization on a democratic basis. Sternly refusing to consider any other question the convention put before the people the single issue of the previous year: "Conservative or Radical control?"[13]

To meet the enthusiasm created by this move, the Republicans could only develop the policy adopted the year previous. By carefully packing their convention, and obtaining the personal attendance of Washington officials, and after a long secret conference of leaders, they were able to restore party harmony. Defeat of the carpet-bagger plan for controlling federal patronage manifested unmistakably the dominance of the liberal wing. Thus the way was prepared for co-operation in the coming national elections with the many whites who did not relish an alliance with the national Democratic party. To these, and to old Whigs especially, the platform extended a cordial and liberal invitation. In state matters, the party's special interest in public education prompted a serious enquiry whether the schools, especially those for the negro, would be safe under continued Conservative control. With Conservatives in possession of the courts, the platform continued, the negro's constitutional right to serve on juries was unquestionably being destroyed; beyond doubt, the operation of the Funding Act would cause a doubling of taxes.[14]

The issue of the campaign that followed was the one

[13] *Whig*, July 20, 22, (address of state committee), 27; *Dispatch*, July 23, August 19, 23; *Enquirer, Dispatch, Whig*, August 30, 31, September 1, 1871. The change in the *Enquirer's* ownership had brought it into fairly close harmony with Governor Walker, above, p. 21. Raleigh T. Daniel as party chairman named Robert L. Montague president, and he appointed William Smith chairman of the committee on business, to which all important matters were referred. This arrangement was at once a recognition of old leaders and a necessary step in identifying the new Conservative party with the old (above, p. 20).

[14] *Whig*, January 13, 17; *Dispatch, Enquirer, Whig*, September 28, 29, 1871.

stated by the Conservatives—"Conservative or Radical rule?" Inspired by the example of their old leaders, the great bulk of the whites voted for the Conservative candidates, and the negroes for the Republican candidates, each regardless of other issues. The Conservatives, consequently, won with an increased majority in both houses.

The policy of the Conservatives, however, did not entirely prevent other issues from having weight; and herein lies a further characteristic of Virginia politics for several years to come. These issues were discussed and roughly decided by the Conservatives in each legislative district separately, and when the district was a close one, not only the regular Conservatives but also the doubtful and apathetic voters had weight. In this campaign such issues were: the public school and local government systems, the number and salary of legislators, the railroad policy, private interest rate, exemption laws, and the Funding Act. How general the discussion was can not be determined; but that it was often vigorous may be inferred from the comment frequently made that the nature of these questions and the ignorance of the voters rendered the local demagogue dangerous. Particularly noteworthy were the arguments advanced against the Funding Act: That it had been passed by the corrupt influence of brokers and speculators; that before any assumption of obligation had been agreed to there should have been a settlement with West Virginia because the debt was "created by the whole state before any division of her territory or any destruction of her property in slaves"; and that it made "the taxes of the rich payable in coupons at far less than par value, while the poor . . . [would] be compelled to pay . . . dollar for dollar." Of course such a method of deciding important questions did not yield the definite and organized expression of popular will ordinarily obtained through political parties. Thus in the present instance only twenty-six of the one hundred and thirty-two members of the previous House were returned; but the exact reasons for the change and the intentions of the new members were not at all clear.[15]

To the legislature thus elected Governor Walker reasserted his fiscal views, December 6, 1871. Reminding the members that "as a legal proposition the interest on the funded debt must unquestionably be paid," he demanded, in substance, that three-fourths of the current revenue should be used for this purpose. Referring lightly to "what may be appropriated for school purposes," he suggested as a substitute for the constitutional appropriation a poll tax of two dollars, prepayment of which should be a suffrage requisite. The governor's belief was, plainly, that if the people wanted free schools, good roads, improved asylums, an agricultural department, and the like, they would submit to higher taxes.[16]

But the legislature forthwith voted, by a majority of 119 to 33 in the two houses, that the operation of the Funding Act be suspended. This action was vetoed by the governor because it was contrary to sound public policy and discriminated against those who had not funded; and this reasoning prevailed with the Senate.[17] Thereupon a bill prohibiting the receipt of coupons for

[15] Cf. *Whig*, October 31, November 1, 10, 1871; January 2, 3, 1872; *Enquirer*, September 1, 18, November 6, 9, 1871; January 8, 1872; *Dispatch*, March 8, 1872; December 19, 1873; Ruffin, *Facts;* C. U. Williams, *Present Financial Status;* C. T. O'Ferrall, *Forty Years of Active Service,* pp. 194 ff.; *Memoirs of Governor William Smith,* p. 276; *Annual Cyc.,* 1871. Richmond Conservatives nominated and elected representatives of the German and Irish elements, *Dispatch, Whig,* September 27, 1871.

[16] Governor, *Message,* December 6, 1871; Auditor, *Report,* 1871. *Cf.* pp. 26, 29.

[17] Sen. *Jour.,* 1871-1872, pp. 88, 111; acts in force March 7, 19, 1872.

taxes was passed, notwithstanding the veto, and the payment of four per cent interest on the whole debt recognized as Virginia's was ordered. But the state supreme court, early in the next legislative session, declared by a vote of three to one that the state must receive for taxes the coupons of all bonds issued under the Funding Act prior to the attempted prohibition because they constituted a contract between the holder and the state.[18] Under this decision a preferred class of bonds, soon known as "consols," was created to the amount of some twenty millions, or about two-thirds of the whole. The legislature deemed it impracticable—as, indeed, it was— to remedy this discrimination against "peelers"[19] by making the interest on them also receivable in payment for taxes, and the holders of consols refused to surrender their privileged position.[20] The governor suggested, and the legislature adopted, a joint resolution petitioning the federal government to assume the whole debt; but the only result of this was a temporary rise in the bond market.[21]

In other respects, also, the legislature pursued a course

[18] Antoni v. Wright, 22 *Grattan*, 833, December 13, 1872. Judge Staples dissented.

[19] Strictly this term applied only to bonds issued between the passage of the prohibiting act and the court's decision; but it will be used for all bonds other than consols.

[20] Under the initiative of the legislature a conference with creditors was attempted; but its only result was a demonstration of bad feeling between legislature and creditors, *Enquirer*, February 19, 21, 22, 1873.

[21] Sen. *Jour.*, 1872-1873, December 16; joint resolution of March 26, 1873; *Whig, Dispatch, Enquirer*, February 18, 1873, and quotations in *Whig* showing division of press. For New York opinion of the stock-jobbing nature of the proposal see *Whig*, February 12, 1873, quoting New York *Advertiser*. Henry A. Wise had favored such a petition by Virginia, West Virginia, and the creditors jointly (B. H. Wise, *Henry A. Wise*, p. 397), and Governor Kemper (*Message*, January 1, 1874), endorsed it on the ground of duty incident to the war. But the plan never had influence other than that indicated above.

44   READJUSTER MOVEMENT IN VIRGINIA

quite antagonistic to the restoration of credit policy. It taxed state bonds on the theory that they were private property; it ordered an investigation of the passage of the Funding Act;[22] it put bonds held by the colleges in a specially favored class;[23] and established, in the interest of farmers and local politicians, the Virginia Agricultural and Mechanical Institute;[24] it repealed the act for a general sale of the state's railroad assets; refused even to consider a somewhat similar plan for disposing of the James River and Kanawha Canal; and resumed the older policy, under which the great era of railroad consolidation and expansion was soon brought to a close.[25] It limited the permissible private interest rate to eight per cent, which was even lower than that allowed in the unamended constitution, rendered easier the redemption of lands held for delinquent taxes, and tried seriously, though in vain, to stave off the threatened defeat of the exemption laws by the state courts.[26] Aided by the general desire of the whites to be rid of an impracticable "Yankee idea," it took the first steps toward amending the local government system.[27]   It

[22] House *Jour.*, 1871-1872; *Dispatch*, March, 1871, *passim; Whig*, August 8, 1877.

[23] An act of February 23, 1867, authorizing payment of full interest on their bonds was continued in force by act ᴏf March 20, 1872, and from time to time thereafter, Second Auditor, *Report*, 1879, p. 10.

[24] *Acts*, 1871-1872, pp. 48, 312. It was to be supported by ᴛhe proceeds from two-thirds of the land scrip donated by Congress in 1862, and by a local appropriation; but state appropriations were of course soon made.

[25] The old railroad wars continued, however, being especially fierce in 1874 and 1875. *Cf. Dispatch, Whig, Enquirer, passim.* They ceased with the appointment of receivers for most of the roads in 1876 and 1877. *Acts*, 1871-1872, p. 45; *Annual Cyc.*, 1872, 1873; *Brown Papers.*

[26] Above; *Acts*, 1871-1872, pp. 72, 99; 1872-1873, pp. 138, 177, 329. The exemption act of June 27, 1870, and the clause of the state constitution on which it was based were declared unconstitutional by the state supreme court in 1872, 22 *Grattan*, 266.

[27] Above, p. 18.

shifted the burden of taxation noticeably from the farmer and the laborer to luxuries and corporate wealth.[28] But it did not increase the revenues nor immediately decrease expenses.

Radical as this legislation was, it probably fell short of the popular wishes. For of the two houses the lower was at once the "fresher from the people" and the more extreme. Moreover, a majority of the legislators represented the upper and middle classes, the negroes and the "odds and ends" having voted for Republicans and Independents who advocated more extreme action in economic and fiscal matters. Did the people of the state, then, wish to repudiate? Some thought so.[29] Certainly, the first step toward repudiating "peelers" had been taken. Yet the legislators intended only to get rid of town and corporate influences and Yankee ideas, to regain control over the state's finances so as to adjust them equitably and rationally, and to give the substantial country people a chance to recover.[30] This was certainly a very natural course for farmers and ex-Confederates to take, and by no means an improper one. On the announcement of the court's decision, however, most of them

28 This was done (1) by permitting revaluation of land and the oyster catch; (2) by imposing taxes on gross receipts of transportation and insurance companies in addition to license and property taxes; (3) by a sales tax, as well as license tax, on liquor. Not all of this was new, but the tendency was decidedly as stated. See *Acts*, 1871-1872 (including extended session).

29 For vote on suspension of funding, see Sen. *Jour.*, 1871-1872, p. 88; *Enquirer*, December 16, 1871; Ruffin, *Facts*. Conservatives favoring suspension were: Thomas J. Christian, A. Fulkerson, C. T. O'Ferrall, F. McMullin, H. H. Riddleberger, Wm. R. Taliaferro, Wm. R. Terry. On prohibiting receipt of coupons for taxes the party vote was: ayes, 81 Conservatives, 33 Republicans, 5 Independents; noes, 32 Conservatives, 1 Republican. The vote on the private interest rate bill was quite similar.

30 See House resolution of December 23, 1871; *Whig*, December 28, 29; *contra*, *Enquirer*, December 20, 1871; *Religious Herald* and *Central Presbyterian*, in *Enquirer*, February 19, 1872.

yielded out of traditional respect; and it was they who
blocked further action of the same character. But
Republicans and Independents and a minority of the
Conservatives, chiefly those from the "Southwest,"
agreed with the dissenting judge[31] that the decision was
wrong in law because under it "liens and mortgages
may be given upon the future revenues of the state, by
statutes assuming the form of contracts"; and with the
Whig[32] that it substantiated an impression begun since
the war that "the law which is dispensed is wanting in
the essential elements of justice and equity."

Thus, by 1872, party lines and policies had become
definitely established. Despite its varied program of
liberalism, democracy, and reform, the Republican party
was controlled, through federal appointees, from Washington, and few besides the negroes were attracted to
it. On the other hand, the Conservative party relied
upon its single promise of native white control; and this
sufficed both to hold together the Bourbons and the
capitalistic interests and to control the state legislature.
The elections of 1871, however, had disclosed a wide
difference of opinion among Conservatives, due in part to
a Confederate reaction, now just beginning, and in part
to divergence of economic and social interests and principles. Especially noteworthy was the legislature's
attack upon the Funding Act. This subsided, however,
when the attempts at undoing the act met defeats at the
hands of the governor and the courts. But the Richmond *Whig* and other Conservatives, especially in the
"Southwest," bitterly condemned governor and courts
as well as the Funding Act. Republicans shared this
hostility.

[31] Judge Staples lived in the "Southwest."
[32] December 17, 18, 1872.

CHAPTER V

"DEBT PAYERS," AND THE ELEMENTS OF DISSATISFACTION, 1874-1877

As the campaigns of 1870 and 1871 fixed unalterably the issue between the Conservatives and the Radicals, so the contest for governor and legislature in 1873 and the events growing immediately out of it sealed the fate of the Republican party until its rejuvenation in the early eighties.[1]

The prospects of the Republicans at the beginning of the campaign were bright. Through their victory over the Conservatives supporting the Liberal-Democratic combination headed by Greeley the year previous, they were enabled to urge with more effect than before the futility of the non-partisan idea. Though the Conservatives quite correctly attributed this defeat to their candidate and not to their party policy, they could conceal neither their factions nor the failure of their fiscal efforts; and so good a politician as Governor Walker declared confidentially that only two Conservatives could be sure of carrying the state that year (1873).[2] Accordingly, being assured of continued support from the federal administration, liberal Republican leaders early took the initiative and by July were able to assemble a state convention marked, as in 1871, by the domination of federal employees and the subordination

[1] See ch. 13.
[2] Letter to W. H. Ruffner, May 7, *Ruffner Papers*. Walker's view, however, proved incorrect. Walker was now recognized as a Conservative.

of the negroes. For governor they nominated Robert
W. Hughes, once an extreme secessionist but now federal district-attorney in the "Southwest," a man of
excellent family, the "brains of his party," and a reputed
favorite of Grant. Carpet-baggers were represented by
C. P. Ramsdell, of Surry, and old Union men by David
Fultz, of the once strongly Whiggish county of Augusta.
In an intelligent and well written platform they offered
to the "Southwest" development of its resources through
outside capital and federal aid; to the railroads, a "free"
policy; and to liberal sentiment, the hospitable reception
of immigrants, exact and impartial justice, and fair elections. As in 1872, they endorsed the administration of
the schools under Supt. William H. Ruffner,[3] Conservative though he was, urging only a more democratic
method of selecting the local trustees. Shifting to meet
the changed situation, they condemned repudiation in
any form and promised compulsory adjustment with
West Virginia through use of the federal courts.[4]

The Conservatives, however, again refused to recognize any issue save negro rule under federal direction.
Their newspapers refrained from expressing gubernatorial preferences, and their convention, marked even
more than in 1871 by the prominence of old leaders, spent
its energies in stately compliments to itself and bitter
denunciation of Radicalism. A brief platform noted the
results of Radical rule in the Southern states, declared
for "exact and impartial justice" to both races, pointed
"with pride" to the school system, promised to co-operate with "Gen. Grant" in cultivating good will
between the sections, and urged the completion of the
James River and Kanawha Canal as a matter of national

[3] Below, p. 60.

[4] *Enquirer, Whig,* July 31, August 1; *Dispatch,* August 7, 1873; *Annual
Cyc.,* 1873.

importance. For governor they named Gen. James L.
Kemper, of the Valley, a soldier of two wars and twice
Speaker, a liberal in politics and a friend of Mahone in
the railroad war. Then, by a dramatic *coup,* they compelled Kemper's closest competitor, Col. R. E. Withers
(now of the "Southwest"), an ex-Bourbon and an enemy
of Mahone, to accept the second place. The ticket was
completed with the name of Raleigh T. Daniel, of Richmond, a lawyer and editor of war-time fame and since
the war the dominating party chairman.[5] Likewise, in
the campaign that followed, the Conservatives permitted
but one issue; with this they colored all the brilliant
liberal speeches of Hughes. Hitherto they had carefully
refused to draw the race line; now, without nominally
changing this policy, they refused in places to enter joint
discussions and by thus "dividing the crowd" compelled
white men to support the Conservative party or repudiate their color. After this the result was never in doubt.
Hughes was overwhelmingly defeated.[6]

The Republican party now began to pay in full for the
indignities which it had attempted to heap upon ex-Confederates. For some time trickery and fraud had been
practiced by the Conservatives and the drawing of the
color line tended to encourage the practice. But such
methods were ever uncertain in their results, they lacked
social respectability and were in direct defiance of stat-

5 Above, pp. 20, 39. The chairmanship of the state committee and
that of the executive committee were hereafter held by different men.

6 *Dispatch,* July 13, August 8, November 4, 5; *Enquirer,* July 18, 20,
August 7, 8; *Whig,* July 17, August 5. 7, 8; November 4, 5, 12, 1873; Withers, *Autobiography,* p. 313. For Mahone's share in the selection of Kemper,
see below, p. 70. That Republicans hoped for assistance from public school
men is indicated by a letter of Hughes to Superintendent Ruffner, April 24,
1873, and by the reported assertion of Ramsdell that Superintendent
Ruffner was not in accord with Conservative policy as to schools; also by
the preparation of John W. Daniel (letter to Ruffner, October 1, 1873),
to meet the move, *Ruffner Papers.*

utes which their sponsors had made.[7] So an amendment
to the suffrage law embedded in the constitution was proposed by the legislature in 1874 and ratified in 1876,
under which failure to pay the poll tax and conviction
for many petty crimes became disqualifications. This
limitation of suffrage, together with the abolition of one-
third of the local offices, was an "undoing of reconstruction" which rendered unnecessary the constitutional convention that would otherwise probably have been called.[8]
As a result, the hold of Republicans, already weakened
in the counties and towns, was now broken completely.
Of the two federal senators chosen by the compromising
legislature of 1869, one had proved to be a good Conservative and the other was replaced by Colonel Withers
in 1875; next year the Conservatives elected all but one
of the members of the House.[9] By the end of Kemper's
administration (1878), therefore, federal appointees had
become not only the dominating leaders of the Republican party but almost the party itself. With this condition of affairs they appeared quite content.

When Governor Kemper began his term, January 1,
1874, Virginia faced not only the effects of a far-reaching
national panic—in her case unrelieved by previous prosperity—but also the fiscal woes inevitably arising from

[7] Knight v. Johnson, Sen. Jour., 1875-1876, Doc. 3; Platt v. Goode, in
C. H. Rowell, Digest of Contested Election Cases; Acts, May 11, 1870;
March 30, 1871; April 30, 1874

[8] Thorpe, 3901, above, pp. 19, 44. A. E. McKinley in "Two Southern
Constitutions" (Political Science Quarterly, IX, p. 671) quite overlooks
this fact. The bulking of the negroes made such laws necessary. The
political motive is evident from the fact that negroes voted against them.
Cf. Dunning, "Undoing of Reconstruction, in Atlantic Monthly,
LXXXVIII, p. 437.

[9] In 1874 and in 1876 ex-Governor Walker was chosen by Conservatives
of the Richmond district, previously represented by the Radicals C. H.
Porter and James A. Smith. At the expiration of his second term he
returned to New York.

previous policies. The legislature of 1870-1871 had
avoided the problem of current debt interest by permitting the greater part of it to be funded. The succeeding
legislature had managed to retard the annual million
dollar inflow of coupons by offering four per cent in cash
and two per cent certificates in exchange for them, while
making their sale for tax-paying purposes difficult.[10] By
means of these devices and the habitual under-payment
of appropriations for other purposes, especially for the
"peeler" debt, the annual deficit of about a million
dollars had been temporarily concealed.[11] But now the
large surplus which had existed at the beginning of
Governor Walker's administration was gone. Nearly a
million dollars in authorized cash payments and half a
million in tax-receivable coupons were outstanding, the
current year would show a deficit of almost another million, the bulk of the state's assets had been bargained
away, and general economic conditions demanded a
decrease, rather than an increase, in taxes.[12]

The fiscal views of the new governor were unknown
at the time of his election, the debt not having been a
campaign issue that year. To the great disgust of the
financial world, however, he attacked the problem at
once, somewhat after the manner of the legislature of
1871-1872. The fundamental need, he said, was a "permanent financial policy." The first essential of this
policy was equality of creditors and uniformity of obligations, and the proper way to obtain these objects was

10 Acts of March 19, 1872 (repealed December 23, 1872); March 13,
1873; December 24, 1872 (prohibiting collecting officers from dealing in
coupons and imposing a broker's license tax on other persons dealing in
them). Only some $300,000 in coupons were turned in for taxes up to
October 1, 1873, Second Auditor, *Report*, 1873.

11 *Message*, March 8, 1870.

12 Auditor, *Report*, 1874. In addition there were $1,800,000 of deferred
interest certificates.

to call a conference of consol holders and induce them to exchange their tax-receivable coupons for, say, four per cent in cash and two per cent in deferred interest certificates. The second essential was prompt payment of interest, for which the necessary money could be obtained only by a more careful administration of the revenue laws, by finding new subjects of taxation, and by reducing expenses in proportion to the state's reduced capacity, through a constitutional convention if necessary.[13]

The legislature endorsed the governor's proposal by authorizing the conference, and named the governor and R. M. T. Hunter, the treasurer, as the state's representatives. At the appointed time, ex-Secretary of the Treasury Hugh McCulloch came to represent part of the British holders; Richmond men and some members of the legislature spoke for most of the other creditors. In a long address the governor portrayed the extreme distress of the people and the heaviness of the state's burdens, coupling with this gloomy picture a severe arraignment of his predecessor for misrepresentation of the facts and waste of the state's assets. Asserting that there was a strong sentiment against the debt entertained by "leading minds," he intimated that the coupons could be successfully fought. On the other hand, he emphasized the desire of the state to be perfectly fair and her ability to meet her obligations if given time for recovery. The creditors' representatives agreed with the governor that the state could pay four per cent now and should soon be able to pay six per cent. They could do no more, however, than resolve that if punctual payment of interest should be guaranteed, those consol holders who had no taxes to pay would, in their opinion, accept the terms

[13] *Messages*, January 1, March 27 (Sen. *Jour.*, 1874, Doc. 17), December 2, 1874 (with appended speech before the conference, Sen. *Jour.*, 1874-1875, Doc. 1).

proposed by the governor.[14] Out of this resolution grew several propositions, more or less authorized, for funding the consol debt. But from the stringency of their terms it was obvious that the holders of consols intended to surrender their position of preferred creditors only for a better one, and that they would permit no relief to holders of "peelers." This attitude they soon made very clear by thrusting upon the treasury a deluge of coupons.[15]

Thus by 1875 two attempts at undoing the Funding Act had been undertaken by the Conservatives, and had failed. Further agitation would probably prove equally futile. It might injure the party; it would handicap business, already sorely distressed and clamoring for a cessation of attacks upon credit, and it would be accompanied by appeals to the whims and passions of the masses, to which the Bourbons, now rapidly recovering their old-time influence, were bitterly opposed. Accordingly, in the opinion of a majority of the legislature and of almost the entire press, nothing remained but to "pay the debt." This view Governor Kemper accepted. And with his acceptance began a united and truly heroic attempt on the part of almost all the upper classes to meet the state's obligations as they stood.

The program of the "debt payers" was divided into three parts: reduction of expenses, increase of revenues, and reorganization of the sinking fund.

[14] *Op. cit.; Dispatch*, November 11, 1874. Senator H. W. Thomas, of Alexandria, presided; James Dooley, of Richmond, was secretary. Seventy-five to eighty per cent of the consols were held outside the state. Below, p. 89.

[15] Sen. *Jour.*, 1874-1875, Doc. 4; *Dispatch*, November II, 18, 1874; Second Auditor, *Report*, 1875. The *Dispatch* (December 18, 1876) advocated a waiting attitude. The *Enquirer* (December 12) believed the whole attempt "a lame demagogic movement." Even the *Whig* (December 3) was unenthusiastic.

State expenses[16] for all "ordinary" purposes from 1850 to 1860, according to Governor Kemper, averaged $588,236; from 1869 to 1875, $1,084,189—an increase of eighty-four per cent with population and territory reduced nearly one-third. Among "extraordinary" expenses, also, there were new and increased items (quite apart from the public debt) the total of which is not easily ascertainable. Some of these items were due to inefficiency and petty graft, often concealed in fees, travelling expenses, and the like. Others, however, were the unavoidable outcome of war and reconstruction. Such were the one hundred and twenty-five per cent increase in "criminal expenses" for which emancipation and the cumbersome judicial system were responsible, and the eighty-seven per cent in legislative costs for which matters of race adjustment, the unprecedented fiscal situation, and the enlarged powers and duties of the General Assembly offered sufficient reason. Such, too, were increases of some $275,000 for public schools and of perhaps $50,000 for the care of lunatics, a class of expenses which popular approval quite as much as positive law rendered unavoidable.[17] This situation the

[16] Local expenses were curtailed through reducing township officers from twelve to eight and giving the legislature control over local debts. *Cf.* above, p. 50.

[17] Governor, *Message*, December 1, 1875; Sen. *Jour.*, 1859-1860, Doc. 33; *Annual Reports*, 1877; "Civis" (B. Puryear, professor in Richmond College) in *Religious Herald*, January 17 to February 28, 1878. The division between "ordinary" and "extraordinary" expenses is largely an arbitrary one; but the comparison made by Kemper appears fair. "Criminal expenses" were allowances made by the state to the county and circuit courts; the penitentiary was an additional expense, the negroes furnishing the great bulk of the inmates. In 1879, 110 lunatics were being kept in jail and other places besides asylums at an expense to the state of $35,000 a year. Emancipation both increased the amount of crime and transferred the policing of the negro from private to public hands; so with lunacy. An illustration of pettiness appears in Sen. *Jour.*, 1877-1878, Doc. 12, where it is reported that of $1,300 appropriated for the encourage-

"debt payers" attacked vigorously, some favoring a return to the standard of 1860 or perhaps even lowering it in proportion to war losses.[18] But the Radicals, insisting that the adoption of more direct penalties and more summary processes would degrade the lower classes, retarded the adoption of a revised criminal code until 1879; then an annual saving of $50,000 was at once shown. Though the legislature as early as 1874 proposed a constitutional amendment reducing its own membership and substituting biennial for annual sessions, this amendment did not become effective until 1880, because, some said, legislators liked Richmond and their easy salaries. Though both Walker and Kemper had earnestly urged more work and fewer clerks in the departmental offices, every effort in this direction was blocked by the "associated influence" of interested persons.[19] There seemed, indeed, to be two fundamental difficulties. The leaders insisted upon treating alike, as equally foreign and objectionable, those expenses which were mere abuses and those which in the long run would prove both popular and productive. Again, some fees and salaries had come to be considered the customary reward of politicians, great and small, and necessary, in the absence of federal patronage, to keep the state out of the hands of the negroes. The result was that a standard of econ-

ment of immigration, $1,000 went for a *Summary of Virginia,* of which libraries received 303 copies, legislators 1,760, and 43 were sold. Half the legislature's time was consumed in private legislation, sometimes for minor matters—empowering a high school to grant certificates of distinction, for example.

[18] Above, p. 20; "Civis," *op. cit.*

[19] *Acts,* 1877-1878, p. 207; *Thorpe,* VII, 3903; Sen. *Jour.,* 1877-1878, Doc. 7; Auditor, *Reports;* Governor, *Message,* December 1, 1877; "Civis," *op. cit.* Under the revised code the first to suffer the penalty of whipping was a white man in Norfolk, and at the hands of a negro constable, *Annual Cyc.,* 1878.

omy severe even to niggardliness[20] was set for new
undertakings without effecting any considerable elimination of abuses or curtailment of expenses.

The tax-paying class believed themselves to be getting
poorer. In 1875, though the full effects of neither the
long period of depreciating prices nor the panic of 1873
had yet been felt, reassessment of realty showed a loss
of twelve per cent as compared with 1870.[21] Unused to
heavy taxes the people believed their burdens already
too great. Every year $7,000,000 of excise taxes were
collected in the state, and, on a per capita basis, the
state's share of the tariff amounted to nearly $6,000,000;
these great sums, the tax-paying class believed, were
paid by the people of the state. Besides, state and local
taxes amounted to over $5,000,000.[22] To increase the
state's revenues was, accordingly, very difficult. Treasurer R. M. T. Hunter devised a tax revision scheme
intended primarily to reach personalty; but, as such a
scheme would affect landowners primarily, it was quietly
dropped, for opinion was all but unanimous that the land-
owners could stand no further burden. Taxes on business licenses were tried as far as the increasing political
importance of the merchant and the doctor permitted.[23]
Capital, notwithstanding its demand for an honest debt
policy, availed itself of every constitutional safeguard,
of old charter exemptions, and of the strong railroad
contingent in the legislature; not until 1879 did it pay

[20] Below, pp. 59 ff. Because of poverty the state was not represented at
the Centennial Exposition.

[21] Act of March 31, 1875; Auditor, *Reports*, 1871, Doc. 9; *ibid.*, 1877,
Doc. 7. The valuations were $279,000,000 and $246,000,000 (currency).

[22] Sen. *Jour.*, 1874-1875, Doc. 1.

[23] See, for example, tax bill of 1874. In 1879, these yielded (exclusive
of licenses to manufacture and sell liquor) $340,000—a very great increase
over 1871.

as much as $120,000.²⁴ Great efforts were made to reach the masses. Thus a dog tax, it was urged, would net large sums; but the legislature gave it only a brief and imperfect trial, for the dogs' owners had votes.²⁵ For a similar reason the suggested increase of the poll tax from one dollar to two was not tried; and the requirement that the dollar tax be paid before voting netted little additional revenue.²⁶ Dr. Moffett, of the Valley, fathered an act for taxing the consumption of liquor which was expected to produce half a million and to solve the whole matter. But the liquor dealers, now an important political factor, fought it so successfully that there was a large loss the first year, only a slight gain the second, and in the third the act was repealed.²⁷

At the beginning of Kemper's administration the state had two sinking funds: one amounting to a million and a half dollars in 1861, but dormant since then; the other created by the act of March 31, 1871, for the reception of proceeds from the public works. Both were invested almost entirely in state bonds. By an act of March 31, 1875, the former fund was revived and consolidated with the latter, and payment of interest on the whole was authorized. The practice immediately arose of investing this interest in the cheaper state securities. This practice was open to the serious objection that the state was paying herself interest in preference to her creditors, and was depreciating their holdings in order to buy them in at a low price. But it

²⁴ For efforts and difficulties see tax bill of 1871-1872 (extended session); act of February 4, 1873; Governor, *Message*, December 3, 1879; Auditor, *Reports, passim.*

²⁵ *Acts*, 1871-1872; 1872-1873; *Whig*, January 3, 20, 1877.

²⁶ Below.

²⁷ *Acts*, 1876-1877, pp. 245, 301; 1878-1879, p. 310; 1879-1880, p. 147; Auditor, *Reports; Enquirer*, March 3, April 1; *Dispatch*, February 7, 1877; January 17, 1879. The motive appears to have been mainly fiscal. Regulation of the business was quite a problem, however, *Whig*, January 5, 1879.

was certainly legal because the constitution required a sinking fund, and it was probably just because it provided a market for peelers at a time when funds were not available for interest on them.[28] Moreover, it seemed to assure their eventual retirement. By 1877 the total of this fund was $5,145,271; by 1879, $5,841,620.[29]

By 1877 in the opinion of Governor Kemper,[30] the fiscal results of these efforts were very encouraging. For the fiscal year 1876-1877, Kemper estimated a net gain of nearly $200,000 over the average for eight years. "It is as clear as a mathematical demonstration," he wrote, "that, if the legislature shall leave the general features of the present revenue system untouched . . . , the current resources of the treasury will hereafter suffice to pay full interest on the entire outstanding debt." But this optimism, so characteristic of debt payers, found little warrant in the auditor's reports of that year. Over four millions of interest were accrued and unpaid on July 1. Presuming an increase of $125,000 in revenues the next year, the annual deficit would still be $600,000.

But this policy of the debt payers, commendable as it

[28] Authorization of four per cent cash (and a two per cent certificate) for interest on the funded and two-thirds the unfunded was made in 1874 and 1878, provided so much could be spared. In 1876, in order to avoid the discussion always occasioned by special authorizations, interest payment was left entirely to the auditor's discretion under the last clause of the general appropriation act, *Acts*, 1874, p. 264; 1874-1875, p. 366; 1875-1876, p. 263. The amount actually paid in cash in 1876 was $158,000, and in 1877, $68,000, Auditor, *Report*, 1876, Doc. 3; *ibid.*, 1877, Doc. 4.

[29] See C. U. Williams, *Present Financial Status of Virginia.* Apparently, in 1879 some $2,000,000 represented the old fund and its invested interest; some $50,000, the bonds of defaulting officials; $1,540,000 had been "purchased by the commissioners" apparently under act of March 31, 1875; and the rest had come from the sales of state assets. See Second Auditor, *Report*, 1873, Doc. C.

[30] *Message*, December 5, 1877. Compare with message of December 6, 1876, for the governor's optimism.

was, contained one serious defect. It did not take into account the elements of dissatisfaction. Three illustrations of this will suffice.

Early as 1873 the farmers had begun to organize in "granges," for the purpose of alleviating the "languishing condition of agricultural interests" "caused in part by the oppression of unequal legislation, both state and national." Strongly opposed at first because they "introduced innovations upon long and well established usages of society" and endangered the Conservative party, these granges by January, 1876, numbered 685 with a membership of 18,783, including many conservative farmers and shrewd politicians. In state meetings, they appointed committees to obtain favorable legislation on transportation, immigration, and the inspection of tobacco and fertilizers. Locally, they attempted to manufacture fertilizers and to do away with the middleman's profits through co-operative stores and agencies. In 1877, however, the legislature had done little for them, the co-operative undertakings were failing, and the membership appeared to be deteriorating, with a consequent passing of leadership into more radical hands.[31]

[31] State Grange, *Proceedings*, 1874, 1876; *Southern Planter and Farmer*, 1872-1876; "Personal Recollection." The long established State Agricultural Society still existed; also local farmers' clubs. Prominent first members were J. W. White, William Taylor, and Lewis E. Harvie. In 1875, M. W. Hazlewood of Richmond (below) became secretary. Other active members were Franklin Stearns, W. H. Mann, C. T. Sutherlin, B. B. Douglass, Mann Page, J. M. Blanton, R. R. Farr (below), Wm. Ambler, Frank G. Ruffin (below). The *Virginia Patron* became the organ of the order. The *Southern Planter* was favorable, but appears never to have endorsed agitation of railroad rates. The promotion of public education was one of its declared objects, but this was not emphasized. Possibly the long and short haul law (*Acts*, 1874-1875, p. 443) procured a reduction of freight charges on grain; but the rates on guano, agricultural lime, etc., were very high and unequal, Sen. *Jour.*, 1878-1879, Doc. 19; Railroad Commissioner, *Report*, 1878. *Cf.* Magruder, *Recent Administration*, ch. 6.

To a majority of the upper classes between 1865 and 1870 the idea of a state system of public education was distinctly objectionable. The institution, they declared, was a foreign one which their conquerors sought to force upon them. Its main purpose was to break down all social ranks and put the negro upon a plane of equality with the whites. It was an experiment too costly to be tried in the impoverished condition of the state. Others, however, ignoring its immediate origin, declared the institution theoretically good and practically a necessity, in view of the breaking down of the old system and the impossibility of fitting it to the negro even if it should be revived. As a sort of compromise between these two views, it had come to be generally agreed by 1869-1871 that since the constitution had been accepted with the provision for schools in it, the experiment ought to be made in good faith. Such was the view of Governor Walker, of Gen. R. E. Lee (then president of Washington College), of the *Whig,* and probably of the *Dispatch.* To this sentiment the legislature of 1870 responded by entrusting the drafting of the school laws and, virtually, the selection of local school officials to the state superintendent, and by electing as state superintendent Rev. Dr. William Henry Ruffner, son of the famous Henry Ruffner,[32] a man of broad intelligence, marked administrative ability, and indomitable energy. Thus at once the schools were removed from the influence of ordinary politics and the foundation was laid for a system surprisingly good and destined rapidly to increase in popularity. Poverty helped; for many a genteel lady and disabled veteran found employment in the schools and threw about them a much-needed atmosphere of respectability. From the first the negroes favored them solidly. The attempted passage in 1874 of Sumner's

[32] See *Branch Historical Papers,* June, 1910.

Civil Rights Bill requiring mixed schools threatened for a moment to put them out of existence; but this was soon forgotten.[33] And though the whites generally thought that the negro's education ought to be paid for by the federal government and a request to that effect was made, still the negro received, on the whole, a reasonable share of the facilities provided.[34] By 1877 nine-tenths of the families of the state were public school patrons, and it was accounted political death for a public man to oppose openly this institution ''of the people.''[35]

But there still remained lurking in the financial situation a serious danger to the schools. At first, land-owners had protested against the ten cent tax imposed by the state and the still larger taxes imposed by the local governments. Appreciating the importance of this landowning class, Superintendent Ruffner at once suggested the substitution of an increased poll tax and a tax on dogs and the consumption of liquor, arguing that many would contribute for schools in this manner though they would not for anything else. The suggested change was not made, but with the increased use of the schools opposition of this character gradually died away, save for the fitful attacks of that old-fashioned organ of the

---

[33] Rhodes, *History of the United States*, VII, 90; State Superintendent, *Report*, 1874. The legislature protested, Poore, *Descriptive Catalogue*, p. 989.

[34] The whites constituting seven-twelfths of the population (according to the census of 1880) received three-fourths of the school funds. But the negroes paid almost no taxes, were more compactly settled. Besides, it was almost impossible to get suitable teachers in sufficient numbers. For aid to the Hampton Normal and Agricultural Institute see acts of February 7, March 19, 1872.

[35] State Superintendent, *Reports*, 1871-1878; *Educational Journal of Virginia*, 1869, 1870; September, 1878; *Dispatch*, July 10, 1877; February 1, 14, 1878. Very effective in harmonizing public sentiment and the new system was the work of the *Educational Journal* of Virginia, of which John B. Minor, of the University of Virginia, was the father, and C. H. Winston, of Richmond College, the chief editor.

farmers who could not change, the *Southern Planter.* Between the schools and the debt, however, the clash grew sharper and sharper. Early as 1873[36] the superintendent, with characteristic foresight, secured the passage of an act requiring the auditor to pay the schools their constitutional quota of state funds in *cash.* Despite this it was discovered in 1876 that there was due the schools down to 1875 nearly $400,000. By 1877 this sum had increased to $526,000, and in September of the next year appeared to be $850,000. If to this amount was added the interest due on the state bonds held by the literary fund, the total "diverted" was over a million.[37] The auditor's excuse was the confusion of the state's bookkeeping and the inadequacy of the revenues. He had, he said, paid the schools more than their *pro rata* share (one-fifth) of the cash received; the government must go on; the obligation to pay the debt was equally as sacred as the schools. Worse still, from the viewpoint of school partisans, the colleges and the religious press, being habitually conservative and tied up in interest with the bond-holding class, urged the moral obligation to pay the debt while speaking of the education of the masses as a luxury.[38] Bourbons took courage, and began to talk of abolishing the new system in favor of the old one. And a prominent debt payer was understood to have said publicly that it would be better to burn the schoolhouses than to permit the state to default in interest payment on the debt. Thus it came about that, while the people were paying the school tax

[36] Act of March 29.

[37] Superintendent, *Reports,* 1876, 1877, 1878; Auditor, *Report,* 1878. Of $8,511,943 cash received by the state from 1873 to 1877, $1,912,266 was paid to the schools.

[38] Second Auditor, *Report,* 1879; *Religious Herald,* 1878, 1879, *passim.* Not all college men agreed with the auditor, *e.g.,* John B. Minor, letter to Ruffner, November 21, 1877, in *Ruffner Papers.*

and the system was growing in popularity, teachers were going unpaid and schools were closing. These facts the state superintendent did not fail to point out, and the politicians, great and small, took notice.[39]

In later years when the "Readjuster" political party had been formed,[40] certain men were often spoken of as "original readjusters." By this it was meant that they had at an early date objected to recognizing the whole debt of the state as valid, and had insisted that it be "re-adjusted." Hints of this view we have met from time to time. It originated, apparently, in a feeling of humiliation and resentment that men who had inflicted loss upon the state, and such Virginians as were now willing to ally themselves with them, should be able to levy tribute upon those who had defended her with their all. The enactment of laws staying the collection of private debts, the setting aside of a share of the public debt for West Virginia, the iniquities of the Funding Act, and the obvious impossibility of meeting its terms, all contributed to emphasize the idea in thoughtful minds.[41]

In the legislature the notable advocates of this view were Massey and Fulkerson,[42] J. Horace Lacy, of Spottsylvania, Moffett, of Rockingham, and Lybrook, of Patrick. They argued[43] that Virginia had been "con-

[39] The situation as to asylums and other public charities was similar to that of the schools. The *Enquirer* (February 4, 1875) estimated the number of the insane unprovided for at 500.

[40] Below, ch. 8.

[41] Above, *passim*.

[42] Below, p. 105.

[43] This is a composite argument. For development of Massey's views compare his letter of 1873, his speech in the House in February, 1875, his pamphlet, *Debts and Taxes*, published in the fall of 1875, and articles in the Staunton *Spectator* in 1877. The speech is in *Virginia Political Pamphlets*, I (Virginia State Library), the others in his "Autobiography." See also Ruffin, *Scrap-Book*, I (Virginia State Library), *An Appeal;* Fulkerson in *Whig*, January 13, 1879.

quered territory'' and therefore, according to the law
of nations, her *ante-bellum* debts devolved upon her
conqueror. If the federal government would not admit
this, then equity demanded that the debt should be
reduced in proportion to the impairment of the security
on which it had been based—one-third for the loss of
West Virginia and one-third for property destroyed by
war, leaving $15,000,000 principal and interest as of 1865.
No recognition of the debt was valid which had been made
between 1865 and 1870, because the state was not then
in possession of her ''sovereignty.'' As for the Funding
Act, its moral force was vitiated by fraud in its passage;
and though the courts had declared it binding, that
decision was wrong in principle because it ''bound the
state's sovereignty,'' and so could justifiably be reversed
or avoided. The ''state's honor'' and ''restoration of
credit'' arguments relied upon by debt payers were alike
purely commercial. Both depended upon ability and
ability was conditioned by the size of the debt. In this
debt, under existing arrangements, was probably included the portion which had been pretendedly set aside
for West Virginia but which was known on the market as
''Virginia deferred.''. In it certainly should be included
the literary and sinking funds. Taxes on ''dogs and
whiskey'' and all the painful expedients of debt payers
they thought simply absurd.

After the failure of the compromise move in 1874,
something like a concerted attack on coupons and a
campaign for publicity had been begun under the lead
of these men. Through the columns of the *Whig*, Col.
Frank G. Ruffin replied in his striking style to the
Council of Foreign Bondholders, London, over the
signature of ''A Virginia Farmer.''[44] Massey sought
to have the legislature ask explicit instructions from the

---

[44] Ruffin, *Scrap-Book*, I.

people as to the terms on which they were willing to compromise with creditors, and in a pamphlet known as "Debts and Taxes" he reprinted his peculiar views previously expressed through the local press.[45] In the legislature, Fulkerson, hoping to bring the Funding Act again before the courts, pushed through the House a bill imposing a tax of twenty-five per cent on coupons,[46] while Massey sought, under guise of protecting the treasury from fraud, to hamper their receipt for taxes.[47] In 1876-1877 similar efforts again met defeat; but the effects of the agitation were seen in resolutions deliberately designed to scale the debt one-half or two-thirds, which were offered by the Independent Stovall and the Radical Curlett.[48] More immediately important were the earnest efforts of careful leaders of the old school, such as R. M. T. Hunter and A. H. H. Stuart, to effect a compromise with creditors;[49] for these men, though far from accepting "original readjuster" principles, inevitably lent an atmosphere of seriousness to the idea of readjustment.

These measures had received support from practically all Republicans, Independents, and "Southwest" Conservatives, from part of the Valley Conservatives, and from individuals and counties here and there with whom times were hard.[50] There was a certain resemblance,

[45] See House resolution, in *Virginia Political Pamphlets*, I; Massey, "Autobiography."

[46] *Enquirer*, March 14, 17; *Dispatch*, March 18, 20, 1875.

[47] *Virginia Political Pamphlets*, I; *Enquirer*, February 11, 1875. Conditions warranted suspicion, see below, p. 62.

[48] House, *Jour.*, 1876-1877, index.

[49] Stuart's effort had the endorsement of William Cullen Bryant, Thurlow Weed, and Peter Cooper, but it netted only a report on war losses, *Whig*, January 11, 13; March 30, 1877. For Hunter see Ruffin, *Scrap-Book*, I.

[50] House vote on Fulkerson's proposal: "Ayes," 21 Radicals, 36 Conservatives, 1 Independent; "Noes," 3 Radicals, 41 Conservatives, 3 Independents (*Dispatch* classification, March 18, 1875). Among Valley

taking them as a group, between these men and Mahone's railroad faction, though the two were by no means identical. They were friendly to the schools. Some of them were prominent in the granges. They had back of them, however, no organization, no strong press support,[51] no great financial interests. At the beginning of 1877 it seemed that this second wave of repudiation, like that of 1867-1868, had been completely beaten off by the determination and influence of "debt payers."

Summarizing, we find that though the Republicans won the national elections of 1870 and 1872, their party was again beaten in the state elections in 1873, and thereafter rapidly declined. This result was due in part to the Confederate reaction and in part to restrictive legislation. In this legislation the influence of Bourbonism, as well as that of politics, was reflected. The fiscal situation had now become acute. Accordingly, when creditors had refused to compromise despite veiled threats from the new governor, Conservative leaders informally adopted a policy of "paying the debt" through decreasing expenses, increasing revenues, and redeeming the cheaper bonds. This policy completed the union between Bourbons and the city capitalistic interests. But, though faithfully pursued for four years, it met only partial success owing at once to depressed economic conditions and to the burden unavoidably imposed by emancipation and the new constitution. Moreover, such a policy involved no attempt at conciliation of the farmers, now seeking defence of their interests

members not voting was Riddleberger. Ross Hamilton (below) and James B. Richmond voted ''aye,'' Lybrook and Allen (below) voted ''no.'' Examples of counties probably influenced by hard times are Spottsylvania, Stafford, Lancaster, and Essex.

   [51] The *Whig* favored compromise, but not Massey's and Fulkerson's methods.

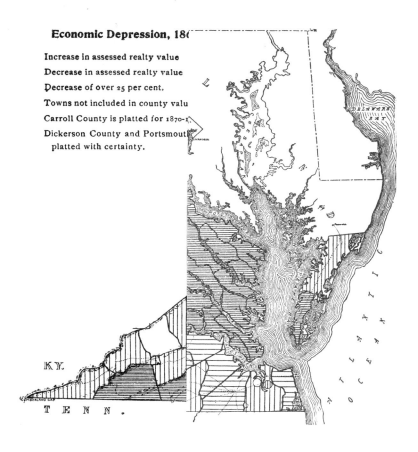

Economic Depression, 18(

Increase in assessed realty value
Decrease in assessed realty value
Decrease of over 25 per cent.
Towns not included in county valu
Carroll County is platted for 1870-1
Dickerson County and Portsmout
  platted with certainty.

in the granges, nor did it appease school partisans to
see "debt payers" and Bourbons united against them.
Believing all other remedies futile, "original readjusters" now openly began not only to demand that the
debt be scaled but also to fight the tax-receivable coupons
in the legislature and the public press with a view to
forcing the issue.

CHAPTER VI

MAHONE AND THE BARBOUR BILL, 1877-1878

Both governor and legislature were to be chosen in 1877. At last, owing to Republican disorganization and apathy,[1] the Conservatives were free to act without the restraining fear of Radical domination. But it was impossible at once to break the habit of years, and the habit had been to refer all issues, save that of race control, to the decision of the legislative districts, and to follow in these districts the leadership of war heroes.[2] Personal and sectional rivalries, therefore, rather than economic and social issues, characterized the gubernatorial race in its earlier stages. The "Southwest" presented Gen. William Terry; the Valley, Colonel Holliday;[3] the Piedmont, Maj. John W. Daniel; the Tidewater, Gen. William B. Taliaferro; while Gen. Fitzhugh Lee's friends urged him as a compromise candidate. None of these expressed, or was expected to express, opinions on the burning economic and social questions of the day, for the convention must be left free to "point with pride," as of old. From this negative attitude the campaign was rescued by the candidacy of General Mahone.

William Mahone[4] was essentially a self-made man.

---

[1] Above, p. 50; below, p. 134.

[2] See above, p. 48.

[3] F. W. M. Holliday was born in Winchester. He studied at Yale and later took a law course at the University of Virginia.

[4] W. L. Royall, *Some Reminiscences;* Withers, *Autobiography;* O'Ferrall, *Forty Years;* Ruffin, *Mahoneism Unveiled; Whig,* November 20, 1879 (being a reprint from the *Old Dominion Magazine*); *New Virginia.*

The son of a poor but respected merchant in one of the older counties, he had been educated at the Virginia Military Institute through the aid of friends. For a time he taught school, then he built railroads, notably the Norfolk and Petersburg of which he became president. Entering the war as colonel, he came out major-general. "Mahone's brigade" was noted for superior equipment and condition, and at Appomattox mustered out more men than any other.[5]

Mahone was perhaps the first in the South to grasp the possibilities of railway consolidation. Out of three loosely connecting and dilapidated roads, he soon created a splendid trunk line nearly crossing the state from east to west, and of this he became president with the munificent salary of $25,000. To this line he diverted from more direct routes the northward-bound cotton of the South to Norfolk, where allied steamships connected. In token of his hopes he called this road the "Atlantic, Mississippi, and Ohio."

To carry out his railroad plans public influence was necessary, and this he sought in ways characteristic of the new generation rather than of the old. Thus he strove to mould public opinion through the *Whig*[6] and perhaps other newspapers, though his control over their ownership was never announced. Always a Conservative, he had been found on each successive inauguration day "close to" the new governor. When special legislation was to be enacted, his unseen hand directed that new institution, the lobby. If a measure was to be defeated, his men were usually in the proper place, whether on legislative committees or in departmental offices. As agents in these matters, he sometimes

[5] Speech of John S. Wise in the convention of 1877 (below). J. H. Lacy in an anti-Mahone speech stated that General Lee had expressed a preference for Mahone as his successor, *Virginia Star*, August 20, 1879.

[6] Above, p. 29, and note.

obtained men already prominent in public life, but more frequently he brought forward new men, perhaps by organizing the "odds and ends" in their communities. And so a "Mahone following" was gradually built up, which was strong enough to be credited with having determined the selection of Kemper for governor.[7]

But Mahone's railroad policy had neglected or injured towns and sections, and these, especially Richmond and the Valley and part of the "Southwest," bore him distinct ill will. Competing interests dubbed him the "Railroad Ishmael."[8] Practical men saw in the financial arrangements of the A. M. & O. with the state[9] little less than a steal. Though weighty in the councils of his party and generous in its support, Mahone so conducted his relations with the Republicans and the Liberals as to suggest a lack of political principle and to create constant suspicion.[10] More than one impartial and thoughtful man despised his legislative methods and deemed his power too great.[11] There was about him, too, an imperiousness of will and manner that had helped to estrange

[7] See *Enquirer*, June 6; *Whig*, May 29, 1876; *Dispatch*, August 3, 1877. The A. M. & O. paid $155,069 for "legal fees, commissions, engraving, bonds, &c." at the time of consolidation, *Dispatch*, October 11, 1879. For Mahone's share in the campaign of 1873 (above, ch. 5) see Withers, *Autobiography*, p. 313; *Whig*, July 7, 9; August 2, 1872; *Nation*, August 14, 1873; *Dispatch*, August 3, 1877; *Enquirer*, June 6; *Whig*, May 29, 1876. Prominent in support of Kemper were Dr. Rives, Dr. Moffett, James Barbour, Joseph Mayo, all of whom favored Mahone's debt views in 1877 (below). N. B. Meade, editor of the *Whig*, became chairman of the Conservative executive committee in 1873.

[8] The phrase was William E. Cameron's. For the fight over the Richmond and Danville Railroad, to which Mahone, Scott, Garrett, and a group of Richmond men were parties, see *Whig*, *Dispatch*, *Enquirer*, April, May, December, 1874. There is virtually no mention of the A. M. & O. in the *American Railroad Journal* from 1870 to 1876.

[9] Above, p. 27, and note.

[10] The *Whig* always favored liberal party lines; so did Kemper, see *Message*, January 1, 1874; above, pp. 38, 48.

[11] *Enquirer*, July 6, 13, 1877; March 31, 1871.

each successive governor and some of his own strongest
followers.[12]   An unfortunate magazine article and the
farcical pretense at a duel which followed led to the
charge that his military reputation was made by the
press and his personal courage was questionable.[13]   Significantly enough, most of the old Bourbons and debt
payers were included in some one of these groups of
detractors.

It was probably with the hope of using the office to
recover his road, now in the hands of a receiver,[14] that
Mahone began his race for the governorship.   Until
July, the arguments advanced in his behalf were distinctive only in the emphasis laid upon the benefits
derived by the state from his business activities.   But
from the first, as the Norfolk *Landmark* said, "No radical candidate was ever pursued with more remorseless
severity."   Had he not destroyed six millions of state
assets, blocked large enterprises, and ruined his road?
Where had he learned statesmanship?   Was it not as
"king of the lobby"?   Would he pledge himself not to
run independently if he failed to obtain the regular
nomination?   The widespread character of this attack
soon showed that the case was one of "Mahone against
the field," and that Mahone would lose unless he could

    12 Norfolk *Landmark*, June 17, 1877; Richmond *Times*, October 9, 1895;
Governor Peirpoint does not appear to have been estranged.

    13 W. L. Royall, *Some Reminiscences*, p. 82; Withers, *Autobiography*,
pp. 307 ff.

    14 Mahone's friends contended that this was the result of a conspiracy
between a representative of English bondholders of the A. M. & O., Bourbons, and the Pennsylvania, C. & O., and B. & O. interests. A desire for
change of management by the English holders and the good relations of
Vice-President Wickham of the C. & O. with the federal and state courts
and Richmond capitalists are indicated by the *American Railroad Journal*,
September, December, 1875; April, June, 1876; October, November, 1877.
In *New Virginia* the statement is made that Mahone was offered the
presidency of the road upon certain conditions.

effect a diversion.[15] Accordingly, early in July, there appeared in the *Whig*[16] and other friendly papers a letter which did not "re-open the debt question,"[17] but which did mark the beginning of Mahone's antagonism to the "debt paying" policy. In this letter he declared, in brief, clear fashion, that to continue "in the present path of inaction" would mean ruin to both state and creditors; that taxes could not be increased; and that "It seems to me the part of practical wisdom, and in direct pursuit of an honorable purpose to deal fairly with the public creditors, that we should seek and insist upon, urge and if necessary demand, a complete readjustment of the debt of the commonwealth and of the annual liabilities thereunder which shall be within the certain and reasonable capacity of the people to pay." Defining his position somewhat further, in another letter[18] he declared "diversion"[19] of the school funds not only a violation of the constitution but also bad public policy and contrary to the wishes of the people. For free schools, he argued, were necessary for the children of soldiers and, significantly, for "the large class of persons recently admitted to the privileges of citizenship."

"The very letter for the times—clear, manly, bold . . .," wrote Colonel Fulkerson,[20] from the "Southwest"

[15] See, for example, *Whig*, March 26 (quoting Staunton *Virginian*), April 23, 21 (quoting Farmville *Mercury*); *Dispatch*, April 6, 30, May 11, June 27, July 2, 5 (quoting Gordonsville *Gazette*); Norfolk *Landmark*, June 19, 20, 1877.

[16] The letter was addressed to M. M. Martin, Charlotte, C. H.

[17] Above, *cf.* pp. 58 ff.; *Dispatch*, July 7, 11 (noting articles by Ruffin in Virginia *Patron*, and *Southern Planter*, and the talk of local candidates); *Whig*, April 17 (Hunter letter).

[18] To Major Alfred R. Courteney, of the Richmond school board, under date June 29, 1877.

[19] Above, p. 62.

[20] *Whig*, October 15, 1882. Massey says that Fulkerson gave Mahone a copy of *Debts and Taxes* and that Mahone was converted thereby, *Autobiography*.

on the appearance of the first of these declarations. "It will elect you governor." The election of delegates had proceeded too far, however, for any such decisive result to be possible. Still, great interest was aroused. The *Enquirer,* speaking for the extreme Bourbon faction, even encouraged the suggestion that the nomination of Mahone might mean the union of the debt-paying Conservatives with the Republicans,[21] for it deemed these letters an appeal to the radical spirit manifesting itself all over the country and, because "levelled at property," an offspring of the "French principles of '93."[22] The *Dispatch,* more diplomatically, tried to break their force by insisting that there was nothing original in Mahone's suggestions, that the convention would, of course, decide what should be done in these matters, and that the nominee would have to abide by its decision.[23] Soon it appeared that "readjustment" had more partisans than "debt payment." All but one of the other candidates declared for it, though with vague qualifications.[24] How a readjustment could be obtained was the question. Mahone had said, "If necessary, demand"; did he mean to *compel* creditors to compromise? And if so, would not this be repudiation? This question Mahone shrewdly left unanswered.

Both the earlier and the later phases of the prelimi-

[21] See quotation from New York *Tribune,* July 29.

[22] July 25, 27, 31. The Lynchburg *Virginian* and the Lexington *Gazette* held similar views.

[23] On the morning of the publication of the debt letter, the *Dispatch* editorially favored debt action by the convention. This, it declared (July 14), was done without knowledge of the letter. It never published the letter.

[24] Only Terry flatly declared for payment of the "last dollar." For views of candidates see *Dispatch,* July 10 (Lee), 31 (Taliaferro and Holliday); *Whig,* July 13 (Terry); *Enquirer,* August 2 (Daniel).

nary campaign were reflected in the convention.[25]   Fourteen hundred delegates, August weather, free liquor, and
unrestrained eloquence marked the celebration by elastic
spirits of a victorious party policy.   Mahone, on the
other hand, was prepared to fight, and there was a dangerous enthusiasm and confidence among his young floor
leaders, Wise, Stringfellow, Cameron, and Riddleberger.
Uniting with other "forcible" readjusters, for the debt
views and the gubernatorial preferences of the delegates
did not always coincide, he endeavored to have the platform adopted first.   But Daniel, Holliday, and Lee
marshalled their forces in joint caucus and prevented
this innovation.   In the balloting, Mahone at first led,
his strength coming chiefly from the "Southside" but
with significant additions from all parts of the state, that
is, from the "solid business men" of Norfolk, the "ward-
heelers of Richmond," and counties wherein the personal influence of a lieutenant was predominant.   Then
Daniel forged ahead, the readjuster "Southwest" swing-
ing to him when its favorite was dropped, rather than to
the former "railroad king," who had once disappointed
them.[26]   Thereupon Mahone in spectacular fashion threw
his strength almost *en masse* to the Valley candidate, who
consequently received the nomination.   By this maneuver Mahone not only established "claims" upon Colonel
Holliday and the Valley but also made the nomination
appear colorless from the viewpoint of readjustment.
Colorless, too, was the platform which urged the use of
"all just and honorable means of bringing about an
adjustment of the obligations of the Commonwealth
which will bring the payment of interest upon the debt

[25] *Enquirer, Whig, Dispatch,* August 5, 10.   Under the editorship of
James Barron Hope, the *Landmark* was strongly for Mahone, understanding that Mahone was not for repudiation.

[26] In not extending the A. M. & O. to Cumberland Gap.

within the resources of the state derived from the present rate of taxation, and so do justice to all classes of
our creditors.'' But it was significant that at last the
Conservative party had taken a stand on the debt
question.

Since the Republicans made no nomination for state
offices, Colonel Holliday and his colleagues were not
called upon during the ensuing campaign to interpret
the Conservative platform.[27] Again, therefore, the
matter was referred to the legislative districts.[28] Here
confusion reigned.

Early as 1870, we find Conservatives standing for
office as Independents.[29] The chief cause of this phenomenon was the temptation to bolt offered to numerous
office-seekers by the eagerness of the negro minority to
vote against regular Conservative nominees. One might
not become a Radical and retain his social standing; but
under the Conservative policy of liberal lines and a
single paramount issue[30] one might occasionally bolt and
yet retain the brand of ''Conservatism.'' The favorite
excuse for bolting was ''ring rule'' and ''court-house

[27] In his letter of acceptance Colonel Holliday merely expressed the hope
that the people would choose men for the legislature who ''have in view
the memories and the resources of Virginia,'' as ''on them in chief measure
will fall the work of solving this question,'' *Enquirer,* September 1. The
Enquirer commented (September 2): ''If [the letter] means any thing it
is that the writer appreciates the necessity for a canvass of the state debt
question within the party.'' The readjusters, however, saw in it a pledge
to leave the decision to the people expressing themselves through the legislature. *Cf.* Riddleberger in *Whig,* March 9, 1880.

[28] *Whig,* August 31, September 1; *Dispatch,* July 31.

[29] *Whig,* November 11; *Enquirer* (quoting Lynchburg *Virginian*),
November 11, 1870; *Dispatch,* November 2, 3, 6, 10, 1875; Knight *v.*
Johnson, Sen. *Jour.,* 1875-1876, Doc. 13; ''Personal Recollections.'' For
dislike of Independents, *cf.* George F. Hoar, *Autobiography,* I, p. 313;
F. Curtis, *The Republican Party,* last chapter; W. L. Fleming, *Civil War
and Reconstruction in Alabama.*

[30] Above, pp. 37, 48.

cliques.'' There was much truth, beyond doubt, in the
implied charge. For with the reaction against Radical
rule, beginning as early as 1871, power had passed very
naturally to old leaders and old families, and there the
''Confederate cult'' tended to keep it. Since this leadership, whether unduly influenced by the bondholding
interests or not, was somewhat self-centered and neglectful of the wishes of the people, the Independents had
pretty generally advocated whatever appeared ''popular'' or savored of ''reform.''[31]

Now in 1877, the conditions which had in the past
called Independents into existence, prevailed to an
unusual degree.[32] The disorganized state of the Republican party[33] rendered negro minorities unprecedentedly
available. Mahone men were complaining, not without reason, of much unfair treatment in the convention primaries. The nation-wide labor agitation
was affecting Virginia cities.[34] Saloon-keepers had a
special grievance in the Moffett ''punch bill,'' which
Mahone, appreciating their power, had taken pains to
characterize as ''class legislation.''[35] The varied program of the more than six hundred granges had created
business antagonisms, which, with some concealment,
were transforming themselves into political factions.[36]
And to the confusion caused by all this was added the
doubtful meaning of the Conservative platform.[37] The
cool-headed *Dispatch* admitted that ''the war brought

[31] Above, p. 65.

[32] *Landmark,* April 8, May 25; *Whig,* July 7, 13 (quoting Portsmouth
Enterprise); *Dispatch,* July 9, 27; August 3; *Enquirer,* July 25; November
4, 6, 27.

[33] Below, p. 38.

[34] The *Whig* sympathized with this move, August 15.

[35] Letter on the debt, above.

[36] ''Personal Recollections.''

[37] On October 7, the *Enquirer* printed correspondence between Major
James Dooley and Gen. Joseph R. Anderson, both of Richmond, the former

changes in the moral sensibilities of the people,'' and feared that ''agitation only tends to increase the public indifference to public honor.'' On the other hand the *Whig* printed, with evident approval, the opinion of an observant correspondent that the Conservative party ''is dead,'' because its leaders either did not know the proper limitations of the words ''public faith'' and ''independent judiciary'' or ''did not choose, from whatever cause, to face the plutocracy that aspires to control, even though it ruin, the people of the state.''[38]

Such conditions were necessarily reflected in the legislative campaigns. Duff Green in the Stafford-King George district, and J. L. Powell in Spottsylvania began Independent attacks on the Fredericksburg ''ring.'' Richmond and Lynchburg had Working Men's tickets. In Henrico, Branch and Atkinson both stood as Conservatives, one for payment of the ''last dollar,'' the other for no increase of taxes. In Albemarle, Massey was the regular nominee for the Senate, while Independents upheld his debt views against the regular nominees for the House. The *Dispatch* opposed Massey because he had once been an Independent, but supported General Starke in Brunswick because, though an Independent, he was for debt payment. In some counties, such as Pittsylvania and Augusta, the Conservatives do not appear to have made any formal nominations. An analysis of the election returns show that twenty-two Independents were elected to the House and that the idea of readjustment had won a sweeping victory.[39]

the author of the Conservative platform, the latter chairman of the committee on resolutions, which showed that neither of them understood the debt plank to endorse ''forcible'' readjustment, nor, indeed, anything similar to the later ''Barbour bill'' (below).

[38] See *Dispatch*, March 20; *Whig*, August 19, 1878.

[39] The ''Southwest'' was solid and the Valley nearly solid. Some of the negroes voted for Independents (who were generally for readjustment),

But whether these results rested upon some deep-seated feeling of dissatisfaction with old methods and issues, as is indicated by the setting aside of old leaders such as William Smith and John Letcher, or upon mere intrigue, as is suggested by the lightness of the vote, is not clear. Nor is it certain, on account of the vagueness of the Conservative platform and the confusion of issues in the local campaigns, just what kind of readjustment was endorsed.[40]

With the assembling of the legislature in December, 1877, the fiscal program of the readjusters became somewhat clearer. From the House finance committee came the "Barbour bill,"[41] which received the support of virtually all the Republicans and Independents and a majority of the Conservatives voting.[42] In its preamble this bill declared that "the preservation of the state government is the first necessity; the constitutional obligation to support the system of public schools, the second; and the payment of the present rate of interest

and some for General Mahone, who consistently supported the regular ticket.

[40] *Whig*, August 29, September 1, 3, November 12, 16, December 18; *Dispatch*, July 9, November 9, 11, 12, 15; *Enquirer*, November 4, 27; Virginia *Star*, October 8, November 10; *Nation*, November 1.

[41] So called from James Barbour (below) chairman of the House finance committee. This committee was appointed by the speaker, H. C. Allen, of the Valley, whom a readjuster conference had endorsed and sustained in full Conservative caucus. There were several such conferences, supposedly secret, *Dispatch* and *Whig*, December 5, 6, 10, 13, 18, 1877. The citation is from the governor's veto message, *op. cit.*

[42] House vote: aye, 20 Independents, 8 Republicans, 43 Conservatives; no, 1 Republican, 39 Conservatives. Voting affirmatively were the Conservatives Farr, Fowler, B. W. Lacy, D. A. Grimsley, Paul, Phlegar, H. C. Slemp, Hoge, Tyler; and the Independents T. L. Michie, L. E. Harvie, and P. B. Starke. Prominent in opposition were: Jos. R. Anderson, W. W. Henry, W. T. Taliaferro, Thos. S. Bocock, Marshall Hanger, John Echols, John T. Lovell, Robert Ryland, Wm. B. Taliaferro. The negative vote was strongest in the cities, Richmond and Norfolk being solidly negative, House *Jour.*, 1877-1878, p. 284; Sen. *Jour.*, p. 296.

on the amount claimed as the principle of the public
debt, the third." Economic conditions, it continued,
forbade an increase of taxes. Therefore, of each fifty
cents collected through the general property tax, twenty-
five must go to the support of the government, ten to
the schools, and fifteen to debt interest; and the parts
thus set aside for the government and the schools must
be paid in money. But Governor Holliday, deeming this
bill only an attempt to rob the creditors and a transfer
of the "vexed and vexing question from the legislature
to the courts," promptly vetoed it.[43] Thereupon, with
the treasury empty and the banks refusing to lend, and
with the Conservative party in danger of disruption,[44]
moderate men came into control, as in 1872. These
moderates, however, could suggest nothing except an
appeal to the creditors for a compromise, the terms of
which they embodied in the "Bocock-Fowler Act."[45]

That the motive behind the Barbour bill was only in
part fiscal is also clear. The wild talk of a "moneyed
aristocracy created by office-holders" and the suspicion
cast upon their integrity, the complaint of the seduction
of readjuster legislators by the "money rings," the
refusal to amend the Moffett act so as to make it efficient,
the suggestion of a constitutional convention to abolish
the veto and revise the debt—all of these reflected the
discontent of the preceding campaign.[46] Moreover, a

43 House *Jour.*, p. 425.

44 Below.

45 Act of March 14, 1878; *Dispatch* and *Whig*, March 14, 15; *Whig*,
March 6, 1878 (statement of auditor). The auditor was directed (*Acts*,
1877-1878, p. 237) to pay the "diverted" school funds in quarterly cash
installments, but he interpreted this to mean, if the cash could be spared,
Report, 1878.

46 *Whig*, December 12, 1877; January 3, 30; February 7, 12; March
2, 15, 1878; *Dispatch*, December 6, 7, 1877. Thirty-five thousand dollars of
bonds were reported to have been abstracted and funded a second time,

determination to control the Conservative party or to disrupt it was indicated when the readjusters not only admitted Independents to their conferences but compelled the full Conservative caucus to do likewise.[47] Most appropriately, the *Enquirer,* which had so consistently preached against "radicalism" and demanded the drawing of strict party lines, expired with 1877.

Immediately after the adjournment of the legislature there began a series of secret conferences among leading readjusters.[48] As a result General Mahone sent to readjuster legislators a circular letter to be signed and returned for publication over their joint signatures. This circular declared that both the veto of the Barbour bill and a recent decision of the state supreme court reaffirming the binding force of the Funding Act and in effect demanding that taxes be increased were in direct defiance of the will of the people taken in accordance with the Conservative platform of the year before, and it urged the people "to take measures to give efficiency and effect to your will, by public meetings, to be held as you may elect, and the organization of committees for each representative [Congressional] district." As "principles of faith," it advised: the sovereignty of the people of the state in matters of taxation, expenditures, and schools; reform and economy in administration; and a constitutional convention.

The immediate purpose of these activities was prob-

but this was the result of an earlier defalcation, Sen. *Jour.,* 1877-1878, Docs. 4, 6.

[47] *Op. cit.*

[48] *Dispatch,* July 5; *Whig,* July 10, 1878. Two committees acted in the matter. The first consisted of H. H. Harrison, Lewis E. Harvie, B. W. Lacy (members of the legislature), and A. Moseley, W. H. Mann, Wm. Mahone (identified with the *Whig*). These activities were suspected but not definitely known until the *Dispatch* published (July 5) the circular with the accompanying "confidential letter." The letter requested a cash contribution.

ably the election of readjuster Congressmen in the fall by identifying the state issue with the national Greenback movement on the ground that both were against "money rings" and their allies the courts. Thus the *Whig's* platform embraced "forcible and irrepressible Readjustment of the state debt" and readjustment of the national debt by paying it in greenbacks, together with the requirement of unanimity for setting aside a law as unconstitutional in either state or federal courts and the thorough purging of both from all impurities "personal or judicial."[49]   At first extreme debt payers and "hard money" men, relying on their control of the Conservative party machinery, were for accepting this challenge and fighting it out on strictly party lines.[50]   A calm survey of the individual districts, however, showed clearly that such a course would probably mean Independent or Radical success in each.[51]   On the other hand, there were many readjusters who were unwilling to desert the Conservative party for that of the "Greenbackers," and some who thought a better fight could be made on the state issue alone.[52]   As the campaign progressed, leading debt payers, notably the sitting members of Congress, endorsed Greenback ideas in a more or less qualified manner.[53]   And so the movement for identifying the state issue with the national Greenback movement failed.   Only two readjusters, and these of the moderate type, were elected to Congress.

Details of the campaign, however, show how thor-

---

[49] May 31, March 20, April 3, 28, July 12.

[50] For example, the Richmond *State* and the Lexington *Gazette*.

[51] *Dispatch*, July 12.

[52] *Dispatch*, May 30, July 12.

[53] *Whig*, August 26 (R. L. T. Beale), 27 (Daniel); September 6 (Johnston).   Only "Ran" Tucker was out and out for "hard money."   General Johnston was a "gold greenbacker."   All the candidates except these two satisfied the *Whig* on the national issue.

oughly the forces of social and political discontent were
disrupting the Conservative organization. In the Richmond district, John S. Wise seemed to have a clear field.
But he belonged to the local Mahone faction which
had long been fighting Gen. Bradley T. Johnson as an
ardent funder and "free" railroad man, and, the *Whig*
insisted, a too skilful manager of party conventions.
Accordingly, friends of General Johnson persuaded
Gen. Joseph E. Johnston to become a candidate in the
belief that Wise would not oppose his old commander.
This belief proved correct.   But the *Whig* in disgust
supported Newman, the "Greenback" candidate, alleg-
ing as an excuse that Johnston was not acceptable to the
people, as shown by the smallness of the primary vote.[54]
In the Valley, John T. Harris, a moderate advocate of
readjustment and greenbacks, was opposed by John
Paul, a more ardent advocate, and by Gen. John Echols,
who was a debt payer and "hard money" man.   Echols
withdrew in Harris's favor, but Paul fought it out
independently.   The banner district for confusion, however, was in the "Southwest."   Here, debt payers said,
the Mahone-Fulkerson-Blair idea was to use the local
officials to supplant the existing party organization.
Part of their forces, however, were diverted by Fayette
McMullin who ran as a Conservative-Independent-
Greenbacker and advocate of federal construction of
the Cumberland Gap railroad.   At the nominating convention a resolution endorsing greenbacks and readjustment was voted down, whereupon the backwoodsmen
left and Col. John B. Richmond was named over
two other aspirants.   Colonel Richmond soon declared

[54] *Whig*, August 2, September 26; Royall, *Some Reminiscences;* "Per-
sonal Recollections" (of Mr. Royall).   Wise had been associated with
Edgar Allen as counsel for Platt, Republican, against John Goode,
Goode Recollections.

himself for "honest" readjustment and greenbacks. General Newberry as an Independent-Greenbacker, a regular Republican, and an Independent Republican completed the list of candidates.[55]

Soon after the elections, there was organized in Richmond a "society to preserve the credit of the state." It was composed of thirty-nine leading citizens, among whom were several representative ministers and two Republican judges. In its open address, this association proposed that similar affiliated societies, without specified restriction as to party or race, should be formed throughout the state, and that each should select and support a "debt paying" candidate for the legislature the following year. The gist of the argument advanced was that an increase of twenty cents in taxes (only a ten per cent increase in the total tax in many counties) would meet all the state's needs, including a sinking fund. "The work proposed is grand," declared the *Dispatch,* and the editor of the *State* was among the associators. But the *Whig* poured upon the "39," and especially upon its "D. D." members, the vials of its wrath.[56] Outside of Richmond the move seems to have been regarded by the Conservatives as a mistake, for it was not only in direct opposition to the pledge of readjustment without increase of taxes, but it also frankly substituted a fiscal issue for old party lines and constituted ministers, bondholders, and federal officials, directors in a matter which people had come to consider chiefly political. Though the plan soon proved abortive, it is significant as showing the loosening of old party ties in the face of the new economic and moral issues,

[55] *Dispatch* and *Whig*, 1878, *passim*, especially August 10, 12, and early November numbers.
[56] It persistently published (*e.g.*, December 17) the amount of coupons used in payment of taxes by the "D. D." members.

and as affording a convenient pretext the year following for the organization of a Readjuster political party.[57]

Thus, in 1877 and 1878, a re-division of political parties along economic and perhaps social lines seemed imminent. The state was virtually bankrupt. There was much talk of "brokers" and "money rings," of "court-house cliques" and "Bourbons"; and a tendency to set aside old leaders was manifesting itself. Independents abounded, representing every phase of discontent, but always opposing the "debt payers." The Republican party was thoroughly disorganized. The overgrown Conservative party, at last forced to face the debt issue, had straddled it. An attempt at "compulsory readjustment" of the debt, thwarted by the veto of the new governor, was succeeded by a campaign for the identification of readjustment with greenbackism as movements of "the people" against the "rings" and "their allies," the courts. In all of this activity the leading spirit seemed to be William Mahone, whom (according to his friends) the rings and the Bourbons had robbed of his railroad and defeated for the governorship in 1877 through "bulldozing" and "trickery."

[57] Robert Beverly was president, A. H. Drewry, vice-president; William L. Royall, fast friend of Bradley T. Johnson and attorney for the bondholders, was secretary. Royall appears to have been the leader. The federal judges were R. W. Hughes and Alexander Rives. Among the ministers were M. D. Hoge, Joshua Peterkin, J. L. M. Curry, J. B. Jeter, and Andrew Broadus. Gen. W. C. Wickham, Republican and C. & O. official, was a member of the executive committee, *Dispatch*, November 29; *Whig*, November 30, December 5, 1878; *Dispatch* and *Whig*, January, 1879 (extracts from state press). Dr. Curry spoke on "Law and Morals" in Mozart Hall, Richmond. The rejection by the *Law Journal* of an able paper attacking the constitutionality of the Funding Act by James Lyons, of Richmond, and the attitude of the *Enquirer* (above) illustrate the feelings of debt payers at this time.

CHAPTER VII

THE "McCULLOCH ACT," AND THE STATE'S CAPACITY, 1878-1879

The compromising spirit manifested by the legislature in the spring of 1878[1] had, by the beginning of its second session, December, 1878, spread to the creditors of the state. Consequently, Governor Holliday was able to transmit, with favorable comment, two propositions, one from prominent New York bankers and brokers,[2] the other from the Council of Foreign Bondholders, of London. In striking contrast to the attitude of four years previous,[3] both pledged their efforts to secure from all creditors a readjustment of the debt on the basis of equity to all and a rate not exceeding four per cent.[4] To reconcile differences in the two propositions and to provide a practical method of giving them effect, the New York interests, acting through The Funding Association of the United States of America,[5] united with the British Council on

[1] Above, p. 79.

[2] L. G. and G. C. Ward signing for Baring Bros. & Co., August Belmont for himself and the Rothschilds, Brown Bros. & Co., Richard Irvin & Co., and Chas. M. Fry, president of the Bank of New York.

[3] Above, p. 52.

[4] Governor, *Message*, December 4, 1878.

[5] Formed about a year previous to handle such debts by Hugh McCulloch, officers of the First National Bank of New York, J. P. Morgan, and others, *Dispatch*, January 3, 1879 (quoting New York *Times*). The British organization included very distinguished names, Sen. *Jour.*, 1879-1880, Doc. 23. For McCulloch's recent residence in England and friendli-

a third proposition, which after various changes[6] (designed to give the appearance of concession, the opposition said) became the "McCulloch bill."

Under this bill the debt was divided into two classes: class I embraced consols and convertible registered bonds; class II consisted of peelers and one-half of the interest unpaid since 1871. These classes might be funded, in the proportion of at least two of the former to one of the latter,[7] into new 10-40 bonds bearing three, four, and five per cent interest for periods of ten, twenty, and thirty years respectively, with tax-receivable coupons attached, neither bonds nor coupons being taxable. The exclusive privilege of funding was given to the British Council and the New York Association above mentioned on condition that they file acceptance of the terms by May 1, 1879, and fund at least eight millions by the following January 1 and at least five millions semi-annually thereafter. With the new bonds should be issued certificates for West Virginia's third of the original debt, acceptance of which constituted a complete and final release of Virginia's obligation therefor. In and after 1885 a special two cent tax was to be levied for the sinking fund, this fund to be used "annually or oftener" for the retirement of the "ten-forties." To insure prompt interest payment the auditor was authorized (under the "Allen amendment")[8] to make

---

ness to the South, see Fleming, *Documentary History of Reconstruction*, I, p. 190; McCulloch, *Men and Measures*, p. 420. For McCulloch's account of the bill see New York *Tribune*, February 5, 1881.

[6] See *Acts*, 1878-1879, p. 29; Sen. *Jour., op. cit.; Whig*, February 6, 7; *Commercial and Financial Chronicle*, January 18, 25; February 15, 1879; Ruffin, *Facts*, etc.; Ruffin, *Scrap-Book*, I (L. E. Harvie in Wytheville *Dispatch*, September 4, 1879); *Fulkerson Papers* (memoranda of Colonel Fulkerson).

[7] The ratio of the outstanding consols and peelers.

[8] Incorporated as section 12 of the bill.

temporary loans and, if unable to do so, to sell, at not less than seventy-five, certificates bearing no interest but receivable for taxes.

Meantime there slumbered in a committee another bill, introduced by D. W. Henkel, a Valley readjuster, which required county and city collectors to reserve out of the taxes paid them in *cash,* subject to the order of school officials only, three-fourths of the county's or city's estimated quota of the state's appropriation to schools. The need for such protection was now very pressing, for half the schools were closing and 100,000 pupils of the year before were being kept at home.[9] Accordingly, when the McCulloch bill had taken shape, the Henkel bill reappeared and, receiving the support of both school partisans and McCulloch bill men, passed both houses without recorded opposition.[10]

March 28, 1879, the McCulloch bill became a law. Its passage was attended by no such scandal as that of the Funding Act.[11] On the contrary, debate was full and

---

[9] State Superintendent, *Reports,* 1878, 1879. In 1877, 73 local superintendents reported a favorable change of public sentiment as to the schools, 37 no change, and none an unfavorable change; in 1878 the figures were 46, 44, and 19, respectively. For hostility to the schools see "Civis" in *Religious Herald,* January, February, 1878; Dr. Dabney in the *Southern Planter,* January, February, 1879; Lynchburg newspapers, spring of 1879 (a local fight).

[10] *Acts,* 1878-1879, p. 264; *Dispatch,* October 29 (W. W. Henry), October 21 (editorial); *Whig,* October 17 and 31 (Ruffner), 1879; February 13, 1885 ("New Virginia"); Ruffin, *Mahoneism Unveiled.* Henkel is thus reported in the Shenandoah *Herald,* March 5: "With the guarantee of this house that the bill providing funds for the public schools [the Henkel bill] will be passed, it affords me pleasure to support the proposition made to the General Assembly by the creditors of the state." The Allen amendment (above) was a counteracting concession. Of twenty members who supported both the Barbour bill and the McCulloch bill, eighteen supported the Henkel bill.

[11] Above, p. 30.

free.[12] The vote[13] of the two houses was large, 104 to 59.
Consistently, the Independents voted against it, 21 to 1.
The Republicans divided evenly. Party considerations[14]
and a belief that the bill contained the best attainable
terms were the influences which, in varying proportions,
won the Conservatives, 99 to 35.

This legislation, the McCulloch and Henkel Acts,[15]
represented the triumph of that moderate move for
readjustment which had manifested itself in 1871 and
1874. It discarded on the one hand the ideas of "state
sovereignty," "will of the people,"[16] and antagonism
to "money rings"; on the other, it recognized the actual
fiscal situation and the existence of new popular necessities. If unhampered by political considerations, would
it settle the debt problem?[17]

A full execution of the McCulloch Act would necessarily bring the state very great fiscal advantages:
immediate relief from the pressure of accumulated
interest and reduction of the interest rate by one-
half, uniformity of obligations, equality of creditors,
and unquestioned release from obligation for West
Virginia's share; ultimately, a saving of at least
$26,000,000[18] in interest. Compared with these any loss

12 *Contra, Whig,* April 3, 4, 1879. Some debt payers, though they supported the act, boldly pointed out serious objections. For example,
Senator Bradley T. Johnson declared it would necessitate an increase of
taxes (*Whig,* October 28, 1879), and the *State* said the Allen amendment
meant "bankruptcy."

13 Sen. *Jour.,* 1878-1879, p. 463; House *Jour.,* p. 546.

14 Below, chs. 8, 9.

15 To these should be added the Moffett liquor law amendment (*Acts,*
1878-1879, p. 36) previously rejected (above, p. 79).

16 For a proposition by Senator Paul to submit the McCulloch act to a
vote of the people see *Whig,* February 25, 1879.

17 The following analysis is the author's. The partisan arguments are
given below, ch. 10.

18 The *Dispatch's* estimate (February 3, 13, 1879) plus one-half the

of taxes on bonds or coupons, the increase in the principal by some two millions, and the annoyance arising from the tax-receivable character of coupons were negligible.

But a full execution of the act depended upon the ability and good faith of the funding monopolists on the one hand, and upon the ability of the state to meet the new interest promptly on the other.

That the first of these requisites existed seems unquestionable in view of the business standing of the promoters, the advantageous terms offered creditors, especially the non-residents,[19] and the endorsement given the scheme by the state and national administrations and the great bulk of the press. Yet it is to be remembered that the associations acted only as agents and with no penalty for non-fulfillment of contract save its cancellation, which would not affect operations already concluded by them. Readjusters at the time doubted the ability of the agents as well as their good intentions, and later asserted that the act was only a stock-jobbing device.[20] For this view, market fluctuations and the cessation of funding on an apparent prospect of full interest payment gave much warrant.[21]

The second requisite for success was much more problematic. The ability of the state to avoid defaulting

interest accrued to September 30, 1878. The new principal would be $31,227,083, the old was $29,367,958, Governor, *Message*, December 3, 1879.

[19] Owning probably two-thirds of the whole, Auditor, *Report*, 1874; William E. Royall, *History of the Virginia Debt Controversy*, p. 6. Such holders of two consols and one peeler would gain in the amount of this principal and lose little of the interest which they were accustomed to receive. Resident holders would lose somewhat, as they had used their coupons for taxes. Non-residents had sold theirs for about seventy-five.

[20] *Whig*, January 18, February 12, 24, 1879; Ruffin, *Facts*, etc.; Massey, *Autobiography*, ch. 2.

[21] Peelers were 25 in July, 41 in December, 1878, 44 in March and July, 1879. For cessation of funding see *Dispatch*, January 9, 1880.

before the funding should be completed, without resort to the endless chain of issuing certificates under the Allen amendment,[22] was exceedingly doubtful. For the act made no provision for arrearages to schools, colleges, and asylums amounting to over a million or for coupons amounting to a million and a half, as of February 1, 1879; the treasury was empty and the banks were not disposed to lend. But presuming that the crisis could have been passed, could the state pay three per cent on the new principal during the next ten years? Taking as a basis of income the revenue of 1878 and assuming that bonds held by the colleges and the literary fund would be converted, Governor Holliday estimated an annual surplus of $350,000; General Mahone,[23] of $115,000. But the reassessment of realty next year was generally expected to bring decided reduction in revenue; this loss Mahone estimated would wipe out the surplus under the governor's estimate and leave a decided deficit under his. Both the severe pruning in the governor's expense estimates[24] and the actual figures of the next year[25] indicate that Mahone was very nearly correct. Certainly the margin was narrow.

The Conservative platform of two years before had declared that there must be no increase of taxes, and the elections following had decidedly supported this

22 In effect, these certificates would be tax-receipts discounted twenty-five per cent for cash. They were to be issued in denominations of one dollar and above, and offered for sale in each county.

23 *Whig*, February 26, 1879. Mahone believed the state would pay three per cent on $32,000,000 provided there were no exemptions, monopoly, etc., and no future increase in the rate. Below, p. 99.

24 *Message*, December 3, 1879. For example, the governor estimated $30,000 as the cost of the legislature annually, as compared with $100,000 from 1850 to 1860, $187,000 from 1869 to 1875, and $120,000 for 1878-1879. Also, he put ''extraordinary'' expenses at the improbably low sum of $74,000. *Cf.* above, p. 54.

25 Below, p. 144.

view.[26] But the foregoing analysis seems to show very clearly that under the new legislation there must be such an increase or the schools would remain stationary and the needs of the impoverished and afflicted remain unmet. Could Virginia stand additional taxation?

Careful study of a mass of evidence indicates that the state, as a whole, had gained decidedly in both population and intrinsic value of property during the decade just ending.[27] The debt of counties and municipalities[28] was but $13,000,000, of which $10,000,000 was owed by towns. Though taxes had increased ten per cent, the ratio of taxation to true wealth, if the census may be trusted, was but .67 as compared with .70 and .62 for the average state and the average Southern state respectively; and the burden *per capita,* though half that of the former, was but little larger than that of the latter.[29]

It had been a great decade for the towns. Thither, with the fall of slavery, had shifted the center of social life. The distribution of supplies to laborers and small farmers through country merchants; the comparatively settled labor and social conditions inviting men and money from within and without; the concentrating tendency of the federal tax on tobacco manufacturing;

[26] Above, p. 78.

[27] Population increased twenty-three per cent according to the tenth census. Reassessment of realty in 1880 showed a decrease of 43 millions, currency, which would be a small increase in gold value. This, owing to popular depression and politics (below, p. 144), was probably too small. The tenth census figures of 693 and 409 millions (currency) for the "true wealth" in 1870 and 1880 respectively are probably worthless. See C. D. Wright, *History and Growth of the U. S. Census,* pp. 53, 57 (note), 58, 162, 173.

[28] Tenth *Census.*

[29] Governor, *Message,* March 27, 1874; Auditor, *Report,* 1880; Tenth *Census,* VII, pp. 18, 20. The census estimate apparently fails to include $700,000 derived from license taxes.

consolidation of railroad management and the development of shipping terminals for through traffic—all these tended to make the town the business center also. Only Petersburg and Fredericksburg of the old towns failed to show gains, and many new ones had sprung into existence.[30]

By selling off piece after piece of his estate and mortgaging the remainder at high rates of interest, the large farmer had been able to repair war losses and secure improved equipment.[31] Through such sales, usually for a small cash payment and a promissory note, the number of farms increased 44,668,[32] or 60 per cent, which meant that this number of "poor whites" and ex-slaves had become independent farmers. Gradually the negro had settled down to something like steady work. So production increased markedly.[33] But only a beginning in adaptation to the new conditions was made. Leaders of public thought were too busy with race politics, and legislators with railroad wars and state finance to provide good roads or agricultural schools or even a respectable department of agriculture to enable the farmer to meet the competition which rail-

[30] P. A. Bruce, in *The South in the Building of the Nation*, X, ch. 1; Arnold, *Tobacco Industry*, ch. 2; *Ruffner Papers*. Manufacturing capital increased from 15 to 27 millions (gold), output from 30 to 51, Tenth *Census*, II, p. xii. For value of figures see Twelfth *Census*, VII, pt. 1, p. xcvii. For influence of tobacco tax see *Dispatch*, January 15, 1879. Richmond's exports increased $300,000 from 1878 to 1879. They were chiefly tobacco and flour, the latter for South America, *ibid.*, January 1. Norfolk had been continually growing, chiefly through shipping and trucking, *Landmark*, January, 1879. Danville and Lynchburg showed an increase in realty values of one hundred per cent. Yet all were small towns, Richmond (the largest) having only some 30,000 inhabitants.

[31] Above, pp. 8, 25, 44. County "land books" and court records are eloquent of the process.

[32] Twelfth *Census*, V, pt. 1, p. 699. Lots under three acres not included in the census would probably offset the speculative investments.

[33] *Ibid.*, pp. 90, 694; Vol. VI, pp. 80, 90.

road extension made inevitable. And so profits were possible only when the general level of prices was high. But coincidently with these processes came a general drop in prices, heavy, long-continued, greater in what the farmer could sell than in what he must buy.[34] Gradually profits disappeared.[35] Laborers were underpaid. Few immigrants came to counterbalance the fearful drain, especially of young men, to the towns or to other states.[36] Land depreciated in value.[37] But the mortgage and the promissory note remained the same, the interest never failed to accrue. In some places taxes were very high,[38] and there was no money to pay them. And so the courts were busy ordering sales and the newspapers printed columns of delinquent tax payers.[39] Thus the market for land almost disappeared, and the new farmer was driven to the wall along with the old.

Now any increase in state taxation would fall pri-

[34] Averages were: 1867-1871, corn 146, wheat 145, tobacco 163; 1877-1880, 76, 105, 135, respectively, *Aldrich Report* (52 Cong., 2 sess., S. R. III, pp. 36, 104 ff.); *cf.* above, p. 59.

[35] The value of total production was eleven per cent less (gold) in 1880 than in 1870, Twelfth *Census*, V, pt. 1, p. 703. See *Whig*, January 6, February 25; *Dispatch*, February 25, June 13, 1879.

[36] Since the census figures for 1870 include West Virginia, the exact changes cannot be given. In 1880, 683,000 natives lived in other states, 62,000 born outside lived in Virginia. The tenth census (I, pt. 3, p. 479) notes the "remarkable tendency" toward outside cities.

[37] *Whig*, July 8; *Dispatch*, August 14, 1879; Commissioner of Agriculture, *Reports* (especially 1880); "Personal Recollections." The sales books of James Roach, auctioneer of Fredericksburg, show that the most frequent price in several counties was $2.50 per acre. For areas of greater depreciation in 1875 see Map III.

[38] The *Whig* (August 8, 1879) enumerated the taxes of a man in Pittsylvania, owning property assessed at $1,000 but worth $500, as follows: state tax, $5; county and railroad debt, $6; county and district schools, $2; state poll, $1; county poll, 50 cents; total, $14.50.

[39] *Whig*, July-November, 1879, *passim;* House *Jour.*, 1878-1879, Doc. 6. The Norfolk *Landmark* had fifteen columns of local delinquents in October, the Portsmouth *Enterprise* (*Whig*, September 15), four columns.

marily on the farmer, for after ten years of experiment two-thirds of the state's revenue came directly from the counties. Any attempt to raise the rate, therefore, would probably have led to evasion or to hardships in very many individual cases. In either event, the debt question would have been as far from settled as ever.

As a result, therefore, of the fiscal situation and of the movements described in the preceding chapter, bondholders and leaders of the Conservative party united to frame and pass in early 1879 the McCulloch and Henkel Acts. The Henkel Act was designed partly to protect the schools. But while the McCulloch Act gave promise of materially lightening the fiscal burden, there was grave doubt whether its terms would be complied with by all of the creditors. Moreover, the state could hardly have met these terms without serious injury to many individuals and continued neglect of important economic and social interests already suffering and restless. The leading classes, however, school men included, gave the act remarkably consistent support.

CHAPTER VIII

THE "READJUSTER" CONVENTION, 1879

At the very time of the enactment of the McCulloch bill, the elements of dissent were forming a new political party for the purpose of defeating that measure.

On the assembling of the legislature in December, 1878, it appeared that the defeats already suffered and the compromising proposals of creditors had rendered some readjusters apathetic: Allen, Moffett, and Fowler, in the opinion of Colonel Fulkerson, were "morose, sore-headed, offish, ill tempered."[1] But among the rest, opinion was unanimous that public sentiment still favored the principles of the Barbour bill and ought to be organized in its behalf. So on motion of Senator John Paul, of the Valley, the drafting of a call for a state convention was tentatively authorized.[2] Then, dispersing for the holidays, the readjusters quickly obtained from local mass meetings, especially in the west, an endorsement of the convention idea.[3] Returning, in two final conferences, Col. A. Fulkerson presiding as usual, they adopted an "Address" drafted by James Barbour, chairman of the executive committee.[4] Asserting that the debt-paying association was "an organized party, openly proclaimed," and that its purpose was

[1] Memorandum of Col. A. Fulkerson, dated "January, 1879," in *Fulkerson Papers.* See above, pp. 81, 85.

[2] *Whig,* December 13, 19, 1878.

[3] *Whig,* January 3, 6, 13 (quoting Bristol *News,* Salem *Register,* Rockbridge *Register*), 16 (for action of Central Greenback Club of Marion).

[4] *Fulkerson Papers.*

to conduct a "crusade against the people" and force them to pay six per cent interest on the whole debt while starving their free schools, this address urged supporters of the principles of the Barbour bill to choose delegates "by county, district, and ward meetings as you may see fit to attend a convention of Readjusters" in Richmond, February 25, and there "take such measures as may seem to you proper to protect your imperilled rights and interests as citizens and tax-payers."[5]

About one-fourth of the legislature favored this action.[6] The "Southwest" furnished 13 of its 26; the Valley, 6 of its 20; the rest of the state, 24 out of 129. The Republicans numbered 4, the Independents, 11. Judged on this basis the group had behind it neither geographical nor political solidarity. Party ties and the possibility of compromise with creditors were too strong. But the *Whig,* assisted by a few small papers, labored earnestly in its behalf, emphasizing the social note as well as the fiscal.[7] And behind the *Whig,* but

[5] *Whig,* January 14, 17; *Dispatch,* January 17, 1879. Fowler and Moffett opposed specific reference to the Barbour bill, *Fulkerson Papers. op. cit.*

[6] Those italicized below voted against the McCulloch Act, those marked (n. v.) did not vote on it. For the convention, Senators *Bliss, Chiles, Fulkerson, Norton, Paul,* Powell (n. v.), *Slemp,* Ward, *Wood;* Delegates *Akers, Barbour, J. R. Carter, Chase, Coleman, Crank, Davidson, Dickerson, Evans, Fauntleroy,* Ficklin, *Frazier, Fulkerson,* Hamilton (n. v.), *H. H. Harrison, Harvie, W. T. James, Kelley, Lady, Lee, McCaul, McConnell, McDaniel, J. H. Smith, Spessard, A. J. Taylor, J. Walker,* Walsh, *J. R. White, Witten, Young.* Against the convention: Senator *Massey;* Delegates Adams, Bernard, Dance, *Fowler, Fry, Fulton,* Goode, *R. N. Harrison,* Henkel, Keyser, *McMullan, Moffett,* Oglesby, Popham, *Wright,* Speaker Allen, *Dispatch,* January 17; Sen. *Jour.,* p. 463; House *Jour.,* 1878-1879, p. 546.

[7] The following program illustrates the *Whig's* position at this time: abolition of the suffrage prerequisite and the whipping post; reduction of the burden of taxation, including the excise tax; bitter arraignment of the "debt-paying association," especially its "D. D." members, as

never showing his hand, was Mahone with the remnants of his railroad following, to whose fiscal views "original readjusters" were already disposed to yield.[8]

The election of delegates began forthwith and continued almost up to convention day, the *Whig* acting as a bureau of information and Samuel Goode as corresponding secretary of the executive committee. The process was necessarily irregular: informal communication among local leaders, a mass-meeting on the monthly "court-day," and the selection of desirable men from each district. Regular party officials appeared only in their private capacity. Negroes played little part. No rule as to numbers was observed. The *Whig* (promptly reducing its semi-weekly subscription rates) desired "a mighty out-pouring of the people." Resolutions reflecting at once the local situation and the editorials of the *Whig* were generally adopted. Some counties deputed members of the legislature; quite a number attempted no action.[9]

This process encountered many difficulties.[10] With few exceptions the leading newspapers were bitterly

"Pharisees"; defence of the schools against Bourbon writers and the debt-paying policy.

[8] *Cf.* below, January 5, 1878 [1879]. Fulkerson wrote: "I hope you will find time at a very early day to write out your idea as to the form of that call. If we attempt an organization, it ought to be made a success, and if successful, it will lead to an early settlement of the debt, for which the people will feel more indebted to you than to any other man in the state," *Whig*, October 15, 1882. In a letter to the Abingdon *Standard*, in *Whig*, January 13, 1879, Colonel Fulkerson expressed a willingness to pay three per cent on a recognized debt of $30,000,000 instead of six per cent on $15,000,000, which was his original idea.

[9] *Whig, Dispatch*, January, February, *passim*. Private papers, now inaccessible, would probably show a more extensive central direction and so lessen the appearance of spontaneity.

[10] *Op. cit.*

hostile,[11] and behind these papers (though as yet silent) were the regular party central organizations. Ridicule was heaped upon the move as the work of chronic bolters and agitators, intended to prevent a settlement of the debt and to advance their own interests, but likely to prove a mere "flash in the pan." The *Dispatch* maintained, with sudden and undignified changes, a veritable black list.[12]   Great parade was made of former readjusters now supporting the pending fiscal legislation. These influences led in some places to apathy, in others to "trickery and bull-dozing." Many elected as delegates refused to serve.   In one county, Funders[13] (led by the judge of the court, it was said) captured the mass-meeting and deputed its Funder legislators.   In another, the "court-house clique" broke up the meeting.   In another, negroes were chosen through the efforts of the Funder senator, the Richmond opposition proposing the plan and furnishing the necessary funds.[14]

On February 25 and 26, some one hundred and seventy-five delegates assembled in Mozart Hall, Richmond.[15]   They came from three cities and fifty-nine counties, the proportion varying from west to east and according to the strength of local leaders.   Politically,

---

[11] The *Landmark* and a few smaller papers insisted upon according the convention the respect due honest men and old allies.

[12] Later separately printed; also printed as an honor roll by the *Whig*.

[13] This name was first used for supporters of the Funding Act, but now for supporters of the McCulloch bill, and in general for the opposition to the readjuster move.

[14] *Whig*, March 1; "Personal Recollections" (William L. Royall).

[15] *Dispatch*, *Whig*, February 26, 27. These figures are estimates. Only a dozen counties whose legislators favored the move were unrepresented; 22 counties whose legislators were opposed sent delegates. Albermarle, home of Massey, sent 23; Petersburg, where Mahone and Cameron lived, 13; New Kent, under the influence of Major V. Vaiden and B. W. Lacy, 13; Barbour's county, Culpeper, 6; while one unaccredited delegate from Portsmouth spoke for all the populous Norfolk region, and one for the four counties of the "Northern Neck."

Conservatives of the liberal brand predominated, with a striking admixture of Republicans, Greenbackers, and Independents of every shade. Socially, there were self-made men, aristocrats, country preachers and doctors, and politicians of the usual types.[16] From Halifax and New Kent came a few negroes. It was a very loquacious body; and the more obscure members did their full share of the talking. Opinion differed on the terms of debt settlement: Mahone favored three per cent on thirty-two millions, some negroes absolute repudiation. But the dominant note was unmistakable: it was a "people's convention" assembled in response to a "wail from the people" to "crystallize the sentiments of the people and enforce them" against the "rings and court-house cliques," "brokers and the broker press." The interests of the white masses and the negroes were one; and they would brook no opposition from treacherous governor or hide-bound courts.

Without serious dissent, a vigorous "Address to the People of Virginia" presented by Senator Riddleberger was adopted. It declared that the people had always desired a definite settlement upon terms as liberal to creditors as conditions permitted. To this end they had accepted the Conservative pledge of 1877 only to find themselves thwarted by the governor. Then arose the

---

[16] For leaders see below, ch. 9. The following were among those reported as present: Albermarle, J. A. Michie, J. H. Smith, W. H. Wood, R. G. Crank; Augusta, D. N. VanLear, Jas. H. Hamilton; Caroline, Thos. A. Welsh, S. J. R. White, Dr. Wright; Culpeper, J. W. Bell; Floyd, A. M. Dickenson; Giles, W. G. Baine; Highland, John Paul; Hanover, W. M. Newman; Henrico, William Taylor; King William, S. D. Gregory; King George, Lawrence Taliaferro; Lee, L. S. Fulkerson, H. C. Slemp; Louisa, Dr. F. F. Brook; Montgomery, E. Esbridge; New Kent, Dr. J. H. Garlick; Nottoway, G. A. Overton; Washington, D. F. Bailey, I. C. Fowler; Warren, John Paul; Wise, H. C. Slemp, Rev. Morgan Lipps; Petersburg, A. Rogers, Jr., S. Bolling; Roanoke, Dr. A. B. McConnell, Lee Willson; Stafford, Duff Green; Smith, F. M. McMullin, George W. Hubble.

"Debt-paying Association" "to take charge of the honor of Virginia, educate you up to the point of virtue from which you have back-slided," and to increase taxes so as "to pay six per cent on the whole debt." Present conditions, fiscal and economic, "certify your inability to assume a higher rate than three per cent, either now or at any future date that can be fixed by a prudent forecast." The agitation ever since the passage of "the iniquitous Funding Bill" shows that to deceive the people again, or to over-estimate their capacity "would be fatal to that repose by which every consideration should be secured." Yet, under the McCulloch bill, "the attempt is made to deprive you of all real relief by a delusive measure, which by exceptions, exemptions and discriminations takes back with one hand what it purports to yield with the other," perpetuates the most objectionable features of the Funding Act and adds others, "all cloaked, veiled and tendered under a pretense of charity." Then the Address, without suggesting any specific method of settlement, laid down as principles the following points: no liability whatever for West Virginia's share; interest on "Virginia's fair proportion" within the revenue derived from the existing rate of taxation after deducting expenses of government and charitable institutions economically administered and liberal appropriations to public schools; no tax-receivable coupons, exemption from taxation, discrimination between creditors, or funding through agencies not under the state's control; and finally, ratification by popular vote, the settlement thereafter being subject to legislative alteration. Not prominent, but very noteworthy, was the charge that the McCulloch bill "stubbornly refuses to acknowledge the necessity to our state of fitting for their exercise those whom the Federal Government invested with all the rights, privileges and immunities of citizenship."

An elaborate plan for permanent organization, likewise presented by Senator Riddleberger, was adopted.[17] Avoiding the too obvious concentration of power under the early Conservative plan and the divided responsibility under the later,[18] this plan retained the strong features of both. For each Congressional district a chairman was to be chosen by the delegates representing it in the convention, and these chairmen (vested with considerable power in local matters) were to constitute the state committee. An executive committee of three was to be named by the president of the convention, and its chairman was to be (ex officio) chairman of the state committee. The plan thus outlined was duly carried out and to the important office of chairman of the executive committee, the president, Major V. Vaiden, appointed General Mahone.

The Readjuster convention of February, 1879, was called for the immediate purpose of opposing the McCulloch bill. Care was taken that both the call and the proceedings of the convention should appear spontaneous. In membership, it was representative of all classes, the great majority being Conservatives, either unknown or noted for party irregularity. The Address denounced the McCulloch bill as an attempt at deception and fraud, declared for no higher taxes, and favored public education and charities, partial repudiation, no

[17] Riddleberger was chairman of the committee on business, which handled all important matters except the permanent organization of the convention (cf. Bourbon plan, above, p. 20). For president, Mahone reported Major V. Vaiden, of New Kent. The temporary officers were Capt. Frank S. Blair and Capt. J. H. McCaul.

[18] Above, pp. 20, 39, 49.

exemptions or special privileges, and a popular referendum. A careful organization after the manner of
political parties was provided for, and General Mahone
was appointed chairman of the executive committee and
thus became the permanent head of the movement.

CHAPTER IX

SECTIONS AND LEADERS, 1879

Thus, under stress of economic and political conditions, the factions which had arisen among the Conservatives gradually lost their identity, until in February, 1879, the old party differences gave way before a clash between "Readjusters" and "Funders."[1] Both in the inception and in the results of the Readjuster Movement, however, one feels the weight of a force that was not altogether due to either business or politics. It may be well, therefore, to pause at this point for a rapid survey of social and political conditions as manifested in each of the "sections" into which the state had long been divided, and in the attitude and policy of the leaders whom these sections followed.

Beyond the Alleghanies lies a triangular group of counties known as the "Southwest."[2] Mountainous and possessed of a strong Scotch-Irish element,[3] this section was democratic in its habits and was drawn toward eastern Tennessee rather than toward eastern Virginia.[4] Before the war, it had never been largely given to slaveholding and in politics it had been always Democratic,

[1] The capitalized term "Readjuster" is here used for the organized party, its members, views, etc. The uncapitalized form, "readjuster," represents the movement in general. The same distinction is maintained between "Funder" and "funder."

[2] Ambler, *Sectionalism;* L. P. Summers, *History of Southwest Virginia;* "Personal Recollections."

[3] There is a smaller German strain.

[4] Slaves constituted sixteen per cent of the population according to the census of 1860; negroes approximately the same in 1880.

in contrast to the slave-holding and Whiggish tendencies of the Tidewater. Personal and party connections, however, together with the influence of slave-ownership upon its valley leaders and the satisfactory internal improvement policy of the state, had tied it strongly to the "East." And so, though unwilling to go out of the Union, in 1861, it had declined to unite with West Virginia and had heartily supported the Southern cause. After the war, the weight of old influences again began to be felt. The large old Whig minority, disgusted at the prospect of an alliance with its former political foe, afforded the Republican party a very considerable native white nucleus.[5] The "Southwest" had no worn-out lands to be marketed through immigration schemes at the state's expense, and no influential moneyed centers. It had no ever present negro problem. It wanted schools and unrestricted suffrage. It wanted money to build railroads and to develop its untouched resources of minerals and timber, and it saw that this money must come from the North. Self-confident, aggressive, and suspicious, it had over and over again registered its protest in the legislature against the prevailing fiscal policy.[6] But the "East" was diplomatic and generous in the distribution of offices, and the "Southwest" remained loyal. Upon the failure of the Republican party, however, party ties had loosened and the clannish disposition of the mountain people asserted itself in personal politics.[7] Dissatisfied,

[5] In a total vote of 21,000 in the eighth Congressional district in 1869 the Republicans received 6,260. Only 4,888 negroes were registered. See Abingdon, *Virginian*, in *Whig*, March 8, 1870, for the feeling as to parties.

[6] Note its vote against the Funding Act and for its repeal, against appropriations for debt interest and for Fulkerson's anti-coupon bill; and its demand for asylums, Sen. *Jour.*, 1871-1872, p. 88; House *Jour.*, 1874, p. 451; *ibid.*, 1874-1875, p. 367; *Dispatch*, March 18, 1875.

[7] *Cf.* p. 82.

Parties, 1873 and 1876

    Conservative

    Republican

    Fluctuating

Towns

Sections (ch. IX and n. 23)

Small capitals are abbreviations
   of county names

democratic, and self-assertive, this section was clearly
a fit soil for the new party.

Best known among the Readjusters in this section was
Col. Abram Fulkerson.[8] Of a family long prominent in
Washington County affairs, he had been educated at the
Virginia Military Institute and, having fought through
the war, had then read law under John W. Johnston.[9]
On the recommendation of Hughes, Mahone had made
him one of the "incorporators" of the A. M. & O., and
thenceforth they had been intimate. Entering the
legislature in 1871, Fulkerson had forthwith become an
opponent of the Funding Act and of the makeshift
policies by which it was supported.[10] To him, as much
as to Massey, was due the ceaseless agitation for readjustment and the "conversion" of Mahone; and it was
he who engineered the preliminary moves in the organization of the new party.[11] He was prepossessing in
personal appearance, good-natured, witty, hard-working,
and, above all, shrewd and determined. Mahone called
him the finest politician in the state; the *Dispatch,* a
"dangerous demagogue." To the people of his section
he now preached, with great effect, of hard times, the
decaying schools, the lunatics in jail; and of the "proud
old funders who are tickled by the Yankee bond-holders,
by the phrase 'honor and credit of the state,' who don't
pay any taxes, and don't care a damn who does."

Between the Alleghanies and the Blue Ridge lies the
"Valley."[12] The upper part contained a notable Scotch-

8 Richmond *Tobacco Plant,* May 3, 1879; *Dispatch,* July 9, 1878, October
23, 1879; Culpeper *Times,* in *Whig,* January 24, 1879; *Whig,* October 15,
1882; Summers, *History of Southwest Virginia; Fulkerson Papers.*

9 Below.

10 But he advocated abolition of the township system. *Cf.* p. 50.

11 Above, p. 80; also ch. 8.

12 Wayland, *German Element in the Shenandoah Valley;* J. A. Waddell,
Annals of Augusta County; Ruffner Papers.

Irish element; the lower, an important German strain. Physiographically, the former looked toward the "Southwest," and the latter toward Maryland and Pennsylvania; mountain passes encouraged both to communicate with the "East." Like the "East," the Valley contained an aristocracy of landowners and office-holders, backed by an increasingly important slave system[13] but modified by intellectual traditions in the upper region and by racial characteristics in the lower. Along the mountain sides flourished a social and economic democracy like that of the "Southwest." Though opposed to secession in 1861, no part of the state had more valiantly supported the Southern arms or come out of the war with greater loss of men and property. Heretofore almost solidly Democratic,[14] it now, during Reconstruction days, became solidly Conservative; the Republicans could not poll even the full negro vote. Already, however, the upper classes had begun to leave their country homes and to settle in the little towns. Here they formed oases of intelligence and sound thinking. But their political strength was lessened. Taking advantage of this situation, the Independents grew in numbers,[15] and flourished on the vote of the negroes and the "odds and ends" of the mountain sides and the little towns. The strength of the Valley remained, however, in its middle-class farmers. No longer confronted by the slave system, these farmers were beginning to display again the "homely habits and unconquerable industry" which would "gradually restore prosperity and intelligence"[16] to the country

[13] In 1860, twenty per cent of the population was black.
[14] With the striking exception of the strongly Scotch-Irish county of Augusta.
[15] Above, p. 38.
[16] W. H. Ruffner, "Sketches of the Lyle Family," in *Washington and Lee Historical Papers*, No. 3.

districts. Though they had no negro problem, were suspicious of the eastern towns, despised the land-poor planters, and were much afraid of high taxes, they were honest, comfortable, and slow to move. Hence the vote of the Valley in the legislature had never been decided on the chief fiscal issues, and its leaders had often shown an uncertain attitude.[17] But Mahone thought that here and in the ''Southwest'' would begin a ''ground swell'' that would sweep the rest of the state.[18]

In this region Harrison Holt Riddleberger was the conspicuous Readjuster leader.[19] Having served well as a Confederate soldier and as editor of the staunchly Democratic *Tenth Legion Banner,* he had entered the House in 1871, and at thirty-two had become state Senator and elector on the Tilden ticket. So far from being an ''original readjuster,'' he had opposed the attempted repeal of the Funding Act in 1872. But his origin, habits, and ambition threw him into opposition to the ruling groups and made him champion of the masses in his section. Thus we find him fighting the Conservative organization and the administration of the schools under Ruffner, Conservative and friend of public education though he was, apparently because he believed that both were too much in the interest of the privileged classes. This attitude soon led him to attack the fiscal policy which the state had adopted both before the war and after, and to endorse the radical doctrine that a decision of the courts against the constitutionality of a law was not binding unless it was unanimous.

[17] Governor Kemper, Congressman Harris, Speaker Allen, Senator Henkel, and to a slighter degree Col. Charles T. O'Ferrall and Governor Holliday, illustrate this tendency.

[18] *Harvie Papers.*

[19] *National Cyclopedia of American Biography; Enquirer,* March 31, 1875; *Whig,* December 3, 1874; ''Personal Recollections''; *Ruffner Papers.*

Next in importance was John Paul,[20] of Rockingham, now just forty years of age. Senator Paul boasted that he had been "raised between two corn rows,"[21] and Funders were fond of pointing to his "well-known rampancy and extravagance." But he possessed, according to his closest political foe, Col. Charles T. O'Ferrall, "all the elements of popularity, strong and magnetic as a speaker, with a splendid record as a soldier and untiring energy." Both of these men had studied law,[22] and now Paul was to become Congressman and federal district judge; Riddleberger, United States Senator.

East of the Blue Ridge lie the Piedmont, Southside, and Tidewater sections.[23] Together they contained two-thirds of the state's population, of which one-half was black. They differed in soil, climate, and products; and before the war they had often differed in politics. The spread of slavery, however, together with the development of inter-communicating trade routes, had knit them firmly together under an aristocratic régime. After the war these sections remained united because their fundamental problems were the same. Of these problems, race adjustment took precedence; and the views of this region became the policy of the state. These views were

[20] *Congressional Directory,* 47 Congress; O'Ferrall, *Forty Years;* Elam, *Mahone and Virginia.*

[21] The reply said to have been made to this assertion of Paul is quite in harmony with the rough and ready discussions of the time: "A pumpkin-head, by G—d!"

[22] Paul studied law at the University of Virginia after the war.

[23] For distribution of the races see map. The "Southside" is the section south of the James. "Piedmont" is often applied to the counties along the Blue Ridge exclusively, the others being called "Midland." As the description of these sections is largely a re-survey of previous chapters, references have been deemed unnecessary. Much help has been derived from "Personal Recollections." *Cf. Nation,* September 13, 1877.

as follows: Economically, the negro must work out his own salvation, unhelped and unhindered; socially, he must remain in a rigidly separate sphere; politically, he might hold office rarely and vote to a limited extent. The rigor of this scheme, however, was modified in many a practical way, for the negro's taxes were light, his schools reasonably good, his teachers often white, and his personal freedom little restrained. His farm lay side by side with the white man's; he traded at the same store as the white man, drank at the same bar, travelled by the same railroad and steamer. When he was accused of crime, white lawyers defended him. His own church and public "hall" rose in every neighborhood, always with white assistance. Grievances the negro undoubtedly had. Punishment by whipping and chains he deemed "class legislation" and "degrading"; and he resented the fact that his insane were thrust into the jails and that jury-service, which he deemed a privilege, was denied him. But for all this, he was fairly content with his position as a whole; only the practical loss of political privileges rankled.

Not less important was the social situation among the whites of the "East." Many of the old plantation class, realizing that the prestige of the plantation was gone, had quickly moved to the near-by towns, making these, as in the Valley, the new intellectual centers. Under the exigencies of reconstruction politics, political leadership, too, passed from the counties and the old leaders gave place to a compromising and practical body of men residing chiefly in the towns—men with strong Northern connections, intent upon the material development of the state, and caring little for "dead issues." Then came the Confederate reaction, bringing prominence and power to "war heroes." While adhering to the views of the old leaders these men deemed themselves practical, and soon formed alliances with the "interests," by conceding to the latter the shaping of economic and fiscal policies though reserving the offices for themselves. Thus "honor" and the "credit of the state" were combined in a new party watchword. Meantime a stronger middle class was forming. To the numerous small farmers were added new landowners, saloon-keepers, small manufacturers, truckers, oyster-planters, cattle-dealers, merchants, self-made lawyers, and not a few solid adventurers from the North. The towns felt their presence: even in Richmond political recognition was accorded the German and Irish elements, and a "bone and sinew" candidate now and again opposed a "Franklin Street man." Still more important were the men of this class in the counties from which the old leaders were departing. Here they rose to prominence in the churches and the numerous fraternal and benevolent associations, shared local political leadership, and even broke into the family circles of the weakened upper classes. As yet, however, their opportunities were greatly restricted; for energy, initiative, and equipment were valued but lightly in comparison with "experience," and in public life offices were deemed "honors." Finally, turning to the lowest classes, we find conditions very bad and very slow to improve. Never had illiteracy been so great or knowledge of public affairs so slight.[24] Obsessed by race prejudice, the lower classes followed party leaders almost as blindly as did the negroes. The abolition of slavery, together with the breaking up of the plantations and the establishment of public schools, unquestionably meant their ultimate emancipation, but only after they had learned to labor intelligently and to save. Meanwhile hard times and competition with

[24] The "pauper" system of schools (ch. II) was discontinued during the war and was never revived.

the freedmen kept them literally bowed to the ground. The more serious minded found solace in the churches, where a Puritan-like religion was preached; others, in the saloons, where drunkenness and brawls were frequent. In the public schools, indeed, they dimly recognized their children's chance for better things. But it was difficult both to pay taxes and to spare the child's labor and the money for his books and clothes. Besides, in some places the schools were closing. Could these masses be aroused so that they would throw off the leadership of the aristocrats and the towns? Before 1877 efforts to this end had been rarely successful and only when disguised by some minor issue. Now, in 1879, Mahone was hopeful, but not sanguine, that the masses might be stirred to a livelier interest in the affairs of the government.

The list of leading Readjusters in the "East" was short but significant. Foremost in the ridge counties was the plebeian farmer and parson, John E. Massey; in the Midland, James Barbour led. Of a family long prominent in the affairs of state and nation, Barbour had battled independently and fearlessly for a more representative party management and against the fiscal policy embodied in the Funding Act.[25] In Richmond, the *Whig* fought almost alone; for the course of John S. Wise was as yet unannounced. In the "Southside," where the densest negro population lay, the self-made Mahone found a powerful ally in his aristocratic fellow townsman, William E. Cameron. An editorial writer of uncommon power, Cameron was also a successful politician, and was now serving his third term as mayor of Petersburg despite its large negro majority. He and John S. Wise, both young, eager, and brilliant, with perhaps a touch of unsteadiness, were destined to be

25 Barbour had been anti-Mahone in the railroad war.

viewed in the North as excellent examples of the anti-Bourbon forces in the movement. From Williamsburg, Dr. Richard Wise, of the well-known Virginia family of that name, co-operated with V. D. Groner,[26] the self-made manager of a great Norfolk steamship line, himself no believer in Readjustment but a friend of Mahone.[27]

While the leading Readjusters of the "East" were thus evenly divided as regards the class from which they sprang, the three most conspicuous and powerful of them were, and claimed to be, "men of the people." William E. Massey[28] called himself "the father of the Readjuster movement." The son of a small farmer and mechanic of Spottsylvania County, he had managed to secure a good education, and having drifted about in Piedmont and the Valley, as teacher, lawyer, and itinerant and regular preacher in turn, he had finally settled as a farmer in Albemarle. Forced repudiation of Confederate bonds (some of which he owned), increased taxes for interest on the compounded state debt, the high private interest rate, and the general suspicion of one who lives remote from the center of things combined to convince him that the interests of the "people" were not being represented at Richmond. Therefore, though sharing the traditional Virginia opposition to a minister's participating in politics, he felt that the situation imposed upon him a moral duty. And so, in 1873, he entered the House to undo the Funding Act. Here, impressed by the indolent and slipshod methods of handling the state's securities, he hit upon the plan of killing the act by creating difficulties in the use of coupons, on the ostensible ground of preventing fraud.

[26] See *Dispatch*, November 15, 1879, June 2, 1881; *State*, 1881.

[27] *Whig*, June 3, 1881.

[28] Massey, *Autobiography;* Contemporary press; "Personal Recollections"; above, p. 63.

The morality of this appeared perfect, for he was an "original readjuster." From the genial simplicity of his looks and the apparent harmlessness of his efforts, the capital city reporters soon dubbed him "Parson." But when, in 1877, the state treasury became empty and the lawyer-farmer urged in a vigorous pamphlet that the affairs of the state be settled as would those of a private bankrupt, men began to say that he would be a strong independent candidate for governor. Save for his fiscal views, however, Massey was a genuine Conservative; only with considerable reluctance did he enter the convention of 1879. But once committed, he acted with remarkable energy. Wandering about the state, he drew large crowds, especially among the farmers. Thoroughly understanding the shallower aspects of finance and the deep feelings of the people, with a marvellous memory for figures and a lack of scruple in using them, full of homely anecdotes and Biblical quotations, occasionally caustic, always imperturbable, he had no peer as a stump-speaker in his own party and rarely met his match among his opponents.

Through its long opposition to policies approved by the leading classes, the Richmond *Whig* had become by 1877 theoretically a democratic paper. In the shaping of this attitude well-born men had played a leading part— Mosely and Meade as editors, Cameron, Ruffin, and Ruffner as contributors. None the less the belief gained ground that for certain purposes at least the *Whig* was but the "personal organ" of General Mahone; and as Mahone and democracy were both unpopular in Richmond, it had ceased to be read in the "best homes" there. Its editor now was W. C. Elam, a plain man of North Carolina and as good a school man "as ever put pen to paper."[29] With Elam the social note was ever promi-

29 W. H. Ruffner to Elam, *Ruffner Papers.*

nent—"the Brokers and the Broker press," the "Scribe and Pharisee" parsons, the office-holding set who "generally train with the court-house clique and always believe that money and position are stronger than the people." In lucid explanation of figures, often combined with unwarranted distortion of them, in effective reiteration of a leading idea in striking language, and in arousing suspicion of his adversaries' motives through insinuation, virulent personal attacks, and often deliberate misrepresentation, he was unexcelled. And for all such utterances of the *Whig,* though a recluse by habit and physically unfit, he held himself strictly accountable, according to the honor code of the "Bourbons" whom he so much affected to despise.[30]

Quite different from the rest was Gen. William Mahone.[31] In him a varied career as soldier, railroad president, and political wire-puller had developed remarkable capacity for intrigue, organization, and command; and an extraordinary energy rendered these powers always available. Possessed of a peculiar personal appearance, a high-pitched voice, and many idiosyncrasies of manner, he presented to the observer few of the characteristics of an orator or party leader. Though he quickly learned the language of the reformer and spoke easily of "the cause" which he came later to interpret as the "regeneration of Virginia," he lacked magnetism and was never genuinely popular with the rank and file. Lieutenants, however, he won easily, especially among young men, and these he inspired with

---

[30] See *Dispatch,* June 24, July 3; *Whig,* February 9, 1880. The Northern Neck *News,* June 11, 1880, has an account of his duel with Col. Thomas Smith, of Fauquier, caused by an editorial assertion (June 1, 1880) that on the collapse of the Confederacy, "the President, Governor, and whole bomb-proof corps grabbed the remaining swag and sneaked away." It is said that Elam after the duel denied the authorship of this.

[31] Above, p. 68.

confidence and aggressiveness. In the campaign of 1879, we hear little of headquarters of committeemen. Mahone was everywhere—planning, speaking, bargaining. It was a new type of leadership, and one with which Funders for four years were utterly unable to cope.

The Funders accorded to none of their number such precedence as was enjoyed among Readjusters by the leaders just described. Of most distinguished *ante-bellum* services was R. M. T. Hunter, state treasurer, who had been opposed to the tax-receivable coupons and had favored a readjustment of the debt in the interest of "peelers," but now deprecated party divisions because, he thought, "the political warfare upon the South has not yet ceased."[32] Although a Confederate of distinguished Virginia family and educated in the school of Calhoun and McDuffie, John W. Johnston had accepted federal appointment as judge in 1869, and from this position had been advanced to the federal Senate by the compromising legislature of 1869-1870. Conducting himself with quiet dignity, however, he managed to escape serious suspicion as to his party integrity, and having become rooted in the regard of the business men of the "East" and of the entire western section, he was now serving his third term.[33] The family and business connections of Robert E. Withers, together with a certain personal charm, political aggressiveness, and the glamour of military service, had caused him to be elected over Hunter in 1874, as the colleague of Johnston.[34] An intense interest in public education led Dr. William H. Ruffner, of Lexington, at first to favor readjustment; but

---

[32] Letter in *Dispatch*, October 4, 1879.
[33] He was elected twice by the legislature chosen in 1869, see above, p. 22. The third time John W. Daniel was his chief opponent.
[34] Withers, *Autobiography*, p. 317.

upon the passage of the Henkel Act, he began to throw
the weight of his strong personality and the prestige of
his office into the Funder scale.[35] All of the Congressmen supported the Funders. Of these, John Randolph
Tucker, of Lexington,[36] was probably the ablest and had
the clearest record for sound fiscal views; John Goode, of
Norfolk, was deemed the most eloquent and popular.
The *Whig* hated Tucker most bitterly for his opinions,
and despised Goode for having broken from his old
alliance with Mahone.[37] A war hero, young, eloquent,
popular, and with a personal defeat chargeable to
Mahone,[38] John W. Daniel, of Lynchburg, was most
active in stumping the state, and successful beyond all
others in uncovering Readjuster plans. An asset of
great moral worth was the eloquent preacher and
future ambassador to Madrid, J. L. M. Curry, professor
in Richmond College.[39] Gen. T. M. Logan, now a railroad promoter of Richmond, and Senator John T.
Lovell, editor of the Warren *Sentinel,* shared the committee leadership; J. Bell Bigger, formerly of Lynchburg, was secretary. Among the newspapers may be
mentioned the Richmond *State,* which inherited the
Bourbon clientage of the *Enquirer,* the Norfolk *Landmark,* which had but recently broken with Mahone and
still insisted upon a discriminating liberalism, and the
Richmond *Dispatch,* now nearing the height of its power
as party organ *par excellence.* To these should be added
the Baptist *Religious Herald* and the Methodist *Christian Advocate,* whose occasional entrance into campaign
controversy, contrary to their usual custom, serves to

[35] *Whig,* January 31; *Dispatch,* October 17, 21, 1879.

[36] Above, p. 81. Mr. Tucker founded the law department of Washington
College just after the Civil War and lectured there for years.

[37] "New Virginia."

[38] Above, p. 74.

[39] Alderman and Gordon, *J. L. M. Curry,* p. 246.

show how dangerous to moral and social order leaders of the upper middle class deemed the new movement. In Gen. W. C. Wickham, of Hanover and Richmond, the Funders had a Republican ally of much influence in his party and of unquestioned business and social standing.[40]

This brief survey of the geographical sections of Virginia at this time shows that the "West," especially the "Southwest," being democratic and unencumbered with a negro problem, was ready to follow the Readjusters, and that in the "East" where the negro though of great importance was an uncertain factor, their chief hope lay in winning ambitious young men or self-made men of the middle class, who were barred from political advancement by the prevailing preference for "experienced" men or war heroes, and who might be counted on to arouse the lower classes of whites. It shows also that though the leaders of the new party were about equally divided between the well-born and the self-made, the two most conspicuous Readjusters were both "men of the people."

[40] Wickham won the rank of brigadier-general in the Confederate army. As a member of the Confederate Congress he advocated a cessation of hostilities in 1864-1865. Because of the friendship of Grant he was useful in the movement of 1869. He was successively president, vice-president, and second vice-president of the C. & O. Railway. See memorial, "A type of the Southern Civilization," by Thomas Nelson Page.

CHAPTER X

THE READJUSTER CAMPAIGN, 1879

The contest for control of the legislature of 1879-1880 began with the Readjuster Convention.[1]

To prevent the enactment of the McCulloch bill,[2] Readjusters of the legislature had already begun to filibuster. But, supported by the bulk of the press and some expressions from the public mass-meetings, Governor Holliday called an extra session. The Conservative state committee met quietly on the night after the call and endorsed the bill.[3] Then the debt-paying association became dormant. Black-lists of the opposition began to appear. And after some three weeks the Funders had secured the great advantage of *une fait accompli.*[4]

Interest centered next on the spring elections for local offices. Control of these through "rings," Readjusters said, formed the very basis of "Bourbon" and "Broker" power. Accordingly, candidates sprang up "as plentiful as the locusts of Egypt." In some places ability to write was the only requisite required. "Handshaking" on county court-days was widely complained of. Incumbents usually won; for in many eastern counties the possibility of Republican success kept the organ-

[1] Ch. 9.
[2] Above, p. 85.
[3] Below.
[4] *Dispatch,* March 5, 6. W. E. Royall took the stump for the Funders and in 1880 established the *Commonwealth* in their interests; Bradley T. Johnson returned to Maryland; C. U. Williams became financial agent for the funding syndicate. *Cf.* p. 81.

izations intact, and in others party regularity was still
esteemed. But the increased number of the disappointed, the acceptance of Readjustment by many of
them, and the bitterness of feeling developed—these
were all favorable to the new move.[5]

Local organization in the interest of the Readjusters
had begun during the convention days when some county
chairmen were appointed by the Congressional district
committees.[6] Early mass-meetings especially in the
democratic "West," had enthusiastically assumed to
endorse, revise, or supplement these appointments, the
standard being usually good community standing.
But soon a dearth of material was met, and mass-
meetings and committees ceased to be reported. Save
for the peripatetic Massey, Readjuster speakers also
became quiet. Encouraged by this and by the apparently successful operation of the McCulloch act, the
Funders exultantly asserted that the move was "dead."
On July 4, however, the *Whig* briefly stated that
the organizing was going on "with vigor." This
was true. Through his power as party chairman,
Mahone had been quietly selecting his men, and late in
July the Funders, to their surprise, faced a compact and
widely extended organization.[7] For these later selections, the qualifications were generally shrewdness and
availability.

The Funders, meantime, were planning to use the
name and organization of the Conservative party. But

[5] *Cf.* above, p. 76. *Dispatch, Whig* (news and editorial columns),
April, May, especially election returns (May 24 ff.); *Virginia Star*, August
23; Northern Neck *News*, June 13.

[6] Above, p. 101. The county (or town) chairman named three associates
from each magisterial district, these smaller groups constituted precinct
or ward committees.

[7] *Whig*, February 27 (list of county chairmen); March 22, 24; April 24;
May 20. The difficulty was admitted by Readjusters, *Whig*, July 23,
October 30 (New York *Herald* interview with Elam).

the Conservative state committee hesitated to take vigorous action. A half-hearted attempt at checking the move early in March had met only derision.[8] The Readjusters, clinging to their place in the old organization,[9] refused to admit that they had left the party;[10] they asserted that the committee held by usurpation and represented rejected principles,[11] and they challenged it to call a state convention.[12] It was, indeed, no slight matter to "read men out of the party"; and the final decision was taken in the face of the vigorous protest of two members and by one less than a majority of the whole committee. On August 6, by a vote of 13 to 2, the McCulloch Act was declared "a great public measure devised and accomplished by the will and judgment of the Conservative party," and support of it was made the test to be applied in local organization and nominations.[13]

Public discussion formed a striking[14] and important feature of the campaign. In March, prominent Readjusters began to invade the precincts of Funder legisla-

[8] By the vote of nine members the Readjusters were declared a "party" and local reorganization in the interests of the McCulloch bill was urged. The *Whig*, March 6 ff., dubbed this "Lord Lovell's lament" from John T. Lovell, over whose signature as chairman the address was published. For unsuccessful attempts at local reorganization see *Whig*, March 22, 24, 26 (quoting Fredericksburg *Recorder* and *Southern Intelligencer*).

[9] For disorganization in consequence, see *Dispatch*, October 23; *Virginia Star*, October 25.

[10] *Cf.* Bourbons in 1869 and debt payers in 1877, above, pp. 21, 36, 73.

[11] "If Readjusters have gone out of the party, where in the devil did the Funders go when they formed an association with Wickham, Rives, and Hughes . . . ?" Abingdon, *Virginian*, in *Whig*, March 11. *Cf.* above, p. 83.

[12] *E.g.*, *Whig*, March 11.

[13] *Dispatch*, *Whig*, August 7. John L. Marye drew the report. Groner and Wise (above) protested. For two later addresses, see *Dispatch*, August 9, 20. Some Funders regretted this action, notably the *Landmark* and the Petersburg *Index-Appeal*.

[14] *Cf.* above, pp. 41, 49.

tors, compelling them to defend themselves and sometimes to call in their more eloquent friends. This attack lasted through May. In August, the Funders "took the stump" in force. Debate then became general and continued until November. The Readjusters used their half dozen strong speakers to great advantage. Beginning in the "Southwest," in the Valley, and in the ridge counties of Piedmont, where discontent was unrestrained by the negro problem, they advanced gradually eastward, singly, by twos, threes, or even fours, as occasion demanded, through the discontented tobacco counties into Tidewater and thence back into the fairly prosperous counties along the upper Potomac, often suddenly returning to some strategic point threatened by the Funders' more numerous artillery. Although new party organs were established and the circulation of the old ones increased, these discussions, often joint and lasting from four to six hours, largely took the place of campaign literature.[15]

At first the Funders assumed a haughty attitude, and relied too much on appeals to sentiment. But the Readjusters asked questions, read figures, and took the offensive; and soon detailed and serious discussions became common. These discussions centered upon three points: the validity of the debt, the McCulloch "settlement," and the purposes of Readjuster party.[16]

[15] For convenient list of newspapers, see *Dispatch*, August 21; *Whig*, January 4, August 5. Ten thousand copies of General Mahone's convention speech were ordered printed. The address of the Readjuster members of the legislature could be had for five dollars per 1000, net. Funders printed the Petersburg address of J. W. Johnston. Examples of new papers are the Giles *True Issue* (Readjuster), and the Northern Neck *News* (Funder).

[16] Among the best reported speeches are those of J. W. Johnston in Norfolk and Petersburg (*Dispatch*, October 2, 11); Ran Tucker in the "Southwest" (Abingdon *Standard*, October 16); Mahone in Richmond (*Whig*, February 25); Blair at Wytheville (*Whig*, May 20); and Massey as collected in his *Autobiography*. See also Conservative committee ad-

The Funders would begin by showing how the debt was originally contracted honorably and for public utilities which still served their purpose.[17] Admitting this, the Readjusters told of how interest had accumulated during war and reconstruction, and of how this had been assumed as an obligation and compounded, under the Funding Act, contrary to every principle of law and equity.[18] But, said the Funders, we are bound for the debt as it stands (less West Virginia's share): legally, even to the extent of our private property, because of our contract; morally, because we are forbidden to steal—the state's honor is that of the individual; commercially, because Wall Street opinion "controls the influx of capital."[19] No state, replied the Readjusters, has ever been compelled to pay against its will. Other states have repudiated without loss of credit or blame from Funders.[20] Are not many of you *private* bankrupts? Is it not rather cowardly to cater to the opinion of those who "having stripped us, think it rascally that we should not submit to be skinned"?[21] "Honor won't buy a breakfast."[22]

dresses (above). Important Funder campaigners not mentioned above were: A. A. Phlegar, called by the Readjusters the "brains of his party in the Southwest"; W. W. Walker, minister and lawyer; C. W. Stringfellow; W. E. Royall (above); Gen. J. A. Walker, commander of the Stonewall Brigade; J. H. Tyler, C. H. O'Ferrall, and P. H. McKinney, later governors; ex-Speaker Allen; Attorney-General J. G. Field, elected as a Readjuster; R. A. Coghill; A. M. Keiley, mayor of Richmond.

[17] This argument was used in the "West" especially, *Dispatch*, July 29 (editorial), August 13 (letters); *Whig*, September 6 (editorial).

[18] While Readjuster opinion continued to differ on the amount the state was not properly bound for, this was always excluded. *Cf.* above, p. 62. Funders urged that emancipation was not an absolute loss to the state, *Whig*, September 5 (W. W. Walker); *Dispatch*, October 2 (J. W. Johnston).

[19] Norfolk *Landmark*, in *Dispatch*, October 17.

[20] *Whig*, October 23, November 3.

[21] *Whig*, February 28.

[22] This phrase, first used by Blair, was much distorted in its applications by the Funders.

The McCulloch Act, asserted the Funders, will settle the question. It gives to creditors even less than does the Barbour bill. Its acceptance by them is clear from the amounts already funded. It brings the debt within the capacity of the state. Even Mahone has admitted,[23] and the auditor's figures clearly demonstrate,[24] that three per cent interest can be paid now without increase of taxes, and before the higher rate begins conditions will so improve that the ten-forties can be replaced by three per cent bonds. Under the Henkel Act, they continued, the schools will receive more than the Barbour bill allowed them; therefore, the leading school officials advocate the new settlement.[25] Through exemptions and special privileges, replied the Readjusters, the ten-forties are equivalent to six per cent bonds. Moreover, the creditors of the state, under this act, would receive only fourteen of the thirty-two millions that the state would have to pay; brokers would get the rest.[26] Comparison cannot be made with the Barbour bill as that was but the first part of the program of 1877-1878.[27] The Funders' estimates are deceptive as usual, the fraud now consisting in making a division between "ordinary" and "extraordinary" expenses and excluding in the process whatever is inconvenient. Actually, there would probably be a deficit of $600,000 yearly for the first ten years under the proposed "settlement."[28] Did not Johnston

[23] Above, p. 99.

[24] Address of Conservative state committee, above, p. 120.

[25] *Landmark*, July 9 (speech of Supt. William F. Fox, president of the Educational Association of Virginia).

[26] See the Godwin-Royall debate at Surry Court House, *Dispatch*, August 28; *Whig*, September 1, October 3.

[27] *Whig*, October 3.

[28] The chief trick in the juggling by which this was obtained lay in confusing the special embarrassments of the funding period (above, p. 90) with permanent conditions. The confusion was very thoroughgoing. See Massey, *Autobiography*, ch. XIV; *Whig*, August 11.

and Phlegar originally admit this? And is not McCulloch reported to have already "given the order" for an issue of certificates under the "Allen amendment" which will cost the state five and a half per cent a month[29] and paralyze the schools? Just wherein lies the justification for believing that ten years will enable us to pay a state tax of ninety cents?[30] Shall the state be thus "bound for forty years"? Shall the people never know anything but debts and taxes and unsatisfied wants?

Questioned as to their political intentions, the Readjusters asserted that this was not a "party fight"; men would next year vote their old tickets.[31] Here, however, they were on the defensive. The Funders were, indeed, forced by campaign exigencies to modify their early emphasis upon the heinousness of "deserting" the Conservative party for an alliance with the Republicans.[32] None the less, they thoroughly ventilated the "records" of the new party leaders.[33] "Look at them all. From leader to corporal, what has any one of them ever done? Absolutely nothing." Massey was a "political parson"; Paul, a "ranter"; Fayette McMullin, "an ignorant, uneducated old man"[34]—all were "disappointed politicians" seeking to "get possession of the state, rob her, and blacken her fair name."[35] And Mahone! had he not virtually robbed the state of assets equivalent to ten millions of state bonds?[36] Did he not, during the last legislature, father a scheme for using the sinking fund

[29] Ibid., September 17. Certificates could be sold at seventy-five and redeemed six months later at par.

[30] Report, in Dispatch, September 2, of Mahone's Charlottesville speech.

[31] For example, Whig, September 10; Blair at Wytheville, Wytheville Dispatch, in Whig, May 20.

[32] See Dispatch, August 28, for a recent local use of this.

[33] Dispatch, July 10 (editorial).

[34] Dispatch, July 23.

[35] Dispatch, July 19; August 8 (quoting Hillsville Virginian).

[36] Royall in Dispatch, October 11, and Abingdon Standard, October 16.

to purchase a railroad and make himself president?[37]
Now compare with these our leaders, they said, both
Senators, all the Congressmen, four ex-governors, the
leading clergymen, nearly all the newspapers at home
and abroad![38] And what will the Readjusters do if they
win? Pack the state courts[39] and attempt to repudiate?
Then we shall have among us federal tax gatherers,
backed by federal troops.[40] The day, replied the Readjusters, when great names carried weight is past.[41] As
for the press, "McCulloch's Republican organs in New
York and his Conservative organs in Virginia play the
same tune. . . . *in hoc signo vinces*—$ is borne on all
the banners of the many against the few.''[42] Office-seek-
ing! How dare the Funders reproach us for this? Has
not Daniel run for "every office in sight," and at last
had a town created that it might bear his name and elect
him mayor?[43] The debt can be readjusted, without any
packing of the courts, by using pressure such as the
Funders are now using upon consol holders.[44]

From their dull talk of sickness and hard times the
people turned to these discussions as to an intellectual
treat, plodding miles, and standing hours in the summer's heat. But they were largely a crude, unread
people, untaught by reconstruction politics to differ
philosophically. Coarse jokes, rude interruptions, sting-
ing personal attacks were relished. Feelings usually ran
high. Among the spectators fights were not infrequent.

---

37 *Dispatch,* September 5 (editorial on authority of Daniel).
38 *Dispatch,* July 28.
39 *Cf.* above, p. 46.
40 Argument used by Royall and Goode and endorsed by the *Dispatch.*
41 *Whig,* September 10 (on candidacy of W. W. Henry); *Virginia Star,*
October 11.
42 *Whig,* February 28.
43 Massey, *Autobiography,* ch. XIV.
44 Elam, New York *Herald,* in *Whig,* October 30.

Often a general "row" seemed imminent. Back to the crossroads store went a vague impression that we did or didn't owe a debt, and a vivid recollection of how some speaker "eat up" his opponent.[45]

Nominations for the one hundred and forty seats[46] in the legislature began early in August. In the "West," Readjusters and Funders conducted themselves like well-established parties of nearly equal quality.[47] In the "East," however, chaos reigned. The Funders had much trouble. Their "Conservative" meetings were often attended by Readjusters—sometimes in good faith, often to force an adjournment or even to dictate the nomination. Many refused to enter the "modern scramble for office." Sometimes faction and the strength of the debt feeling compelled them to postpone nominations, set aside old favorites, and honor converted Readjusters.[48] But, on the whole, their selections were decidedly representative of the successful upper classes. In Readjuster conventions, on the other hand, one could note an unusual proportion of new men and ruined representatives of old ruling families, and many Independents and Republicans. Here some excellent nominations

[45] "Personal Recollections"; *Dispatch,* August 28 (Surry); *Virginia Star,* November 1; *Whig,* June 12 (Grayson *Clipper*); October 18 (Rockingham). At least two were shot in quarrels. For duelling later, see above, p. 114.

[46] The full number of both houses under constitutional amendment of 1876, *Thorpe,* VII, 3902.

[47] The Funders were somewhat superior socially and in past political honors especially in the Valley. In six counties of the "Southwest" and one of the Valley there were Independents.

[48] *Whig,* October 1 (Grayson); *Dispatch,* October 8 (King William); *Whig,* March 22, 24, 26, April 19, and Virginia *Star,* August 13 (Stafford); *Whig,* September 6, and *Dispatch,* September 15 (Patrick-Henry); Virginia *Star,* August 23, October 1 (Fredericksburg-Spottsylvania); *Dispatch,* October 6 (Prince George-Surry).

were made[49] and some exceedingly bad ones.[50] The latter were due in part to the dearth of suitable material and in part to the attempt to win the colored vote.

Influenced by the opposition of President Hayes to repudiation in any form, the Republican state leaders early expressed their personal approval of the McCulloch Act. On the other hand, they hoped that the negro would be kept out of the campaign, lest, perhaps, he learn to follow other leaders.[51] With this the Funders were, of course, content.[52] The negroes, however, as far as they had any opinion on the subject, were opposed to paying the debt. It had been created by their old masters, it interfered with schools and asylums, and it necessitated a tax on whiskey. Moreover, it was generally supported by their political opponents and opposed by the local Independent and Republican leaders whom they were wont to follow. Still, fear of estranging the whites and, in many cases, the habit of years impelled the Readjusters to seek this vote very cautiously. True, the negroes who had come to their convention had been received courteously, and had been accorded in the address a vague recognition of their desires as to schools, suffrage, and taxes. But, taunted with these facts, the Readjusters half apologized; saying that to break the color line had been originally one of the aims of the Conservative party; that the debt question must be settled by votes, and they preferred the "honest

[49] *E.g.*, the "Gallant" Col. Bob Mayo, of Westmoreland, and J. T. Stovall, formerly Conservative chairman in Patrick-Henry.

[50] This analysis is based on a detailed study of two Tidewater and two Piedmont counties and the returns for the House (*Dispatch*, November 16), supplemented by a mass of press notes.

[51] *Cf.* above, pp. 50, 83. *Whig*, March 3 (views of President Hayes), July 12, 30 (quoting Rockbridge *Enterprise*); August 20 (*Southern Intelligencer*); below, p. 135 (purported Mahone-Cameron arrangement).

[52] *Whig*, March 22; *Dispatch*, August 9, November 15 (quoting).

negro'' to ''Bourbon Republicans''; that the Funders had counted upon ''bagging them all'' through their association with ''Rives and Co.''; and that it was due to Bourbon trickery and broker money that negro delegates had come to their convention at all.[53] Accordingly, confused by divided leadership and little sought by either side, the negroes were generally apathetic.[54] But with September the situation changed sharply. Beginning, apparently, with an insinuating speech of Massey's in Petersburg, the Readjusters spread rumors that they would grant the colored men more ''rights'' and that the Funders meant to increase the poll tax to three dollars and ''bind'' them for forty years. Churches and societies were called in to spread and enforce these rumors.[55] Republicans, some of them negroes, were supported for the legislature in at least twelve counties and one town. The Funders at once countered by appeals to the negro pride in their ''best men'' and by confusing local situations. They spoke from the same platform with hired negro speakers, established clubs, ran Republican candidates to split the vote of the Readjusters, and in at least six counties voted themselves for Republicans, two of whom were negroes. Moreover, private citizens pledged themselves to pay any increase in the poll tax. Rumor had it that ''Broker money'' was plentiful,[56] and both state and national Republican leaders now lent their active assistance to the unusual attempt to save the negro from unscrupulous and designing men.[57]

[53] Above, pp. 83, 99.
[54] *Landmark,* September 10 (quoting *Southern Intelligencer*).
[55] *Dispatch,* September 17, 30, October 8, 10, 14; Virginia *Star,* September 13; *Dispatch,* November 15 (quoting Cameron in New York *Herald*).
[56] *Whig,* September 30; October 10, 17, 18, 28; Northern Neck *News,* October 10; *Virginia Star,* October 29.
[57] Frederick Douglass endorsed the McCulloch Act and President Hayes

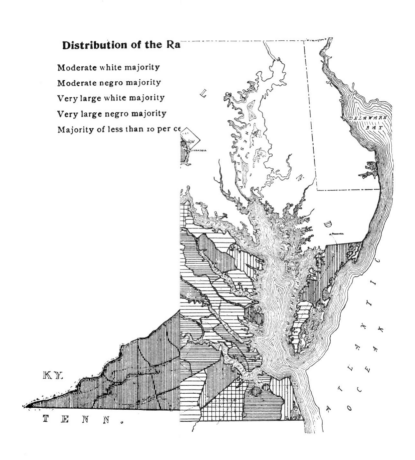

Distribution of the Ra

Moderate white majority

Moderate negro majority

Very large white majority

Very large negro majority

Majority of less than 10 per ce

The campaign closed amid great confusion and excitement. With three sets of candidates in the field for both House and Senate (as often was the case), bargains could be made with lightning rapidity. Petersburg negroes were wild, their women urging them on, firmly believing that the McCulloch Act would "place their children in bondage for forty years to pay a debt created to hang John Brown."[58] The Funder executive committee had suggested "confidentially" that care be taken to have "one reliable person" at each voting place.[59] "Vote or die; and have your vote counted, or give short shift to those who seek to prevent," counselled the *Whig*.[60]

By a vote of 82,000 to 61,000 the Readjusters won fifty-six delegates and twenty-four senators.[61] The surprise and mortification of the Funders was intense: rascality had won; the negro was the cause; the world must know that tax payers and *real Virginians* had voted to pay the debt. In this view the outside press concurred with unusual unanimity.[62] The Readjusters

authorized Judge Hughes to telegraph his endorsement to Colonel Popham (clerk of the federal court and editor of the *Southern Intelligencer*). But the negroes considered the Douglass letter a forgery and Hayes the supplanter of Grant. The Republican state executive committee urged support of all "straight-out" Republican candidates, *Whig*, October 16, 29, 30; November 1.

58 Petersburg *Index-Appeal*, in *Dispatch*, November 11.

59 *Whig*, September 30.

60 *Whig*, October 27.

61 In the Senate, of 30 Funders, 5 were re-elected, of 13 Readjusters, 7 were re-elected and 2 replaced by other Readjusters, *Whig*, November 12. The smallness of the vote (figures are for delegates) was due to poor Funder management, the perplexity of the negro, and to the Readjusters' having no candidates in some districts (*e.g.*, Richmond) owing to lack of time and funds, *Whig*, October 30.

62 *Dispatch*, *Whig*, Northern Neck *News*, *passim*. The New York *Tribune* was an exception.

denying all of these assertions claimed a majority of
both races.

Analysis of the returns[63]—and the much larger vote
of 1881 was substantially similar[64]—shows that the white
and Conservative "West"[65] and the negro and Republican districts of the "East" had in the main gone
Readjuster; the prevailingly Conservative and white
counties of the western and northern Piedmont, Funder.
The towns, even the little villages, usually went Funder;[66]
the districts surrounding them, Readjuster. Several
counties of the "East" distinguished from their neighbors by large white majorities and a reputation for
"backwardness" were, suggestively, Readjuster.[67] The
sectional, racial, and class feeling which thus appear back
of the returns, were probably assisted directly by the
degree of long continued economic depression; for while
the map shows very mixed results, of twenty counties
selected for the heaviness of realty depreciation, fourteen went Readjuster, and in only six of these did the
negro predominate numerically.[68] Possibly one-fourth
of the negroes and 40,000 whites, for one reason or
another, left their regular parties.[69]

[63] *Cf.* maps.

[64] Seven House districts changed each way.

[65] The "Southwest" elected 18 Readjusters to 3 Funders; the Valley,
11 Readjusters to 6 Funders.

[66] Petersburg and Norfolk were Readjuster; Portsmouth, a tie. In 1881
Norfolk and Portsmouth were Funder; Danville, Readjuster.

[67] *E.g.*, Stafford, Richmond, Spottsylvania, Fairfax.

[68] The map is for the years from 1860 to 1875; for valuation in 1880,
see below, p. 144. Of towns, only Petersburg and Fredericksburg showed
losses.

[69] This estimate is based on a study of individual districts. *Cf. Whig,
Dispatch,* November, December, *passim.* The Readjuster vote in the
"West" was 23,000. In Norfolk, 169 negroes voted; the Funder white
majority was 131, *Landmark,* in *Whig,* November 10, 16. From districts
with a negro majority of ten per cent or more, 20 Readjusters and 12

In their local organization the Readjusters utilized the multifarious factions already existing. On the other hand, the "Funders"—as supporters of the McCulloch Act were called—controlled the old Conservative party organization, and through its central committee soon "read out" all Conservatives who opposed the McCulloch Act. Public joint-discussions characterized all stages of the campaign, the Funders appealing to "honor" and "party fidelity"; the Readjusters urging hard times and the sins of brokers and Bourbons. Late in the campaign the Readjusters bid for the negro vote, and obtained it through promises of more "rights," despite the combined efforts of the "Conservatives" and the more prominent Republicans. The election returns indicate that the Readjusters won through the combination of the negroes and the "West," aided by acute and long-continued economic distress. At best, however, the vote was light.

Funders were returned. Similar white majorities sent 28 Readjusters and 26 Funders; the rest, 10 and 4 respectively.

CHAPTER XI

NATIONAL INFLUENCES: THE READJUSTER–REPUBLICAN ALLIANCE, 1880-1881

Owing to opposition from the governor, the legislature accomplished little during the session of 1879-1880 beyond indicating with greater clearness the Readjuster program. Before this program could be completed in 1881-1882,[1] a policy in national affairs began to appear which, though in many respects not an integral part of the Readjuster Movement, gave it a national importance and profoundly modified its later course.

From 1869 to 1877 Virginia's touch with the Union had been slight. By carefully maintaining a formal obedience to reconstruction laws, the dominant Conservative party had been able to avoid serious interference from Washington, federal supervisors of elections appearing rarely, federal troops but once.[2] This was undeniably good. But the persistence with which the Republicans endeavored to regulate the domestic affairs of the South and the manifest partisanship back of it, together with the unending carping of Republican statesmen and press,[3] had naturally transformed the Demo-

[1] See ch. XII.

[2] At Petersburg, November, 1876, Governor, *Message*, December, 1876. The *Dispatch* (October 2, 1881) charged Mahone with responsibility for the conditions which led to their use.

[3] The following editorial from the New York *Times* (January 5, 1880) is by no means an extreme illustration: "The old slave masters must domineer and tyrannize; they must keep the colored man in subjection and misery; they must raise a barrier of intolerance against enlightened

cratic preference of a majority of the whites into a
fixed conviction that a decent man could under no
circumstances be a Republican. Because this conviction
subserved home rule by the fittest, the leaders of the
Conservative party did not hesitate to foster it by every
means in their power, often by language and conduct so
extreme as to obscure the reasonableness of their main
position.[4] Nor did the quality of the Virginia Republicans or the blindness and ineffectiveness with which
they followed Grant afford any considerable correction
to the excesses of this sentiment. Inevitably, therefore,
the Conservative party had gradually abandoned its
semi-independent position and become a branch of the
national Democratic party—not so much a partner as
a handmaid, faithful and unassuming.[5] No Virginian
influenced either national politics or national legislation:
the detested tobacco tax and the un-Virginian office-
holders remained, proofs of isolation and impotence.

ideas, and fight against the incursion of those who would work for free
institutions. . . . But one great change they must recognize. They can
never again tyrannize over the nation. . . . The civilization of the South
is of the past. . . . It must go down, and the sooner the better for the
South and the better for the nation.''

[4] The following editorial from the *Enquirer* (July 3, 1877) is by no
means extreme: ''What was 'treason,' 'rebellion' and 'the old secession
spirit' a few years ago . . . is now 'Bourbonism.' . . . Let us glance
briefly at the history of Southern 'Bourbonism.' First, What has it done
for our own state? . . . A steadfast adherence to principles, an unswerving
devotion to the constitution, a refusal to kiss the hand that smote us, has
built up a pure government and brought us to the threshold of a new era
of prosperity. Second, What has it done for the nation? It has vindicated
the right to self-government. . . . It is Southern 'Bourbonism' that inspired the cry that now rings out all over the land as a warning to
radicalism, 'Thus far shalt thou go and no farther.' . . . The vanished
'Rebel' has stood a bulwark against the treason of the victor.''

[5] Greeley was accepted in 1872 on account of the similarity of the
Democratic-Liberal union to the Conservative party at that date. The
state convention of 1876 neither expressed opinions on national issues
(aside from reconstruction) nor instructed for presidential nominees.

Other states followed Virginia's method and example, and by 1876 the South was "solid" in political thought and action.[6] This solidarity, however commendable its origin may have been,[7] was objectionable alike to Liberals and to Radicals in the North: to the Radicals, because it was a victory of "Rebel Brigadiers" dangerous to both party and Union; to the Liberals, because it meant the perpetuation of sectionalism and race prejudice.[8] Accordingly, as the representative of the Liberals, President Hayes attempted in 1877 to break this solidarity by removing its more obvious causes,[9] and by offering place to Southern Democrats who would share in his administration. In Virginia conditions were not unfavorable, for *ante-bellum* leaders were largely gone and old national issues were dormant,[10] the Conservative party was overgrown and the Republican discredited, while on tariff and money questions opinion was far from being unanimous. The attempt, however, proved

[6] New York *Herald*, January 10, October 22, 1869; *Enquirer*, November 11, 1877; *Nation*, August 4, 1876, April 5, 1877; Dunning, *Reconstruction*, p. 303.

[7] *Cf. Nation*, 1869, 1873, *passim.*

[8] An additional objection was the very modern one of Southern influence in the national convention. *Cf.* Cincinnati *Gazette*, in *Dispatch*, January 1, 1879.

[9] The presence of federal troops and the active participation of federal officials in politics, Sparks, *National Development*, ch. 8; Dunning, *Reconstruction*, p. 211. The president's idea was not new, see *Dispatch, Enquirer, Landmark*, 1874, *passim.* "Assessment" of federal employees for partisan purposes seems to have been approved or tolerated by Hayes, *Annual Cyc.,* 1882, art. "Congress."

[10] The legislature and the Conservative party sought to make use of the federal treasury. Examples are: joint resolutions for an American university and an American printing-house for the blind (1870-1871), for assumption of all state debts, and for appropriation of the net public land revenue to education (1879-1880); party requests for completion of the James River and Kanawha Canal (1873); press endorsement of federal aid in the construction of the Texas Pacific Railroad (*Whig, Enquirer, passim*).

disastrous. For while the liberal "outs," largely the
Mahone following,[11] maintained an open mind and
possibly a receptive disposition, the other wing, to which
the president made his appeal, repelled him with hot
Bourbon wrath or cold partisan calculation.[12] In other
Southern states the result was the same.[13]

The next attempt to detach Virginia from the solid
South was due to influences that President Hayes and
the independent opinion of the North would gladly have
discredited. Senators Conkling, Cameron, and Logan,
highly incensed at the threatened injury to the political
machines, were plotting to retain the old system and
restore Republican control over Congress by electing
Grant for a third term.[14] In the fall of 1879, ex-Senator
Simon Cameron quietly came to Richmond and made
secret arrangements with Mahone. In accordance with
these arrangements the Republicans of the legislature
helped to elect Mahone to the federal Senate, despite the
efforts of the Funders to effect a different combination.[15]

[11] See *Whig, Landmark*, April, 1877, *passim*, including quotations from
the Petersburg *Index-Appeal. Cf.* above, ch. 6.

[12] J. L. M. Curry (above) was offered a place in the cabinet, Alderman
and Gordon, *J. L. M. Curry*, ch. 14. The *Enquirer* demanded that those
who took his "pay for treason" be visited with the "social terror," see
February 27, March 10, 24. The *Dispatch* urged the danger of Radical
rule and the possibilities of an alliance of interest with the West, see
especially April 13. Dr. Curry's declination was based on grounds of
broad policy.

[13] *Cf.* Mayes, *Lamar*, p. 319.

[14] Sparks, *National Development*, pp. 167 ff.; Cooper, *American Politics*,
I, 242; Conkling, *Roscoe Conkling*, chs. 29, 30, 31; W. S. Kerr, *Senator
John Sherman*, chs. 45, 46. Don Cameron, son of ex-Senator Simon
Cameron, the boss of Pennsylvania, was now Senator and chairman of the
Republican national committee. He was credited with originating the idea
by the *Nation*, September 7, 1882.

[15] Cooper, *American Politics*, I, p. 263. Mr. Cooper was chairman of the
Pennsylvania state committee, a consistent Republican and a ring man.
His story is confirmed by Withers, *Autobiography*, p. 386, and by contem-
porary suspicion, *e.g.*, New York *Times*, April 22, 1880. The Funders sup-

Soon the old rumor was revived that the Readjusters would support Grant the next year; but this rumor, as late as November 7, was branded by the *Whig* as a "stupendous falsehood."

Whether in accordance with the Cameron agreement or not, Mahone in 1880 adopted a curious and tortuous policy. He first suggested, early in the year, that the Readjusters nominate independent Congressional candidates and an independent electoral ticket, "uncommitted to any National party or its candidate, and instructed to vote together in the electoral college as may seem best to them for Virginia, for the South, and for the Union"; to which the *Whig* added the gloss that "if the vote should be close between the National parties [as in 1876], the Readjuster Electors, if elected, would be in a commanding position well worth striving for."[16] Meantime, however, the North was diligently encouraged to believe that the debt issue was but a pretext under cover of which the color line had been broken and "Bourbonism" was being overthrown;[17] and this belief was widely held, especially among the friends of Grant.[18] When, therefore, after a short but vigorous Sherman campaign,[19] Grant appeared to be the decided choice of the Virginia Republicans, Mahone deliberately advocated

ported the "Ross Hamilton" bill proposed by the negro of that name and drawn, it was said, by Congressman Dezendorf and other Republicans, *Dispatch*, February 28, 29, 1880.

[16] *Whig*, January 31; *Dispatch*, February 2, 3 (quoting Mahone interviews in Philadelphia *Press* and New York *Herald*). The *Whig* recalled the original function of electors.

[17] *Op. cit.; Dispatch*, November 15, 1879 (Cameron interview).

[18] New York *Times*, April 22, 28, July 7; New York *Tribune*, February 2, 3, April 22; *Nation*, March 3, 4, April 29.

[19] The New York *Times* (January 24, February 17) charged, giving names and places, that Sherman tried to effect fusion in the Congressional districts and to win votes for himself by extensive use of the treasury patronage. The *Tribune* denied this.

fusion on the basis of six Readjuster and five Republican
electors pledged to Grant. But, despite the strategy of
the party chairman,[20] and the pleas of the Lewises[21] and
the *Southern Intelligencer* (hitherto Funder), the Republican convention, controlled by office-holders and guided
by Gen. W. C. Wickham, Mahone's *quondam* railroad
antagonist, voted fusion down, though only by a very
narrow majority and after an all-night session, during
which, it was said, a stampede for the Mahone fusion
plan was averted only by a false fire alarm.[22] Undaunted,
Mahone then called a Readjuster convention which
nominated an electoral ticket pledged to Hancock;[23] and
having attempted unsuccessfully to fuse this with the
regular Hancock ticket, he supported it to the end.[24]
None the less, the Readjuster candidates for Congress
took so unhesitating a stand for the upbuilding of the
material interests of the commonwealth, through protective tariffs and internal improvements at national
expense, and expressed such fervent thanks that the day
had come when the proud Bourbon was beneath the feet
of the common white man, that the Republican national
committee urged their support in several districts.[25]
But the "intense prejudice for maintaining democratic

[20] C. P. Ramsdell and James Brady, chairman and secretary respectively,
published their resignation on the issue of Hayes's civil service order
(above) but did not call the committee to receive it. Following the precedent afforded by the national Republican committee, they now resumed
their places, and called a convention, small, early, and in the heart of the
white and Readjuster Valley, *Southern Intelligencer*, December 17, 1879,
January 3, 19, 1880.

[21] Ex-Senator John F. Lewis and his brother, L. L. Lewis, then federal
district attorney.

[22] *Dispatch, Whig*, New York *Times*, April 23; *Nation*, April 29, 1880.

[23] *Whig, State*, New York *Times*, July 7, 8; *Nation*, July 15, 1880.

[24] *State*, October 18, 22, 28, November 1; *Nation*, October 28, November
1, 1880.

[25] *Whig*, June 5; *State*, October, November, *passim*, 1880; Address of
Straight-out Republicans, 1884; *New Virginia*.

supremacy" and the "solid phalanx in which the colored
people were marched to the polls and voted—contributed
to produce consternation and a stampede."[26] Readjusters polled only 30,000 votes for president. They
maintained their organization unimpaired, however,
and sent Fulkerson and Paul to the House of Representatives at Washington. "I can not be dismayed,"
wrote Mahone, "nor deterred from adherence to principle. . . . The duty of the hour is organization and
preparation for the fight ahead."[27]

At the special session of Congress of March, 1881,
Mahone entered the Senate and by his vote gave the
Republicans control over its organization.[28] The Republicans, in turn, nominated Riddleberger and George C.
Gorham[29] for sergeant-at-arms and clerk of the Senate
respectively, and gave Mahone the chairmanship of one
committee and a commanding position on three others.
These acts precipitated prolonged and vigorous discus-
sion. Renouncing any obligation to act with the
Democratic party because he had been elected as a
Readjuster, Mahone declared himself still a Democrat,
but utterly opposed to Bourbon control through tyranny
of public opinion and suppression of the negro vote.
The Democrats sought to show that the Republicans
were buying help from a party traitor and repudiator.
But the president sent him flowers and Senators Logan,
Hoar,[30] and Cameron rushed to his defence. A speech

[26] Mahone to Harvie, November 5, 1880.

[27] *Op. cit.*

[28] *Cong. Record*, 47 Cong., Special Sess., pp. 5, 22, 33, 55, 85, 137, 176;
New York *Times*, March 7, 10, 15, 16; New York *Tribune*, March 15;
Mayes, *J. Q. L. Lamar*, ch. 25; Hill, *Senator B. H. Hill of Georgia;*
Cooper, *American Politics*, III, p. 207.

[29] Gorham had been serviceable in securing Republican co-operation in
the legislature of 1879-1880. See also below, p. 154.

[30] Yet Mr. Hoar says (*Autobiography*, II, p. 160): "With the exception of Reverdy Johnson, of Maryland, there is no record of a single manly

of Cameron's was significant. The desire to elect
Riddleberger, he said, was "something higher and
above" a mere effort to reward party friends and control
the organization of the Senate. It concerned the coming
political contest in Virginia. It will be the best proof
that could be given of the confidence which the Republican party has in all true men who uphold the laws, of
its respect for them, and desire to co-operate with them.
"All that we ask is that they shall stand with us in favor
of securing to each lawful voter the right to cast one
free and unintimidated vote, and to have it honestly
counted." If this be done, "the Solid South is a thing
of the past."

The campaign for governor and legislature (1881)
had, indeed, already begun. Warned by the strength
of Democratic sentiment displayed the year before
among the Readjusters, Mahone announced in January
that the maneuvers of 1880 had been merely incidental,
and that the main issue would be the same as in 1879.[31]
The state convention early in June reiterated this
announcement, adding to the issues railroad regulation
in the interest of the people and a formal condemnation
of suffrage restrictions. Significantly enough, however,
the convention dared to join to these democratic principles an endorsement of federal aid in the development
of mining and manufacturing. The state ticket, too,
presented a nicely calculated balance: "There's Cameron, he's for the Democrats; and there's Lewis, he's
for the negroes; and there's Blair, he's for the Greenback lunatics," commented the *Dispatch*.[32] Then was

remonstrance, or expression of disapproval, from the lips of any prominent
Southern man'' against election frauds in the South. Nor does he mention
Mahone in his autobiography.

[31] *Whig*, January 4, 14, 1881.

[32] June 4. For the elimination of Massey, see below, p. 152. John S.
Wise was the choice of Richmond Readjusters for governor.

seen much running of Republicans to and from Washington, the result of which was that the "Coalitionist" faction endorsed the "Anti-Bourbon, or Liberal, Party," along with the payment of "every dollar [of the debt] honestly due," and the "Straight-outs" soon withdrew the ticket which recollections of the year before had induced them to put into the field without the usual authorization.[33]

The response of the Funders to these movements was significant.[34] They accepted Readjuster ideas[35] as to the schools by pledging the payment of all funds appropriated "by the constitution or otherwise." They promised "equality of right and exact justice to all men," including specifically fair elections and jury service of both races. They coupled the name of James Barbour with that of John W. Daniel on their state ticket, and agreed to use all "lawful and constitutional means in [their] power to secure the settlement of the debt upon the basis of a three per cent bond," with but one class of creditors and without increase of taxes. Having thus minimized the differences between the two factions of the old party, they rang the charge of a corrupt Republican alliance, and, as the campaign progressed, cautiously urged, under the leadership of A. M. Keiley, the re-establishment of race lines in politics. The Readjusters countered vigorously: W. E. Cameron boldly talked of carrying "Africa into the war"; federal appointments favorable to Mahone began to be reported; and soon, with the succession of Arthur to the presidency, removals took place in his interest,[36] and Senator

33 For full account see *Annual Cyc.*, 1881.

34 *Dispatch, State*, June 2, 1881. *Cf. Dispatch*, November 15, 1879. The Conservative debt plank was almost identical with that advocated by Mahone in 1879.

35 Below, p. 160.

36 Gorham is reported to have said in 1882 that Garfield insisted on

Cameron "passed around the hat" among the revenue
officials throughout the country.[37]   But the net result
was a fuller vote rather than any change from the
alignment of 1879; for the issues of that year had not
been settled. And the victory was similar to that of
1879.

Thus, before the new and victorious party could do
more than indicate clearly its program in state affairs,
two external forces began to attract it toward Republicanism. These forces were the sentiment of liberalism
and the exigencies of machine politicians. That the
latter would determine its ultimate course was asserted
by many thoughtful men. In the second contest for
control of the state, however, the Readjusters won on the
same issues as in the first: a larger vote indicating
greater popular interest and better organization.

treating Mahone as a Republican Senator if he continued to support
Republicans in the Senate, *Dispatch,* October 12, 1882. Mahone stated that
he received little federal help before Arthur's administration, New York
Times, November 20, 1881. Blaine at first opposed him. On September 22
the *Nation* said, ''News has been coming in for some time that Federal
officers are being removed for refusing to act with Mahone and the Readjusters,'' and gave specific instances. *Cf.* Sparks, *National Development,*
p. 328.

[37] Cooper, *American Politics,* I, p. 264; *Nation,* June 2, 9, 16, 23, 30,
August 18; *Annual Cyc.,* 1881.

CHAPTER XII

THE READJUSTERS IN POWER, 1879-1883

The period of Readjuster control over the legislature, from December, 1879, to December, 1883, proved to be a period of Readjuster supremacy in all departments. During the first two years the Readjusters were, indeed, hampered by a Funder governor, and insurgents clogged the machinery for the greater part of the last two years.[1] Some have claimed, too, that much of what was done was due to influences discussed in the preceding chapter and should be credited to "Mahoneism," not to Readjustment. None the less, a great deal was accomplished during these years, and little of it without the consent of those whom the Readjusters had freely chosen to lead them.

Of Readjuster legislation, "An act for the preservation of the credit of the state," commonly called the "Riddleberger bill,"[2] formed the very heart. Vetoed by Governor Holliday in 1880 as in flat defiance of both state and federal courts and contrary to "the spirit which has ever moved and inspired the traditions of the commonwealth,"[3] this bill was remodelled and two years later received the signature of Governor Cameron.[4] One-third of the principal and accrued interest, as of

---

[1] The governor's term began with January.

[2] In *Whig*, February 10, 1880.

[3] Sen. *Jour.*, 1879-1880, p. 440.

[4] Act of February 14, 1882. For character of amendments, see below.

July 1, 1863, was set aside for West Virginia.[5] By deducting from the remaining principal all sums paid through the sinking funds since that date, the debt principal was found to be $16,843,034. The total interest unpaid to July 1, 1863, and since accruing on the corrected principal was $25,743,268; deducting sums paid or assumed in some other form the balance of interest due was $4,192,343. The total debt (including the literary fund)[6] was therefore declared to be $21,035,-377,[7] as of July 1, 1882. New eighteen-fifty bonds, dated July 1, 1882, and bearing three per cent interest payable in lawful money, were offered in exchange for the various classes of outstanding indebtedness, the ratio of exchange being determined by subtracting from the amount of each class the interest on it already paid.[8] Payment of interest on the debt in any other form was forbidden. The new bonds became known as "Riddlebergers."

As a supplement to this act, two "coupon-killers" had already been passed. These forbade tax collectors, under pain of heavy penalties, to receive coupons except "for verification" before a jury of the county and when accompanied by the amount of the taxes in cash; upon the establishment of their genuineness the cash would be refunded. The remedy offered for the breach of contract[9] would, it was thought, satisfy the courts; the difficulty and cost of proving the genuineness of coupons, clipped from bonds held abroad perhaps, would prevent

5 West Virginia entered the Union June 20, 1863. Certificates of indebtedness "to be accounted for by the state of West Virginia, without recourse upon this commonwealth" were given.

6 Principal, $1,428,245; interest, $602,016, Second Auditor, *Report,* 1881.

7 Approximately, a scaling of ten millions.

8 Consols would exchange at 53, ten-forties at 60, peelers at 69, etc.

9 Above, p. 43.

their deluging the treasury and tend to encourage conversion of consols and ten-forties into Riddlebergers.[10] Thus the long-desired uniformity and definiteness of obligations, and an adequate reduction in the annual interest burden, seemed assured for the not distant future.

While readjusting the debt, the legislature also began a readjustment of taxation. In this matter, the wretchedness of the existing system might well have authorized a thoroughgoing revision. No more serious purpose appears to have been entertained, however, than to lighten for the time the burden of the laborer and the farmer, and to gain some partisan advantage thereby. Thus the new measures declared that the poll tax need no longer be paid before voting, substituted the older and lighter liquor license plan for the Moffett law,[11] reduced the tax rate on general property from fifty to forty cents, and ordered a reassessment of realty under conditions which resulted in a diminution of $13,000,-000.[12] To offset the loss in revenue thus entailed, an effort was made to reach corporate wealth; and this effort, it should be recorded, was serious and eventually successful.[13] The energetic measures taken to collect delinquent taxes, to compel county treasurers or their

[10] Acts of January 14 and January 26, 1882. See above, pp. 42, 65, for origin of this method of attack.

[11] Above, p. 57; *Acts*, 1879-1880, p. 147. Fulkerson introduced the bill at the request of the liquor dealers, *Whig*, January 16, 1880.

[12] *Acts*, 1881-1882, p. 497. The old plan was used, but by Readjuster appointees and with extended opportunities for local revision, *cf.* above, p. 91.

[13] *Cf.* above, p. 56, [Douglas S. Freeman], *Report of the Virginia Tax Commission* (1911), appendix, ch. 6; Magruder, *Recent Administration*, p. 175. The taxable value of railroads in 1880 was $9,876,000; in 1885, $35,955,000.

sureties to settle,[14] and to adjust old claims of the state against the railroads[15] were of similar importance, for they enabled the Readjusters to punish enemies and reward friends, and produced a temporary abundance of funds. These funds the legislature proceeded to spend with an abandon but little short of recklessness.[16]

The direction which the liberality of the legislature took was significant. Public education received such generous treatment that some feared the ruin of the denominational schools.[17] The Riddleberger act put the literary fund in the most favored class of creditors and directed that the interest in arrears be paid in cash to the amount of $378,000. The state tax rate for schools was not reduced; local boards were authorized to tax railroad and telegraph property for their support; and, under the "Granstaff" act, the percentage of the schools' estimated quota of state taxes to be retained by local authorities was increased to ninety.[18] The full claim of the schools to taxes previously "diverted" was admitted, and regular quarterly payments of $25,000 and

[14] Auditor, *Reports*, 1880, 1881; *Acts*, 1879-1880, pp. 74, 136, 293, 299.

[15] *Acts*, 1881-1882, pp. 76, 400, 490. Thus ended the state's ownership in railroads, with the exception of the R. F. & P. stock, which is still retained and is exceedingly profitable, and some minor properties sold in 1882-1883. The A. M. & O. sale (below) was generally conceded a good bargain for the state. The Richmond and Danville was permitted to redeem an amply secured debt of $420,000, due four years later, with "Riddle-bergers" worth about 50. The requirement that this road surrender its exemption from taxation appears to have been a condition attached to the issue of new stock, and not a part of the sales bargain.

[16] For contemporary discussion of wastefulness from the Readjuster standpoint, see the reply of John S. Wise to Holmes Conrad, in *Whig*, September 25, 1883. At that date the treasury contained one and one-half millions.

[17] Richmond *Christian Advocate*, January 26, 1882. Colleges were given special privileges later, *Acts*, 1881-1882, p. 203.

[18] *Cf.* above, p. 87; *Acts*, 1881-1882, pp. 166, 203, 233.

a special payment of $400,000 thereon were directed.[19] This $400,000 was secured from the settlement of the A. M. & O. claims. The remaining $100,000, derived from the same source, was granted, together with a fixed annuity, to a negro "Normal and Collegiate Institute,"[20] the construction and operation of which were quickly begun. Altogether, public schools received from the state annually about $600,000, as against less than $400,000 annually from 1870 to 1877.[21] For lunatic asylums approximately $250,000 a year was spent, as compared with $190,000 in 1879 (when special attention had been given them), and a new building for the colored insane was virtually completed.[22] Nor did the maimed Confederate soldier lose any part of his customary paltry donation.[23]

If this legislation, while primarily fiscal, had an important social significance, still more did a multitude of other measures, passed or nearly passed, tend to subserve the interests of the masses and to break the power of wealth and established privilege.[24] The poll tax, imposed originally for the benefit of schools which should train citizens to vote but converted by Bourbons and debt payers into a restriction on suffrage, was repealed.[25]

[19] *Cf.* above, p. 62; *Acts*, 1881-1882, pp. 203, 473.

[20] *Ibid.*, p. 286. Apparently this money should have been used to reduce the debt. Above, p. 19.

[21] Auditor, *Reports*, 1877, 1880 to 1883. The estimates are the author's.

[22] Auditor, *Reports;* reports of asylums, in *Annual Reports*, 1884; *Acts*, 1881-1882, p. 246. The new asylum had been long projected. The Southwestern Asylum (white) might be credited to Readjuster influence, *Acts*, 1883-1884, p. 692.

[23] Auditor, *Reports, passim.* The total average annual payment was about $10,000. It had been very irregularly made.

[24] There is an excellent, though partisan, summary by B. B. Munford in *State*, September 13, 1889.

[25] Funders aided in the final stages from party motives and because of

The whipping-post was abolished; mechanics were better secured in their wages; foreign insurance companies were put under a stricter bond;[26] and benevolent and fraternal organizations were chartered by the score, among them a "Labor Association of Lynchburg." N. W. Hazelwood, in behalf of the state grange, championed bills to prevent fraud in the manufacture of fertilizers, to establish experiment stations, to provide state supervision over the warehousing and sampling of tobacco, and to regulate the rates and management of the railroads.[27]   Lady pushed a commissioner-of-sales bill which would have transferred the management of property to be sold under judicial decree from the supposedly grasping lawyers to special state officials.   Heretofore, especially in 1877-1879, the legislature had gladly removed disabilities incurred for duelling; henceforth, state officials must make oath that they would never participate, directly or indirectly, in this relic of past customs.[28]

The state administrative departments, wrote Massey, just after the victory of 1879, must be put "in sympathy with the people." "If I can exert any influence," declared Mahone, "not one of them [the present officials] shall go unexpelled—and that quickly."[29] In this view the

the corruption to which it gave rise, see below, p. 156; *Whig*, January 23, 1880, September 25, 1883 (John S. Wise); *Dispatch*, April 7; *State*, April 22, 1882. Fulkerson was patron of the repeal. The vote on ratification was 107,303, to 66,131.

26 *Acts*, 1879-1880, pp. 81, 87.

27 *House Bills*, 1881-1882. Hazlewood was secretary of the grange and a member of the legislature. Duff Green presented the railroad bill. For ulterior purpose, see below, p. 158.

28 *Acts*, 1881-1882, p. 404. Hazlewood favored a more extreme measure, *House Bills*, 1881-1882, No. 207.

29 Letters to Colonel Harvie, November 10, 11, 1879, *Harvie Papers*. For method of selecting officials see below.

legislature unanimously concurred. By common consent Massey became auditor. The energy and ability which he brought to this important office, long slothfully and incompetently administered by an appointee of Governor Peirpoint, justified the selection.[30] His successor, S. Brown Allen, however, was a "Mahone man," and proved an entirely unsatisfactory official. A scheme devised by Massey for the collection of delinquent taxes became in the hands of both, but especially of Allen, a powerful and sometimes corrupting political asset.[31] C. M. Reynolds and T. T. Fauntleroy, "original read-justers," received the easy places of treasurer and secretary of the commonwealth. They served acceptably[32] until 1882, when they were replaced by the "Mahone men," D. R. Reverly and W. C. Elam. Gen. Asa Rogers, long second auditor and as such directly in charge of the debt and the school funds, became railroad commissioner, and H. H. Dyson, a Republican, took his place. Despite the protests of even Republican friends of public education, Superintendent Ruffner was replaced at the end of his term by R. R. Farr—a severely ironic commentary upon the sincerity or the intelligence of Read-juster interest in the schools.[33]

With startling directness the legislature declared vacant the controlling boards of the several state asylums and colleges; and in some instances even ven-

[30] Massey, *Autobiography*, ch. 15; House *Jour.*, 1881-1882, December 16; comparison of auditors' reports. Auditor Taylor was in large part the victim of circumstances.

[31] Sen. *Jour.*, 1883-1884, Docs. 27, 30; House *Jour.*, 1883-1884 and 1884, Index.

[32] Sen. *Jour.*, 1881-1882, Doc. 20. The selection of Fauntleroy was criticised by the *Dispatch*, which had previously commended him.

[33] Massey, *Autobiography*, p. 204; Ruffin, *Mahoneism;* House *Jour.*, 1883-1884, Index; *Ruffner Papers* (letters of Gen. S. C. Armstrong, president of the Hampton School, to Ruffner, 1881).

tured to order an immediate reorganization of the institution affected.[34] For this the general excuse was "Bourbon" inefficiency and lack of sympathy with the masses.
There was truth in the charge; but under the new
régime the improvement in efficiency was not as noticeable as the amount of petty extravagance and humiliat-
ing partisanship.[35] So, too, the old county and city
school superintendents, who had been selected mainly
because of their moral and scholastic qualifications, were
largely replaced by men of energy in close "touch with
the people." But as the new appointees used their
energies primarily in the service of the party and the
superintendent and the county judge controlled the local
boards of school trustees, which selected the teachers,
the entire school system began to feel, what had been so
long feared, the vicious influence of politics unabashed.[36]

Nor were the courts spared. For a century they had
been citadels of conservatism and respectability. They
were wont to be affected by politics only remotely. Because of the character of the judges, extra-judicial
powers had been given them in matters requiring impartial and scrupulously honest attention, such as the
appointment of election officials and assessors and the
selection of school trustees. Most of them, however, held
Funder views; besides, Readjusters needed the power
and prestige of their offices. So the legislature retired
all of the supreme court judges and about three-fourths
of the county and corporation judges as their terms
expired, and was with difficulty prevented from vacating
the circuit courts under the pretense of redistricting.
The new supreme court judges served full terms without

[34] *Acts,* March 9, 1880; February 15, March 3, April 7, 14, 1882.
[35] Reports of superintendents and boards in *Annual Reports;* Sen. *Jour.,*
1883-1884, Docs. 32, 33.
[36] Sen. and House *Journals,* 1881-1882, Index; below, p. 167.

discredit. But the scarcity of Readjuster lawyers, party exigencies, and the refusal of some Funder lawyers to accept Readjuster appointment led to many unsatisfactory and some scandalous selections. By 1884, six appointees had resigned under pressure, one had been removed, and six had died. In the opinion of some competent observers, no other action of the Readjusters produced such deep dissatisfaction as did this.[37]

That the legislature sent self-made men to the national senate was perhaps accidental. Through their energy and their willingness to exchange deciding votes for federal patronage, however, these Senators gave to Virginia a prominence and an influence which she had not possessed for more than a generation. Neither Mahone nor Riddleberger spoke frequently, being immersed in state politics most of the time. Both advocated a high protective tariff, Mahone having much to do with the notorious iron schedule in the Tariff Act of 1883. Both advocated liberalism, Mahone to the extent of vilifying a large part of his constituents. But in neither of these positive attitudes did they represent the most intelligent and substantial citizens of their state or rise to the level of national statesmanship.[38]

[37] Massey, *Autobiography*, p. 217; Senate and House *Journals*, 1879-1880, 1881-1882, 1883-1884, Index; *Whig* and *Dispatch, passim;* Royall, *Virginia State Debt Controversy*, ch. 5. Convenient lists may be found in the *Warrock-Richardson Almanack*. Supreme court judges were: Robert A. Richardson, T. T. Fauntleroy, L. L. Lewis (below), B. W. Lacy, D. A. Hinton. Prominent among county judges not removed were John W. Bell, Jos. H. Sherrard, William H. Mann. Prominent new appointees were J. R. McDaniel, Jas. M. Gregory, Edmund Waddill, F. S. C. Hunter, William R. Taliaferro, A. M. Lybrook, Robert Mayo. Prominent as corporation judges were Thos. S. Atkins, A. C. Holliday, D. J. Godwin, N. B. Meade, S. B. French. That some were illegally retired was strongly maintained.

[38] Above, p. 138. Mahone voted on but 7 of the 22 matters deemed worthy of a recorded vote by the *Annual Cyc.* He was one of the conferees, "placed there at a late hour," who raised the duty on iron ore from 50 to 75 cents, *Annual Cyc.*, 1883, art. "Congress."

If one views the legislation of this period as a whole, its resemblances to the ultra-democratic ideas imbedded in the constitution is at once apparent. So, too, the comparative absence of well-known names among the holders of office and the prominence of hitherto obscure men bring to mind the carpet-bagger and scalawag régime. One striking exception, however, presents itself, and that is the attitude toward the negro. Though the needs and wishes of the freedmen now had much more weight than during the preceding decade, no effort was made to "elevate" them by special legislation. Even the election laws remain unchanged. Appointment to office they did indeed receive, but only as "our faithful allies" and never very frequently.[39] If a second democratic revolution was in truth under way, the forces controlling it were the farmers and the poor whites and the aspiring middle class leaders.

Both the rapidity of legislation and the character and activities of appointees were largely due to the authority exercised by General Mahone. The Readjusters had, in fact, been developing a "machine," of which Mahone was by 1882 the absolute "boss."[40]

The stages of this development are clear. The convention of 1879[41] lodged party control in a state committee representative of the Congressional district delegations. The legislative caucus that followed emphasized this oligarchical tendency by apportioning the state patronage to the Congressional districts, the positions to be

---

[39] Below, p. 163.

[40] "A member of the Legislature" [Holmes Conrad], *Mahoneism Unveiled*, in Ruffin, *Scrap-Book*, II (originally published in the Winchester *Times*, 1883); A. M. Lybrook's letter in *Dispatch*, September 12, 1882; Ruffin, *Mahoneism Unveiled* and *An Appeal;* Munford's letter in *State*, September 13, 1889. *Cf.* Massey, *Autobiography*, ch. 17.

[41] Above, p. 101.

filled on nomination by the legislators therefrom.[42] Thus
a corps of leaders, salaried and uniformly distributed,
was assured. As the single chairman of the party, however, as well as its most distinguished member and the
owner of the *Whig,* Mahone from the first exercised
unusual influence, to which was added early in 1880 the
prestige of a United States Senator-elect. To him, therefore, was generally conceded the task of "talking over"
those who were dissatisfied with the action of the "committee on spoils," as the caucus apportionment committee was aptly termed; and from this fact it is reasonable to infer that he was consulted in advance of the
apportionment. But thus far the authority which he
wielded was only such as any capable leader might
obtain and was perhaps little greater than that enjoyed
by "Parson" Massey, "the most popular man in the
party." After his successful début in the Senate, however, Mahone advanced by bold and rapid strides to
complete control. First, by clever manipulation of the
state convention, he secured the defeat of Massey's
gubernatorial aspirations, and thereby sidetracked his
only rival. Then, strengthened by this victory and by
the open and vigorous support of President Arthur, he
quietly obtained from the candidates for the legislature
a written "pledge," "under seal," to "stand by the
Readjuster party" and to go into the party caucus and

[42] Fulkerson presided. Massey, who had been defeated, was made an
honorary member. Judge B. W. Lacy, of New Kent, became speaker, and
P. H. McCaul, clerk of the House; Gen. W. M. Elliott became president
pro tem., and C. H. Causey, of Nansemond, clerk of the Senate; A. J.
Taylor and C. M. Webber (editor of the Salem *Register*) became sergeants-
at-arms. Riddleberger and Paul were active in patronage arrangements.
Much to their annoyance, the *Dispatch* managed to report these meetings
quite fully.

abide by its results.[43] After the elections, in a preliminary conference of leaders selected by himself, the work
of the legislature was mapped out; and, when the legislature assembled, this program was gradually unfolded for
adoption in the caucus under rules of procedure which its
members were bluffed into accepting, and which, some
of them asserted, they were not allowed even to read.
The revolt followed of the "Big Four," as four members
of the caucus who had not given the pledge came to be
called;[44] and as a result of this revolt most of the measures objectionable to even a few Readjuster legislators
failed of passage. But the "Big Four" and their
backers were quickly "read out of the party." Nor was
Mahone's supremacy questioned again for two years.

This machine, as has been suggested above, rested

[43] Lybrook, *op. cit.* The procedure followed in obtaining the pledge is
illustrative of Mahone's indirect methods. The "Judge" addressed below
was Lybrook. "Fernald" was the Republican collector of internal revenue
at Danville.

"U. S. Internal Revenue Office,
Danville, Va., Sept. 14, 1881.

Dear Judge.—I send you herewith two 'pledges' to sign one and have
the party nominee for your county to sign the other one, and return to me,
and I will forward them to Gen. Mahone, *who directs me to do this.*

Of course it is nothing for an honest man to do and sign his hand to his
faith. Please attend to this promptly.

Fernald.''

"Patrick Co., Virginia,
.... 1881.

"I hereby pledge myself to stand by the Readjuster party and platform, and to go into caucus with the Readjuster members of the Legislature,
and vote for all measures, nominees and candidates to be elected by the
Legislature that meets in Richmond, as the caucus may agree upon.

Given under my hand and seal this .... day of Sept., A. D., 1881.''

[44] Senators S. H. Newberry, of Bland, and P. G. Hale, of Grayson,
formerly Conservatives, and A. M. Lybrook, of Patrick, and B. F. Williams,
of Nottoway, formerly Republicans. It is the popular opinion in Virginia
that these men saved the day.

primarily upon its control over the patronage, state and national. The extent of state patronage has already been indicated.[45] Equally important was the national patronage. In round numbers, the treasury service employed two hundred men at an annual salary of $400,000, the post-office department, 1,700 postmasters at $150,000. Connected with the federal courts were some seventy men.[46] The navy yard at Portsmouth was a large and unfailing employer at critical times. In the prevailing scarcity of money and dearth of business enthusiasm, these positions were all deemed highly desirable, and therefore worth working for. Moreover, their holders could be "assessed" regularly and with confidence. So, too, could Virginia's quota of the employees in Washington.[47] And to these sources of strength should be added the sympathetic support of the *National Republican,* of Washington, under the editorship of Gorham and Assistant Postmaster General Hatton.[48]

A second reason for the facility with which Mahone established machine control is found not so much in the character of the Readjuster leaders or in the enthusiasm which their plans aroused, though each of these was contributory, as in the possession of the negro vote. Trained by the slave system to unquestioning obedience, the colored men had easily learned to follow political bosses during reconstruction days. Being gregarious by instinct, they almost always moved *en masse.* And since their ignorance was stupendous and their credulity childlike, flattery, bribery, and threats were sufficient

[45] Above.

[46] *Register of U. S. Officials,* 1879.

[47] New York *Herald,* in *Dispatch,* October 22, 1882.

[48] Above, p. 138; New York *Tribune,* June 5, 1883. Hatton was later postmaster general.

to win them—one was under no necessity of inventing a *reason* for the course they were advised to take.[49] There were, indeed, important offsets to these advantages: their inability to move without white leadership, for example, and the perpetual danger of provoking a recrudescence of race politics. But these disadvantages did not become operative until 1883.

The manner in which Mahone used his control over the machine is striking. Indeed, in the opinion of some it constituted the most important phase of the Readjuster movement. Illustrations abound. Thus, despite the pledges of two state conventions, the Riddleberger Act was not submitted to the people, nor did it directly repudiate war and reconstruction interest on the debt, both of which the Republicans of the North thought unwise.[50] To gerrymander Congressional districts even to the extent of making 187,000 people in a white district equivalent to 132,000 in a black district was perhaps not unusual; but to avow the partisan motive and to express open regret that only eight "administration" representatives could be thus assured was rather startling.[51] The second mortgage bond which Mahone himself had executed as president of the A. M. & O. he induced the

[49] The following was printed by the *Dispatch* as a speech of W. L. Fernald delivered at Halifax Court House: "It does those Funder overseers so much good to see a *nigger's* back whipped. Every time they see a nigger's back cut, they jump up and clap their heels together like game cocks. . . . You will see colored judges and lawyers in that court house, and you will have good schools if the Readjusters succeed. . . . When a colored man comes out against the Readjuster party, he has sold himself. A man who goes against his race and color is *a damned scoundrel.* . . . Some will say, what will become of the Republican party if we all go over to the Readjusters? There is nothing in a name except the smell. . . . My office looks Africa because I have so many colored people in it."

[50] The terms of the debt settlement are, however, in the author's opinion, substantially the same as those of the first Riddleberger bill, which were endorsed by the people in the election of 1881.

[51] The *Whig's* utterances are referred to.

board of public works to compromise for $500,000 in cash, and the legislature ratified the arrangement, as the schools needed the money.[52] Two bank note companies, the American and the Kendall, bid for the printing of "Riddlebergers"; the legislature awarded the contract to the lower bidder, but the other contributed $5,000 to the campaign fund and the legislature had to change its decision.[53] During President Arthur's administration some two hundred federal appointments were changed at Mahone's request;[54] fear controlled the rest. With entire openness, state employees resident in Richmond were "assessed" for campaign purposes at five per cent of their annual salary; federal employees, indirectly, at two per cent of theirs. The auditor appointed collectors of delinquent taxes with power to name their own deputies. To these collectors, receipts for the payment of the poll tax were sent, signed in blank. The Readjuster voter was handed a receipt as he entered the booth and, in 1882, federal supervisors of elections guaranteed its acceptance as a prerequisite for voting. Such voters were supposed to return the receipts; but the collector was not always bonded, and did not always render an account to the auditor.[55]

Party leaders Mahone paid well: negroes in the Norfolk region received from $300 to $500 each; men of a higher type were rewarded with public favors not always of an unquestionable character.[56] Activity was

---

[52] Above.

[53] *Dispatch, State,* April, 1882. The state was forced to pay the Kendall Company also. In 1885 the second auditor bought the rejected bonds at auction from an express company for $17.75, Sen. *Jour.,* 1885-1886, Doc. 10.

[54] Estimate in "New Virginia," in *Whig,* March 28, 1885.

[55] Above; Sen. *Jour.,* 1883-1884, Doc. 27; contested election cases of O'Ferrall *v.* Paul (House Misc. Docs., 48 Cong., 1 Sess., No. 16), and Massey *v.* Wise (*ibid.,* No. 2*i*, pts. 1 and 2); O'Ferrall, *Forty Years.*

[56] Ex-Congressman Dezendorf to D. B. Eaton, in New York *Tribune,*

demanded of all office-holders. Thus, the superintendent of an insane asylum not only distributed poll tax
receipts but also bought the institution's provisions and
used its teams in the interest of the party;[57] and the
Norfolk postmaster and his assistant were reported to
be usually away on party business.[58] Mahone bossed
rather than guided: men said that he went into the
auditor's office and appointed or removed tax collectors
as if the auditor were his absent clerk; the sheriff of
Pittsylvania made affidavit that Mahone telegraphed
his removal;[59] Col. Frank G. Ruffin, long a "power" in
the Conservative party and a staunch supporter of
coalition, for protesting against assessment and the
"pledge" lost his clerkship.[60]   Massey alleges[61] that the
gubernatorial nomination was offered him on the condition of absolute obedience to Mahone, such as Wise
and Cameron had promised. Conventions usually merely
registered his will: that of 1881 adopted a platform
which he had sent the day before to Wall Street;[62] in
1884, having named the temporary chairman and,
through him, the permanent chairman, Mahone reported
from a single committee a plan of party organization, a
platform, delegates to the national convention, and
electors—all of which the convention ratified.[63]

Not content with this power, Mahone contemplated
vast extensions and a greater concentration of the

May 14, 1883. Dezendorf was anti-Mahone; John Goode calls him "able."
For favors see Ruffin, *Scrap-Book*, II, p. 174; Munford, *op. cit.*

[57] Unanimous report of bi-partisan committee, Sen. *Jour.*, 1883-1884,
Docs. 32, 33.

[58] Dezendorf, *op. cit.*

[59] *Dispatch*, February 8, 1883.

[60] *Ibid.*, July 6, 9, 1882.

[61] *Autobiography*, ch. 17.

[62] *Dispatch*, June 8, 1881.

[63] *Ibid.*, April 24, 1884. Col. William Lamb was temporary chairman,
Brown Allen permanent chairman.

state patronage. Of this purpose the measures defeated
by the "Big Four"[64] give ample proof. To concentrate
patronage was one of the aims of the bill creating the
office of commissioner of sales in each county and giving
him the power virtually of controlling the local newspaper through the advertising business of the office.[65]
Such, too, would have been the result of the attempt to
create a railroad commission with power not only to
examine all books, papers, and employees, and to make
rates and enforce them, but also to dismiss for cause
any officer or employee.[66] These proposed offices were
to be filled, not by popular election or even by legislative
election, but by the governor.[67] Similarly, although the
district school trustees were already under Readjuster
control through their election by local boards on which
Readjusters had an appointive majority, none the less
an effort was made to transfer their selection to the state
board of education, the members of which all held office
in Richmond. Rumor had it that the sheriffs, too, now
elective and the most important of the county officers,
would soon be named at the state capitol. According to
Colonel Ruffin, if these attempts had succeeded, 42,620
adults, drawing $18,300,000 yearly, would have become
virtually subject to Mahone.

This concentration of power and its further extension
Mahone and those closest to him defended, by insisting
that it was necessary to break up the "rings" and to
keep them broken in order that "Bourbon Democrats
and Bourbon Republicans" might be overthrown and the
"regeneration of Virginia" accomplished. And such

---

[64] Above.

[65] *House Bills*, 1881-1882, No. 259. The newspaper provision does not
appear in this bill in its first form.

[66] *Ibid.*, No. 121.

[67] *Scrap-Book*, II, p. 174. Sheriffs are not included.

reasoning undoubtedly had its weight, especially at first. But the written evidence, supported by a well-defined tradition among both Democrats and Republicans today, indicates clearly that the main object of Mahone's ambition was to perpetuate the power of the machine and that this was deemed a sufficient end in itself.

What, then, are the significant features of the Readjuster period of control? On the one hand, an attempt at democratization through legislation and appointments; on the other, the development of a new political machine. The legislation was mostly economic and social, intended to subserve the interests of the masses and to break the power of the privileged classes. Much of it was progressive and sound, in line with the best tendencies of the reconstruction period. That it involved repudiation was unfortunate but probably necessary in view of the position taken by the preferred creditors. In appointments, the balance of opportunity between well-known and unknown men was redressed; even the negroes received recognition. But if the conception of offices as "honors" was dead, that of office as opportunity for public service had not been attained; instead, men served the party. That the organization of the party quickly became a machine was due in part to the circumstances of its origin and its possession of the negro vote; in part, to the skill of General Mahone and his control of the federal patronage. As the machine became perfected, it shaped both appointments and legislation more and more to suit its own ends, until it became a very real and a very debasing tyranny.

CHAPTER XIII

THE END OF READJUSTMENT, 1883-1885

With 1882 the character of Readjuster legislation and appointments ceased to be a topic of prime political interest. To put Virginia in the Republican column was now clearly Mahone's chief object; to "redeem the state" gradually became the single aim of the Conservative management. In the struggle Readjuster ideas and tactics were taken over by the victorious Conservatives, soon called Democrats, and thus they survived. Simultaneously the improvement in economic conditions became apparent.

The story need not detain us long. In April, 1882, as the spokesman of the anti-Mahone Readjusters, Massey began to "lay the matter before the people" in characteristic fashion.[1] His chief contention was that the legitimate work of the Readjuster party had been accomplished and that Mahone's purpose now was to "bind the state and hand her over to the Republicans." Others, including Fulkerson, followed. But the regularly constituted Funder leaders in Virginia were in no position to profit by this diversion—their personal interests were too closely involved, their knowledge of the inner workings of the Readjusters too intimate for

[1] Above, p. 152; Massey, *Autobiography*, chs. 17 to 20; "A. Fulkerson's Account of his Stewardship as a Congressman delivered at Abingdon," in *Fulkerson Papers;* addresses of the "Big Four" and the "Readjuster Members of the Legislature" (*cf.* Lybrook on the accuracy of this claim to authorship) in *Annual Cyc.*, 1882; Lybrook, *Mahoneism;* Ruffin, *An Appeal.*

a broad and statesmanlike view. Remote from the cauldron of Richmond politics, however, the Democratic leaders in Washington saw the opportunity. Quietly seizing the party reins, they encouraged Massey to become an independent candidate for Congressman-at-large and then induced the state committee to give their action a passive endorsement. Likewise, under the same influences, several Congressional districts informally adopted conciliatory policies. But the breach in the old party's ranks proved too wide and the workings of the Mahone-Republican machine too powerful, for such spontaneous and irregular methods. Though it was a "Democratic year," the "Coalitionists" won five of the eight districts, and Wise defeated Massey by 5,000 votes in a total of 193,000 cast. With Mahone in the Senate and Riddleberger about to join him there, the "Solid South" was unmistakably broken. This result was attained by a combination of boss, patronage, and negroes—a combination that might easily be effected in almost any Southern state.[2]

With spirits thoroughly chastened by successive defeats, Funder congressmen, press, and local leaders now, for the first time, deliberately went to the rank and file for advice. In the widespread discussion that ensued a Conservative policy was gradually shaped for use in the legislative campaign of 1883: first of all, an unequivocal and formal renunciation of the Funder claim to a monopoly of Conservatism; secondly, a revivifying of the issue by which warring factions had so long

[2] *Cf.* ch. 11. Throughout the South, wrote "Vates" in the Boston *Post* (*Whig*, July 4), the negroes and the bosses are coming together, and "the hour is big with fate." The *Nation* thought the movement "likely to spread through the South," January 12, May 25. The *Dispatch* feared (July 12) Mahone's success "will give such an impetus to the Coalition movement that the arrest of that movement between now and 1884 may be impossible."

been held together; and, thirdly, a new leadership which should be at once popular and efficient. Accordingly, the state committee early in the year agreed to call a state convention and named as the place, not Richmond, but Staunton, in the heart of the white and Readjuster Valley. In the election of delegates to this convention, the committee announced, "all Conservative Democrats are equally entitled to participate."[3] Fortune aided the venture. For in March came the decision of the highest federal court sustaining "Coupon-Killer, Number One" and thereby the Readjuster debt settlement.[4] Some Funders, indeed, to whom the decision was almost incredible, sought loopholes in the rather confused reasoning of the court; but others welcomed the opportunity for an honorable retreat, and soon the great majority declared the matter ended.[5] Satisfied, many Readjusters now entered the convention and shared its honors with their old, but hitherto preferred, party friends. The platform, formally accepting the Readjuster settlement, rang the emphasis upon "Mahoneism"; and upon the walls of the convention hall one could read "THIS WAY, FREEMEN!" With a word of praise the old leaders were set aside, and a complete reorganization after the Mahone model was

[3] "What Fulkerson did for a convention," manuscript in the handwriting of Colonel Fulkerson, *Fulkerson Papers; Dispatch,* February 15.

[4] Antoni *v.* Greenhow, 17 U. S. *Rep.* 769; *Annual Cyc.,* 1883, Art. "Obligation of Contracts"; Royall, *Virginia Debt Controversy,* ch. 6. The grounds were that the remedy offered by the state for breach of contract was "substantially equivalent to that in force when the coupons were issued," and that this remedy was the "one which the state has chosen to give, and the only one therefore, which the courts of the United States are authorized to administer." Chief Justice Waite rested his decision on the first named ground, Justice Matthews on the second, Justices Bradley, Woods, and Gray concurred in both. Justices Field and Harlan dissented.

[5] *Dispatch,* March 6; *Dispatch* and *State, passim* (citations). That a belief in a conspiracy between Mahone and the Republican justices had weight (Royall, *op. cit.*) is not evident from the Richmond press.

planned. To the chairmanship of the party, with its enlarged powers and duties, the convention unanimously elected John S. Barbour, a railroad man and a Funder, but one of those who had inspired and directed the new party policy. Before the convention Barbour stated that he "didn't believe much in still-hunting with a brass band, nor had he much faith in committees. Nor in platforms." In token of the burying of old issues the name "Democrat" was now, for the first time, formally taken.[6]

Despite the consequent Democratic enthusiasm and activity,[7] however, the result of the campaign was still in doubt when the "Danville riot" gave to the Democrats a most convincing argument for the overthrow of Mahoneism.[8] The circumstances were these: Early in 1883, Governor Cameron appointed two negroes as school trustees in Richmond, and negro mass-meetings endorsed the act.[9] Many Conservatives thereupon urged that race lines be drawn. To this, however, many, especially of the ex-Readjuster following, would not consent.[10]

[6] *Dispatch, State, Whig,* July 25, 26; above, p. 101; *Dispatch,* July 28; *Whig,* November 7. Barbour was a brother of James Barbour, above, p. 111.

[7] The Democrats were aided by the opposition of Straight-outs. Mahone was handicapped by the desertion of lieutenants, see letters of Congressman Dezendorf, also editorials, in New York *Tribune,* May 14 ff.; also interview of Mahone in same, June 8. Apparently Mahone had to threaten Arthur with the loss of Virginia's vote in the national Republican convention next year, *ibid.,* June 5, 13.

[8] *Dispatch* and *Whig,* November 3-9; *"New Virginia";* O'Ferrall, *Forty Years,* p. 294; "Personal Recollections." O'Ferrall gives the year as 1885.

[9] *Dispatch,* May, June, July, *passim.* Another negro trustee had been appointed in Lunenburg by Cameron, *State,* March 8. Kemper had done the same, *Whig,* October 3. But "Africanization" was not feared under him.

[10] Opposition to drawing the color line was greatest in the Norfolk region, where "fusion" had already begun. Many favored support of negro schools from funds contributed by negroes only.

But as the campaign grew warmer, the Democrats resorted to "dividing the crowd" on public occasions, and in many places the negroes were wrought up to a state of extreme excitement by the speeches of Republican leaders. A climax was reached in Danville. In this little "Southside" town, the whites paid $38,000 of the $40,000 taxes. But the negroes were in a majority and, aided by a new town charter which they had obtained from the "pledged" legislature, they secured a majority of the council, over which a carpet-bagger presided. All the justices of the peace, four of the nine policemen, the health officer, the weigh-master and the clerk of the market, together with twenty of the twenty-four renters of stalls in the market, were negroes. It was just such an "Africanization" as had been feared in Reconstruction days, and predicted time and again as the necessary outcome of Mahoneism. On the Saturday night preceding election day (Tuesday), a street brawl led to a "riot," in which a few whites and blacks were killed. The governor called out the militia and order was soon restored. But forthwith flaming posters told the story to the whites of the "Southwest"; and in Lynchburg a mass-meeting unanimously resolved, upon motion of the stern old Bourbon, Gen. Jubal A. Early, that "the negroes must know that they are to behave themselves and keep in their proper places." After this the result of the election was no longer in doubt. The whites turned out as never before, and the Democrats, by a majority of 18,000 in 267,000 counted, won nearly two-thirds of both houses. From all over the South came congratulations, the sincerity of which no one denied.[11]

[11] Two hundred and sixty-seven thousand votes were counted in 1883; 193,000 in 1882; 213,000 in 1881. The Democratic majority was 18,000 as against a Republican majority of 13,000 in 1881 and 5,000 in 1882.

The legislature thus elected quickly demonstrated how completely the old debt issue had ceased to be a matter of political importance. Recalling how for thirteen years this question had "profoundly agitated the people of Virginia . . . resulting in political contests which have convulsed the popular mind, given repeated and ruinous shocks to the business interests of the state, retarded prosperity, and threatened the safety of the people"; how a "large body of the citizens and tax-payers" had made "persistent, repeated, and earnest but unavailing efforts to effect and carry out a settlement, by which a much larger sum would have been recognized and assumed by the state than has been assumed by the 'Riddleberger Bill' "; and how the people had endorsed this bill at three successive elections and the highest courts had declared it valid, the legislature resolved that "any expectation that any settlement of the debt, upon any other basis, will ever be made or tolerated by the people of Virginia, is absolutely illusory and hopeless," and that the interests of both creditors and the state required its complete acceptance by both. Not a vote was recorded against this resolution. The Readjuster Democrat Newberry introduced it in the Senate, the Funder Democrat William A. Anderson in the House. Among those who voted for it were A. Koiner and W. C. Wickham, ex-chairmen of the Funder wings of the Conservative and Republican parties respectively.[12] Governor Cameron signed it. Moreover, laws suggested by the governor and designed

There was undoubtedly a great deal of fraud. In most places Mahone controlled the election of judges; and his state board of canvassers refused to go behind the returns. Half the "Southwest," two-thirds of the Valley, and all the cities but Norfolk and Petersburg went Democratic.

[12] *Acts*, 1883-1884, p. 7; House and Senate *Journals*.

to make the Riddleberger Act and the "Coupon Killers"
more effective were enacted without difficulty.[13]

Nor did the legislature undo or attempt to undo any
of the other economic and social legislation of the
Readjusters, the more liberal suffrage, the larger appropriations for schools and charities, the lower and fairer
taxes, and the abolition of the whipping-post. On the
contrary, it desired to supplement and extend them all.[14]
For such legislation was, unquestionably, the "will of
the people."

If in these matters the legislature followed the Readjuster creed, still more did it acknowledge the influence
of the Mahone system in its political activities. Acting
upon the pointed advice of the new state committee,[15]
individual members forbore to seek offices for themselves, and the caucus smoothly and equitably apportioned the patronage.[16] Next, by prompt and vigorous
efforts, the Democratic majority in each house was
increased to two-thirds.[17] Then the task of breaking
the grip of the machine was begun. The governor's
share in the appointment of the commissioner of agriculture and of the capitol police was taken away.[18] The
boards of all the asylums were declared vacant and the
appointment of their members was transferred from the

[13] Governor, *Message*, December, 1883; *Acts*, 1883-1884, pp. 504, 527;
Acts, 1884 (extra session), p. 163.

[14] Above, ch. 12. *Cf.* the white female normal school in the "Southside" and the lunatic asylum in the "Southwest," *Acts*, 1883-1884, pp.
417, 692. The House directed that a bill for separate negro teachers and
trustees for negro schools be reported, but nothing resulted, House
Jour., p. 86.

[15] *Dispatch*, November 23, 25, 1883.

[16] Especially pleasing was the selection of Col. Frank G. Ruffin as
second auditor, the officer in charge of public debt operations and of the
literary fund and member of the board of public works.

[17] "*New Virgina*"; Ruffin, *Scrap-Book*, II, p. 224.

[18] House *Jour.*, 1883-1884, pp. 274, 752, 754.

governor to the board of public works.[19] Over the heads
of the county superintendents of schools was held a
threat of fine and loss of office for active participation
in politics.[20] The appointment of school trustees was
taken from the boards, composed each of county judge,
superintendent, and commonwealth's attorney, and given
to new boards elected by the legislature.[21] Registrars,
judges, and clerks of elections were treated in a similar
fashion, without any adequate provision being made for
representation of both parties.[22] The charters of towns
were changed so as to require new registration of voters
and otherwise to aid Democratic control.[23] The state
was redistricted for Congress, not indeed with such
disregard of numerical equality as Mahone had shown,
but with such obvious political bias that the governor
declared the new arrangement would give one party
seven or eight of the ten representatives on the basis
of the nearly balanced vote at the last Congressional
election.[24] To justify such strenuous and high-handed
procedure, and to obtain material for the next campaign,
as well as to bring the guilty to bar, partisan investigations were made into every cranny of Mahoneite
official activity. These investigations brought to light
a mass of incompetence, petty graft, and violent partisanship, and some gross mismanagement. Yet on the
whole it may be said that the tone of the reports was
rather judicial than partisan and though the terror of
prosecution was held over some, the object in the end
seemed to be to prevent and reclaim rather than to
punish. Upon the public records, the legislature spread

[19] *Acts*, 1883-1884, p. 155; House *Jour.*, pp. 482-513.
[20] *Acts*, 1883-1884, pp. 684, 698.
[21] *Ibid.*, p. 177; 1884 (special session), p. 119.
[22] Sen. *Jour.*, 1884, p. 23; Acts of August 25, November 29, 1884.
[23] Norfolk, Portsmouth, Danville, Petersburg.
[24] House *Jour.*, 1883-1884, p. 556.

a demand that Mahone, as the instigator of strife between the races, a traitor to the party that had elected him, and a traducer of the state he represented, should resign his seat in the United States Senate. And it sat at this work, at intervals, till past the November elections of 1884, with no little inconvenience to its members and at the risk of a popular reaction.[25]

Meantime Mahone fought what was perhaps his most brilliant campaign. In point of intelligence and respectability the "Coalitionist" state convention of April 23, 1885, was undoubtedly the strongest that he had ever got together. A flag of the United States draped the chairman's platform, and around the arch behind, one could read, "With malice to none, with charity to all." Matters moved with clock-like precision. Governor Cameron's administration was endorsed "like a flash," even though the governor himself pleaded indisposition to the demand for a "speech." Tremendous cheers greeted "Mahone, the black man's friend." "With all the dramatic effect he could bring to bear," Mahone read the platform. In it for the first time the name Republican was officially taken—"the Republican party of Virginia." No mention was made of Readjustment; the emphasis was laid upon liberalism, in state as well as nation. Despite the spirited objection of some who preferred Blaine, the delegates to the national convention were instructed to vote as a unit for Arthur: "We are for Arthur because Arthur is for us" ran the convention slogan which the delegation carried to Chicago. In the only important contest which came before the national convention, the Mahone delegates won over the "Straight-out." And when Wise and Riddleberger, so rumor had it, hoped to weaken Mahone by a rather precipitate "break" to Blaine, the successful candidate

25 *Dispatch*, March 8, July 29; *State*, March 5, 6, November 29, 1884.

sent word that "Arthur could not have been a better
friend to General Mahone than he would be." None the
less, at the elections, the Cleveland ticket won by 6,000
in 284,000 votes counted. Republicans cried fraud,
corruption, intimidation, and claimed the state by
15,000. Fraud there undoubtedly was, but by Republicans as well as by Democrats. That eighty-five per
cent of the total possible vote was counted seems to
disprove the charge of extensive intimidation. Acceptance of Readjuster views by the Democrats, the race
line, and the probability of national Democratic success,
together with the smoother workings of the new
machinery, would seem to account sufficiently for the
great increase in the Democratic vote.

With discriminating firmness the Cleveland administration at once proceeded to remove or suppress all
Republican postmasters and revenue officials who had
been unduly active in state politics—one of the things
for which Cleveland had been elected, the *Nation*
declared. By the middle of July, 1885, the task was
fairly complete in the opinion of even so interested an
observer as Chairman Barbour. There remained,
accordingly, only the governorship to be "redeemed."
For this position the Democrats pitted Fitzhugh Lee
against John S. Wise, who still maintained a semi-independent allegiance to Mahone. So worn out were the
old issues that both parties sought new ones, and these
were usually ultra-democratic. Thus both endorsed
"local option" in the matter of liquor licenses, both
advocated increased pensions for Confederate soldiers
and free text-books for the public schools, and both
promised a variety of things calculated to win the labor
vote. National interest was again aroused: because, said
the New York *Tribune*, Virginia was the only Southern
state where even a semblance of fair elections was main-

tained; because, said the *Nation,* "the whole nation is humiliated when any state is debased by the domination of such a boss." For the first time, Republicans of national prominence came down to speak, notably, Sherman and Foraker. Wise polled only 2,000 fewer votes than Blaine had received the year before. But Barbour and Lee raised the Democratic vote 6,000 above that cast for Cleveland. The legislature, too, was overwhelmingly Democratic. So was its successor. And so Daniel and Barbour soon superseded Mahone and Riddleberger in the Senate.

A new and happier era had now clearly arrived. Economic conditions were much better than in 1879. Realty assessments showed an increase of thirty-six millions—more than fifteen per cent, and the tax burden of the farmer was proportionately fairer than of old.[26] There were no railroads now in the hands of receivers. Charters for new and *bona fide* enterprises were being issued in large numbers. The lower middle class continued to increase in numbers and in wealth; over ninety-six per cent of the 300,000 tithables paid less than twenty-five dollars each in taxes. Newspapers had increased in size, number, and circulation; they no longer abounded in huge lists of delinquent taxpayers or in cries from the distressed. Schools were firmly established. In 1886, the literary fund was converted into more than a million of Riddlebergers. A normal school for the whites and another for the colored, the former presided over by Dr. Ruffner during its first years, were receiving regular, if inadequate, assistance. By an act of 1884, appropriations for disabled Confederate soldiers had been increased one-half. There was a disposition to continue

[26] Realty now contributed thirty-six per cent of the total revenue, as against fifty-nine per cent in 1871.

work on the asylum problem until no insane person should be confined with criminals.

Old sectional antipathies among the upper classes had been greatly modified. Scalawags and carpet-baggers were almost entirely things of the past; their Mahoneite successors were at last muzzled. For the first time in almost a generation, "real Virginians" now had a share in the national government. They helped in the making of the laws, and they alone executed the laws within the state. They had the ear of the president. They even represented the nation abroad. With manifest pleasure, they saw the independent political opinion of the North approving their political position, and they rejoiced that the commercial world at last understood and applauded the "Bourbon" stand for the fiscal honor of the state. They found parental pride in the applause with which Fitzhugh Lee was welcomed during the presidential inaugural parade, and their press chronicled without unfavorable comment the fact that in the following July he spoke at Bunker Hill. Warmed now by the generous attitude of Grant at Appomattox and again in 1869, a Democratic convention paused, on news of his death, to adopt resolutions of respect and sympathy. "Surely," said the *Dispatch,* "we have a united country." "Best of all," said the *Whig,* in summing up Colonel Elam's interpretation of the Readjuster Movement, "it gave us that political regeneration which makes us New Virginians indeed, by transforming us from mere Virginians and Southerners into American citizens."

But the fiscal situation was still serious. All except one of the state's former holdings in internal improvement companies were gone. The revenues, even after the reassessment of realty in 1885, showed but little increase over those of 1875. They could scarcely be increased. For even if a statesmanlike policy would permit the imposition of a greater burden upon the masses, political conditions would not: Mahone, men said, had "corrupted the people." Nor could the tendency to reach out and tax capital be pursued far; for capital had not entirely forgiven the repudiating state, and, besides, the Democratic party must draw upon capital in order to maintain its control. On the other hand, there were new and increased expenses. Some of these were temporary: the extra legislative expenses, for example, and possibly the increased criminal expenses. But others were unquestionably permanent: such as those for schools, asylums, and pensions. In general, it was quite clear that any increase, present or prospective, in the revenues of the state, as compared with the period of 1877-1879, was fully offset by present and prospective expenses that, for all practical purposes, could not be avoided. Obviously, the debt was still an important consideration. Even under a complete funding into "Riddlebergers" the interest would be hard to meet. So far, however, less than five millions had been funded, and creditors showed no inclination to increase the amount. But public sentiment on this question was almost unanimous now. When part of the legislation supplementing the "Coupon-Killers" was declared unconstitutional, other was contrived. Business men refused to use the old coupons, lawyers to take coupon cases. The bondholders did, indeed, make a strong and spectacular legal fight, during which attorneys for both sides were in turn sent to prison for contempt.[27] But by degrees it became clear that the state was slowly winning: between 1883 and 1890 the maximum amount of coupons received at the treasury for one year was $258,938, the minimum,

[27] For an account by the most energetic and daring of the bondholders' counsel, see Royall, *Some Reminiscences.*

$40,540. So the holders of consols and ten-forties yielded. By agreeing to the act of February 20, 1892, they accepted the essential principles of the Riddle-berger Act.[28] The new bonds were known as "cen-turies"; the act, as "the settlement." There remained the task of compelling West Virginia to settle with creditors for her share of the old debt; this was a moral obligation assumed as part of "the settlement." But the economic and fiscal problem of Virginia was at last solved.

Though Mahone's control over the state was never restored, the Republican party retained its newly won supremacy in over one-half of the "Southwest" and about one-third of the Valley and in the cities of Nor-folk and Petersburg. It was more strongly entrenched than of old in the rest of the "Southwest" and the Valley. In the "East" it once more controlled in most of the counties with large negro majorities and in some cases where the negroes were not in the majority. Improvement in Republican leadership was noteworthy throughout the state. But the quality of its masses improved little in the "East." Over this party Mahone's personal domination continued, though his most trusted lieutenants left him. Defeat did not crush his spirit or destroy his unique prestige in national politics.

The Democratic party in Virginia did not recede from

[28] See Governor, *Message*, January 14, 1892, and accompanying docu-ments. The commission representing Virginia consisted of P. W. McKinney, R. H. Cardwell, H. T. Wickham, J. Hoge Tyler, Taylor Berry, W. D. Dabney, and Robert H. Tyler. F. P. Olcott was chairman of the bond-holders' committee. Grover Cleveland, Thomas F. Bayard, E. J. Phelps, George S. Coe, and George G. Williams constituted an "advisory board for the creditors." Some points which the Readjusters had insisted upon were not incorporated in the settlement, e.g., subjection of the new bonds to taxation.

174 READJUSTER MOVEMENT IN VIRGINIA

its newly assumed preference for popular wants as
against the interests of the creditors. Nor for fifteen
years did it dare again legally to restrict the suffrage
though disgust with the negro voter became more and
more profound. The new plan of organization and the
new methods of conducting campaigns were not abandoned. The new leaders were not discarded. If in time
control became unduly concentrated and dangerously
close to large business interests, it was never again distinctly Bourbon or neglectful of the new man and the
young man. When the national Populistic movement
came, the way had already been prepared for its acceptance by the Democrats. In short, the Democratic party,
as compared with the old Conservative party, its predecessor, was new in organization, methods, ideals, and
leadership. These changes, constituting a compromise
between "Radicalism" and the "Old Régime," would
probably have come without the "Readjuster Movement." But to tell how they did occur has been the
purpose of this study.

CONCLUSION

Post-bellum Virginia history may be said to end with 1885: the ten or twenty years succeeding constitute an appendix, which may be included or omitted without material difference.

The task of the period (and its test) was internal readjustment—readjustment of the state's economic and social policies, of private enterprises and ideals, and of the relations of races, classes, and sections.

Most of these problems were solved with but little friction owing to the domination of Conservatism. For Conservatism was not only a political party, it was also a social code and a state of mind which bound the whites to united and temperate action. The solution was accomplished, however, under a condition of stress—of potential conflict between aristocratic and democratic forces. The aristocratic forces comprised partisans of the old régime, weakened by emancipation, indeed, but strengthened by firm alliance with capitalistic interests and by the gradual development of an "old soldier" cult. The democratic forces were the "West" and the "new" men whom war and reconstruction had thrust forward in the "East." They included also the "poor whites" and the freedmen; but these groups were usually impotent because of race antagonism.

The Radicalism of reconstruction days and the Readjuster Movement a decade later were both democratic protests against the domination of Conservatism. Radicalism, however, was largely obstructive of genuine democratic advance because it was exotic and rested upon force, and because it alienated the "West" through its attitude toward the negro. The Readjuster Movement, on the other hand, was native in origin, and its democracy was meant primarily for the whites, the negroes being considered inferior allies. Each succeeded a well-defined aristocratic movement, and each ended in a compromise whereby Conservatism became more democratic and more progressive.

On detailed analysis, the Readjuster Movement exhibits a political, an economic, and a social phase. Not until the breakdown of reconstruction politics, through the continued defeat of the Republican party and the overgrowth of the Conservative, could independent opinion make headway. Then the union of Conservative "outs" with the Republican fragments as "Readjusters" was feasible. This, in turn, paved the way for an enlarged and rejuvenated Republican party and, indirectly, for a Democratic party that was smaller but better organized and more liberally led than its Conservative predecessor.

It was economic depression that led most directly through the consequent fiscal embarrassment and general discontent, to the reception of the inciting principle of the movement. This principle, that the state's creditors should be compelled to share in the general loss occasioned by war and reconstruction, gave the movement its name. Other things being equal, it was supported by the hardest-pressed individuals and communities. Eventually it became, through general acquiescence, the basis of debt settlement. Organized just as the lowest point of depression was passed, the movement ended soon after the turn of the tide had become obvious.

Socially, the movement aimed at a government in closer "touch with the people." It sought, specifically, taxation according to ability, unrestricted manhood suffrage, abolition of the special privileges of bondholders, "brokers," and officeholding "rings," and equalization of opportunity through elementary state socialism. The leaders were mainly self-made men of the middle class, marked by energy and political shrewdness. Their methods included agitation, disregard of precedent and judicial decisions, a spoils organization, and, eventually, a boss. The response of the white masses was loud and strong in the democratic "West"; in the "East," doubtful and hesitating. The end of the movement found many "new" men in prominent places. It also found the "will of the people" accepted as the criterion of public policies, and the discovery and organization of that will recognized as the first duty of party leaders. For a short time the negro seemed about to become a part of this political "people"; but the habit of implicit obedience to overseers and a boss proved too strong. These results seemed to necessitate, and to anticipate, the elimination of the negro as a voter and a wider extension of the state's social activities, especially in education.

Lastly, our study affords an illustration of the interplay of local independent movements and national politics. Undoubtedly Greenbackism aided in the inception of Readjustment, and Readjustment prepared the soil for Populism in Virginia. On the other hand, Republican supporters of the national credit and of the great private "interests" aided repudiation in Virginia; and the combination of ignorance in Virginia and federal patronage under a boss made possible the only political breach yet made in the new "Solid South."

BIBLIOGRAPHICAL NOTE

This note indicates the nature of the material used. No attempt is made at a complete enumeration.

MONOGRAPHS

C. H. Ambler, *Sectionalism in Virginia from 1776 to 1861* (1910), H. J. Eckenrode, *Political History of Virginia during the Reconstruction* (1904), and J. P. McConnell, *Negroes and Their Treatment in Virginia, 1865-1867* (1909), furnish the political background subject to the limitations implied in their titles. G. W. Dyer, *Democracy in the South before the Civil War* (1905) is incomplete but suggestive. For the economic and social side the above, B. W. Arnold, *History of the Tobacco Industry in Virginia from 1860 to 1894* (1897), and the contributions of Bruce, Dyer, Clark and others in *The South in the Building of the Nation* (1909) have been used. William A. Scott, *The Repudiation of State Debts* (1893) roughly sketches the debt history to 1893. George W. Green in Lalor's *Cyclopedia of Political Science,* article "Repudiation," and R. P. Porter in the *History of State Debts* (Vol. VII of the tenth census) give useful summaries of debatable figures. Semi-historical in its treatment is F. A. Magruder, *Recent Administration in Virginia* (1912), which appeared too late to be of any considerable service. A. D. Mayo, *Common School Education in the South* (Commissioner of Education, Report, 1901, I, Ch. XI) gives a convenient and suggestive account, largely of the work of Dr. Sears, down to 1876.

AUTOBIOGRAPHIES, MEMOIRS, ETC.

As yet works of this character either end with the war or keep as far as possible from Virginian movements and conditions. There are some exceptions. Wm. L. Royall, *History of the Virginia Debt Controversy* (1897) is the work of a native attorney for the bondholders; his *Some Reminiscences* (1909) presents the mature views of an ardent young participant of the old school. Col. R. E. Withers, Lieutenant-Governor and United States Senator, hated Mahone as much as he could hate anyone, and his delightful *Autobiography of an Octogenarian* (1907) reflects this as well as some slight lapses of memory. Governor Charles T. O'Ferrall came from west of the Blue Ridge and in the early '70's was a Readjuster—perhaps this, perhaps his native kindliness, tempered the tone of his *Forty Years of Active Service* (1904). John Goode, Congressman and president of the last constitutional convention, was in the thick of most of the political fights, but his *Recollections of a Lifetime* (1906) tells little of them. *The Autobiography of John E. Massey* (1909) is valuable for the spirit of Massey and for his writings and speeches, but it is marred by the failure of the editor to indicate which parts of it are of her composition; much of it appears to be compiled from the Richmond *Whig*. Alderman and Gordon, *J. L. M. Curry;* T. C. Johnson, *Robert L. Dabney;* and *Memoirs of Gov. William Smith,* contain important material. Of outsiders who touch Virginia affairs, A. K. McClure (*Recollections of Half a Century* and *The South: Its Industrial, Financial and Political Conditions,* 1886) and Hugh McCulloch (*Men and Measures*) are consistently friendly to the anti-Readjuster, or Funder, element, with whom they were at times associated in business; T. C. Platt (*Autobiography*) saw only Republican machine interests; James G. Blaine (*Twenty Years in Congress*) and John Sherman (*Recollections of Forty Years*) changed sides and views according to party exigencies.

CONTEMPORARY UNOFFICIAL PUBLICATIONS

The State press mirrors, but with much concealment and distortion, every feature of the period. To an unusual degree the Richmond newspapers dominated the rest. Long before the war, began the rivalry of the *Enquirer* and the *Whig*, both dictators of opinion, while the *Dispatch* was an humble gatherer of news. After the war, the news capacity, business sense, and

political instinct of the *Dispatch* made it (under the direction
of Ellyson and Cowardin) the most prosperous and influential.
The *Enquirer* became the organ of the bondholding and aristocratic faction, suspending in 1877.   The *State*, founded in 1875
by J. Hampden Chamberlayne and edited by himself and
Packard Beirne, succeeded after a fashion to the *Enquirer's*
views and clientage.   The *Whig* identified itself with the Readjuster movement and the fortunes of General Mahone, and expired in 1888.   The Virginia State Library has preserved and
listed these; slight gaps may be filled at the Congressional
Library, with the apparent exceptions of the *Whig* of 1875 and
the *Enquirer* of July-November, 1876.   Others preserved and
listed in the Virginia State Library are: *The Southern Planter
and Farmer* (1872-1876); *The Commonwealth* (Funder, daily,
William L. Royal editor, February-July, 1880); *The Religious
Herald* (Baptist, weekly, 1870-1882—other numbers in the
library of Richmond College); the *Southern Churchman* (Epis-
copalian, weekly, 1880-1882); the *Educational Journal of Virginia* (organ of the Virginia Educational Association after
November, 1869, edited by C. H. Winston, monthly; later the
semi-official and then the official organ of the state board of education).   Preserved and listed by the Norfolk public library are:
The Norfolk Landmark (Conservative, liberal, daily, James Barron Hope editor, M. Glennan managing editor) and *The Norfolk Ledger* (Conservative, daily).   Typical town papers are
The Virginia Herald (1871) and *The Virginia Star* (1877-1879),
Conservative semi-weekly, Fredericksburg, which were loaned
to me by Judge A. T. Embrey of that town.   The Northern Neck
News (1880, weekly, Conservative, edited in part by Wm. A.
Jones, preserved in its office at Warsaw) is representative of the
country newspapers.   No Republican state papers appear to
be extant except the *Southern Intelligencer* (1880, Richmond,
daily, John R. Popham editor, in the Virginia State Library)
and the Valley *Virginian* (1881-1884, Staunton, H. H. Riddleberger editor, weekly, in the Congressional Library).   Of outside papers the *Nation* is valuable for the independent (though
ill-informed) Northern view.   New York dailies followed political situations closely but not with either accuracy or fairness.

Even more partisan was the *National Republican* (Washington), a "Mahone sheet." The magazine literature (which treats the legal side of the debt question chiefly) is unimportant; it is sufficiently indicated in Scott, *Repudiation of State Debts*, pp. 272-274. Few pamphlets of the earlier period remain; many of the later have recently come to the State Library. The views of Readjusters who refused to follow Mahone into the Republican party are presented with great fullness by Frank G. Ruffin[1] and, to a less extent, by A. M. Lybrook,[2] the former previously a Democrat, the latter previously a Republican. Gilbert C. Walker and C. U. Williams present early Funder opinions on the debt. *"New Virginia"* (published originally in the *Whig* in 1885 and probably the work of its editor, W. C. Elam, or of S. B. French) gives a review of the entire period in the light in which Mahone wished the North to see it. This was loaned me by Judge Goolrick, of Fredericksburg. The others are in the Virginia State Library. *American Politics* (1882) by Thomas V. Cooper and Hector T. Fenton, of Pennsylvania, contains an unusually bold statement of the Camerons' share in the events of the later period. Nine editions of this book were issued by 1885 with the account unchanged. For election returns and party affiliations of legislators the *Warrock-Richardson Almanac* is invaluable. The *Proceedings* of the State Grange (State Library, 1874-1876) should be studied in connection with the *Southern Planter*.

OFFICIAL PUBLICATIONS

The usual state publications are practically complete in the State Library. They are often badly digested and partisan. The *Annual Reports of Boards, Officers and Institutions* contain: Reports of the Auditor, the Second Auditor, the Treasurer,

---

[1] His pamphlets, largely reprints of newspaper articles, are cited as: *Mahoneism Unveiled* (no date, probably 1882); *An Appeal* (1883); *Facts, etc.* (1885, "Facts, Thoughts and Conclusions in regard to the Public Debt of Virginia"). Colonel Ruffin is unusually accurate in his facts and thoroughly honest. His *Scrap-Book* in five volumes is also in the State Library.

[2] Judge Lybrook's pamphlet (cited as *Mahonism Unveiled*) is a reprint of his letter to the *Dispatch* (1882).

the State Superintendent of Public Instruction (also published separately as *Virginia School Reports*) and the various boards of which the Sinking Fund Commission, the Board of Public Works (continued by the Railroad Commissioner from 1877 and published separately), and the trustees of various asylums, colleges, etc., are most important. *House Bills, 1881-1882,* is incomplete but valuable. There is an *Index to the Acts of the Assembly* in their manuscript form (in which they are known as "Enrolled Bills"). The House and Senate *Journals* contain the governor's messages and other documents, usually as an appendix. Major "Jed" Hotchkiss published under authority of the legislature a *Summary of Virginia, Geographical and Political,* which is valuable for its maps. Contested elections for state officers were occasionally presented as House or Senate documents; those for federal offices are easily accessible through C. H. Rowell's *Historical and Legal Digest.* The figures given in the returns of the United States census officials cannot be considered more than approximations, as these officials were often untrustworthy. The *Ku Klux Committee Report* (House *Reports,* 42 Cong., 2d sess., no. 22, pt. 1) is negatively valuable.

MANUSCRIPTS

The large collection of *Ruffner Papers* was placed unreservedly at my disposal by Dr. and Mrs. R. F. Campbell, of Asheville, N. C. For selections from the *Fulkerson Papers* and the *Dickinson Papers,* I am indebted to Mr. S. V. Fulkerson, of Bristol, Virginia, and Miss Camilla Dickinson, of Richmond. J. Willcox Brown, of Afton, Virginia, has recently deposited with the Virginia State Library a collection of manuscript articles, in the nature of recollections, by himself. The *Harvie Papers,* discovered by Prof. C. H. Ambler and deposited in the State Library by Dr. Armistead G. Taylor,[3] contain letters from Gen. William Mahone and other Readjusters to Col. Lewis E. Harvie, of Amelia County and Richmond. The large and carefully preserved collection of *Mahone Papers,* hitherto inacces-

---

[3] See Report of the Virginia State Library for 1913-1914, p. 7.

sible to students, was, through the courtesy of Mr. and Mrs. W. L. McGill, placed at my disposal for consultation on crucial points. The state *Land Books* are invaluable for an understanding of economic conditions. Under the enlightened and energetic policy of the State Library's present management other similar material will probably soon be available.

"PERSONAL RECOLLECTIONS"

Under this title are entered memoranda of conversations with men who were participants in the situation described but whose names it is not advisable to give at present.

INDEX

INDEX

DATE DUE			

Detroit

Documentary History of American Cities

Tamara K. Hareven and
Stephan Thernstrom, Series Editors

Detroit

Edited
by
Melvin G.
Holli

Series
Editors:
Tamara K.
Hareven
and
Stephan
Thernstrom

New Viewpoints

A Division of Franklin Watts   New York   London   1976

Library of Congress Cataloging in Publication Data
Main entry under title:

Detroit.

  (Documentary history of American cities)
  Includes index.
  1. Detroit—History. 2. Detroit—History—
Sources. I. Holli, Melvin G.
F574.D4D23   977.4'34   76–24802
ISBN 0–531–05385–7
ISBN 0–531–05591–4 (pbk.)

New Viewpoints
A Division of Franklin Watts
730 Fifth Avenue
New York, New York 10019

CONTENTS

Contents   **xi**

APPENDIX
Tables

Maps and Figures

INDEX

Foreword

"There has been an earthquake in the automobile world and the temples of the industry—from the Volkswagen lair in Wolfsburg, West Germany, to the giant factories in Detroit and Tokyo—are still trembling," wrote *The New York Times* on 7 April 1974. The "Pride of Detroit," the gas-guzzling, five-thousand-pound, chrome-plated brontosaur had been rendered obsolete by the new oil age. The whirlwinds of change that swept out of the sheikhdoms of Araby shook the titans of Detroit—Ford, Chrysler, and General Motors—unlike any single event of the twentieth century. The ten-miles-to-the-gallon behemoths of the pre-oil-embargo days, like anachronisms from past times, seemed doomed to extinction. The natural selection likely to be practiced by cost-wise consumers, and killing changes in prices at the gas pump decreed by the seers of Washington, will probably drive out of the auto-agency sales-rooms the Pride of Detroit and relegate it to the role of museum exhibit piece. No longer can we say with confidence, "Ford's in his flivver. All's well with the world."

This study covers the entire span of Detroit's history from its founding by the first Cadillac in 1701 to what may be the period of the last Cadillac as the energy and petroleum crisis continues to unfold.

In the beginning Detroit was an extension of Montreal and the French maritime settlements for the exploitation of furs and riches in the New World. Detroit's entrepôt importance derived much from its presence on one of the continent's longest inland water-ways and on one of the eighteenth century's most important lines of commerce reaching into the North American interior. Its name, *de troit,* translates as "strait" and describes the narrow connecting waters between lakes Erie and Huron, which were of military significance for checking the incursions of the English and the Iroquois Indians into French domain. The city was planted on the highest bank, on the narrowest part of the river, which the French measured by cannon as only "one gunshot" across.

The French brought to Detroit an archaic social system called seigniorialism which, although it may have possessed certain military advantages, was not attuned to the rapid commercial advances being made in English-speaking North America. French-speaking elements remained the principal population group in Detroit until early in the nineteenth century.

As Detroit's population grew more heterogeneous in the 1840s and 1850s, the city also became more cosmopolitan and was confronted by more complex social and cultural conflicts issuing from this diversity. The "School Question" of 1853 was a significant force in shaping political and social attitudes of Detroiters toward new cultural groups and in determining the social composition of political parties.

During the two decades following 1850 Detroit was predominantly a commercial city. By 1855 Detroit had achieved a high plateau of mercantile development and had high hopes of becoming the commercial emporium of mid-America. City boosters and leading civic men were heralded as farsighted Jasons who sought the golden fleece of commerce for their respective cities. Detroit's industrial "takeoff" was well under way during the 1870s, which was a critical decade in changing the economic and social character of the city. Between 1880 and 1890 Detroit had a diversified and balanced industrial base that twentieth-century urban planners would envy. Detroit was a medium-sized city with nothing unique in its industrial base to predict or explain the meteoric and dramatic changes that came after 1902. This fact is often lost sight of by writers who have ransacked Detroit's past in search of forerunners of the dynaflow, the chrome bumper, and other technological innovations that might have destined Detroit to become the motor-town capital of America. Detroit's principal contribution to the automobile is not to be found in its inventive spirit or in its geography but, rather, in the entrepreneurial efforts of a few early motorcar assemblers. Any rational observer of the American city scene in 1900 would probably have predicted that the automobile industry would develop in a more advanced industrial city than Detroit.

Although Detroit had grown enormously in population before

the turn of the century, its social geography and spatial arrangements remained peculiarly preindustrial. The upper classes remained near the center and core of the city, and would continue to do so after 1900. The poor and newcomers were not crammed into central ghettos but were scattered from the waterfront to the outskirts, often living on cheap land on the periphery. Often lost sight of by many city chroniclers is the fact that Detroit from 1860 to 1890 was a Teutonic city, with Germans as the leading foreign-born group. Their presence would be felt in many ways, including stormy prohibition and temperance battles.

The impact of the automobile industry upon Detroit was immense and seemingly permanent. By 1919 the modern and enduring character of twentieth-century Detroit was fixed. The city was, is, and probably will be for the foreseeable future dominated by this single industry. A basic industry as all-pervasive as motor vehicle manufacturing was to Detroit affected the social and political character of the city: it influenced the city's language and metaphors, the subjects treated in its newspapers and magazines, and its law enforcement practices, and provided the leadership for municipal reform and civic endeavors. Auto factories acted as powerful magnets drawing to Detroit elements almost totally absent from its population and imparted to the city a more working-class and blue-collar character than to most cities in its population class. The overwhelming influence of a single industry with low skills requirements had a significant and measurable impact upon Detroit's population structure and character. Detroit was much less a service-oriented and more a blue-collar city than its fourth population rank would suggest.

The auto industry also brought to Detroit a sharply fluctuating "boom-and-bust" business cycle, exaggerating the peaks and troughs experienced by the national economy. During the prosperous twenties, booze, vice, and gangster rowdyism characterized the brash new city that had pushed up from thirteenth to fourth in rank in just two decades. Motorcar metaphors continued to pervade the literature about Detroit, which was described as "Utopia on Wheels" and "Dynamic Detroit," but by 1930 the city was sadly "out of gear." The city fell from superaffluence to grim poverty with the boom-and-bust cycle again exaggerated in one-industry towns such as Detroit—when the national economy was beset by a cold, Detroit normally caught pneumonia. From a 1929 peak the number of wage earners plunged 40 percent by 1933.

The dramatic and far-reaching events of the 1930s saw workers take mass and collective actions that would permanently alter the structure and nature of labor relations. The critical turning point for organizing mass-production workers into unions occurred in the 1937 sitdown strikes at General Motors, which brought national attention to a new and stunning strike technique. A feeble and new union, the United Automobile Workers, was the David that struck down the Goliath of American industry, and the shock waves reverberated from coast to coast. After 1937 the mass-production industries in autos, steel, and rubber would lose much of the overweening and awesome power they had exercised over the worker. The sit-down victory was clearly the most significant single event in the labor history of the Detroit region, and in mass-production industry in the nation. The ripples from the sit-down would continue to be felt in our own time, when civil rights workers and college-student protesters would adopt the sit-down but call it the "sit-in."

The impact of the Detroit-based automobile industry upon politics was tremendous. Under the UAW the Democratic party was liberalized and the state's health, welfare, and education programs were updated and modernized. The Republican party became a captive of automobile management, which transformed the GOP's old-fashioned patronage orientation into a keenness for social and economic issues and programmatic politics. Both big business and big labor entered city and state politics, not for the traditional rewards, but to control, shape, and influence the state's social and economic policy. The all-pervading nature of the automobile industry stunted diversification and discouraged the growth of research and new technologies that would have attracted electronic, computer, and missile work to Detroit in the 1950s. The opportunities for diversification and for achieving a more balanced economic base were missed because, as one writer saw it, Detroit "let the space age pass her by" by concentrating almost exclusively upon automobile production.

So powerful were the forces of urban disruption that high hourly wage scales and strong representation in the auto unions by

Negroes were not sufficient to check the firestorm that swept Detroit in 1967. Liberals, planners, and city watchers were rudely disabused of the comfortable notion "that it couldn't happen here." Since the late sixties, race seems to be at the center of a majority of conflicts and encounters in the auto plants.

Hardly had the wounds and abrasions of the 1967 riot begun to heal than the school busing issue struck Detroit with full force, rubbing raw the wounds of past discontents and opening up new areas of harsh conflict. The United States Supreme Court resolved the question, at least temporarily, in a five-to-four decision in July 1974 against city-suburban busing as a cure for Detroit's school-segregation problems.

The resurgence of ethnicity in Detroit complicated considerably the problems of dealing with a factionalized and fractured city. By 1970 the rebirth of national identities was a fact of life that urban policy-makers and public officials had to be prepared to contend with. Although ethnicity was perceived by many critics only as a divisive force (tearing apart and fragmenting society), that judgment is premature and fails to appreciate the positive potential of this puzzling phenomenon. Unlike the explosive nationalisms of the nineteenth century, ethnicity was something less than an all-encompassing folk culture of blood and soil. Ethnicity among second- and third-generation Americans has more the character of a subsidiary and secondary loyalty, stronger perhaps than associational memberships, but clearly falling short of the militant nationalisms of the nineteenth century. Ethnicity also possessed reintegrative possibilities by slowing the course of social and neighborhood disintegration and by helping people to rediscover their place and heritage in society, clearly important core components in a broader system of social relationships.

M. G. H.

Detroit

PART ONE

FRENCH TRADING POST TO AMERICAN TOWN, 1701–1850

> Our fort is one arpent square without the bastions, very
> advantageously situated on an eminence. . . . We took
> care to put it at the very narrowest part of the River,
> which is one gunshot (across) being everywhere else a
> good half-quarter of a league; and if the post is in-
> habited, the ground is very good there for building
> eventually a large town.
>
> —Alphonse de Tonty
> 1 September 1701

Introduction

North America's principal colonial cities were founded primarily
as imperial outposts to stimulate trade and regulate commerce
in the best interests of the mother country. The prevailing mer-
cantilist design placed these seaboard cities into a feeder system
that provided raw materials for the homeland and a limited market for manufactured goods. The planting of American towns
was done with a keen eye for good harbors, timbered coasts
for ship stores, and rivers that drained potential hinterland areas.
If any single influence can be identified as dominant, then commerce was the key factor that explains the siting of American sea-
ports in the seventeenth century.[1]

America's interior cities were founded for similar reasons, for Detroit was an extension of Montreal and the French maritime settlements of the North Atlantic coast. French traders, missionaries, and soldiers had penetrated deep into the interior of North America by waterways such as the Saint Lawrence River, the Great Lakes, and the Mississippi River. Their aim was to capture for France the fur trade, and to lay claim to French dominion and to whatever future riches might be unearthed there. Unlike New York or Boston, Detroit was not located on a natural break in the line of transportation. Although Detroit stood alongside one of the eighteenth-century's longest and most important lines of commerce, military considerations determined its actual physical site. The French were fearful of interloping in the fur trade and hoped to check English traders from Albany and to contain their fierce Iroquois allies, who were adept at disrupting the peltry traffic. For this purpose the straits, or *de troit,* on the connecting waters between lakes Huron and Erie proved strategically attractive. Although considerably south of the historic French routeway into the lakes country, the straits formed a natural bottleneck from which to interdict the unwelcome incursions from the east and south. The military significance of this location was underscored by its founder, Antoine de la Mothe Cadillac, who chose the highest bank on the narrowest part of the river, a distance that the French measured by cannon as only "one gunshot" across.[2]

Having convinced the crown and the colonial ministry of the efficacy of his plan, Cadillac set out in 1701 to erect Fort Pontchartrain du Detroit. His letter written in 1700 explains the factors that persuaded policy-makers in France to plant an outpost there. Although he was not unmindful of personal profits, Cadillac's vision of the future settlement extended beyond that of the typical garrison way station. As commandant he hoped to induce permanent settlers with religious, educational, and medical institutions and to enlarge the colony by interracial marriage. Miscegenation would also win the loyalty and fealty of the Indians through blood lines, Cadillac believed.

Newly established Detroit lacked agricultural self-sufficiency for several years and during its first century often suffered severe food shortages. Although some Indian maize was cultivated locally, the quantity was never sufficient to provision the fur traffic or to meet the community's needs. The town produced few tools and even fewer services except those necessary for the prosecution of long-range, intercontinental trade with metropolitan Europe. The settlement's trade was lubricated by brandy, guns, and blankets fabricated in France, and later England, and in some instances distant Montreal. Its tributary area extended hundreds of miles into the interior, where valuable furs were gathered for grading, and sale in Detroit and transshipment to Europe. If a city's reach can be considered a gauge of its metropolitan status, then eighteenth-century Detroit's standing was far above what its numbers would indicate, or its services justify. Like most North American cities Detroit was part of a capitalistic venture and depended upon the export of some valuable staple into the Atlantic trade.

The principal instrument for integrating the French *habitant* into North American settlement was seigniorialism. As a system of social organization seigniorialism was in a state of decay that would lead to its extinction in the mother country while at the same time it was revived to bloom again in the New World. Old France's seigniorialism was not perfectly replicated in New France, but was adjusted to the fur trade and to some extent reshaped by social and environmental factors present in North America.[3]

Detroit, as a part of New France and then Upper Canada, shared all of the disabilities, or privileges, if one prefers, of the *ancien régime*. La Mothe Cadillac's installation in 1701 as commandant, seignior, and in 1707 as fur factor of Detroit is a classic example of the imposition of a premodern social system upon a people and a large geographic area at a time when northwestern Atlantic nation-states were well advanced into the first important phases of social and economic modernization. Cadillac granted lands by feudal tenure, required from his vassals the customary prerequisites and emoluments, engrossed to himself the feudal monopolies of the gristmill, and licensed and regulated all commerce and trade. This imposition of an archaïc social system occurred one half century after Yankee settlers of Massachusetts (as shown by Sumner C. Powell's *Puritan Village*) had abandoned communal land tenure and moved toward a modernized form of holding landed wealth: freehold tenure. These two differ-

ent modes for holding the community's most tangible forms of
wealth, for organizing society, and for conducting commerce
capture clearly some of the most vital and important differences
between modernizing and premodern societies.[4]

Seigniorialism also adjusted to the Detroit Indian trade. Its
most lucrative aspect, the fur traffic, was controlled by the seignior and commandant. He was given a monopoly on the sale of
gunpowder, wine, and brandy and authorized to regulate the flow
of peltries by issuing licenses to the beaver country as well as
supplying permissions to Montreal for provisions. The result was
that during the French period almost all beaver pelts moved
under the seal of the commandant and his associates or, later,
successors. Residents of Detroit were banned from trafficking in
goods from Montreal except for their own consumption and some
incidental Indian trade. The *habitants'* least-encumbered right
was that of raising food for their own subsistence. On his fief the
rights to minerals, timber, firewood, and stone were reserved by
the seignior or the king. The raw muscles and backs of voyageurs
did not escape exaction, either. They were required by their permits to carry in each canoe from Montreal 150 pounds of freeload
cargo for the fort commandant.[5]

The overall effect of such a social system seemed to be the
retardation of Detroit's economic development. During the slow
period of transition, roughly from 1800 to 1850, the profound
influence of a century of French Canadian seigniorialism became
more apparent. As one of our documents, Bela Hubbard's "Reminiscence," shows, seigniorialism as a system of land ownership
appeared to have hampered the *habitants'* productive energies from
the time of its first implementation in Detroit in 1707. French
officials and traders, later their English counterparts, and then
American observers had from the beginning of the eighteenth century complained repeatedly of the *habitants'* "crude" and "slov-
enly" methods of cultivation and their "shiftlessness and lack of
consistent industry." The critics usually called for Yankee farmers
whose knowledge of agriculture would make the fields rich with
production and transform the Detroit region's food deficit into a
food surplus.[6]

The *habitants* were clearly subsistence farmers, and inefficient
ones at that. The agricultural revolution of the eighteenth cen-

tury had passed them by. They left much of their acreage uncultivated, continued to use the fallow-field system when it was in discard elsewhere, and neglected the soil when its fertility was exhausted. They were also charged, by Bela Hubbard and others, with dumping their manure on ice-covered rivers to be rid of it and with employing an inefficient and shallow plow that barely cut the crust of the soil. The result was that Detroit continued to pay high prices for staple foods that had to be transported across the lake from the upper parts of the states of New York, Pennsylvania, and Ohio as late as the first quarter of the nineteenth century.

Nor was the *habitants'* ownership of prime river and lake frontage in Detroit to benefit them very much during the great influx of newcomers in the 1830s and 1840s. Although windfall profits were to be made, relatively few Frenchmen became wealthy by their ownership of real estate when the population of Detroit mushroomed from 2,200 people in 1830 to 21,000 in 1850. It seemed as if Henry George's "unearned increment" seldom fell into French pockets. The most prominent and wealthiest land speculators were newcomer Yankees and New Yorkers like Lewis Cass of New Hampshire, who parlayed a $12,000 purchase in 1816 into a $100,000 sale in 1836. When poor agricultural conditions in the East and "Michigan fever" in the West pushed and pulled thousands of New Yorkers and New Englanders into the region, newcomers, and not the old settlers, were the beneficiaries of the boom.[7]

Neither was the French *habitant* culture able to withstand the invasion of the aggressive, literate, and institutionally mature "cultural imperialism" of the Yankee. The liabilities of few schools, high illiteracy rates, and no newspapers that could sustain themselves could not be offset by a rich oral tradition. Even that, lamented the foremost student of Detroit's *habitant* culture, was left to the "pen of the Englishman." By the time the French found the "stuff for books, it was English books that enlisted their attention." [8]

Finally the forces of demography began to work against the French after 1824. Their majoritarian position of the preceding 125 years was threatened by a new immigration. Relatively static population figures had favored the French. Although Detroit had about 500 or 600 people by 1760, very little growth had occurred by a half century later in 1810, when population was pegged at 770. The population managed to reach only 2,200 by 1830. The next four years, however, saw the population double and then double again, so that by 1838 the city had about 9,000 people. Very little of this new growth came from the French. Although most estimates put the proportion of the French population at about one-half in 1830, by 1834 they had shrunk to about one-sixth. Their share of the civic and political offices (never proportionate to their numbers in population) declined markedly after 1835. Even when they had comprised a majority of the city's population in the 1820s, they had never held political offices commensurate to their numbers. The *habitants* faded quietly from the social and political scene after 1835, and by 1850 they were the forgotten element in Detroit politics, noticeable only for occasional opposition to free public schools and the antislavery and temperance movements.[9]

Free schools, slavery, and prohibitionism were the burning public questions in the 1840s and 1850s. The principal proponents for reform on these issues were New Englanders, or as Walter March called them, the "strict sober-sides from the land of Jonathan Edwards." The increasingly heterogeneous character of Detroit in the 1840s would bring new groups into new conflicts. The encounters did not engage Yankees against the old French *habitant* as directly as it did against the newcomer Irish. The Irish brand of Catholicism, which had been forged by centuries of Anglo-Irish strife and bitter historical memories of Protestant oppression, was an instrument honed for ethnic and religious conflict more than was the easygoing Catholicism of the French, who gave their religion a charming and relaxed air of churchianity. The entire social style of old French Detroit was in decline by 1840, but fortunately keen observers such as March and Hubbard recounted for posterity (see our documents) some of the richness of that earlier period. The last physical vestiges of the French presence in architecture and language were rapidly vanishing, as the *Detroit Gazetteer* selection records in 1840. By then the French were being displaced as the principal Roman Catholics in Detroit, and by 1850 the Irish had become the largest foreign-born group in the city. The newcomer Irish came to resemble their religious antagonists, Yankee Protestants of New England antecedents, demanding devoutness, intolerant of religious differences, and determined to use the political system in shaping the larger society to their own interests.

The city's public schools provided the focal point of Detroit's first serious religious and cultural clash. The "Bible war" occurred in 1844 and was resolved in 1845. The free public schools were barely two years old when ultra-Protestants triggered a serious fight over the incorporation of Bible readings into the course of study, an event that endangered the existence of the public system.

The free public schools had been established by the cooperation of Protestant and Catholic leaders. Dr. Zina Pitcher had conducted a survey that had demonstrated the need for tax-supported education. Pitcher, a Protestant New Yorker and then mayor, had joined with Father Martin Kundig, a most influential and highly regarded Catholic priest, to win public and city council support for the schools. John R. Williams, a prominent old Detroiter of French ancestry, had presided over the meeting that sought legislative authorization; he had also helped to draft the final enabling legislation that in 1842 laid the legal foundation for Detroit's tax-supported schools. Although the effort to establish free public schools had a strong Yankee Protestant flavor about it, Catholic spokesmen had played a vitally important role in gaining public approval from some reluctant segments of the community.[10]

Hardly had the fledgling system come into being than it was at the center of a storm of controversy. Beginning in the spring of 1844 and continuing into 1845, ultra-Protestant elements prosecuted a vigorous public campaign seeking to include Bible readings in the public school curriculum. The minority report (reprinted here) unfairly arraigns the school board majority for being negligent in its Christian duty to prescribe Bible readings in school and for being, by that reasoning, thereby "opposed" to the Bible. Although a majority of the board members were Protestants, they resisted for reasons cited in the majority report. It was impolitic and impractical, they argued, to impose a Protestant version of the Bible upon Catholics as well as others who stood in strong opposition. The board majority warned that dissatisfied religious groups might unite with tax enemies of the school

to destroy it. They recommended against the adoption of Bible
readings in December 1844. Yet ultra-Protestant church groups
persisted in applying pressure, and in February 1845 the board
of education capitulated with a permissive regulation that admitted to schools the reading of either the Protestant or Catholic
version of the Bible, but without interpretive commentary or
proselytizing (as one of our selections points out).

The second outbreak in the growing religious and cultural
cleavage surfaced in 1853 and became known as the "School
Question." It was a formative event in shaping the political and
social attitudes of Detroiters. During the 1840s, when newcomer
Irish and German immigrants were becoming more numerous, they
were also becoming more assertive. They found a sympathetic
ear in Detroit Bishop Peter Paul Lefevre, a Belgium-born, Saint
Louis–ordained priest with few cultural ties to the older *habitant*
community. Attentive to these new groups and their enlarged political influence, Bishop Lefevre initiated a larger conflict by demanding a pro rata share of public school revenue for Catholic
schools and also unleashed a campaign against expanded public
improvements in the city. The church opposed a program for paving in the central section of the city that abutted onto church
property, the replacing of an old and inadequate waterworks
with a new one, and the construction of a public almshouse. On
this occasion Detroit Catholics were less the targets than the aggressors. The bishop entered into the municipal fray by leading
a hostile demonstration into the city council chambers. A chastened common council slashed its city improvements program
from $400,000 to $250,000. These improvements would have cost
the church additionally in the way of taxes through special assessments, and deprived the church's charity hospital of city revenue
for care of public charges, once a public almshouse was built.[11]

Simultaneously Bishop Lefevre pressed for the diversion of
public school money for Catholic schools, and this was the issue
upon which the 1853 city election turned. The political atmosphere was supercharged with partisan and theological passions.
The bishop was reported as impolitically calling the public schools
"godless," "infidel," and atheistic, and his more fervent partisans assumed a no-compromise posture on fund diversion. Protestants responded with equal heat, resurrecting the imagery of the

religious wars of Europe. They perceived in the church the "cloven hoof," the "scarlet woman," and Satan in the guise of priestly robes. On a more rational level, some of them expressed a genuine apprehension about the preservation of the public schools, which they believed fund diversion endangered. For the most part political spokesmen on both sides indulged in intemperate, abusive, and vituperative rhetoric, reliving and discharging Old World hatreds upon one another. The two selections from the *Detroit Free Press* capture some of the sulfur and brimstone and religio-political turbulence of that campaign.[12]

Fortunately, and almost incredibly in view of the heat of the campaign, no traditional election-day rioting occurred. The regular Democrats who represented the Catholic party in this dispute were soundly defeated by the Independent ticket composed of splinter Democrats and Whigs, most of whom were Protestants but with a few disgruntled Catholics joining them. Providentially, the political system seemed to work as theorists believed it should, since it absorbed much of the religious and ethnic hostility and channeled it toward the ballot box, where conflict became rhetorical, ritualized, and symbolic. Detroit was spared from the street unrest, Bible riots, and school wars that some cities suffered.

The cultural and religious implications of this conflict had a far-reaching effect. Historians such as Ronald Formisano have pointed out that these religiocultural cleavages would contribute significantly toward shaping the social composition and ideological perceptions of the modern political party system. As conflicts of this type became ritualized through the ballot box, Protestants and Catholics would increasingly come to regard one another as negative referents in choosing their historic party preferences.

The increasing cultural and ethnic heterogeneity would end the old harmony whereby a broadly shared sense of community had made it possible to accommodate religious and ethnic differences. When Yankee Protestants sought to impose their cultural and social values upon newcomer Irish and Germans, they met not only stiff and vocal resistance but aggressive counterproposals that had been conspicuously absent from the older French *habitant* generation. Thus Detroit had experienced its first bout with urbanization and its disruptive cosmopolitan influences. The onset of ethnic and cultural conflict signaled the end of one era for

Detroit and the beginning of another. The two periods overlap, and the decade 1840–50 best approximates the division between them.

NOTES—PART ONE

1. Carl Bridenbaugh, *Cities in the Wilderness: The First Century of Urban Life in America, 1625–1742* (New York, 1955), pp. 3–6; Charles N. Glaab and A. Theodore Brown, *A History of Urban America* (New York, 1967), p. 3.

2. Charles R. Tuttle, *General History of the State of Michigan* (Detroit, 1874), pp. 112–14; Harold A. Innis, *The Fur Trade in Canada* (New Haven, 1962), pp. 53–55.

Alphonse de Tonty to ?, 1 September 1701, Cadillac Papers, *Michigan Pioneer and Historical Society Collections* 33: 131. For question of authorship of letter see Jean Delanglez, "The Genesis and Building of Detroit," *Mid-America* 30 (April 1948): 94, n. 44.

3. William B. Munro, *The Seigniorial System in Canada* (New York, 1907), pp. 12–13.

4. Land in Detroit was first granted *en seigneurie* but in 1716 changed to *en censive* (or *roture*). The latter carried the same feudal duties with the exception of a smaller alienation fine. Munro, *Seigniorial System in Canada,* p. 79; Sumner C. Powell, *Puritan Village: The Formation of a New England Town* (Garden City, 1965), pp. 171 ff.

5. "Clauses and Conditions Expressed in the Concessions Granted by M. de la Mothe Cadillac at Detroit," 4 November 1721, *Michigan Pioneer and Historical Society Collections* 33: 686–87; "Reply of Gatineau to the Petition of the Inhabitants of Detroit to the Intendant of New France, October 21, 1726," in *Collections of the State Historical Society of Wisconsin* 3: 171–75; Almon E. Parkins, *The Historical Geography of Detroit* (Lansing, 1918), pp. 55, 66.

6. Munro, *Documents Relating to Seigniorial Tenure,* 39, 70; "Reply of Gatineau to the Petition of the Inhabitants of Detroit to the Intendant of New France, October 21, 1726"; "A Selection of George Croghan's Letters and Journals Relating to Tours into the Western Country—November 16, 1750–November, 1765"; Jacob Lindley, "Expedition to Detroit, 1793," *Michigan Pioneer and Historical Society Collections* 17: 594.

7. "Assessment and Tax List, 1864 Special Income Tax for District I Michigan" (manuscript, National Archives, Washington, D.C.). For the 1844 real and personal property tax assessment for the Detroit elite, see Alexandra U. McCoy, "Political Affiliations of American Economic Elites,

Wayne County, Michigan, 1844, 1860, as a Test Case" (Ph.D. diss., Wayne State University, 1965), pp. 56–61. George N. Fuller, "Detroit Michigan's Capital One Hundred Years Ago," *Michigan History Magazine* 20 (Winter 1936): 9, 13. Idem., *Economic and Social Beginnings of Michigan* (Lansing, 1916), p. 131. For the influence of ethnocultural factors on banking, see William G. Shade, *Banks or No Banks: The Money Issue in Western Politics, 1832–1865* (Detroit, 1972), pp. 17–19, 33–38.

8. M. Carrie W. Hamlin, "Old French Traditions," *Michigan Pioneer and Historical Society Collections* 4: 70; Richard C. Ford, "The French-Canadians in Michigan," *Michigan History Magazine,* 27 (Spring 1943): 257.

9. Leigh G. Cooper, "Influences of the French Inhabitants of Detroit upon its Early Political Life," *Michigan History Magazine* 4 (January 1920): 299–304; *Detroit Gazette,* 8 August 1817, reprinted in Silas Farmer, *History of Detroit and Michigan* (Detroit, 1890), pp. 715–16; Ronald P. Formisano, "The Social Bases of American Voting Behavior, Wayne County, Michigan, 1837–1852, as a Test Case" (Ph.D. diss., Wayne State University, 1966), pp. 396, 408, 410, 414.

10. William D. Wilkins, "Traditions and Reminiscences of the Public Schools of Detroit," *Michigan Pioneer and Historical Society Collections* 1 (1877): 454–57; Arthur B. Moehlman, *Public Education in Detroit* (Bloomington, Ill., 1925), pp. 73–78, 86–88.

11. *Detroit Daily Advertiser,* 26 February 1843, 1, 4 March 1843; *Detroit Free Press,* 1, 2, 5, 6 March 1853.

12. *Detroit Free Press,* 8 March 1853; Ronald P. Formisano, *The Birth of Mass Political Parties: Michigan, 1827–1861* (Princeton, 1971), pp. 222–27, 165–94.

Cadillac's Plan for Detroit, 18 October 1700

Antoine de La Mothe Cadillac was born in France in 1658 and died there in 1730. He had served in New France as a commandant at a remote northern fur station and then persuaded the French government to found a larger post and colony at the site of Detroit. He envisioned more than a trade rendezvous for annual fur-buying. Cadillac proposed a full-fledged, self-supporting community with a wide range of skills and services for the fur domain. During his years in Detroit, Cadillac invested much of his own money and effort into constructing the nucleus for a town in a new world—in addition to bringing seeds, fruit trees, and domestic animals, he had constructed a gristmill, brewery, icehouse, warehouse, a fort, a lodging house, and a church. However, commandant Cadillac's strong will resulted in much bickering with subordinate officials, and quarrels with the Beaver Company over control of the fur monopoly and with the Jesuit missionaries over sale of brandy to the Indians. The result was that his tenure as Detroit commandant, which had begun in 1701, ended in 1710 with his removal and appointment as governor of Louisiana.

*The document that follows, a letter from Cadillac to the French minister of the colonies, is from the Cadillac Papers, edited by C. M. Burton (*Michigan Pioneer and Historical Society Collections *33 [1904]: 96–101).*

October 18, 1700
Minister of the Colonies
Count Pontchartrain

Sir:

It is my duty to give you an exact account of all that I have done regarding the establishment of Detroit since it was referred to you at the time when I was in France, and concerning which you were good enough to converse with me.

M. de Pontchartrain having referred it this year to MM de Calliere and de Champigny to press it on at once, provided there were no important objections, they both approved of it and retained me to carry out the establishment of this Strait which separates Lake Huron from Lake Erie.

It is greatly to be feared that the execution of this scheme has been delayed too long, from the news we have that the English have fortified themselves on a river which discharges itself into Lake Ontario, and that they will extend their posts toward Lake Erie.

If our Colony were not full of envy, disunion, cabal and intrigue, no opposition would have been offered to taking possession of a post [which is] so advantageous that, if it were separated from all those we [now] have, we should be compelled in a short time to abandon all; for it is that alone which will make the Colony and its commerce entirely safe, and cause the certain ruin of the English colonies. For that reason it is very important that it should not pass into other hands, which would be inevitable if we deferred taking it any longer.

The objections which have been raised also at the wrong time, in the belief that this post might cause us to be forever at war with the Iroquois, are now removed by the peace which has been concluded with them. That tribe was not in a position to keep up the war any longer, and will not be able to begin it again very soon; therefore there could not be a more suitable time for establishing Detroit, which will be fortified more quickly than the Iroquois can make up the loss of their numbers.

It is an incontestable fact, that the strength of the savages lies in the remoteness of the French, and that ours increases against them with our proximity. For it is certain that, with a little Indian corn, these people have no difficulty in traversing two hundred leagues to come and take some one's life by stealth; and when we want to get to their lands, we are obliged to provide ourselves with stores of all kinds and to make great preparations, which involves the King in extraordinary expenses, and always with very little effect since it is like beating drums to catch hares.

But, on the contrary, when we are the neighbors of that tribe and are within easy reach of them, they will be kept in awe and will find themselves forced to maintain peace since they will be unable to do otherwise unless they wish to ruin themselves irretrievably.

It would be in vain to establish this post if they would not comply with my memorandum; for if only a garrison pure and simple were kept up there, it would be liable to the revolutions which usually take place in frontier posts, and it would make no impression on the minds of the Iroquois and of our allies, and much less still those of the English.

In order to succeed thoroughly, it would be well (in my opinion) to adopt the following measures.

1.

To go and station ourselves there with a hundred men, one half of whom should be soldiers and the other Canadians. In order to

carry out this expedition with all necessary despatch, and to un-
deceive the Englishmen at once as to [their] having any claim there
and to take from them all hope of establishing any relations with
our allies, this strength is sufficient for the first year. For this
number is absolutely necessary to me for fortifying [the place] and
for taking the proper steps for the subsistence of those who wish to
settle there subsequently.

2.

The year after, the fort being secure from insult, it is well to allow
twenty or thirty families to settle there, and to bring their cattle
and other necessary things which they will willingly do at their own
cost and expense; and this may be continued as it is permitted in
all the other settlements of the Colony.

3.

It is no less necessary that the King should send two hundred picked
men who should, as far as may be, be of different trades and also
rather young.

4.

It is not advisable that I, any more than the other officers, soldiers
and inhabitants, should do any trade with the savages, in order to
take away from the people of the other established posts their cause
for complaint, as to which they are very active. But [it is advisable]
to unite this business to that of the general company which is
formed; in which [case] it will keep up a warehouse to supply all
the goods needed by the savages, our allies, and the Iroquois, while
letting them have them at a better price than in the past, which can
easily be done by conveying them by boats. But as it would be impossible for me to live without doing any trading and with only the
1000 livres pay which I have, which will barely suffice for making
the head men of the savages eat and drink at my table so as to
attach them to our interests by this good treatment, I hope you will
be so good to me as to inform M. de Pontchartrain of the indispensable necessity for increasing it [i. e. the pay], lest I should
become absolutely unable to continue my services in the style due
to His Majesty.

5.

We must establish at this post missionaries of different communities such as Jesuits and other Fathers, and ecclesiastics of the foreign missions; they are laborers in the vineyard, and should be received without distinction to labor at the vine of the Lord, with orders in particular to teach the young savages the French language, [that] being the only means to civilize and humanize them, and to instil into their hearts and their minds the law of religion and of the monarch. We take wild beasts at their birth, birds in their nests, to tame them and set them free. But in order to succeed better in that, it would be necessary for the King to favor these same missionaries with his bounty and his alms, in proportion as they instruct the children of the Savages at their houses, on the evidence which the Commandant and other officers give of it.

6.

The third or fourth year we shall be able to set Ursulines there, or other nuns, to whom His Majesty could grant the same favors.

7.

It would be important that there should be a hospital for sick or infirm Savages, for there is nothing more urgent for gaining their friendship than the care taken of them in their illnesses. The hospitallers of Montreal seem to me well fitted for that, because they know beforehand the temper and the preferences of the Savages [from] often having them with them.

8.

It would be absolutely necessary also to allow the soldiers and Canadians to marry the savage maidens when they have been instructed in religion and know the French language which they will learn all the more eagerly (provided we labor carefully to that end) because they always prefer a Frenchman for a husband to any savage whatever, though I know no other reason for it than the most ordinary one, namely that strangers are preferred, or, it were better to say, it is a secret of the Almighty Power.

9.

Marriages of this kind will strengthen the friendship of these tribes, as the alliances of the Romans perpetuated peace with the Sabines through the intervention of the women whom the former had taken from the others.

We shall find, in the execution of this scheme, not only the glory of His Majesty but also that of God magnificently extended; for by this means his worship and his religion will be established in the midst of the tribes, and the deplorable sacrifices which they offer to Baal entirely abolished.

I am unable to tell you fully enough how my enemies have bestirred themselves to take away from me the honor of carrying out my scheme; and this appears not to have ceased. But MM. de Caliere and de Champigny have not opposed it; on the contrary they have retained me for that so as to begin it next spring. When it was seen that they had resolved on this, everything possible was done to persuade them that my memorandum is impracticable, and I have seen twenty parties formed to upset it. I venture to assure you there is nothing to fear and that everything will be favorable to this undertaking; I [will] answer for it with my life. Monsieur de Pontchartrain will no sooner have given his decision than the whole country will applaud it, according to the policy of all men, who are very glad to find difficulties in all that does not originate with them.

As I am taking my son with me to Detroit, I beg the Minister to be so good as to grant him an ensigncy or an order for the first vacancy; that of my company has been given to the son of M. de Ramezay, with which I am satisfied. I hope you will have the kindness to say a word in my favor to M. de Pontchartrain regarding it. As I was one of the ten who were chosen by the Colony to settle its concerns, we have approved the agreement made by Pascaud with M. de Roddes, but have rejected the one made with M. Bourlay and his partners as being too burdensome and insupportable for the reasons which are noted on it, and to which you will no doubt give [your] attention as well as Monsieur Amelot who is very acute. The Colony sends two persons for the matters which concern it, and to manage the sale of the beaver skins; instructions have been given them, and there is reason to hope that they will conform to them, and that they will do their duty better than the first [men sent].

Permit me to assure you that I am, with deep respect

Monsieur
Your very humble and very obedient servant
Lamothe Cadillac

The Social Style and Spirit of Habitant Detroit, 1820s

Orlando B. Wilcox (1826–1907) was born and lived his early years in Detroit, until the 1840s, when he matriculated at West Point and was graduated in 1846. Although most of his adult life was occupied as a professional soldier, he returned after the Mexican border campaign to Detroit in 1854 to practice law until 1861. During those years, under the pen name Walter March, he completed a recollection of his childhood in early Detroit, which was published in an autobiographically derived novel. Although the novel's plot is fictional, the descriptions of early Detroit are not. The sights and sensations of a racially mixed community and the delightful insouciance and social style of the French habitant are accurately depicted and represented with compassion. Wilcox's descriptions are substantially supported by the available records, which exist in abundance, but which are fragmentary and nowhere capture the spirit of the old habitant society at such a sustained length or as sympathetically as this piece does. The selection covers Detroit of the 1820s up to about 1835, when Yankee invasion set the stage for additional changes in Detroit. The selection is derived from Shoepac Recollections: A Way Side Glimpse of American Life *(New York, 1856).*

Our City

Ours was a little antiquated city. Its inhabitants were mostly French. At the time I came upon the stage of events, the transition to a modern American town had scarcely commenced. The body of the population was still of the *ancien régime.* The few Americans were officers, or ex-officers, of either the general or territorial government, and their families, relations, dependents, and friends, whom they had persuaded to venture beyond the "jumping-off place," as Buffalo was then termed. The spirit of emigration had not been fully aroused; and the spirit of speculation, if felt at all, was confined to the fur-traders, a class made up of all nations.

I cannot compare the society more nearly than to that of some principal East India Company station in a city of Hindostan. There were the governor of the territory and his family, the judicial, executive, and military functionaries, with their families and dependents; like subahdar, nabobs, begums, and the lesser lights—traders and natives, French, Indian, and half-breed. But one could not well imagine a pleasanter state of feeling than mutually existed, with sufficient distinction between the different castes of classes to prevent wrangling, and yet sufficient community of interest, prejudice, and pleasure to make everybody sociable. The French gave a tone of gaiety—the military, both elevation and hospitality. There were balls, where everybody danced with everybody's wife and daughter. There were theatricals, where the most dignified gentlemen took parts. It may be a mere whim, but I think I never have elsewhere met such easy polish and affability among gentlemen. There was no touchiness about position in the social scale, and consequently neither stiffness nor affectation; and to this day, the same easy grace of manner is notable among the sons and daughters of the good old city. . . .

Yet there he would behold the Frenchman, riding in his two-wheeled cart to market with white fish and onions, and screaming rascally *patois*. Or he might observe a wedding procession, of the same mercurial race, driving through the principal—or rather only —avenue, at full speed to church, two and two, in little antique *caliches;* the bride, of course, dressed in white, but wearing no bonnet, though rejoicing in a veil that sweeps the ground, and her bridesmaids driving after as bonnetless as herself—a happy state of things to which the dear ladies of the present day are fast returning.

As he sauntered along up the street, he would see old-fashioned buildings, stores and dwellings forming a promiscuous row, with high gables and dormer-windows, roofs peaked like Vandyke hats, with their edges notched and painted red, and doors panelled into four parts, and opening by subdivisions, like modern window-shutters. Motley groups, consisting of French, Americans, and Indians, sit with their sociable pipes enjoying confabulations made up of words, nods, shrugs, and the impenetrable "ugh! ugh!" of the taciturn red man. Peeping into the halls and rooms as he passed, he might here and there discern a carpet, but generally the floors were covered with Indian mats. The shops would be filled with bales of furs, gaudy-colored calicoes—known as Indian calicoes—mococks of maple sugar, broidered with painted porcupine quills, deerskins, moccasins, and Indian trinkets; few such, however, as are now palmed off upon the curious and credulous stranger at Niagara. . . .

Pleasantries

Ah! that was a happy time for everybody. Our little community was not yet divided on the question of Bibles in schools, or wine on the side-boards. Slavery was little talked of, and as for disunion—the mere word was considered, by the veriest *Kenuck,* as a profanation of human language.

But as settlers from New England began to thicken among us—*Bostonians* they were indiscriminately denominated—it gradually came to light that our lively little community were scarce a grain better than the wicked, nay than the very heathen; witness the fiddling and dancing on Sunday evenings (and pleasant Sunday evenings they were deemed by us, in our dreadful ignorance), wherever there was any little neighborhood of French people—on the great wide porch, or beneath trees on the grass; or, if in the house, with the doors and windows thrown wide open. And there were the prettiest and most mischievous-eyed French girls, dancing away for dear life with the good-looking, frank-mannered *voyageurs,* or *courreurs de bois,* in their red, yellow, or green sashes, long black hair, and blue calico shirts. Such abominations attracted the "growing attention" of the strict sober-sides from the land of Jonathan Edwards, as he passed these dens of Apollyon, on his way to the place where prayer was wont to be made. Then was there not racing to church the year round, and racing home again? And were there not regular trotting matches on the afternoons of the great days of the church, which brought the people in from the country, up and down the river? Especially, was there ever anything like it in the winter season, when the wicked river would even wink at these atrocities by freezing over, so that nothing was seen on Sunday afternoons but carioles turned up in front, in a curl like a skate, gliding, or rather flying, over the ice, two and two? The little Canadian ponies held their tails up in the air like banners, and their noses protruding into the clouds, or snorting

between their legs—they trotting like mad, while the *garcons*
whooped like Indians, shouting, *whey! avance! arriez!* ever and
anon stealing a flashing kiss from the bright demoiselles at their
sides.

Then on Easter morning, was not the church-yard of St. Ann's
fairly riotous with boys cracking painted eggs? Nay, in the same
precincts, were not idolatries frequently committed? Was not the
Host carried in procession by chanting Jesuits and nuns, to a high
mound called Mount Calvary, where there was a huge cross, and
beneath which lay the tomb of our Saviour? Doubt not that these
abominations smelt in the nostrils of the sons of the Puritans.

But, in the time of my boyhood, the feud had not taken any
religious turn among the boys, who, I must confess, were very far
behind the boys of the present day, and knew little of religious
controversies, and talked not dogmatically of these, nor of the various ologies in which the present juvenile generation are so good
and wise. . . .

The Vicar of St. Ann's was the pious and polished old mission-
ary, Father Robert. Where this son of the Scarlet Lady hid his
cloven foot, I never knew; for of all men he was beloved in our
community—even among the *unco good* Protestants. He was celebrated in the Catholic annals of the Northwest for his learning,
self-devotion, and enthusiasm. He was the first to do honor to
the neglected remains of Father Marquette, the explorer of the
Mississippi. He established the first newspaper; though, whether
this was an act of grace and Christian charity, some of the Berke-
leys of the day may be disposed to doubt. He was likewise entrusted with our interests at the seat of the Federal Government,
as our territorial deputy to Congress, and was acknowledged by
everybody at home as the best-hearted and most agreeable of
men. He did good Protestants the honor to respect their heretical
prejudices, and was a frequent visitor at their houses.

"Ah! Mrs. March," he would sometimes say to my mother with
great politeness, "if all Protestants were as good Catholics as you,
there would be no trouble in the world."

Good old man! he died before the evil days drew nigh, or ere
the men came who would have known him not.

There was yet wanting in our cup another element of happy dis-

cord considered now indispensable in every well-organized city—
the foreigner question. We scarcely knew what foreigners were,
except as brethren in pursuit of fortune and happiness. The
Frenchman who left his cherries to the birds, his sheep to the dogs,
and his fish-seine to *le diable,* for the purpose of shouldering his
musket at the call of General Hull, would have been astonished
to have been branded as a foreigner. And as for the English or
Scotch fur trader, whose packs had been pillaged by the British
at Mackinaw, whose money had flowed freely as his blood would
have flowed in defence of the town, and who cursed "Old Hull"
as a traitor, or pitied him as a coward—not one ever thought of
him as a foreigner. In fact we all dwelt together harmoniously, to
the best of my recollection, and knew no more distinction of blood
or nationality than they are innocently supposed to know in
heaven. . . .

The Institutions and Culture of Old French Detroit, 1830s and 1840s

> I listen in vain for the melodies which were once the
> prelude to many joyous hours of early manhood. But,
> instead, my ear is larumed by the shriek of the steam-
> whistle and the laborious snort of the propeller. All an-
> nounce that on these shores and waters the age of the
> practical, hard-working, money-getting Yankee is upon
> us, and that the careless, laughter-loving Frenchman's
> day is over.
>
> —Bela Hubbard

*Bela Hubbard (1814–96) came to Detroit in 1835 and settled on
what was then the outskirts of the city at a site called Springwells.
He was at various times an assistant geologist for the state and*

editor of an agricultural publication, but became best known for his civic and cultural contributions in Detroit. He was a memorialist of standing both in the state and the city. Hubbard examined the principal social and economic institutions of the French and, in some cases, saw them in an unfavorable light when compared to their Yankee successors. Yet he was not completely out of sympathy with the ancien régime, *as can be seen. He had a keen sense that an epoch in the city's history had passed and tried to preserve it by making the single most extensive canvass of the institutional structure of the old French society of Detroit. Our selection was drawn from the* Michigan Pioneer and Historical Society Collections *(1 [1877]: 350–67) and covers the 1830s and 1840s, the twilight years of the French society in Detroit.*

While the colonists on the Detroit retained many of the characteristics of their countrymen in the old world, modifications necessarily took place in the adaptation to so different an abode. Taking possession of a vast wilderness, families neither gathered into hamlets, as is the custom of the peasantry of France, nor did they seek an independent existence, like the backwoodsmen of New England stock; but their dwellings, each on its own farm, were in such close proximity as almost to constitute a continuous village for many miles of river shore. Originally motives of protection against the savages, and afterwards those of social intercourse, led to this near neighborhood.

Land Titles and Farms
The original titles to these lands were variously derived. Of those below the city as far as the River Rouge (three miles), three are from grants of the Marquis de Quesne, Governor-General of Louisiana and Canada, 1740; ten from Marquis de la Jousire, vested with like powers, 1750. Ten others are from Indian deeds of gift, subsequent to the occupancy by the English—1770 to 1780 —confirmed by the British commandant. Two of the French grants actually received confirmation of the king, although this was required by the *Contume de Paris,* which was the law of the country. Permits to occupy were sometimes granted by the French commandants. These grants and rights of occupancy were confirmed by the United States Government, early in the present century,

through a commission, sitting at Detroit, and upon these patents were issued. The tracts thus confirmed vary in width from two to five arpents and were about eighty arpents in length.[1]

I have heard old inhabitants say they could shout to each other from their door steps. And this mode of telegraphic message, passing rapidly from house to house, served the purpose of modern methods, in case of apprehended danger, and even for social converse.

An American backwoodsman thinks settlements crowd too close upon him—that he has not elbow room enough if a neighbor establishes himself within a mile of the spot which he has selected for his hearthstone. A Frenchman so situated would die of *ennui*. He must have facilities for regular and frequent intercourse with his neighbors; and, as roads are execrable in a new country, he best accomplishes his object by fixing his habitations upon the streams—highways that nature has created. The canoe is his carry-all; in it he and his family move easily, at all times, to and from even distant settlements. What glorious opportunities for the gratification of these desires was presented by those grand highways of the new world!

From the water also came a large part of his food; for fishing and trapping were more favorite employments than agriculture. The object of the first settlers being the fur trade and Indian traffic, these lakes and rivers supplied a natural channel through which those operations were conducted.

It was along the chain of the mighty lakes and rivers of our continent that France sought to maintain her foothold in America by the erection of forts, at points widely separated, but selected with wonderful foresight. In the vicinity of, and under the protection of these, were the early settlements made. As this protection became less needed, as the Indian trade declined, or was further removed, the peasant farmers made more distant settlements. They retained, however, the practice of inhabiting only the banks of streams, accessible from the great lakes. I know of no original French settlement which is not so situated.

As a hunter the French settler had none of the renown of the

1. The arpent is a measure of length, as well as area, the side of which is 192 feet 3 inches.

American backwoodsman, but to his skill in trapping the great fur companies of Canada owed a large part of the smaller peltries that were so considerable a source of their revenues.

Like the beaver and muskrat, the Canadian not unfrequently lived almost in the water of his favorite streams and marshes, and built his cabin in a spot which could be approached only by canoe. The dwellers in habitations so little superior in architecture and site to the houses which these ingenious little architects contrive for their accommodation, in their native marshes, and denoting so little higher degree of mental advancement, deserved the *soubriquet* bestowed upon them by the contemptuous Yankee, of "Muskrat Frenchmen."

French Agriculture

We have seen that the kind of enterprise which characterized the French emigrant was very different from that which marked the Anglo-Saxon settlers, which has converted the wilderness into fertile fields, and, almost in a single life-time, constituted this nation one of the formidable powers of the earth.

After more than a century of settlement, the farms along the Straits exhibited only a narrow strip of cultivation. This rarely extended half a mile from the water's edge. From their doors the family had a view of the untrimmed forest, where the deer roamed, and wild beasts prowled, frequently to the very barn-yards.

Even this limited extent of field received very imperfect culture. It was almost never manured, and, so little was high culture understood or regarded, that instances are well known where farmers, whose manure heaps had accumulated to an inconvenient degree about their barns, adopted the most ready means of relief by carting the incumbrance on to the ice in winter. The offensive material was thus washed away, without further trouble, when the ice broke up in the spring. I declare, on undoubted authority, that in some cases even the barns were removed, to avoid the piles that had accumulated.

This limited agricultural improvement did not originate from the extreme subdivision of the land, for each proprietor possessed acres enough; though his farm, in its proportion of length to breadth, bore a resemblance to his pipe stem.

As this great national interest flourished so little under the kind of encouragement bestowed by the French Government, it may be curious to compare the terms by which grants of land were bestowed by the commandants, with the tenure by which, under the fostering care of the present government, each householder may secure a homestead. One runs in this wise: "The granter was bound to pay a rent of fifteen livres a year in peltries to the Crown forever; to assist in planting a May-pole, on each May-day, before the door of the Mansion House. He was forbidden to buy or sell articles of merchandise carried to or from Montreal, through servants, clerks or foreigners; to work at the business of a blacksmith; to sell brandy to the Indians, or to mortgage the land, without consent of the government. The Crown reserved all minerals and timber for military purposes. The grantor reserved the right of hunting rabbits, partridges, and pheasants. All the grain raised was to be ground at the manor wind-mill, where toll was to be given, according to the custom of Paris. On every sale of land a tax was levied, and the government reserved the right to take precedence of any buyer, at the price offered." In so many restrictions we see one reason why agriculture, as an independent pursuit, should not flourish.

Farm Implements

Having spoken so disparagingly of French agriculture, it is but just to observe that the Canadians were speedy to adopt the superior implements and modes of cultivation used by the Anglo-Saxon settlers; and the present generation see little difference between the tools and the methods belonging to the one or the other. But half a century ago the old methods were still practiced.

The *cart* was the universal vehicle for farm and family use, wagons being unknown. The *plow* was of wood, except the share. Its long beam and handles extended ten or twelve feet, and it had a wooden mould-board. In front were two wheels, also of wood, of different sizes; a small one to run on the unplowed side, and a larger one in the furrow. There were neither chains nor whiffle-tree; oxen were fastened by a pole, which had a hinged attachment to the beam. And very good though shallow plowing was performed by this rude but ingenious implement.

Both oxen and horses were employed in the various operations. The harness was very simple, and constructed of withes or twisted raw-hide. No yoke was used, but a rope of the kind mentioned was passed around the oxens' horns, and they pushed with their heads. It was maintained, by those who employed this seemingly singular method, that it was the most natural and effective, and gave greater freedom of action to the cattle. Possibly scientific agriculturists of the present day may get a useful hint from the simple ideas of the olden times.

The *hoe* was a very heavy iron implement, having a long shank. It was the same that was used by the Indians, after the introduction of iron among them. The latter never plowed, and were ignorant of the method of laying out the field in parallel rows; hills of corn being planted without regard to regularity, though at tolerably uniform distances. And though the Frenchmen used the plow effectively, their ordinary mode of planting corn was precisely that of the Indians.

French Vehicles

The winter *carry-all* was a strong but narrow box, placed upon runners, which spread widely and were iron shod. Sometimes these were adorned with fancy heads. The thills, which were of hickory or ash, were so fixed as to spring outwardly, and when the horse was harnessed in, the ends were brought together and tied. The strain, consequently, prevented any rubbing against the horse's sides, and allowed a large liberty of action, which was of great service to their keen trotters and pacers. It was constructed for two persons only, although a seat for a third was sometimes placed in front. Horses were sometimes driven *tandem*.

The *traineau* was of rougher construction, made for work, and the runners did not spread. . . .

French Homesteads

From the consideration which we have bestowed upon the agriculture of the early French settlers on the Detroit, we turn naturally to their homesteads. We often form some judgment of a people from the houses they live in.

The better class of dwellings of the French habitans were of quite a substantial character, considered as mere timber structures. They were built of logs, squared and covered with clapboards, and the roofs shingled with cedar. They were of one or two stories, according to the need or ability of the owner, but were never ambitious. Generally they were one *full* story, the upper or half story being chiefly within the roof, which was high and lighted by small dormer windows, projecting on the front and rear sides. The entrance was in the center, and a hall ran from front to rear. A low and perfectly plain veranda was another usual feature.

One of the oldest and most noted structures of this class was the "Cass house," which had been used by several of the Territorial Governors of Michigan, and exhibited many marks of the tomahawk and bullet, received during the Indian wars. It stood on the Cass farm, and was built of cedar logs, weather-boarded; about fifty feet front and one story in height, with step roof. A heavy stone chimney rose out of the center. The position, when I first saw it, was very beautiful. It was upon the immediate bank of the river, here quite abrupt and high, and shadowed with trees. No wharf or building obstructed the view, which commanded many miles of the river channel and shores, and in the rear were smiling gardens and green slopes, between which flowed the little river "Savoyard," since diverted into a covered sewer. This old mansion is still a comfortable dwelling, or dwellings, on Larned street. It stands but little removed from its old site, but in front and in rear are stony streets, thickly lined with houses. It is remote from the present border of the river, and its time-honored character is lost in new boards and white paint. Its age is probably not less than 150 years.

Another old domicil of the times of French regime—the Lafferty house—stood half a mile below, and was torn down in 1861, to give place to structures better suited to the wants of modern times. It was erected in 1747, and was, at the time of its destruction, in excellent preservation; the timbers heavy and solid, and the stone chimney exhibiting the large, open fireplace which marked an age of hospitality and good cheer.

The Knaggs house, another well known mansion, was for several years my own residence. It consists of two parts; one a low structure of a single story, with an attic, and containing two rooms and a pantry. It is of unknown age, and, like the Cass house, bears marks of Indian outrages. The other portion is of comparatively modern date, and consists of three considerable rooms, separated by a central hall. It has a second half story, with dormer windows, and also windows in the gables, and is throughout well finished. The front door is umbraged by a square portico, which had seats, and commanded a delightful look-out upon the river, in its immediate front. Both parts of the mansion are built of squared pine timbers, clapboarded. The newer portion had, when I took possession, a coat of paint, white in front, red in the rear. If there had ever been paint on the older portion it had long disappeared. The panes of glass throughout all the windows were a curiosity, being of a size entirely disused and no longer sold by dealers,—six and a half by seven and a half inches.

I will allude to another and one of the few French mansions in the city,—the old "Campau house." It is built upon the foundations of the original dwelling burned down by the fire which consumed the entire city in 1805.

Though an interesting relic and a good specimen of its class, it belongs to the present century. It will give a good idea of the contrast between the old town and the new to state that the avenue of 120 feet wide upon which this house fronts, corresponds here with the old St. Ann street, on which it formerly stood, but which, though the longest street of old Detroit, had a width of only thirty feet.

Few such memorials of the "good old days" now remain in this vicinity; but on the Canada side of the channel comparatively little change has taken place in the appearance and condition of many old French homesteads. The village of Sandwich wears much of the old-time character, and a dreamy quiet pervades the place, worthy of Sleepy Hollow, and singularly in contrast with the bustling, wide-awake activity which distinguishes most American villages.

Most French dwellings had yards, fenced by pickets of red cedar. These were often ten or twelve feet in height, and were intended, and often served, as a stockade for protection during the troubles of the war times, as well as against wolves.

Some of these defenses were standing along the river, between my house and the town, as late as 1837, and consisted of very closely set, large and mostly round posts, which were generally still sound. They were so deeply sunk that the ax was used, rather than the spade, when their removal became expedient. Few, if any, of these posts can now be seen in this vicinity, but the stumps of many still remain as landmarks of a past age, below the soil, where the ax has left them.

Another feature of the old settlements has disappeared,—the *wind-mills,* which once marked every few miles of river shore, and were an animating part of its picturesque scenery.

These institutions of primitive times were in full operation down to the stirring period of Yankee improvements, 1836–7. Until then there were no flouring mills of any other description within many miles, though we have the authority of Judge Campbell for stating that a water-mill was built as early as 1734 on May's creek, below the city, and one on Mill or Conner's creek, above, and that, as late as 1830, one was standing in ruins upon Bloody Run, where it is crossed by Jefferson avenue.

The wind-mills served sufficiently well all the needs of the French era; but with the advent of larger wants more capable structures were demanded. The neglected wind-mills fell to decay, and at the present time a few only survive in ruins.

From these brief notices of the dwellings of the French land-owners, it will, doubtless, and with truth, be concluded that the occupants lived in reasonable style and comfort, and that the personal appearance of our French progenitors corresponded to the simple and comfortable character of their homesteads.

Costumes

The gentlemen's dress of the olden time, in winter, consisted of colored shirt, with vest and pantaloons, or leggings. A belt or sash held up the pants, and over all was worn a *capote,* or heavy blanket coat, with a sack or loose cap attached; that was thrown back or over the head, as required. The latter extremity was bound with a colored handkerchief, while the lower were protected by shoe-pacs and sometimes moccasins.

On dress occasions the sash was richly ornamented with beads, in the Indian fashion, and sometimes was of wampum. It was spread widely over the body, outside the coat, and tied behind, the ends hanging down two feet or more. In warm weather pantaloons were worn without vest, and were sustained by a belt, generally of leather. The feet were bare, and hats of straw completed the covering.

The voyageurs, or boatmen, often wore shirts over the trowsers, made of leather, with ruffles in the bosom made of the same material. They had bright colored cloth caps, which hung over on one side and terminated with a tassel.

The dress of the women consisted of short gowns or *habits,* falling no lower than the knee, and showing the petticoats, which reached to the feet; and they had ample straw hats. For cold weather they had fur hats or bonnets. They received the fashions from Montreal, but the changes were so slight that probably less variation had occurred in a century than takes place in the costume of our modern belles in a single year. In fact, the costume I have described continued always unchanged, from the earliest period down to the time of my own personal observation. The straw hat maintains its repute even yet as a permanent and wholesome style abroad, its merits having given it a wide adoption; and it would be well if, in other particulars, the convenient fashions of our Canadian dames could be preserved.

Society
The French people continued to preserve, down to a very recent date, a good degree of their ancient character. There was much of the "beau monde" at the rival but neighborly cities of Detroit and Monroe, and a constant intercourse was kept up, until the preponderance of the former city and the overwhelming influx of foreigners.

Amusements were of the social rather than literary kind, and the social virtues never shone more brightly among any people. Nor were these confined to their own kin, but were extended to the newly come, of whatever nationality. The old habitans of the better class still retain a vivid recollection of those happy days, and will tell that no people ever enjoyed life so keenly.

During the winter—which comprised nearly half the year—the settlements on the Detroit and River Raisin were almost shut out from the eastern world. Vessels and river craft were all laid up; railroads were not in being; and travel to the nearest Eastern cities was a long and painful journey. I have myself known Detroit to be without a New York mail for more than two weeks at a time, and have found it a week's journey, traveling by ordinary stage, day and night, through Canada to Buffalo. This was the season for French gayety and resource to display themselves. No aid from foreign sources was needed to make the winter pass pleasantly. And who could surpass the French for parties, balls, and merry-makings!

At these were gathered, especially, the young of both sexes, who kept up, until a late hour in the morning, that fascinating amusement, of whose saltatory mazes a Frenchman never tires; and here were exchanged glances from those lustrous black eyes, so suited to brunette complexions, and which lighted up even the most ordinary face, like native diamonds sparkling through their rusty covering. And, indeed, the demoiselles were not to be despised for graces of face and figure; for though the men mostly had long thin visages, scarcely in keeping with their fun-loving propensities, the girls were both plump and handsome.

During the period of depression which followed the speculations of 1836, when a general stagnation and gloom overspread the whole land, there was no lack of French gayety.

In the winter of 1841, when times were at their worst, this was manifested, even to an unusual degree, in numerous balls and other social gatherings. With a characteristic tinge of superstition, the French considered this unusual gayety ominous of approaching war, or other calamity, and that they were impelled to it by some secret and uncontrollable impulse. Perhaps philosophy may find a more reasonable solution. I relate the fact only.

Amusements

Sundays, as in all Roman Catholic countries, were holidays, and were improved as such to much greater extent, among the Canadians of half or even quarter of a century ago, than now among their descendants. Possibly they were spent quite as innocently, though more noise and hilarity prevailed. The parents and daughters of the family traveled to church in sober jog-trot style enough, in carts drawn by a single pony. But the young men went mounted on their nags, and returned in the grand style, racing, with whoop and hurrah!

In the winter these races were exchanged for trotting matches on the ice, in their light home-made carry-alls. . . .

Seldom have I witnessed a more animating spectacle than that of a large canoe belonging to the Hudson Bay Company, manned by a dozen voyageurs—the company's agents seated in the center

—propelled with magic velocity, as if instinct with life, every paddle keeping time to the chorus that rang far and wide over the waters.

But times have changed, and with them have passed from our midst the voyageur and his song. French gayety is rapidly ebbing into more sober channels. Even the priests have set their faces against balls and merry-makings!

As I call up these reminiscences, with the same noble river in my view, I listen in vain for the melodies which were once the prelude to many joyous hours of early manhood. But instead, my ear is larumed by the shriek of the steam-whistle and the laborious snort of the propeller.

All announce that on these shores and waters the age of the practical, hard-working, money-getting Yankee is upon us, and that the careless, laughter-loving Frenchman's day is over.

Detroit in 1838: An Urban Inventory

Detroit was the capital of Michigan from 1838 to 1847, when the state house was moved to interior Lansing. When Michigan entered the union in 1837, John T. Blois (1809–86), a Latin teacher and private-school proprietor, recognized the need for a solid, factual gazetteer to disabuse future investors and settlers of the false notion that the southern peninsula and Detroit were located in a miasma of mosquitoes and uninhabitable swamps.

This is the earliest comprehensive picture of the physical aspects of Detroit. Much can be perceived from this selection, but what is especially clear is the fact that important economic changes tended to approximate demographic and social changes under way in Detroit. The decline of the French habitant *seemed to occur almost simultaneously with that of the fur trade. Although Detroit was still primarily a raw-material producer with a "passive economy," by 1838 furs had been replaced by salted fish as the leading export. Like other regional gateways Detroit also profited considerably from the transient business of provisioning and lodging immigrants. Yet the future had been presaged, for Detroit had already made a modest start in wholesaling, which would become an economic mainstay as Detroit emerged into its next period as a commercial city.*

This selection is drawn from the Gazetteer of the State of Michigan *(1840, pp. 271–80).*

Detroit city, port of entry, seat of justice for Wayne county, and capital of the State of Michigan, has a healthy and beautiful location on the west bank of a strait of the same name, upon a site elevated 30 feet above its surface, of which, and the surrounding country, it commands extensive views. It is seven miles below the outlet of Lake St. Clair, and 18 above the western extremity of Lake Erie. . . .

For the distance of a mile upon the river, and for three-fourths of a mile extending back, it is more or less densely settled. The plan of the city is rather uncouth and laboured, with much mathematical ingenuity, better suited, it is acknowledged, to flatter the fancy than to promote practical utility. Upon the river, and for 1,200 feet back, it is rectangular—in the rear of this, triangular. The streets are spacious. Among the more noted are the eight avenues: viz: Madison Avenue, Michigan Grand Avenue, and Washington Grand Avenue, each 200 feet wide: Woodward Avenue, Monroe Avenue, Miami Avenue, Macomb Avenue, and Jefferson Avenue, each 120 feet wide; all except Michigan, Monroe, and Jefferson, terminating at one point called the Grand Circus. The other streets are 60 feet wide, and generally cross at right angles. Atwater street, upon the river, Woodbridge street, running parallel with it upon the declivity, are mostly occupied by stores and dealers in the heavier articles of merchandise. Woodward avenue, leading from the river at right angles, to Jefferson avenue, through Campus Martius and the central part of the city, is becoming of increased importance, and ranks among the first of the business streets. The principal street running with the course of the river upon the summit of the declivity, and through the central and most densely populated part of the city, is Jefferson avenue. Upon this are most of the public and private offices located, as well as the fancy and dry goods stores, and the dealers in the lighter articles of merchandise. This is a beautiful and pleasant street, and will compare with the most noted streets of any of our western cities. There are several convenient public squares, the most noted of which is the *Campus Martius*. . . .

Of the ancient style of the French buildings, scarcely a vestige remains. The city is mostly built of wood, and in a manner to accommodate its emigrant population, which it is supposed composes one half or two thirds of the city. Stores and dwellings of this class are often constructed upon leased grounds, and so constructed as to be easily removed; and it is a common occurrence to see one or more buildings removing from one part of the city to another, as the convenience of their owners requires. Although these temporary structures form no inconsiderable portion of the city, there are many permanent dwellings, not disproportionate to the number of *resident* citizens, built in a respectable style; and a few elegant private mansions. There are several extensive blocks of stores, constructed of brick, in a style and permanence highly creditable to the appearance of the city. Considering the enterprising and fluctuating nature of the great mass of the population, the city has altogether a cheerful and comely appearance, and, aside from the trifling inconveniences mentioned, inviting to the emigrant; and it has not a few outward indications of high cultivated taste and refinement.

The most interesting of the public buildings are, the capitol, the city hall, St. Paul's church, the presbyterian church, the baptist church, the cathedral of St. Anne, and the bank of Michigan. . . .

Detroit contains eight churches—one, each, for presbyterians, episcopalians, methodists, baptists, German Lutherans, and one for the colored population, the latter of which is ministered to by clergymen of different denominations. The Roman catholics have two churches—one for the French, and one to accommodate the English, Irish, and German population. There are four banks, with an aggregate capital of $2,250,000; 3 markets; a theatre, museum, circus, a public garden, State penitentiary and county jail; government magazine; mechanics' hall; four printing offices, three of which issue 9 newspapers, viz. 3 dailies, a tri-weekly, and 4 weeklies, one of which is a religious paper,—and a monthly periodical devoted to the cause of education. Of the larger mercantile establishments, may be numbered 27 dry goods stores, 25 grocery, and grocery and provision stores, 14 hardware stores, 7 clothing stores, 8 silversmiths and jewelry stores, 8 druggist stores, 10 extensive forwarding and commission stores, 3 bookstores, and the repository of the American Sunday School Union. There are 27 lawyers and 22 physicians. Among the various public offices, are, a distributing post office for the State; office of the collector of customs; office of the department of Indian affairs; the public land office; and the office of the board of internal improvements.

The markets are usually well supplied. For a few years past, Ohio, Indiana, and Upper Canada have furnished the greater portion of the cattle slaughtered here. The fish market is not only the most abundantly supplied, but one of the best in the Western States.

There are several extensive manufactories. There is a large steam saw mill, sash factory, edge tool manufactory, 3 iron foundries, a brass foundry, and 2 breweries.

The *Detroit Iron Foundery* has attached thereto, a foundery, finishing, pattern, and boiler shops, calculated to manufacture extensively all kinds of castings, mill irons, mill gearing, steam engines, &c., and it employs from 25 to 30 workmen. The *Michigan Iron Foundery* is nearly as extensive, and employs from 18 to 25 workmen. The City Brewery, owned by Thomas J. Owen, Esq., built in 1837, at an expense of $20,000, is the largest west of Albany. The main building is of brick, 40 feet by 140, and three stories high. It is capable of brewing 25,000 barrels annually, which would require for consumption from 80,000 to 100,000 bushels of barley. The *Detroit Brewery* is also an extensive establishment that does a large business.

There are several charitable institutions, which reflect much credit upon the city, and upon their benevolent founders. There are two orphan asylums, one under the patronage of the catholics, and the other of the protestants. The latter is a handsome two story brick edifice, situated a mile and a half above the city, erected through the influence and benevolence of the ladies of Detroit.

The ladies' free school society (protestant), supports three schools, by receiving indigent children of every denomination, furnishing books, and educating them gratuitously. Average number, 200. Among the other charitable institutions, are the St. Clare English and German free school (catholic), and the French female charity school. They average about 40 pupils. The hospital and poor house are supported by the county. . . .

The census taken to first of March, 1834, showed that, of a population of 4,968, 777 were under 15 years, and 251 between 15 and 20, making 1,028, or about one-fifth of the population of the city. There were then 12 schools, and 448 children in attendance.

During the present season there have been established seven school districts within the city. Agreeably to the census taken first January, 1838, the total number of children under 15 years was 3,156; of 5 and under 15, 1,842; of 15 and under 21, 1,199; total under 21, 4,355, or near one-half the population of the city.

Detroit is in need of a well selected public library. There are many private libraries which are respectable. There is a circulating library of 1,000 volumes. The Detroit Young men's society have a library of 1,200 volumes. The Michigan State library, at the capitol, contains 1,900 volumes. The legislature have appropriated $1,000 per annum for five years to its enlargement.

Detroit, often denominated "the city of the Straits," is the great commercial mart and emporium for the State. It is peculiarly well situated for commerce, and has ever been the centre of trade, especially of the fur trade, for a large section of this north-western region. The fur trade, however, having decreased with the increase of population, is now comparatively inconsiderable. The American fur company have an agency here, but the value of the trade, being one of the secrets of the company, is entirely unknown to the public. The value and amount of the various kinds of merchandize sold are uncertain. It is sufficient to say, the several stores before mentioned are mostly those doing an extensive business in each respective line, and are but a part, when the smaller establishments are enumerated. The city trade is quite disproportionate to that from the country. Many of the interior merchants make their entire purchases here, while others come to the city to replenish their stock. It is estimated by different merchants that from one-half to three-fifths of the merchandise sold goes to the interior. The exports to other States are comparatively inconsiderable. The principal article is fish. An illicit trade is, and has been for many years, carried on to a great extent upon the frontier, in detriment, not only to the city trade, but to the revenue of government.

Western emigration has been a great resource of support to the city for several years past. Of this, Detroit has been the principal avenue, or rather the portal to the interior. It is the season of open navigation, usually eight months of the year, that activity and business prevail.

Detroit is deeply engaged in the lake trade, and it has been the seat of considerable ship building. The first steamboat, called the *"Walk-in-the-water,"* arrived at this city the 11th of August, 1818. The amount of shipping belonging to this port was 849 tons; the value of exports was $69,330, and of imports $15,611. In 1825, the number of arrivals was 270, and an equal number of clearances. In 1829, the export trade of the city and the ports north and south of it, was estimated at nearly $400,000, of which $325,000 were supposed to be furs and peltries. Aggregate tonnage owned in Detroit in 1830, 995 tons; in 1834, 4,000 tons. The number of arrivals and clearances in 1834, was (not including those vessels navigating in the district only) 2,112. From data received through the custom house of this port, we find in 1837, the aggregate number of vessels of every description owned in the city 47, amounting to 5,164 tons, including the following descriptions and aggregate tonnage, viz: 10 steamboats amounting to 2,184 tons; 3 brigs, 560 tons; 26 schooners, 2,200 tons; 8 sloops, 220 tons. The total amount of wharf made is 5,900 feet. From calculations made in 1836, it was estimated, for seven months navigation, that, of the steamboats navigating the lake waters, "two of the first class and one of the second, arrived and departed daily; the former averaging 200 passengers each way, and 50 tons import freight,—the latter 50 passengers and 20 tons import freight." Of the other lake vessels, "an average of three arrived and cleared daily, averaging each way ten passengers and 100 tons import freight." The profits realized during this season upon steamboats were estimated at from 50 to 70 per cent, and upon schooners from 80 to 100 per cent. . . .

In 1810, the population of the city was 770; in 1818, 1,110—

596 males, 444 females; in 1820, 1,442–887 males, 488 females, 67 colored; in 1828, 1,517; in 1830, 2,222; in 1834, 4,968–2,904 males, 2,064 females; on the first of January, 1838, 9,278.

Detroit in Transition: Ethnic and Cultural Conflict, 1844 – 45, 1853

The documents illustrating the "Bible war" and the "School Question" cover the years 1844–45 and 1853 and relate to the basic problem of a growing religious and ethnic cleavage in Detroit. Documents A and B follow the conflict over the use of Bible readings in the public schools and the apparent resolution of that question in 1845. The selections are from the Reports of the Committee of the Board of Education, 1844 *(1844, pp. 3–12) and the* Detroit Advertiser *(6 February 1845).*

Documents C and D indicate that the Bible-readings conflict was not settled in 1845 but was only the symptom of a growing ethnocultural cleavage that rose again in 1853 under the name of the "School Question." That and the related issues resolved themselves in a climactic municipal election in 1853 that established the pattern of settling future conflict in the political arena.

Both documents are from the Detroit Free Press *(4, 5 March 1853).*

"BIBLE WAR"

(A)
Admission of the Protestant Bible into the Schools, 1844

In accordance with a Resolution adopted by the aforesaid board December 2d, 1844, the following is presented to the Public:

At a special meeting of the Board of Education, held on Monday, Dec., 2d 1844, Members present, Messrs. Gage, Farmer, Higgins, Taylor, Barstow, Robb, Williams, Watson, O'Callahan and Hulbert, (10).

After transacting the ordinary business, the committee on School Books, to whom was referred, at a previous meeting, a petition signed by a large and respectable portion of tax paying inhabitants of the city of Detroit, praying for the introduction of the Bible into the public schools, presented two reports,—a majority and minority, with corresponding resolutions appended to each, the former signed by Messrs. Barstow & Taylor, and adverse to the prayer of said petitioners, the latter signed by J. Farmer, Esq. and favorable thereto, both petitions were received by the board, action was had on the majority Report and resolution which resulted in its adoption by the following vote, Ayes, Messrs. Barstow, Taylor, Robb, Williams, Watson, and O'Callahan, (6). Nays, Messrs. Farmer, Gage, Higgins and Hulbert, (4). . . .

At a meeting of the board June 13th, 1844, the following Petition was referred, by motion of Mr. Hulbert, to the committee on school books with instructions to report.

PETITION, TO THE BOARD OF EDUCATION OF THE CITY OF DETROIT. Your petitioners, inhabitants of this city, and taxable inhabitants thereof, respectfully represent, that it is with regret they have learned, that among the licensed books admitted into the district schools, the Bible has not found a place, and that its introduction by a Teacher, has been most promptly and sedulously resisted,—we earnestly desire that such a just ground of reproach should no longer have foundation, and pray the teachers of the several districts, be at liberty to introduce it into the schools, and use it for the reading of the scholars, as they may judge expedient. We are not disposed to dictate what edition of the English Bible shall be preferred; there is but one English translation of it, that is not Sectarian—the common version translated by the authority of King James, and generally

Under these considerations, we feel we should not act a faithful part as citizens of this community—as anxious for the welfare of society—as attached to our country, and as contributors, by our Taxes, to the public schools, if we refrained from urging the adoption of the Bible as a book to be read in them, at the direction of the teacher—and declaring to you that it is so vital to the interests of Education, and of the social state, that we shall be unwilling any longer to consent to be taxed for the support of Schools devoid of what we feel so indispensable to the public good. We deprecate Sectarianism. The exclusion of the Bible makes our Schools Sectarian, and contributes immensely to the growth of Sectarianism. As parents, guardians, . . . we therefore respectfully present our Petition for your serious consideration.

JNO HULBERT, Secretary

Majority Report

The Committee on School Books, to whom was referred the Petition of a large number of the Citizens of Detroit, requesting that the Teachers of the several schools, under the direction of this Board, be at liberty to introduce the Bible into their respective schools and use it, for the teaching of the scholars, as they may deem expedient, and that the English Bible, as translated under the authority of James I of England, be the edition so authorized to be used, Respectfully report,—

That they have had the subject, referred to them, under consideration, and have given it that deliberation which its intrinsic importance, and the number and character of the petitioners, have demanded.

Your committee fully agree with the petitioners in the high estimate which they put upon the Bible. It is the Book, above every other, entitled to the respect and reverence of all, and its free and general circulation, among all classes of the community, is not only a right secured by the very genius of our institutions, but one which no human laws have any power to intermeddle with, or, in any way to restrain. Religious liberty is essential to the enjoyment of civil liberty. Indeed, there can be no such things as liberty at all where every man is not permitted to worship God after the dictates of his own heart and to have free access to all those sources of information which throw light upon his relations to God and define his moral and religious duties. The right to read the Bible is in this country therefore secured to all, and there is no power in this Board to limit or restrain it.

The state of facts in this city with regard to this at present, much agitated subject, is peculiar and very different from that of any other city where it has arisen. In the first place our Roman Catholic population is not only more numerous than in other cities, but it is the oldest we have. It stands therefore, in this latter respect, at least, upon an equal footing with the Protestant population. Again, our system is a new one, just adopted, and in the adoption of which all have united and participated. The Catholic and Protestant population were equally active and ardent in obtaining the passage of this law and carrying it into effect. And again, ours is purely a local system, confined to this city, and not extending to other portions of the state. We have, then, here a system of voluntary taxation, self-imposed, in the adoption of which all denomination of christians have united.

To your committee, therefore, it has seemed evident (and this view has they think governed the action of the Board) that in order, under the above state of facts, to sustain the system at all, it must be based upon some common ground which will be mutually satisfactory to all, and that the introduction of any features repugnant to the religious views of any one large class must inevitably result in its destruction. For it seemed to them clear, as it yet does, that the dissatisfied class uniting with the open and secret enemies of the system would be able, if not to destroy it at once, to interpose obstacles, to create uncertainty and to engender bickering and bad passions which would eventually mix themselves up with party strife and the clamor of demagogues, so that the system would become paralyzed and useless, and finally be abandoned.

It was in view of these difficulties, and if possible to fix upon such a course of action as all would be satisfied with, that the course since acted upon was adopted. That is the whole subject of religion and the use of the Bible received no direct action. . . .

Our school system is menaced. The great interests of education in this city are in danger. And if we can, we are bound to avert these dangers. How can we, how shall we do so, consistent with justice and duty? We think there must be concession on both sides, and that a rigid tenacity in insisting to have this subject settled in their own way, and no other, on either part, must result in making the system a source of general contention, and recrimination, and finally entirely overturning what will have already been rendered worthless and unworthy of preservation.

Resolved, That it is not expedient to grant the prayer of the Petitioners, by which they demand the adoption of the Protestant version of the Bible only, to the exclusion of the Catholic, to be used in the schools under the direction of the Board.

Resolved, That it is not expedient to introduce any alteration of our School system during the present School year, and that whatever action may be had, should have reference to, and take effect only on the commencement of a new School year.

SAMUEL BARSTOW
ELISHA TAYLOR

(B)
Admission of Both the Protestant and Catholic Bibles into the Schools, 1845

"Resolved, that there is nothing in the rules or by-laws at all conflicting with the right of any teacher in the employment of this board opening his or her school by reading, without note or comment, from any version of the Bible they may choose, either Catholic or Protestant.

Resolved, that the teacher who shall in any way note, comment, or remark, in his or her school, upon a passage of Scripture read therein, or other passage of Scripture, shall be removed from his or her school upon proof being made to the committee of his or her school; the decision of said committee, however, being subject to the action of the Board."

"SCHOOL QUESTION" AND THE CITY ELECTION, 1853

(C)
"The Present Crisis," The Catholic Position on Politics, School, and the Church

Mr. Editor: Sir:—

For the last few weeks the minds of the citizens of this city have been unusually excited by matters relating to our primary schools. This excitement has been increasing, until it now threatens violence, at the approaching charter election. It has communicated itself to the country, and every arrival thence brings the intelligence of increasing murmurs of agitated feeling upon this subject there. The cause of this excitement connects itself closely with the religious feelings of the community, and thereby becomes doubly dangerous, however paradoxical this may appear. For it is a well established fact, that the religious prejudices of any community, when aroused become the most bitter, intolerant and malignant of the human heart. I have been, Mr. Editor, a looker on only, abstaining from all participation in the causes which have produced this state of feeling, and I have watched the progress thereof with much solicitude and anxiety. I have observed that it has been fomented and fanned into flame, chiefly, by a certain paper published in this city, and that, too, in a manner which, to any unprejudiced, reflecting person, unmoved by the excitement around him, appears unmanly, ungenerous, unprincipled, uncharitable, unchristian, bigoted, profane, incendiary and devilish. . . .

It is fresh in the minds of all, that during the last winter a meeting of the citizens of this city was called at the City Hall, to consider upon certain questions relating to certain improvements in the city, which affected, materially, the interests of the Catholic churches of this city and vicinity. Of the propriety of those improvements, great difference of opinion existed among the citizens. As I understand it, the Bishop of said churches is the trustee or administrator of the temporalities of the churches in his diocese. As such, he saw fit to appear before said meeting in person, rather than by proxy, to defend that which had been placed in his keeping. Howmuchsoever the propriety of this course of the Bishop may be questioned, yet no one will deny his right of doing as he did.—While a portion of his fellow citizens accord to him honesty of purpose and uprightness of motive, in so doing, they yet condemn his conduct as injudicious under the circumstances. But there are others, of a baser sort, who, actuated by hatred to the Catholics in general, and democratic Catholics in particular, seized with avidity upon this occasion to strike a malignant blow at democracy, by creating and bringing into action a violent and intolerant spirit of opposition and destruction to the Catholic clergy and members of their churches, a great portion of whom are democrats, thus arraying one portion of the democratic party against another—calculating and mischievously operating upon the well known tendency of one religious sect to denounce another of a different creed.—The press, aforesaid, literally teemed with abuse of the Bishop and the Catholic clergy, and its depraved editor administered daily his disgusting and incendiary articles to the excited and perverted tastes of its

readers.[1] In the mean time, the legislature of this State, being then in session, was respectfully and legitimately petitioned to amend the primary school laws. With the Catholics, it is a duty to educate their youth in the principles of their religion. This they could not do at the schools of the city, as they were then conducted. They had conscientious scruples to sending their children to those schools. They therefore desired that the portion of school money to which they would be entitled, provided they sent to those schools, might by law be diverted and expended upon schools where their children could be taught in their peculiar faith. Their petition to the legislature was to this effect, but the petition was denied by that body. And here I will say that, in my humble opinion, the legislature acted wisely.

It is said (and I wish not to deny it) that the Bishop attended upon the legislature, and used his best endeavors to carry out the wishes of a large (and hitherto considered respectable) portion of the inhabitants of this city. For this he has been denounced in no measured terms, although he has done no more than has been done, at almost every session of the legislature, by other professing christians and christian teachers. His conduct was watched and his motives maligned, and the distempered imaginations of his enemies saw nothing in all his moves, but dark designs, the most dangerous to the welfare of the people of this State.—Soon after came the nominations for city officers. Here again was discovered the deep and damnable course of him of the cloven foot, in the person of the Bishop, or his Priests. He, or they, had been seen on a parochial visit to some of his people, and straightway the tocsin of alarm was sounded and rung throughout the city. A new stroke of policy was discovered by the knowing ones, the object of the Catholics, to wit: the utter destruction of the common schools was to be gained by nominating their chosen champions to the office of school inspectors—thus placing the Board of Education within their control. But the mountain labored and brought forth a mouse. . . .

In wards where a majority of the nominating caucus was admitted to be Catholic, even there, staunch adherents to the common schools were nominated to the office of school inspectors, and this, too, without any opposition. I write what I know. And in wards where the Catholics have not the slightest hope of electing their chosen friends, there have been nominated Catholics. So far, indeed, from the history of the nominations showing any concerted design on the part of the Catholics to secure the control of the school Board of this city, that the contrary rather appears. But nothing short of annihilation of the Catholics would appease the wrath and satisfy the desires of some; neither would the object of their desires be accomplished, if the matter was to rest here. The ball must be kept in motion. A new ticket must be made, whereby the democratic party should be divided against itself. And a new ticket was made. This new ticket is composed of good men, so far as I know them. Of the two tickets presented to the electors of this city, I have nothing to say. My object is not to defend, eulogize, or attack either. Neither is it to champion the cause of the Catholics, or any other denomination of christians; but it is, if possible, to aid in appeasing wrath and dissension—to counteract the baneful influence of a reckless press, that would gladly see the fires of persecution kindled, and the city laid in ruins, than to lose the object of its unhallowed desires. . . .

Beware, then, my fellow citizens, that you be riven not to your own injury and discomfiture; and beware, also, that you do not that which, in your cooler moments, your own conscience will condemn. . . .

At the polls you are called upon by it to place the mark of Cain upon the foreheads of the fathers of this city. Examine well before you take this fatal step. Reflect upon the matter, and take a retrospective view of the history of this excitement, and act the part of freemen, and prove yourselves worthy of the liberties you now enjoy.

JUSTICE

(D)
"The Independent Ticket: The Issues Presented,"
The Protestant and "Independent" Position

It is asserted by some of the opponents of the independent ticket that there are no such issues involved in the coming election as are claimed by its friends.

In December last, a committee, appointed by the Common Council after great deliberation, reported in favor of certain amendments to the city charter, and, at the same time, the Board of Trustees of the Water Works reported in favor of a bill for providing for the completion and management of the Water Works. The principal charter amendments were: 1st. To more clearly define the powers of the Common Council in paving streets, at the expense of the adjoining land owners; and, 2d. To provide for the establishment of a city alms house, in connection with a work house. The Water Works bill provided for the organization of a Board to have the control of the Water Works, with power to borrow not to exceed $400,000 to complete them. As to the 1st amendment, making sidewalks and paving streets is one of the necessities of a new and growing city; and following the example of older cities, Detroit has expended $200,000 in this work, raised by assessments on the adjoining land owners. This is the usual and equitable mode. Why should land owners in the back part of the city, where the streets will not be paved for many years, if ever, pay for paving Jefferson avenue. A city alms house, too, is a great need. The poor are numerous, and mainly Catholic. They have an invincible repugnance to going to the county poor house, and mainly because of the want of religious privileges. And they are now supported, with little comfort, and at great expense, and a city alms house would at once provide a comfortable and economical refuge. The water works are utterly inadequate to supply the growing city with water, and, from year to year, are running the city heavily in debt. The subject had been submitted to E. A. Brush, Henry Ledyard, Shubael Conant, W. R. Noyes, and J. A. Van Dyke—all men of eminent business capacity, of unsullied integrity and deeply devoted to the best interests of the city. They reported the bill alluded to. Their view was, that by establishing a new reservoir, procuring new engines, and enlarging the supply of water to meet the full wants of the city, the water rents would pay the interest on the whole cost, and provide a sinking fund to pay off the principal. But to meet this expense in the outset, it was necessary to pledge the credit of the city, but with the well grounded expectation that not one cent would ever be raised by general tax.

All these propositions challenged examination and discussion, and the fullest opposition was the unquestioned right of all. Bishop Lefevre opposed all of the proposed measures; and for fair, legitimate opposition, no one could censure him, however much they might question his wisdom. His motives for this opposition were to some extent apparent. He represents the property of the Catholic Church, which is very large, immensely valuable, and situated in the very heart of the city. A large proportion of it is exempt from general taxation, being used for educational and religious purposes. If paving is done by general tax, his taxes will be far lighter than if it is paid for by assessments on adjoining property; and then, too, much less of it would probably be done. He now denies the right of the city to assess the property benefitted, and has a bill in chancery pending, involving the question. Hence, his opposition to the first amendment.

The alms house system would cut off the revenue which his charity hospital now derives from the city, which, during the last eleven months, was $643.38, and would, of course, cause a tax for the erection of the buildings, of which he would have to pay his proportion; for, although so much of his property is exempt, yet the taxes on church property for 1852 exceeded $1,000—so great is its value. His opposition to the water works improvement seems to have its origin in some vague and indefinite fears that it might, in some way, cause taxation, and in the spirit of opposition, to improvement, which has ever characterized ecclesiastic property-holders.

All of these questions were purely secular, and affecting the Bishop and the Catholic population only as they affected every other citizen. They involved no principle affecting liberty of vested rights. On the Sunday before the propositions were to be submitted to the Common Council, availing himself of his spiritual power to advance his secular ends, he made from the pulpit an inflammatory appeal to his people, holding up these measures in the most odious light, as tyrannical and oppressive, and summoned his auditory to appear before the Council, and defend their rights.—They came, an angry, heated mass—not to protest—not to reason—but to over-awe. The Council adjourned. The meeting of Wednesday night followed—a fierce, tumultuous mob of the most ignorant and excitable of the Bishop's followers, led on by the Bishop himself—their passions aroused to a perfect phrenzy,

by his violent appeals and bitter vituperations. The Common
Council and the Legislature were dared to act against such an
expression of popular feeling. Resistance to the proposed law, if
enacted, was distinctly preached; and the legitimate threat was
made of hurling votes against those who should dare to support
the proposed measures. The more intelligent of the people were
disgusted with the Bishop's course, but they did not choose openly
to oppose him.

The Council showed themselves men, and quietly recommended the proposed amendments.—Then came the ridiculous
pilgrimage of the Bishop and Priests to Lansing. In all this, Bishop
Lefevre has placed himself in an attitude of violent hostility to
the Common Council and city improvement; and by this exercise
of his spiritual power, has, to a great extent, arrayed his people,
especially the more ignorant of them, on the same side. It has
become with him a question of power, as well as of interest. He
must carry the day, or lose influence.

So on the school question, his position is undeniable. Our
noble schools are denounced as "godless"—"infidel"—and the
system as "the essence of tyranny." His people are commanded
not to send their children to these unholy places. The destruction
of these schools, from his own avowed principles, would be a
high religious duty; and in no way could their destruction be more
effectually accomplished, than by filling the Board of Education
with the enemies of the schools.

The Bishop, and those who act with him, have taken open
ground upon both of these questions. They have boldly threatened to bring the crushing power of Catholic votes to bear upon
those who will not aid them, and to "wipe from the political history of the state" those who dare oppose them. They have fairly
entered the political arena with their spiritual powers. They make
their claim, and in the language of their champion, "H.O.B." in
the *Free Press,* "they will have it—no more—no less;" or in the
language of "Justice," another champion, in Wednesday's *Free
Press,* they find an "obstacle in the shape of state common
schools," which they intend to remove by "wisdom, perseverance
and patience." With these fixed purposes of throwing obstacles
in the way of city improvements, and of breaking up the "godless"
and "infidel" schools, and that by political action, what would

they naturally do? They understand perfectly the machinery of party politics—the power of caucusses. They would naturally seize upon this machinery, and use it for their own purposes. Have they done so?

Now, while, as we have said, many of the Catholics disapprove of the Bishop's course, others in large numbers, gave themselves up to the guidance of the Bishop and his agents, and sought to control the caucusses. The several ward meetings were fixed for the same evening. The 8th ward caucus was altered to the afternoon; and for what, except to give the 8th ward boys an opportunity to attend the meetings in the other wards? They did attend. At an early hour most of the caucusses were filled with Irish Catholics, who had every thing their own way. They acted in concert with entire unanimity, so far as the offices of aldermen and school inspectors were concerned. It was, too, an intelligent pre-concert. Look at the result. In four out of eight wards, Catholics are nominated for school inspectors, and in a fifth, a Protestant opposed to free schools. Why is this? Is it owing to their peculiar fitness for the post, or their devotion to the schools and the interests of education? Look at the list and answer. Look also at the fact that, if the caucus nominees are elected, the Catholics will have the practical control of the Board of Education. Why do they seek this? Those who sympathize with the Bishop cannot send their children there, nor can they seek their success. It can only be to embarrass and cripple them. No one objects to their having a representation in the Board; but so long as they cannot support the schools, why should they seek to control them, except to destroy!

Aldermen were nominated in five of the wards, under the same influence. Their antecedents, their affinities, or their known opinions, made them acceptable to the power behind and greater than the caucus.

Look at the delegates to the City Convention. Was there no concert in their selection? For instance, in the 2d ward, was it not a foregone conclusion, long before the caucus assembled, that O'Callaghan, Shaunessy, and Moynahan should be the delegates? Whence issued the decree, except from the Bishop and his agents? There was no deliberative choice in the caucus; their action was forestalled.

But how do you know the Bishop had any thing to do with all this?—where is the proof?—it is asked. The proof is apparent to those who can put this and that together. The Bishop has an object to accomplish—to arrest city improvements; and destroy free schools. He has plainly threatened to use the Catholic vote to accomplish this object. A portion of the Catholics rush in masses, to the caucusses, get the control of them, and make nominations satisfactory to the Bishop, and not unfavorable to his projects.

But, it is asked, how do you know the nominees are not right upon these subjects? Where is your proof? Why not interrogate them? The most satisfactory proof to every reflecting mind is the characters and position of the men—their affinities—their known opinions—their susceptibility to be influenced by motives which may be brought to bear upon them by the Bishop.

Word pledges are but mere ropes of sand. An artless man is he who cannot "keep the promise to the ear, and break it to the hope."

The policy of remaining quiet, until what we have just reason to apprehend, is accomplished, because we have no technical proof that these men, nominated under such circumstances, and by such influences, are on the wrong side of these questions, is the policy of weakness and treachery.

I have not written because I question the full right of the Bishop and his friends to carry their points through the ballot box, nor to argue the merits of the city improvements and school question, but to show that these questions are involved in the present canvass. The Bishop has threatened to carry his points through the ballot box, and he is now executing his threat. Let those who are opposed to his plans, see to it that he does not succeed.

The democratic party proscribe no man for his country or his religion. They have never shown distrust of naturalized citizens or Catholics; but when a Catholic Bishop descends to the political arena, and undertakes to seize the machinery of the democratic party, to carry out his measures, it is time for protest, and, if necessary, for rebellion against caucusses thus controlled. . . .

We would make the same resistance to any other sect who were making the same effort. Had Bishop McCoskry or Dr. Duffield pursued the same course that has been pursued by Bishop Lefevre, the public indignation would have been equally intense, and had a band of Presbyterians, by pre-concert, got possession of the caucusses, and made nominations to carry out peculiar views of their own, where would have been the present supporters of the so-called regular ticket?—

A TRUE DEMOCRAT

PART TWO

COMMERCIAL TO INDUSTRIAL CITY, 1850–1900

The western trade is a prize worthy of those who would struggle for the colossal commercial power of America. A city sustained by that trade, can never languish; for the increase of production of the western states is almost boundless. Its city must be far greater than even Alexandria or Thebes.

—*The Merchant's Magazine*
February 1846

Yet the creation of a system of manufactures by which we should retain at home hundreds of thousands of dollars now annually sent abroad . . . [would] do more to advance her real prosperity than almost any other branch of industry.

—*Detroit Daily Advertiser*
18 February 1860

Unorganized, untaught, uncared for, seemingly unambitious, strangers in a strange land, with every waking hour devoted to satisfying the needs and desires of the physical man, these people seem scarcely to realize their humanity.

—Springwells brickyard laborers,
described in *First Annual Report
of the Bureau of Labor and Industrial
Statistics* (Lansing, 1884)

Introduction

Detroit between 1850 and 1870 was predominantly a commercial city. So much of Detroit's history has been written during the city's industrial "takeoff" or during its later meteoric rise to motortown metropolis that scholars, writers, and collectors of sources have often lost sight of the economic life of preindustrial Detroit, or else they have compressed it into an interesting and romantic episode involving trappers, Indians, and pioneers or, alternately, treated it patronizingly as a transition state or a prelude to a preordained destiny that was motor town. Detroit's commercial economy for 1850 to 1870 has been ignored, and the primitive and primary industries and trade-serving manufactures of that period have been viewed largely as foundation stones for building a factory town. Primary-processing industries have been ransacked by writers in search of basic skills that would somehow contribute knowledge increments that made for technological breakthroughs such as the self-starter, the internal-combustion engine, or chrome bumper or dynaflow drive. Unfortunately, the basic technologies that transformed the "City of the Strait" into a capital city of the motor realm are not to be found in an earlier Detroit. The innovations that brought about the automotive revolution were not tied to any city or, for that matter, any nation but were, rather, international. Detroit's contribution cannot be explained by geographic or technological determinism as well as it can by the happy accidents of entrepreneurship. Sam Slick of Slickville, Yankee peddler, is as much an ancestor of modern Detroit as the German and French claimants for invention of the internal-combustion engine.

Detroit by 1855 had reached a high plateau of commercial development whereby the outstate business with agricultural settlements had replaced trafficking in furs as the main line business. Specialization had begun to overtake the wholesalers and retailers. Whereas formerly merchants had maintained general merchandise with a mixed line of staples, dry goods, hardware, and leather stock, by 1855 they had begun to specialize in a single line or two of goods. Exclusive dry goods sellers, carpet stores, drug and medicine vendors, and crockery, hardware and leather stores were doing business in the city. The men who vended such goods often became rich, as had Zachariah Chandler, and were sent on to the United States Senate or, at a more modest level were elected mayor, as was merchant William W. Wheaton.[1] The modern viewer of high-technology and mass-industry Detroit must be puzzled by the thought that merchant princes and jobbers of "country goods" like Chandler, freshwater commodores and lake shippers like Oliver Newberry, and drug preparers and potion mixers like Jacob Farrand constituted the mainstream of the economy and the city's venerable elite up to 1870.[2] Wholesale trading and retailing were the two most prominent and economically vital functions of a mercantile city like Detroit. Robert Roberts drew a sketch of an exemplary business establishment that had attained a scale of employment and operation that few manufacturing industries would reach during the next decade.

> The store has a free stone front, is four stories high, occupies a front of fifty feet, and extending in depth one hundred feet, comprising ten rooms, each twenty-five feet in width and one hundred feet in depth and an area of 25,000 square feet, all of which are filled to their utmost capacity with foreign and domestic dry goods, carpets, cloths, millinery and clothing,—in addition to which the firm occupy a store-house in the rear. The retail rooms are four in number, finished in the most gorgeous style. About three hundred gas lights are required to light the several apartments. From sixty to seventy-five salesmen and from one hundred to one hundred and fifty persons altogether are employed in the several departments, and including those outside, seamsters and seamstresses, the firm give employment to about six hundred persons. Their invoices of merchandise imported during the year 1854 amounted to more than seven hundred thousand dollars.
>
> This store was recently refitted and opened for the fall trade, with an invoice of goods amounting to over four hundred thousand dollars.[3]

Commercial Detroit, like most of its mercantile neighbors, went to great lengths to stress why the advantages accruing from its location, the resources at its command, and the skill of merchants had destined it to become the commercial emporium of mid-America. One has but to read the puffery of midwestern city boosters to conclude that there existed a basic formula for writing such boosterism that could be transferred from city to city with only a few name changes. Writers composed ecstatic prose on the size and length of warehouses, new railroad lines being constructed or projected, and the hoped-for trade they would bring. Docks and wharves were noted, tonnage of vessels was enumerated, and the class and motive power specified (propeller, steam, or schooner); the leading civic men who invested in shipping were celebrated as farsighted Jasons who sought the prize of the golden fleece of commerce for their respective cities. Wool clip, shingles, lath, tanned hides, and barrels of fish were measured and weighed with precision each year, and their weight added cubits to the stature of the city, boosters believed. The bounty of nature when packed into a barrel, whether whitefish or wood ashes, was celebrated with heroic gusto by boards of trade and mercantile exchanges. Every city lusted for the title of commercial emporium for some region no matter how small, whether a state or perhaps just a county.

Detroit was a typical commercial city and measured and published its imports, exports, and customs receipts for all to behold its commercial splendor. Its export columns burgeoned with ashes by the cask, beef, butter, copper, whitefish, hides and skins, sawed lumber, barrel staves, tallow, live pigs, dressed hogs, and sheep clip. Exports were broken down and enumerated in every conceivable way and by every mode of transport—ship, rail, and dray line. Imports were gauged with equal care and enumerated in great detail. The 1854 Reciprocity Treaty with Canada was hailed as a godsend that would increase business and trade. Vessel arrivals and clearances were also listed by foreign and domestic entries in separate columns. Vessels owned and licensed in the Detroit district and servicing the lake trade were identified by owner and city, listed and numbered and shown by tonnage and class (such as steamer, propeller, bark, schooner), and schedules and itineraries published. The opening of the navigation season in Detroit was an event that was duly noted and examined each year in comparison to the opening dates for the previous twenty years. An unusually early or late opening generally called for an explanatory comment. Detroiters knew that navigable waterways pumped life-giving commerce into their city.[4]

One of the earliest and most durable mainstays for export was fish. Almost any sketch of Detroit written before 1870 devoted a page or two and sometimes several columns of information on Detroit's fishery, particularly that delicacy of delicacies, the whitefish.[5] Generally, in these accounts it was incumbent upon the writer to acclaim the great export range of the commodity. Detroit's foremost commercial chronicler claimed that it was "no uncommon thing" to see Detroit whitefish "advertised in St. Louis, Cincinnati, Louisville, and Natchez; and on the other hand in New York, and Boston, while they also show themselves at Salem and Marblehead, the very head quarters of the mackerel fisheries." The whitefish was considered the "prince of the freshwater fish," and to fully honor this gustatory and commercial delight, Roberts in his *Sketches* printed stanzas of verse.

> All friends to good living by tureen and dish,
> Concur in exalting this prince of a fish;
> So fine in a platter, so tempting a fry,
> So rich on a gridiron, so sweet in a pie,
> That even before it the salmon must fall
> And that mighty bonne-bouche, of the land beaver's tail.

> This fish is a subject so dainty and white,
> To show in a lecture, to eat or to write,
> To raise up my voice or to raise up my knife,
> 'Tis a morsel alike for the gourmand or faster;
> White, white as a tablet of pure alabaster!

> Its beauty or flavor no person can doubt,
> When seen in the water, or tasted without,
> And all the dispute that opinion ere makes
> Of this king of lake fishes, this "deer of the lakes,"
> Regards not its choiceness to ponder or sup,
> But the best mode of dressing and serving it up.

Detroiters estimated their annual catch in 1855 at one hundred thousand barrels. Seafaring colonial Boston had been no less solicitous of its cod fishery.

The manufacturing that existed was often handicraft, or involved processing of farm products, and was primary manufacturing connected with commerce and trade. The scale was small. Professor Allan Pred has referred to these mercantile city manufacturers as "entrepôt manufactures" in that they often resulted from trade directly or indirectly or served some aspect of a larger commerce. Tanning leather, grinding grain, and sawing lumber were direct outgrowths of Detroit's hinterland exports. The tanning of leather is also a good example of first-stage manufacturing that required minimum skill and no machinery and that capitalized upon the abundance of raw materials. Raw skins and hides were stacked and interleaved with oak or hemlock bark and placed into a vat filled with water to cure, and the tannin did the rest. Although primitive, this kind of primary manufacture increased the value of raw material exported. Barrel staves, boxes, lath, lumber, edge tool making, iron hitches, forged products, and wagon and carriage making were all city-serving and trade-serving industries and commonly found in commercial cities. Shipbuilding, cooperage, and printing fell into the same category of "commerce-serving manufacture." The assembly of barrels, kegs, casks, and wooden boxes was an important primary service for commerce. The cooperage industry was widely dispersed to save on the transport cost of bulky, expensive-to-ship containers. In a somewhat similar fashion, breweries and bakeries in a pre-preservative age were local, city-serving, handicraft industries and seldom entered into a broader export trade before 1870. Thus, during the 1860s nothing of either the manufacturing scale or export magnitude of Massachusetts' mill towns could be found in Detroit.[6]

Detroit's one exogenous item that was produced for a national market was copper smelted from Lake Superior ores. Although smelting had many of the elements of a heavy, modern industry that was not commerce-serving, it failed to form the nucleus for nonferrous metal manufacturing, for by 1880 the smelters moved north to mine heads in the "Copper Country" and copper smelting declined to insignificance. Detroit's efforts toward a large-scale steel industry also had an early head start when the Midwest's first Bessemer steel was smelted and produced in 1864 in suburban Wyandotte. That innovative industry fizzled in the early 1870s and Detroit failed to develop a ferro-industrial complex. What was left of small charcoal-smelting became obsolescent with the onset of coke smelting, and, as the forests vanished, charcoal smelting in the Detroit region vanished also.[7] Thus, some of the most spectacular initial thrusts toward what could have ushered Detroit into its "paleotechnic phase" were blunted or diverted. Detroit during the 1870s was still a raw-material processor, boasting of its commercial prowess, but rapidly expanding the base of its manufacturing enterprises.

The decade beginning in 1870 was a critical one of important industrial change. The first significant break with Detroit's reliance upon commerce became evident. The number of manufacturing jobs, for example, took a quantum jump upward from 1,363 in 1860 to 10,612 jobs in 1870, an increase that more than tripled the rate of population growth. The amount of capital invested in manufacturing increased from $1.5 million to $24.6 million and the value of the finished product from $2.1 million in 1860 to $21.8 million in 1870. Detroit's industrial takeoff was well under way, and the momentum of 1870 had carried it through a depression which temporarily slowed growth but did not alter its direction, which was toward manufacturing expansion.[8]

By 1880 the number of manufacturing jobs in Detroit had increased to 16,110 and Detroit had achieved a balance and diversity in its manufacturing that twentieth-century Detroit urban planners would envy. In 1880 Detroit's eight leading products by value ranged from $1 million to $2.5 million, with the manufacture of products from iron and steel at the top and boots and shoes at the bottom of the $1 million–plus class. Tobacco and cigars were a close second, only a few thousand dollars less than the leader in annual worth. Men's clothing ranked third in product value, which was in excess of $2 million. Still strongly represented in Detroit's manufacturing picture and ranking ninth through eleventh in product value were printing and publishing, bread baking, and shipbuilding, all old commerce-serving and city-serving industries. Detroit's industries of 1880, unlike its early copper and iron episodes, provided a solid base for growth, and the industrial picture for 1890 was an enlargement upon that of 1880. The number of manufacturing jobs took another quantum jump and more than doubled to 34,535. Detroit then ranked seventeenth in value of its manufactures among American cities, and fourteenth in population.[9]

By 1900 Detroit was an established medium-sized manufacturing city with nothing unique in its manufacturing base to explain the dramatic and meteoric changes that would occur after 1904. The same industrial base existed in several cities. In fact, any careful rational analysis of skills and supplies would probably have caused an observer to predict that the automobile industry would develop in a more advanced industrial city than Detroit. The number of wheelwrights, wagon makers, or marine engineers there was not a decisive asset. These skills were widely distributed. Far more important in bringing the industry in concentrated form to Detroit were the accidents of birth and the presence of several gifted individuals and pioneer auto assemblers. Neither was the scale achieved by automobile manufacturing a natural outgrowth of Detroit's turn-of-the-century industrial base. Detroit had slowly crept up the industrial scale from nineteenth city in 1880 to seventeenth city in 1890 and finally to sixteenth place in 1900, a three-notch move in twenty years. Under the influence of the automobile, Detroit shot from sixteenth rank in 1900 to fourth rank in 1914, a great leap forward over twelve other industrial cities in only fourteen years. Under the heat of this great expansion many of Detroit's older industries withered. Railroad car building, for example, the city's most important industry in 1890, was in a state of advanced atrophy by 1910.[10] The widespread development and importation of new skills and the restructuring and remaking of Detroit's entire industrial complex after 1900 would attest to the revolutionary impact of motor vehicle manufacturing.

Detroit grew enormously under the pressures of a steady flow of new immigrants and increasing industrial expansion. Yet, surprisingly enough, the social geography and spatial arrangements of class and ethnicity remained peculiarly preindustrial. Perhaps it was the onset of rapid industrialization that caught the city unprepared to rearrange itself in accordance with an industrial social geography. Perhaps, too, it was the reflection of an inadequate transit system to shuttle white-collar professionals to distant suburbs. The fashionable districts were Woodward Avenue in uptown and Jefferson Avenue on the waterfront. A classical preindustrial living pattern persisted by which the upper classes remained at and near the center and core of Detroit and would continue to do so until after the turn of the century.[11]

The poor and newcomers, on the other hand, were not crammed into the central ghettos but scattered from the waterfront to the unorganized districts on the outskirts, often living on cheap land on the periphery. They were also there in part because that is where space-consuming, heavy-labor, and low-profit margin industries such as brickmaking were located. In any event, Detroit's suburban locations had not been taken over by the favored classes, as our selection covering Springwells illustrates. Only three and one-half miles from city hall, Springwells, an innermost suburb, was the location of Polish, Bohemian, and German poor who lived in their shantytowns interwoven among the dusty kilns, brickyards, and lumberyards that covered the low-lying land on Detroit's outskirts. Hanging on to the margins of life, these workers eked out a precarious existence from seasonal and often unpredictable work. As an inspector for the Michigan Bureau of Labor and Industrial Statistics observed, they were "unorganized, untaught, uncared for, seemingly unambitious, strangers in a strange land, with every waking hour devoted to satisfying the needs and desires of the physical man, these people seem scarcely to realize their own humanity." This scene that the state inspector depicted was not the exception, for it could be viewed in the same building-supply industries in other parts of Detroit and in other cities of the state.

Women and child workers were at the nether end of the spectrum in wages, working hours, and health and safety conditions. Even in the best hotels, servants who did not have access to the kitchen were often served "broken victuals" left over from the guests. The conditions most of them faced were deplorable. As the labor inspector, Mrs. Ella Whipple, observed, "As a rule, the cheapest food, the poorest beds, and the hardest work with long hours is what was found to be the lot of women and children in the hotels of Detroit." Dry goods stores, candy and cigar manufactories were scarcely any better. The best conditions for women and child workers, according to the bureau, were the laundries (because they were clean), the pharmaceutical company, and the telephone exchange.

Industrial growth was accompanied by growing population and increasing diversity. The Yankee New England influence over Detroit was challenged and strained and modified by new ethnic and nationality elements that would help to shape the cultural character of Detroit. By 1850 the Irish had become the largest foreign-born group (3,289), comprising about one out of seven Detroiters; Irish settlement had become visible during the 1840s, and it was during this decade that Detroit's "Corktown" was established. The Irish were surpassed in 1860 by the Germans, who became the largest foreign-born group in Detroit and would remain so until 1900. The German proportion of the city's foreign-born population increased from 36 percent in 1870 to 43 percent in 1890, which was not only the census peak for Germans but also the largest proportion recorded for any single foreign-born group in Detroit's census history. This was very much Germany's half century in Detroit. This was also the heyday of Germanic influence in other Great Lakes cities such as Cleveland, Chicago, and Milwaukee. Evidences of German cultural presence abounded in Detroit: saengerfests, bunds, vereins, Turner and Arbeiter halls, newspapers and publishing activity, a German-language theater, lyceums, picnics on national holidays, a large German business district on the east side, and a growing and vigorous voice in city politics. German representatives on the city council had become increasingly visible in the 1880s. By 1884, of the city's twenty-six aldermen at least seven were German-Americans, and that number would increase to fourteen by 1891.[12]

German-Americans were also in the forefront in the "personal liberty" battle versus the temperance and prohibitionist ranks. The fact that the leading drys continued to be the sons and grandsons of the "strict sober-sides from the land of Jonathan Edwards" and generally Republican in sympathy drove German voters and businessmen deeper into the ranks of the Democratic party. In 1887 the prohibitionist forces, with the help of a sympathetic Republican governor, undertook a major drive to abolish all liquor selling by a constitutional amendment that was to be put before the electorate in April, 1887. Earlier efforts to dry up the state through legislative acts had failed. A constitutional amendment, the drys reasoned, was the only sure way to withstand court tests and frustrate the noncompliance stratagems of the pro-liquor forces.

Detroit Germans provided the organizational framework through the united German associations to raise a war chest and mount a statewide campaign through affiliated German societies to defeat the amendment. As our document shows, not only were the initial meetings of the antiprohibitionists held in German halls but German was the *lingua franca* of the movement. In the closing weeks the campaign soon broadened out to include non-Germanic elements, native-born Americans, blacks, and others. This counterattack succeeded in defeating the prohibition amendment by the thinnest statewide vote, 184,305 to 178,470. The wets won overwhelmingly in Detroit, where they swamped the prohibitionists by a seven-to-one margin.[13]

Still the Republican party continued its open flirtation with the temperance elements and went on in the fall mayoralty elections of 1887 to sustain one of the worst defeats in Detroit in the party's history. This rout of a temperance-tinged candidate seared through the marrow of Detroit's bone-dry Republicanism unlike anything else of the decade.

As Professors Paul Kleppner and Richard Jensen have shown, the prohibition question involved much more than merely trafficking in or consuming spirituous beverages. It was one of the key points in the ethnocultural tensions that pitted pietistic, native-born Protestants and their evangelical Scandinavian allies against newcomer Germans, Irish, and other Catholic groups. This factor created divisions within the community and was one of the measures, along with religious intolerance, that kept Catholic newcomers apart from native-born elements and in opposition political parties.[14]

Yet, beginning in 1889 with Mayor Hazen S. Pingree's election, the city GOP would undergo a vast political remodeling whereby ethnics, Catholics, and lower-income groups would be invited by the mayor, by recognition on the ticket, and by the appeals of the mayor's reform programs to alter their political allegiances from the Democratic to the Republican. A revitalized city party was able to overcome some of the obstacles such as temperance and Apaism. Pingree's efforts were vindicated by 1895 when the Republicans had broken away from the Democrats a sizable bloc of Catholic and immigrant voters. The realignment showed in the national and state elections of 1896 when the Republicans swept the city and made inroads into hitherto Democratic precincts and wards.[15] A political transformation had been effected. Our selection "Mayor Pingree Reforms Detroit, 1890–97" also captures some of the vigor and style with which Detroit's dynamic mayor prosecuted reform.

NOTES—PART TWO

1. Robert E. Roberts, *Sketches of the City of Detroit, 1855* (Detroit, 1855), p. 18.

2. *Detroit in History and Commerce* (Detroit, 1881), p. 13.

3. Roberts, *Sketches*, p. 18.

4. "Commercial Cities and Towns of the United States, Detroit," *The Merchants' Magazine* 20 (March 1849): 281–84; "Commercial and Industrial Cities of the United States: Detroit," *Hunt's Merchants' Magazine* 38 (May 1858): 576–81.

5. See for example, "Detroit," *Hunt's Merchants' Magazine* 35 (October 1856): 561–66.

6. Allan R. Pred, *The Spatial Dynamics of U.S. Urban-Industrial Growth, 1800–1914* (Cambridge, 1966), pp. 143–75; Willis F. Dunbar, "The Speeding Tempo of Urbanization," *Michigan History Magazine* 35 (September 1951): 292–93; Almon E. Parkins, *The Historical Geography of Detroit* (Lansing, 1918), p. 288.

7. Parkins, *Detroit*, pp. 293–95, 299–300.

8. *Abstract of the Twelfth Census of the U.S., 1900* (Washington, 1904), p. 354. For 1850 and 1860 see Irma C. Bielenberg, "Economic Detroit, 1860–1870" (M.A. thesis, Wayne State University 1939), p. 143. Sidney Glazer, *Detroit: A Study in Urban Development* (New York, 1965), pp. 50, 51.

9. Ibid.

10. William Stocking, "Industries of By-Gone Days," *Detroiter* 16 (28 December 1925): 9.

11. Eric Kocher, "Economic and Physical Growth of Detroit, 1701–1935," (mimeograph copy in University of Michigan Historical Collections).

12. Justin B. Galford, "The Foreign Born and Urban Growth in the Great Lakes, 1850–1950: A Study of Chicago, Cleveland, Detroit, and Milwaukee" (Ph.D. diss., New York University, 1957), pp. 172, 174, 187,

188, 299; Jo Ellen Vinyard, "Inland Urban Immigrants: The Detroit Irish, 1850," *Michigan History Magazine* 57 (Summer 1973): 122; Melvin G. Holli, *Reform in Detroit: Hazen S. Pingree and Urban Politics* (New York, 1969), p. 10. For increasing ethnic and racial tension, see David M. Katzman, *Before the Ghetto: Black Detroit in the Nineteenth Century* (Urbana, Ill., 1973), pp. 44–47.

13. *Detroit Free Press,* 28 March 1887, 5 April 1887; A. D. P. Van Buren, "Our Temperance Conflict," *Michigan Pioneer and Historical Society Collections* 12 (1889): 403–5.

14. Paul Kleppner, *The Cross of Culture: A Social Analysis of Midwestern Politics, 1850–1900* (New York, 1970); Richard J. Jensen, *The Winning of the Midwest: Social and Political Conflict, 1888–1896* (Chicago, 1971).

15. Holli, *Reform in Detroit,* pp. 125–56.

Detroit As Recalled by a Merchant

Jacob S. Farrand (1815–90), one of the founders and pioneers of the wholesale drug business, came to the Detroit area in 1825. He began as a clerk in a drugstore in 1830, became a partner in 1835, and records in this reminiscence the evolution of the business community in mercantile Detroit. Farrand points out the important role of wholesalers and jobbers and merchant-shippers during Detroit's commercial phase.

The document is drawn from Detroit in History and Commerce *(Detroit, 1891, pp. 11–15).*

REMINISCENCES OF JACOB S. FARRAND

A few weeks before his death the late Jacob S. Farrand gave the following narrative to the publishers of this book. It is printed verbatim, in his own peculiar style. The sketch of the life of Mr. Farrand may be found in connection with the history of the drug firm of Farrand, Williams & Clark:—

"I was brought here by my father with the rest of the family in May, 1825, on the old steamer Superior, the only steamer then on the lakes anywhere. That was in the early days of steam-ship movements. My first business venture was made February 5th, 1830, when I entered the drug store of Rice & Bingham, as clerk, in my fifteenth year, and I have been continuously identified with the drug trade ever since."

"Tell us something of your methods of conducting business in those early days."

"Well—Dr. Justin Rice—I don't know the time he came here, but Edward Bingham came from Hudson, New York, in the year 1828, and the firm was Rice & Bingham from 1828 onward. I entered their store as a clerk in February, 1830. The day I was twenty years old I was made a partner of Mr. Bingham. At that time we did not have as much money in circulation as we have now. We had mighty little money then. We began keeping our accounts from January to January and settled once a year. Orders were given where we desired to pay men, and all that. The payment of men was done in those days very largely with orders."

"Were not payments made very often in furs?"

"Of course there were dealers in furs at that time, but it was not everybody that dealt in furs. James Abbott was the agent of the American Fur Company here and there were others that dealt in furs, but if anyone came in who wanted to sell you furs they were referred to some fur dealer because the common dealer would not know what the furs were worth."

"What was the population of Detroit at that time?"

"When I came here it was about 1,500; in 1830 the National Census made it 2,222, I think. The location of the town was principally down by the river. Our store was on Jefferson avenue, next to the corner where Burnham, Stoepel & Company are now. It was a little building next to the corner. At that time the river bank was up this way further than it is now somewhat; Atwater street was at the water at that time; that was the river front then. The market was right in the middle of Woodward avenue, facing Jefferson—toward the river. The market was an open market where the French people from Canada and from our side came and sold their apples and pears and produce. Beef was sold there also, cut up in stalls. The whipping post was in front of the market."

"Did you ever see a man whipped there?"

"I remember the sheriff whipped a man there, but I didn't see that done. I forget what offence he had committed, but such offenders were whipped for misdemeanors such as we would put them in prison for twenty or forty days now. Business was done in general stores then different from what it is now. All the drug stores sold groceries as well as drugs. The drug store of Chapin & Owen was in the block below us and they sold groceries, and Hinchman & Company, their successors, sell groceries yet. We kept groceries until way along in 1865 or 1866. There was not wholesale business done at that time and no manufacturing to speak of. The Bank of Michigan, where the First National Bank now is, was at that time located at the corner of Jefferson avenue and Randolph street, and that building—the First National Bank Building—was built by the Bank of Michigan, out of wild cat money in 1837 or 1838. That is one of the oldest landmarks left. The first manufacturing was introduced here much later than that. I think Chapin & Owen did the leading business in the drug line at that time. We had very little trade with the Indians in those days. We bought our goods in New York, and brought them up here by canal and lake. We went to New York once a year to buy goods; sometimes twice. Of course it took a good while to go down and buy and get the goods back again by canal. The Erie canal was not opened until late in 1825 or 1826, and goods had to be teamed through from Albany to Buffalo, and it took some three months for them to get goods up here. Collecting bills was quite as disagreeable in those days as it is at present. Levi Cook, a leading dry goods dealer on Jefferson avenue, had a way of doing it peculiar to himself. In the spring when he started off for New York, he left a list of the accounts which had not been paid and told his clerks to sue them in his absence. By the time his new goods got here all was forgotten; they were all good friends again; his old debts had been collected and he saved himself the annoyance of it and retained his trade. That was the way he collected his debts; the boys took all the scolding and it was all over when he got home.

"Property was sold by the acre here in those days and it was very cheap. This house we are now sitting in was away out in the woods." (Mr. Farrand's residence, 457 Woodward avenue.—Ed.) "Why, that lot where Newcomb & Endicott are, when I was in the Common Council I had to look up some titles there and we had quite a time about it. The lot was given to one of the men who lost his house and lot when everything was obliterated and there were no records here, and one of those lots on which the building stands which is now occupied by Newcomb, Endicott & Company, was sold for ten dollars, and those lots where Mr. Sheley's three stores are, between Newcomb, Endicott & Company's and State street, Mr. Sheley bought—sixty feet front, running back to the alley—of a man who went to Wisconsin, and paid him only twelve hundred dollars for it, with the idea that I was to have half of it that I might build a house on it. I was living in Mr. Sheley's house at that time on the lot since occupied by the old church which has just been torn down. But I could not raise the money to make the payment of six hundred dollars until the property was worth more, and so I never took it, for it came to be worth a great deal more than that. But he bought that property for twelve hundred dollars and built his house on it and lived there till he went up to his present residence on Stimpson Place. I guess that transaction was as late as 1844."

"Can you tell when the jobbing business began here—the whole-sale business in any line of trade?"

"Zach Chandler came here in 1833, and when he got up to the amount of fifty thousand dollars a year it was considered a most extraordinary thing and was talked of over the whole town. That was in the wholesale dry goods business which included carpets and such things. Yes, fifty thousand dollars was considered an enormous business and he didn't get his business worked up to that amount before 1850. He was the most successful merchant here during the time he was in business."

"Did he have drummers—how did he sell his goods through-out the country?"

"He did most of the drumming himself. He would get onto his horse and go off to the country selling goods and leave his clerks home to run the business in his absence. Zach Chandler was about the first man who went out from Detroit. He would go to Pontiac and Flint, Ypsilanti, Marshall and Kalamazoo on horseback. They were little places to be sure. There were no railroads in the early days of business here in Detroit and the roads were simply awful. All the business of the city was located on Jefferson avenue, which was the main street. The old American Fur Company was down where H.P. Baldwin 2nd's store is now. Baldwin and Chandler went down there and bought the old Abbott property. James Abbott was agent of the Fur Company, and Post Master here at one time. After Jackson got to be President, Abbott was removed."

"What was the method of getting the mail?"

"Well, when my father came here in the fall of 1824, he took a contract for furnishing Detroit with water. He walked around Lake Erie, came up through Ohio, and went back through Canada. The mail was brought through the Black Swamp in Ohio, on a man's back. My father kept in sight of that man to find his way to Toledo and walked all the way. There were two steamers on the Lake in 1824. 'Walk-in-the-Water' was lost in 1821, down near Buffalo in a storm. Of course the 'Superior' then brought the mail by the same route. She would make two trips a week from here to Buffalo and we got our mail twice a week from the East. In the winter it came around by stage, through Ohio. I don't know how soon it came by stage; I don't recollect that; but, of course, the mails were pretty scarce here and pretty old when they got here. When they came in everybody flocked to the post office, the drivers of the mail coaches tooting their horns and having a great time. The mails from the west came on horseback. I carried the mail myself from Ann Arbor to Detroit in 1827 and 1828."

"Whom do you think has been the most valuable man in the days gone by, to the commerce of Detroit?"

"Now that is a pretty hard question, but I can answer some of it. From 1825 onward Oliver Newberry was the largest owner of vessels for years and years. Old Admiral Newberry, he was called. He had more vessels here than any other man or than any firm, and there were more vessels registered in Detroit than in Buffalo for years—at least it was said so, and I guess it was so. One trip was made from here that I must tell you about. I can't tell you the year it was, but word came down here after the vessels were laid up that the people would starve before spring on the Island of Mackinaw and there was an appeal made to Newberry and his sailors to see if they would not go up there in December to take these people some pork and flour for the winter. Augustus McKinstry and Bob Wagstaff said they would go if they could get the sailors. Newberry said that he would let them have a vessel. Of course, there could not be any insurance. They got a crew and they took the sails out of Newberry's warehouse, tumbled in the freight very fast one day, and went up the river, being towed by a little river steamer into Lake Huron, and they went to Mackinaw between Christmas and New Years, and returned, I think, on the seventh day, having had a successful trip, delivered their freight and laid the vessel up again. I think that was one of the most valiant things ever done. Wagstaff's son is up here on Lake Huron somewheres, in one of the life-saving crews; I saw him last spring just before he started off, I think that was a wonderful trip."

"Then you think Newberry was more important to the commerce of Detroit than any man of recent date?"

"In proportion, I do; he was the founder of the shipping interests of Detroit. He was an uncle of John S. Newberry and a brother of Henry Newberry, who went to Chicago when Chicago began to loom up and who kept a dry goods store here, just where the First National Bank is, and he went to Chicago and made enough money to be able to leave that city two or three million dollars for the Library that we have heard about lately. I can remember when business was entirely confined to Jefferson avenue, and when it was considered a wonderful thing and very presumptuous for a man to move his business from the avenue. Old Robert Smart leased Charles Merrill that corner which is now called the Merrill Block, and then it was built out to Larned street. That was about the first break that was made out Woodward avenue. Then, on the 10th of January, 1854, the old First Presbyterian Church burned down. It was located corner of Larned and Woodward avenue. My store at that time was just north of it. Our store was built in 1852, and Holmes & Company had a double store north of mine. Holmes had the largest dry goods store in this city then. That was in 1852 and about the time when the first business venture was made up Woodward avenue."

Commercial Detroit, 1859

Detroit in 1859 was primarily a commercial city celebrating its imports and exports, its lake commerce, and its country trade. This survey points up the insignificance of manufacturing but also shows that Detroiters were thinking in terms of smelting and refining iron and copper from the Lake Superior district. Changes

in the structure of Detroit's commerce were already under way by 1859 and were reducing the city's tributary area. Even with a diminished hinterland, Detroit conducted a lively trade within the state and the Lake Superior country.
Our selection is drawn from Hunt's Merchants' Magazine *(16 [April 1860]: 422–34).*

Detroit is not, like Chicago, a grain center, or focus for provision trade, like Cincinnati; but it occupies most important position at the head of lake navigation, where the St. Mary's Canal, the Western railroads, and the Canada lines meet the lake tonnage, bringing together a surprising amount of business.

It is almost unnecessary to state that Detroit is located on the right bank of the Detroit River, seven miles below Lake St. Clair, and eighteen miles above the mouth of the river, where it empties into Lake Erie. . . .

The streets are wide and well paved, and the buildings are good, though not altogether of the most modern style. The city is well lighted with gas, and abundantly supplied with pure water. Probably the best line of docks on the whole chain of lakes is found here. Our warehouses also, are immense and conveniently arranged for a very extensive shipping business. Five distinct lines of railroads center here, and these, taken with our position with regard to the lakes, highly favor us for business. The population of the city, at different periods during the last half century, is thus shown:

1820	1,442	1853	34,406
1830	2,222	1854	40,373
1834	4,973	1855	51,000
1837	7,763	1856	59,000
1840	9,102	1857	66,000
1845	10,948	1858	70,000
1850	21,057	1859	75,000

We derive many interesting statistics of the city from the report of the Secretary of the Board of Water Commissioners, a document prepared with much care and published last July. From this we find the total number of families in the city, (not including those boarding at hotels and private boarding houses,) to be 8,464.

The value of taxable property at the time the canvass was made was $15,766,591, and the total real and personal, taxable and exempt, is put at $28,141,591. In 1856 the valuation was $13,757,583; in 1858, $10,741,657.

According to the same report, the increase in the number of buildings in this city in 1859 over the number in 1858 was 342, besides which, there were at the time the report was made, 228 buildings in process of construction. Since then numerous others have been commenced to our certain knowledge, indicating the healthy and vigorous growth of our city.

Our shipping interests rank among the most important on the whole chain of lakes, as does our trade with the Lake Superior country, in which we are more extensively engaged than any other lake port, and our fish trade is by no means unimportant. We conclude this sketch of our trade by presenting tables showing the imports and exports for the year:—

Total Imports and Exports by Rail and Lake for the Year 1859

	Imports	Exports
Alcohol, bbls	2,216	1,562
Apples, bbls	8,449	4,567
Ashes, casks	3,886	4,631
Beans, bush	7,163	380
Bacon, (bulk) lbs	834,088	
Bacon, boxes	200	403
Barley, bush	55,698	
Bark, cords	2,783	
Beef, bbls	20,886	21,709
Beeswax, lbs	3,859	13,088
Broom corn, bales	2,781	2,799
Buckwheat, bush	197	170
Butter, lbs	1,116,306	502,989
Cattle, No	23,946	19,793
Coffee, bags	8,372	
Coal, tons	22,004	1,811
Copper, bbls	3,669	3,389
Copper, tons	2,731	2,492
Cranberries, bbls	291	387
Dried fruit, pkgs	1,111	230

	Imports	Exports
Dressed hogs, No	21,945	17,382
Eggs, bbls	2,983	733
Fish, bbls	14,637	22,012
Flour, bbls	602,140	478,918
Furs, pkgs	1,210	1,165
Glass, bxs	22,575	
Hams & shoulder, bbls	2,384	1,735
Hams & shoulder, tos	146	1,565
Highwines, bbls	5,746	534
Hides, No	114,167	84,766
Hops, bales	73	89
Hogs, No	97,766	84,710
Hay, tons	233	98
Iron, tons	1,602	1,075
Iron, bars	53,862	1,318
Iron, bdls	16,565	
Iron (pig & scrap) ts	1,170	612
Iron ore, tons	2,137	
Lard, tos	551	2,813
Lard, bbls	8,402	3,068
Leather, rolls	2,337	3,173
Lath, M	320	6,047
Lumber, M	3,073	34,524
Lime, bbls	2,852	235
Malt, sacks	5,813	
Meal	9,151	3,115
Millstuffs	80,859	3,475
Maple sugar, lbs	44,852	7,589
Nails, kegs	41,293	375
Oats, bush	73,364	24,816
Oil, bbls	317	213
Paper, bbls	9,737	
Pelts	3,504	1,450
Peas, bush	602	110
Plaster, tons	5,210	28
Potatoes, bags	18,709	36,327
Pork, bbls	30,841	8,529
Posts, No	3,482	7,797

	Imports	Exports
Rags, bales	13,638	2,798
Railroad iron, bars	8,415	2,467
Rye, bush	6,955	
Salt, bbls	52,203	9,218
Salt, (bulk), tons	83	
Seed, bags	13,494	8,678
Shingles, M	5,905	17,118
Sheep, No	6,337	8,161
Skins, bdls	3,008	2,867
Stone, cords	3,524	755
Staves, M	1,596	4,182
Sugar, hhds	9,846	
Sugar, bbls	8,795	
Tallow, bbls	8,249	6,849
Tobacco, hhds	1,550	
Tobacco, other pkgs	2,340	
Tea, half chests	10,346	
Water lime, bbls	9,740	30
Wheat, bush	723,404	400,457
Whisky, bbls	869	65
Wool, lbs	3,362,630	3,758,104
Wool, cords	9,046	

With regard to the general commerce of the lakes, we hold an important position. Every vessel from the upper to the lower lakes, or *vice versa,* must of necessity pass our very doors. A vessel leaving Buffalo for Chicago, or from Chicago or Milwaukee for Buffalo or Oswego, after being lost sight of for several days, first reports her safety and progress at Detroit, and this being the first and only place of importance at which such vessel can touch without going out of her course, it is rendered the most desirable point on the whole chain of lakes for refitting and provisioning. The number of vessels that have thus passed Detroit during the season just closed, is thus reported by Captain J.W. Hall, who has, with commendable public spirit, kept a complete register of all such passages:—

Number of Vessels Passing Detroit, 1859

	No. times		No. times
Steamers passed up	194	Steamers passed down	195
Propellers "	492	Propellers "	503
Barks "	273	Barks "	284
Brigs "	295	Brigs "	314
Schooners "	1,811	Schooners "	1,825
Total number up	3,065	Total number down	3,121

Greatest number passed up in one day, 85; greatest number down, 73.

The passages through the Welland Canal for the season, show a falling off as compared with last year. The following are the figures:—

1859	2,589	1858	3,726

Our citizens are, very naturally, largely interested in the shipping trade, owning, it is stated, nearly nineteen-twentieths of the entire tonnage of the district. The figures for the whole have been kindly furnished by the Deputy Collector of this port. It will be seen that there is a steady increase:—

Number and Tonnage of Vessels Owned in the District of Detroit, Dec. 31, 1859

	Number	Tons	95th
Steamers	73	29,175	02
Propellers	32	6,090	81
Barks	4	1,337	08
Brigs	7	1,877	75
Schooner	131	19,671	56
Scows, and all others	136	4,332	68
Total	383	62,485	05
In 1857	301	52,991	50
Increase in two years	82	9,493	50

The largest vessel in the district is the steamer Western World, 2,002 tons. There are, besides her, nine others measuring over

1,000 tons each, twenty-one measuring over 400 tons, fifty-eight measuring over 200 tons, seventy measuring over 100 tons, one hundred and sixty-three measuring over 20 tons, and sixty-one measuring under 20 tons.

It is stated that there are at present upwards of one thousand six hundred vessels navigating the whole northwestern lakes, the aggregate burden of which is near half a million tons. . . .

As a wool-growing State Michigan ranks among the first in the Union. Heretofore Ohio has taken the palm among her sister States of the West for the superior quality of the wool produced, but the clip of 1859 has shown Michigan to be fully her equal in this respect. As a financial resource our wool crop is of immense importance. The clip of 1859 is estimated to equal at least 4,000,000 pounds, which, at 42½ cents, the average price realized for it, would produce the round sum of $1,700,000 or nearly a *million and three-quarter dollars.*

In 1850 the wool product is shown by the United States census, to have been 2,043,283 pounds; assuming our estimate of this year's clip to be correct, the amount raised, it will be seen, has doubled in ten years.

The principal buyers of our wool are Eastern manufacturers and speculators. These purchase through brokers in Detroit, and these again through agents in every town and village in the State. Thus the greater part of our wool crop passes through this city on its way east. The whole does not, however, Toledo and Monroe being shipping points for large quantities. The receipts and shipments at this port have been as follows:—

Receipts and Shipments of Wool for a Series of Years

	Receipts	Shipments
1854		2,367,600
1855		3,362,600
1856		
1857	2,679,633	3,661,790
1858	2,035,743	2,891,400
1859	3,362,639	3,758,104

. . . The northern half of the lower peninsula of Michigan, it is well-known, is one immense forest of valuable timber, the manufacturing of which into lumber affords employment to thousands of laborers, and to millions of capital. Nearly every stream that empties into the great lakes that form our boundaries, first performs its duty as the motive power to a greater or less number of saw mills, or as the great highway on which huge rafts of timber seek to escape from the dark and dreary solitude of their native forests to the daylight of civilization and utility.

We design here to speak more particularly of our own connection as a city with these interests. With the lumber trade of the western shore we have nothing to do, Chicago and Milwaukee absorb the whole; Saginaw and other manufacturing points on the eastern shores make Albany their market direct; while the territory lying along the shore of Lake Huron and the St. Clair River and lake may justly be considered as coming under our influence and control. To be sure, all the lumber that is made in this tract is not landed on our docks, but our capitalists are largely interested in the mills that manufacture it. Detroit is the mart at which their supplies are obtained, and in many instances the point at which their business is transacted, and from this region are obtained all the logs used by the eight immense manufacturing establishments in actual operation within our city limits. . . .

The shipments by lake from this port for the season have been as follows:—

Shipments of Lumber for 1859

	Lumber, feet.	Lath, M.	Shingles
March	757,000	325,000	1,342,000
April	3,145,000	101,000	2,601,000
May	6,445,000	1,924,000	3,790,000
June	5,709,000	1,250,000	1,759,000
July	5,019,000	569,000	864,000
August	4,896,000	513,000	2,225,000
September	2,577,000	425,000	1,064,000
October	3,418,000	472,000	2,936,000
November	2,070,000	258,000	340,000
December	458,000		107,000
Total	34,494,000	5,701,000	17,118,000
Last Year	76,537,000	13,491,000	36,647,000

Of the stock on hand a year ago, we have no account, though it was probably larger than the present stock. Hence, the difference between the shipments and the amount manufactured and received will show something less than the amount used here and shipped into the country. The figures, so far as we have them, stand thus:—

Receipts	feet	3,066,000
Manufactured		42,000,000
Total		45,066,000
Deduct shipments		34,494,000
Consumed and on hand		10,572,000

The season opened last spring with a firm market, it being well known that the supply of logs was short, and generally believed that with the harvesting of a bountiful wheat crop, there would spring up an active demand for lumber. At this time the demand greatly exceeded the supply. Dealers were anxious to contract ahead to almost an unlimited extent, and on every hand manufacturers had decidedly the advantage.

The natural consequence was, summer logging was extensively resorted to; mills ran night and day; the receipts at all the principal markets began largely to increase, and by the 1st July a reaction had set in, cargoes then went a-begging; prices declined, and soon all the bright prospects of the early spring had completely vanished. Since then the market has been very quiet.

The wholesale dry goods trade of this city is principally in the hands of three large establishments, each of which has abundant means, and is doing an extensive business. A fourth we learn is soon about to go into operation. There are also a few of our largest retail houses that do an extensive jobbing business in connection with their city trade. The Custom-house books show that twenty-five of our city dealers are importers, to a greater or less extent, of foreign goods.

The New York market, during the season of navigation, is sought for teas, coffees, spices, refined sugars, &c., and a part of the stock of sugars and molasses, on account of the low rates of freight. It is accessible also at all seasons by railroad, by two competing lines. There is also direct conveyance between this city and Pittsburg, Cincinnati, Louisville, and St. Louis, giving the advantage of those markets, and also placing us in direct communication with New Orleans. The bulk of raw sugars and molasses have been bought at Cincinnati and Louisville, but some of our grocerymen have purchased a portion of their supplies directly at New Orleans. The latter market, however, can only be resorted to advantageously at certain seasons after a new crop is in, when sugars are freely offered on the levee, or on large plantations. A residence of some months in the winter, and a thorough acquaintance with the market, together with large purchases, are necessary, to make a direct trade with that city profitable. Considerable cash capital, or facilities for raising money, are also necessary for a direct trade with New Orleans, as sugars are sold only for cash or short drafts on New York.

The stock of groceries kept in Detroit is generally quite large in proportion to the sales. Prices have averaged as low here for the past seven years, especially for sugars, as in New York. Competition is always quite active here, and the leading merchants of Michigan rely much upon this market for their supplies of groceries. When country dealers can purchase their stock of groceries here, they frequently buy also their entire stocks of dry goods, hardware, &c.

The extent of country which furnishes customers to this market, is limited to the State of Michigan and the western shores of Canada.

The stability of grocery houses in Detroit is worthy of remark; there have been but few changes during the last eight or ten years, except by adding new members to firms, or occasionally by the establishment of a new house. There are now engaged in the business six firms that deal in dry groceries, seven that include liquors with groceries, and five that trade in groceries and drugs.

The following table of importations gives some idea of the present extent of the trade:—

Receipts of Groceries for the Year 1859.

Sugar from New York.		Sugar from New Orleans.		Coffee.	Tea.
Hhds.	Bbls.	Hhds.	Bbls.	Bags.	Hf. chests
1,538	8,308	4,051	487	8,372	10,346

. . . The quantity of teas imported into the market has been very large. There are several good judges of teas in the grocery trade, who make it a leading article.

The stock of coffee kept in this market is always large, and is always sold at a nominal profit. By reference to New York price lists, it will be seen that the difference in prices barely covers transportation and waste.

The usual credit of four months was uniformly given in Detroit until within the last four or five years, since which, sugars, molasses, and such goods as are bought for cash, have been sold only for cash, or on 30 or 60 days time—other articles of groceries are now sold on 90 days or four months time. Credits have always been more liberal here than in most other Western cities, and goods are sold in open account. Notes are not usually required as in many other cities. It would, however, be found advantageous to merchants if the system of taking negotiable notes could be adopted, as it would be equivalent to an increase of capital.

There is no part of the American continent, and we might almost say of the world, where iron ore is found in as large quantities, and of as superior a quality, as in the State of Michigan. In the neighborhood of Marquette, on the upper peninsula, there exist immense beds of ore, lying entirely above the surface of the ground, and yielding from 65 to 70 percent of pure iron. The ease with which these beds are worked, the entire absence of all the risk incident to other mining enterprises, the extraordinary richness of the ore, and the superior quality of the iron produced, have all, since their discovery, strongly recommended them to the notice of capitalists, and to-day, few of our natural resources are being more rapidly developed, or with more satisfactory results. The remarkable strength and tenacity of this iron have caused it to be extensively used in connection with the poorest ores of Ohio and Pennsylvania, to improve the quality of the iron produced from them. The furnaces of the Mahoning Valley, in particular, use enormous quantities, without which they would be unable to manufacture a metal of quality sufficiently good to enter into competition with the product of other works. For these purposes thousands of tons are now annually shipped to Erie and Cleveland. At Wyandotte, Detroit, and Marquette, are in operation extensive works for smelting and blooming iron, at which, of course, the unmixed Lake Superior ore is used, and an iron is produced believed to be inferior to none. A railroad has been constructed from the mines to the lake shore at Marquette, over which, within the few months that it has been in operation, over eighty thousand tons of ore have been transported. At that port there has scarcely been a time during the past season of navigation when there have not been from ten to twenty vessels lying at the docks either loading or awaiting their turn to do so. These facts shadow forth the future importance of this iron trade.

The existence of copper on the shores of Lake Superior in large quantities was known at an early day; but it was not till 1844, that any systematic explorations were made, with a view to mining. The Indian titles had been extinguished two years previously—in 1842. Mining regularly began in 1845, in which year the Pittsburg and Boston Company commenced operations at the Cliff. The Minnesota mine was first worked in 1848. In 1855, the opening of the canal gave an impetus to mining operations which since have been steadily progressing. The number of Lake Superior copper mining companies now in existence exceed one hundred and twenty. The mining region is divided into three districts, known respectively as the Ontonagon District, the Portage Lake District, and the Keweenaw Point District. The shipments from these for a series of years, as far as we can ascertain, have been as follows, the amounts being given in tons:— [1]

District.	1853	1854	1855	1856	1857	1858	1859
Ontonagon			1,984	2,767	3,190	2,676	2,664
Portage Lake			315	462	704	1,163	1,661
Keweenaw			2,245	2,128	2,200	2,186	
Total	2,535	3,500	4,544	5,357	6,094	6,025	

. . . There are at present nine establishments for the smelting of copper on the continent, eight of which are in the United States— the ninth in Canada as above noted. The locations are as follows: —Detroit, Michigan; Cleveland, Ohio; Pittsburg, Pennsylvania;

1. The copper shipments by individual districts were not available for 1853 and 1854. Aggregate figures are from the entire Michigan Copper Range.—ED.

Baltimore, Maryland; Bergen, New York; East Boston, Massachusetts; New Haven, Connecticut.

At Baltimore there are two establishments, which makes the eight. These Baltimore works are employed exclusively on South American copper. The Detroit works, of all, are the most extensive.

Industrial Detroit: Fifty Years of Industrial Progress

William Stocking, 1840–1930, a well-known newspaperman and commercial writer, chronicles the main outlines of industrial growth in Detroit for this period.

The selection is drawn from Michigan History Magazine *(10 [October 1926]: 609–16), and is reprinted by permission of the Michigan Department of State.*

April 29, 1874, the Detroit *Post,* of which, by the way, the writer of this article was then managing editor, published a supplement of 36 long columns descriptive of the manufacturing industries of the city. Its summing up gave the following as the value of the product in some of the leading classes; manufactures of iron and other metals not otherwise classified, $11,128,500, tobacco and cigars, $4,000,000, flour and feed mills, $1,830,000, breweries and malt houses, $1,116,000, lasts and shoes, $986,000, furniture, $725,000, stoves, $625,000, boiler shops, $585,000.

The changes in the character of Detroit's industries since then are the most interesting feature of its marvelous growth. There has been the rapid rise and subsequent decadence of some classes, astonishing supremacy of others and fluctuations of still others. In 1874 the saw mill industry of Wayne County was already on the decline. The river front opposite and below the city had been the site of numerous mills for sawing pine lumber and had laid the foundations for a number of comfortable fortunes. The Moffat Block and the Penobscot Building are permanent contributions to the city from the fortunes thus made. In 1874 there were 45 saw mills on the river or in the interior of the county operated by steam and five by water. Some of them were small. The total cut of lumber was 74,000,000 feet, valued at $1,443,650. This class of mills has totally disappeared from the river front, but planing mills and sash, door and blind factories have much more than taken their place.

The first blast furnace in the country west of Pittsburgh was set up in Hamtramck by Dr. George B. Russel in 1856. As "The Hamtramck Iron Works," it was one of the most conspicuous landmarks of East Detroit till 1905. About the same time the Eureka Iron & Steel Works and the Wyandotte Rolling Mills were established by Capt. E. B. Ward in Wyandotte, west of the city. The first steel rails rolled in this country and the first Bessemer steel made in the country came from these plants. In 1874 they were the largest single industry operated by Detroit capital and there were predictions that this would become one of the great iron and steel centers of the country. But after Captain Ward's death the Rolling Mills fell upon evil times, the stockholders of the iron works disagreed, part of them took their capital to Chicago and the Wyandotte works were finally abandoned. For many years the fleets of huge iron ore carriers steamed in majestic procession past the very doors of Detroit but left hardly a ton of their cargoes on her docks. The twin blast furnaces on Zug Island and the immense works begun and contemplated by Henry Ford further up the Rouge have revived the hope that this district will yet attain prominence in this respect.

Among the large industries in Detroit in 1874 was that of car building. This afterwards became the largest single line of manufacture in the city. It started in 1853 when George B. Russel and others secured premises on the Gratiot Road and built cars for the Detroit and Pontiac Railroad. In 1874 the existing plants were those owned by the Pullman Car Company in the block bounded by Crogham, St. Aubin and Macomb Streets and the D. & M. Railway, the Detroit Car Company's extensive works on Adair St., the Michigan Car Company at Grand Trunk Junction, the Grand Trunk shops on the river front and the Michigan Central Car

Shops. To these were subsequently added the Peninsular Car Works, the building of logging cars by the Russel Wheel and Foundry Co., car wheel and other subsidiary corporations, and building and repair work by the Detroit United Railway. This industry reached its maximum in 1907 when it employed about 7,000 men and had a product valued at $28,000,000. Since then the decline has been rapid. Only one of the large plants remains in commission, the Peninsular. In the distribution of work by the American Car and Foundry Co., of which this is one of the constituent parts, it is devoted mainly to general foundry work and to specialties other than car building. In the course of events the Grand Trunk work was moved to Port Huron or Battle Creek, the Pullman Car Works to the neighborhood of Chicago and part of the Michigan Central works to Jackson, while the Michigan Car Works and their subsidiaries were abandoned. Aside from a moderate amount of work done by the two electric railway systems, this once great industry is but little more than a memory.

Aside from car building and the older blast furnaces and iron works, a few other industries that were prominent 50 years ago have declined or passed away. The Waterbury and Detroit Copper Co., was then doing a very prosperous business in smelting Lake Superior ores at the "Copper Dock" in Springwells. The business soon afterwards moved to Lake Linden near the source of the ore supply. The Detroit Locomotive Works, then one of the largest foundry and machine shop establishments in the West, gradually wound up the business, though part of its capital went into what are now the Buhl Malleable Works. The Detroit Safe Co. wound up its business and the Diamond Match Co. abandoned this field. The once prominent furniture business has within the past ten years very rapidly declined. The malt and brewery business was large and prosperous from 1874 till 1918, but is now, according to a fiction of law, a thing of the past.

A few of the industries that were prominent in 1874 have added to Detroit's fame and prosperity continuously since that time. The first brass foundry in the city was established by Solomon Davie in 1833. In 1855 the business was purchased by Andew Harvey and is still in existence at the same location on Woodbridge St., the present title of the firm being A. Harvey's Sons. The growth of this industry has been continuous and it received a great impetus when the automobile came into the field, requiring a number of brass parts. Tubal Cain, the ancient "instructor of every artifice in brass," has now many thousand worthy followers manipulating this oldest of composite metals. There are now in the city two large brass and copper rolling mills and over 50 companies that make or manipulate the metal with a product valued at over $50,000,000. Detroit is now the second city in the country in this industry.

Stove making in Detroit dates back to 1861 when Jeremiah and James Dwyer, brothers, with Edwin S. Barbour and others incorporated the Detroit Stove Works. In 1871 the Michigan Stove Company was organized with Charles Ducharme as President, Jeremiah Dwyer, vice president and general manager, and George H. Barbour, Secretary. The Peninsular Stove Company was incorporated in 1881 and three or four smaller companies followed later. For over half a century this has been one of the most stable and prosperous of Detroit's industries. The works have rarely closed down nor often skipped a dividend. For 40 years Detroit companies in this line have led those of every other city in the country in the number of styles made, the territory covered by their trade, and the volume of their business. An interesting fact in this connection is the extent to which the families of the original founders have retained their connection with the business. The names of Dwyer, Barbour and Ducharme frequently occur in the lists of officers of the three large companies.

There are a number of other lines of manufacture in which a single small establishment was functioning in 1874 but which loom large in the present business of Detroit. Berry Bros. had a small establishment on Leib St. It has grown in the same location until now it is the largest varnish factory in the country. The Detroit Dry Dock Co., represented a business which was started at the foot of Orleans street in the '50's. It has operated continuously at the same location with additional yards on other sites. It has built almost every type of vessel including the largest and finest passenger sidewheeler that ever floated on any waters. In 1874 Samuel F. Hodge was running a business which has since developed into the Great Lakes Engineering Works, builders of many of the largest freighters on the Lakes. For 20 years past Detroit has divided with the Cleveland district the major part of vessel construction on the Lakes.

Race Riot of 1863

The race riot of 1863 was a manifestation of increasing ethnic and racial heterogeneity in nineteenth-century Detroit, and it also exhibited the power of an external event such as the national epidemic of riots to afflict a city. It reflected as well the general frustration with the war, racism, and the fears and concerns over job security by the foreign-born. Yet the rational basis for the latter seemed very thin indeed. Blacks comprised only 3 percent of the city's population in 1860 and were not a major source of competition for casual, domestic, or industrial work. The demand for skilled and unskilled labor was largely met by newcomer Irish and Germans who viewed blacks unfavorably and found in the Faulkner affair an opportunity to vent their insecurities.

This was a classic urban riot with interracial violence pitting white aggressors against black victims. The riot was precipitated by a guilty verdict against a Negro, Thomas Faulkner, who was accused of molesting and raping two girls, one white, one black. An enraged mob was thwarted in its attempt to lynch Faulkner and went on a wild rampage of burning, looting, and abusing and even killing blacks. Ironically, Faulkner may not have been a Negro but was possibly of Spanish-Indian extraction. He was later cleared of the charges against him and restored to freedom. The selections are drawn from A Thrilling Narrative from the Lips of the Sufferers of the Late Detroit Riot, March 6, 1863 *(reprint ed., Hattiesburg, Miss., 1964).*

THE CAUSE OF THE RIOT.

Thomas Faulkner, charged of committing the outrages upon Ellen Hover, a colored girl and also a white girl, was to all intents a white man. This is beyond doubt, for he was a regular voter, and the journals of the city that understood his politics state that he voted the Democratic ticket. And an old veteran of over one hundred years of age declares, that in conversing with F. he said: "If he thought he had one drop of colored blood in his veins, if he could, he would let it out." And this was the man that caused the mob on colored men!

On the 6th of March an organized mob made their way from the jail down Beaubien street. They were yelling like demons, and crying "kill all the d—d niggers." In the cooper shop, just below Lafayette street, were five men working, namely: ROBERT BEN-NETTE, JOSHUA BOYD, SOLOMON HOUSTON, LEWIS HOUSTON, MARCUS DALE. These men were busy at work in the shop until the mob made an attack upon the shop. The windows were soon broken and the doors forced open. The men in the cooper shop were determined to resist any that might attempt to come in. The mob discovered this, and did not attempt to come in, but stood off and threw stones and bricks into the windows, a perfect shower. There happened to be one old shot gun in the shop, a couple of discharges from which drove the mob back from the shop. The dwelling house was attached to the shop, in which were three women and four children, namely: MRS. REYNOLDS, MRS. BONN and one child, MRS. DALE and three children.

Some ten minutes after the mob had fallen back from the shop, they made a rush upon the house in which were the women and children. The men in the shop seeing this, rushed out of the shop into the house to protect the women and children. The windows of the houses were soon all broken in; stones and bricks came into the house like hail. The women and children were dodging from one room to another to escape the stones. The men frequently stood before the women and children to shield them from the stones. Very soon after the men went from the shop into the house, the shop was set on fire by the mob. There were plenty of shavings in the shop, which facilitated the burning. The flames soon reached the house in which were the women and children. The mob by this time had completely surrounded the building. Mrs. Reynolds attempted to go out at the back door but could not get out, for hundreds of stones were flying at that part of the building. Mr. Dale, in shielding his wife, got a blow in the face with a stone, which his wife might have gotten had he not stood before her. Some person outside was heard to say "the women will be protected—no protection for the men." Hearing this, Mr. Dale told the women to go out at the front door. Mrs. Dale seeing the blood running from her husband's face, said my dear you are bleeding—you will be killed. Said he to her, go out with your children; they say there is protection for the women, but none for the men. I will look out for myself. Mrs. Bonn started for the door, with her child in her arms, followed by Mrs. Dale, with one child in her arms and two children hanging to her. Mrs. Reynolds next followed. When the women approached the door, some fiend in human shape drew back a large club to strike them, but some spectators, having within them a spark of humanity, rushed to the women and rescued them—drawn probably by the screams of Mrs. Bonn. After the women had got out, the men, one by one, made their way out—were knocked down with stones when they came out, and beaten. Father Clark happened to be in the house, was beaten after he came out. The last one who came out was Mr. Dale. When he came out into the back yard the heat was so intense that he came near being overcome by it—he had his face badly burned. When he came out of the door some twenty dirty-looking Irishmen rushed at him with clubs, crying "kill the nager." But being thoughtful enough to come out with something in his hands, and having a good deal of physical strength he made them get back, and he got out without receiving further injuries. Three families living in the building near the cooper shop, lost all they had; namely, MR. REYNOLDS, MR. DALE and MR. BONN.

The mob, not satisfied with burning the cooper shop, and building adjacent, proceeded up Fort and Lafayette streets, robbing and burning some fifteen houses belonging to colored people.

Of the men who were in the cooper shop one has died from wounds received; namely, JOSHUA BOYD.

M. DALE

The mob, in its first appearance to me, was a parcel of fellows runing up Lafayette street after two or three colored men.

They then returned back and in a short time I saw a tremendous crowd coming up Croghan street on drays, wagons, and foot, with kegs of beer on their wagons, and rushed for the prison. Here they crowded thick and heavy. After this, while I was standing on the corner, with half a dozen other gentlemen, a rifle ball came whistling over our heads. After which we heard several shots, but only one ball passing us. In a short time after this there came one fellow down saying, "I am shot in the thigh." And another came with his finger partly shot off. A few minutes after that another ruffian came down, saying: "If we are got to be killed up for niggers then we will kill every nigger in this town." A very little while after this we could hear them speaking up near the jail, and appeared to be drinking, but I was unable to hear what they said. This done, they gave a most fiendish yell and started down Beaubien street. On reaching Croghan street, a couple of houses west on Beaubien street, they commenced throwing, and before they reached my residence clubs, brick, and missiles of every description flew like hail. Myself and several others were standing on the side-walk, but were compelled to hasten in and close our doors, while the mob passed my house with their clubs and bricks flying into my windows and doors, sweeping out light and sash!

They then approached my door in large numbers, where I stood with my gun, and another friend with an axe, but on seeing us, they fell back. They approached four times determined to enter my door, but I raised my gun at each time and they fell back. In the mean time part of the mob passed on down Beaubien street. After the principal part had passed, I rushed up my stairs looking to see what they were doing, and heard the shattering of windows and slashing of boards. In a few moments I saw them at Whitney Reynolds, a few doors below Lafayette street. Mr. R. is a cooper; had his shop and residence on the same lot, and was the largest colored coopering establishment in the city—employing a number of hands regular.

I could see from the windows men striking with axe, spade, clubs, &c, just as you could see men thrashing wheat. A sight the most revolting, to see innocent men, women and children, all without respect to age or sex, being pounded in the most brutal manner.

Sickened with the sight, I sat down in deep solicitude in relation to what the night would bring forth; for to human appearance it seemed as if Satan was loose, and his children were free to do whatever he might direct without fear of the city authority.

THOMAS BUCKNER.

.   .   .   .   .

LEWIS PEARCE—I was at the cooper shop and when the mob attacked us, and while we stayed in there the mob did not dare to come in, but commenced with great fury on the dwelling-house. We then went there to defend the women and children. As soon as we left the shop they set it on fire.

All the while they were throwing stones and other missiles. I was knocked down by a stone in the yard while the house was burning, and when I came to myself enough to know anything, I found the flames so intense that I would soon be burned to death, unless I had some shelter; so I drew a wheelbarrow over me, that fortunately was just there. I was unable to walk, and there I lay till a couple of policemen came to me and dragged me out, and took me outside of the lot, and turned me loose. I then staggered over to Mrs. Jones', being weak from the blows and loss of blood. I had not been there but a few moments before they came and said to me: "Get out of there." It was, as I suppose, the same two men who took me out from under the wheelbarrow. I found it impossible to get away; so I got out into the privy to conceal myself, and soon a couple of fellows—one a man in soldier's clothes, and the other a man who sold in the market, named Dollar—came to me and brought me out on St. Antoine street, beating me all the way along, the mob behind me throwing at me, and some pelting me with stones and sticks till they got me to Croghan street; and there they fell on me, and with kicks and clubs, beat me till they thought life was extinct, and then went off and left me for dead! My head was bruised so that for weeks my head and ears run with corruption. My knee cap was broke right in two by a stroke from some weapon. My body was so bruised that for two days I vomited nothing but pure blood; but, through the mercy of the Lord, I am now getting better, but never shall overcome the effects of the injuries I have received.

[From the Detroit Advertiser and Tribune]

A Sermon for the Times—The Victims of the Late Riot

Rev. S. S. Hunting, of the Lafayette Street Unitarian Church preached a sermon on Sunday evening, which was eminently appropriate to the times. We have not room to give more than an extract or two, embracing some statistics, relating more particularly to the unfortunate victims of the late riot. Mr. Hunting had taken the pains to procure a number of interesting facts concerning the occupation and character of the sufferers, and has embodied them in a definite statement, which we think may be regarded as authentic. We copy as follows:

Mr. Charles Fletcher had been sawing wood for a widow on Miami avenue, though a carpenter by trade. His house was burned on Lafayette street. Returning home, and not understanding the nature of the excitement, he was immediately driven from his house, was chased out the back alley as by a herd of tigers—by persons carrying poles and every kind of weapon which could be seized. He sought protection in a tannery, was driven into a vat, into water up to his waist and then was protected by the occupant, and went up stairs. Two of the blood-thirsty mob found an entrance and attacked him there, when he escaped down the stairs and fell directly into the midst of a dozen or more brutal persons, who knocked him down and left him senseless. After a while he was taken away by two white men.

This industrious, inoffensive citizen was thus beset as if he were a wolf, and brutally beaten. He has a wife and one child.

Mr. Lewis Houston was a laborer in the cooper shop, and when it was attacked he made his escape through the back alley behind the fence; but was discovered when he came out upon St. Antoine street, and was immediately beset, knocked down, and terribly beaten.

He arose, was helped along the sidewalk by two white men, and the mob seeing it, rushed up and some one gave him a blow on his head that he fell to the ground. Almost senseless, he was helped to the jail, and was there turned over to Dr. Stewart, (a colored physician,) who dressed his wounds. His wife was sent for, and finally succeeded in getting him home, though constantly beset by the boys, crying out, "kill the d—d nigger." His recovery seems to be doubtful. He is injured for life. He has a wife and family.

Mr. Boyd, who has died, escaped from slavery in Western Virginia since the war began. He was a industrious man, earning his daily bread, and saving money to liberate his family.

Mr. Robert H. Bennett was at the cooper's shop, and barely escaped alive. He rushed through the crowd, was shot at, was stoned and clubbed, struck on his legs, fell down five times from the effect of the blows upon him, and at length reached the Biddle House, and was heartlessly ordered not to enter by the Clerk, which order he summarily disobeyed, and forced his way in, bleeding as if he had been butchered, and entered the dining-room, where he met the proprietor of the house, who nobly protected him.

Suburban Workers:
The Springwells Brickyards,
1883

This selection on the workers of Detroit's suburban Springwells was the first report of the Michigan commissioner of labor. Patterned after its Massachusetts counterpart, the Michigan bureau sought to collect and assemble systematic information related to the "laboring class." The gubernatorial initiative that created the bureau envisioned that the commissioner of labor might become a spokesman for the inarticulate or, as the report put it, "those seldom found in our halls of legislation to speak for themselves." The bureau provided much information that in future years laid the basis for reform laws.

This look at the laboring class at Springwells in 1883 is the first penetrating ray of official daylight into the gray lives of marginal and foreign-born workers in the Detroit metropolitan area.

The document is drawn from the First Annual Report of the

Bureau of Labor and Industrial Statistics *(Lansing, 1884, pp. 179–81)*.

Our examination into the conditions of the laboring classes has necessarily been confined to a few localities, and in these we have not deemed it best to report individual cases, further than to give the information contained in our tabulations. . . .

Take for example the brickyard laborers at Springwells in Wayne county.

These brickyards are twelve or fourteen in number, and situated from three to four miles from the city hall.

As nearly as we can ascertain, they employ from 200 to 300 men during the season, which commences in April and terminates about the middle of October.

The men employed are almost entirely of the foreign element, consisting of Poles, Prussians, and Germans, from the various States of the German Empire.

They are mainly healthy men, in the prime of life, ranging in age from 19 to 40, of fine physique, and giving little evidence of the laborious character of their employment and the coarseness of their domestic life.

In working these brick-fields, the men are, with one exception, mainly employed under what is technically known as the "stent system," or piece work.

Under this system they commence work at 4 o'clock in the morning, working until about 9:30, when a recess is taken until about 12, resuming work till 4 P. M., making about nine hours. During this time each man turns out, with the aid of machinery, about four yards, or 32,000 bricks—two yards in the morning, and two in the afternoon. Women and children, where such are employed, are now set to work *"hacking,"* or piling the bricks in rows, to the height of about five feet, leaving spaces between for the circulation of the air. The women are employed from three to six hours a day, according to the output of the men, and earn from 40 to 60 cents a day.

Some of the children employed are of tender age, in some cases not over 7, usually helping the mother, and working the same number of hours; but children of 10 and upwards are frequently employed from sunrise to sundown. In the making of brick, no particular mechanical skill is required, quickness and hard work being the most essential requisites.

The men are classified as molders, pit-shovelers, burners, hackers, wheelers, loaders, &c. Here, as in everything else, machinery has superseded the old method. In the yard of Greusel & Co. the piece work system does not prevail, all the men being employed at day wages. Under the piece work or *"stent system,"* the average wages are from $40 to $50 a month, for days of nine hours, but the work is very laborious. In working by the day, they start at 5 o'clock in the morning, stop one-half hour for breakfast and about an hour for dinner, quitting at from 6 to 7 in the evening, thus making 11 or 12 hours a day. Some few are employed as yardmen, whose business it is to load wagons, plaster kilns, watch and tend fires, and who work from 4 A. M. to 8 P. M., Sunday and Saturday alike. The brickyards running but six months in the year, these men have to seek employment elsewhere in winter. Some go to the car shops, some on the railroad, but they are mostly re-employed by the brick-bosses at a reduced rate of pay, and an increased number of hours. When re-employed they are either sent to the stables as teamsters, or into the woods to chop, by the cord, the next year's supply of firewood for the kilns. As teamsters they receive $1.00 per day, commencing work at 3:30 A. M., making three loads to the city, and returning to the stables about 8 at night.

As nearly as we could ascertain, this rule prevails in all yards except that of Greusel & Co., where but two loads per day are made, the men working but eleven to twelve hours a day. But as a limited number only can be employed as teamsters, the majority are sent into the woods chopping, their average earnings ranging from 50 to 70 cents a day, exclusive of the large amount of time necessarily lost by cold, wet, sickness, &c. The meagre wages paid in the winter season, and great loss of time consequent upon the severity of the weather, probably account for the appalling poverty and squalidity of the poor brickyard laborers. The destitution and wretchedness of life is rendered much more apparent at the brickyards, by reason of the filthy, dilapidated, little hovels into which the laborer is crowded. These usually consist of one room and a shed, and are built of ten-foot boards, standing on end, with the floor raised about two feet, making a room eight feet high, by about ten feet square. As their families will average about six persons, this gives 100 square, or 800 cubic feet to the family, or 133 cubic feet to each member, hardly more space than would be allotted to a family in the saloon of an ocean steamer. Generally they are plastered inside, but dimly lighted, with broken glass and sash, approachable only through mud during a great part of the year, often tilted up at various angles by frost, never painted, and perfect sieves for the chilling blasts of winter. Standing on mud banks, along the edges of stagnant pools, with door opening directly into the room, their extreme wretchedness, as human habitations, may well be imagined.

At the yard of Greusel & Co., the dwellings are two story, each family having two rooms, access to the upper one being by step ladder and trap-door, but they are unplastered, and without even inside sheathing. That such dwellings should be erected, and that these people are permitted to reside in them, are matters equally astonishing. The occupants are comparatively youthful, and have young families; but in families having grown up sons and daughters, they occupy beds ranged side by side, in the same room, delicacy being, apparently, an unknown element here, and the common decencies of life hardly observed. The furniture usually consists of two beds, a cook stove, a few wooden chairs, a cupboard, a pot, a kettle, and a few tin pans, with occasionally a bag of potatoes and a barrel of flour. They eat largely of animal food, chiefly pork, taking the blood, entrails, heads, lungs, liver, and boiling them into unsavory messes. But although living in apparent violation of the simplest laws of health, the people are strong, robust, and of good constitution. In no case could we discover the slightest trace of theft, debauchery, or intoxication. Beyond the breviary or missal of the church service, no trace of literature exists among them. Unorganized, untaught, uncared for, seemingly unambitious, strangers in a strange land, with every waking hour devoted to satisfying the needs and desires of the physical man, these people seem scarcely to realize their humanity.

These surroundings and conditions are not peculiar to the locality or to the occupations named.

They are more apparent there because of the separation of

the industry in which these people are engaged from others of a different character, and because of the congregation of enterprises of like character bringing numbers together.

We find the same conditions at Wyandotte, in Detroit, in the Saginaw Valley, and elsewhere.

In our cities they send their wives and children into our streets and alleys and backyards, gathering paper, fuel, and garbage. At the tearing down of an old building, or tearing up of an old pavement, they appear in swarms, as if by magic, and carry away the rubbish, which they use for fire wood and for building additions to their tenements.

The inmates of our houses of correction and our prisons are better fed, more comfortably clad and housed than these people are. . . . What wonder is it, then, that these men sometimes become desperate and resort to rash measures?

Voluntary Admissions to the Detroit House of Correction, 1883

A peculiar and often unrecognized welfare institution was the city or county jail. Unemployed men, transients down on their luck, and those at the end of their legitimate or illegitimate vocations found in the jail temporary lodging or a "good place to winter." As Judge John Miner pointed out, the number applying for voluntary admission to jail seemed to vary with the business cycle and the demand for labor. The fact that the native-born dominated over the foreign-born among the applicants enumerated in this selection is not necessarily an index of greater want by natives, but may simply reflect greater knowledge about a less-exploited source of welfare.

The document is from the First Annual Report of the Bureau of Labor and Industrial Statistics *(Lansing, 1884, pp. 190–92).*

In reply to a letter addressed to Hon. John Miner, police justice of the city of Detroit, he says:

"It is true that during the fall and winter months individuals voluntarily apply for commitment to the Detroit House of Correction. I regret that the time at my disposal prevents my making such an examination . . . as would justify any estimate or average such as would be of any value.

"I can say, however, in a general way, that the numbers vary in different years greatly, and from observation should say that such applications bear a pretty close relation to the state of the demand for Labor in the country.

"For the period between December 3, 1883, and December 20, 1883, inclusive, there have been sixty-two (62) such applications and commitments."

We afterwards obtained the names of those who had been committed upon their own application during the month of December, 1883, prepared a blank for that purpose and had them interviewed, with the following result:

Where Born.	No.	Where Born.	No.
Canada	5	Prussia	2
England	7	Scotland	1
Ireland	14	United States	50
Germany	6		
Whole number			85

Number in each vocation named.			
Bakers	2	Iron workers	1
Blacksmiths	1	Laborers	30
Brakemen	1	Machinists	1
Brush-makers	1	Millers	1
Cabinet-makers	1	Painters	5
Carriage repairers	1	Printers	1
Cigar-makers	3	Seamen	19
Coopers	1	Shoemakers	3
Farm laborers	6	Stone-masons	2
Glass-blowers	1	Teamsters	1
Iron moulders	2	Weavers	1

Length of time in Michigan.

One to three days	6	One to eleven months	22
One to six weeks	23	One to thirty-one years	34

Length of time in Detroit.

One to five days	26	One to nine months	15
One to three weeks	32	One to thirty-one years	12

Length of time in United States.

One day	1	One to ten years	17
One to ten months	6	Sixteen to fifty-one years	61

Length of time out of work.

Two days	1	One to six months	35
One to three weeks	45	One year	1

Ages.

Sixteen to twenty-one years	22	Thirty-one to forty years	23
Twenty-two to thirty years	35	Forty-five to fifty-six years	5

Six of the number had before applied and were committed, and twenty-five had been convicted, here or elsewhere, one or more times for various crimes, as follows:

Drunkenness	10	Vagrancy	1
Larceny	4	Desertion	1
Burglary	2	Not at school	1
Assault and battery	2	Not given	4

Married, 7; unmarried, 78; having children, 4.

When asked why they applied for commitment to the house of correction they replied as follows:

Thirty-four claimed that they "had no work, no money, were sick;" or "hungry," or "hard up and went to the police station for lodging and was advised by the officer to come up here;" or "was persuaded to come up here;" or "was bounced up here;" or "was committed for staying at the station over night;" or "was told that I would have to go up if I stayed over night;" or "asked for night's lodging and was given three months for it;" five stated that they had "no money, no work, and came to avoid a worse fate;" four "wanted to get some place to stay out of the cold;" two claimed to have been guilty of no crime but being out of employment; three, that they had "no work, no money, and no home;" six, that they had "no work, no money; were sick or hungry, got discouraged trying to find work, and preferred this to being a criminal;" three, that they had no work, or were sick, and was told by outsiders that this was a good place to winter; two no work, no money; could not get home, did not want to steal; two, that they could get no work, and wanted some place to stop; another said that he was out of work and did not want to bum around the country; another, "I had to come here or starve or commit crime; could not get work for my board;" another "came to the city to buy tools, got drunk and was robbed; applied at station for lodging and was advised by the officer to come up here;" another, "was shipwrecked and lost all I had; no work, no money;" another "had the horrors and wanted to get away from temptation so as to straighten up;" others said that they were "out of money, had no prospect of anything but crime or starvation;" or "destitute of friends and money;" or "no means of support;" or "preferred this to begging;" or "no money and no work;" or "offered to work for my board and no one wanted me."

Upon inquiry of the Police Department it was stated that it is the practice at the station to afford temporary lodging to applicants, but where the applications become chronic they are regarded as vagrants.

The above includes statements from nearly all of those committed. It will be borne in mind that twenty-five of the number had heretofore been convicted of crime, some of them several times, and that six of the others had been committed before upon their own application. It is but fair to presume that at least a majority of these thirty-one are not only improvident, but that they are there at the end of an unsuccessful season in illegitimate avocations. It is also fair to presume that quite a number of the balance are in their present condition because of profligate habits. But is it not equally fair to presume that quite a number have told the truth, and that they are there because of a glut in the Labor market?

Women Wage Workers, 1891

Working conditions for women and children were more often than not brutalizing, grossly exploitative, and their work environments were loathsome with filth and often dangerous to the health of workers. Wages were meager and hours long. The exceptions to such conditions were too often exceptions in the work picture in Detroit—the pharmaceutical manufacturer, the telephone exchange, and the laundries were unfortunately not the principal employers of women and children.

Mrs. Ella Whipple's report of conditions in Detroit is drawn from the Nineteenth Annual Report of the Bureau of Labor and Industrial Statistics *(Lansing, 1902, pp. 163–67).*

MRS. WHIPPLE'S REPORT.

Lansing, Michigan, January 1, 1902.

HON. SCOTT GRISWOLD,
    Commissioner of Labor, Lansing, Michigan:
    DEAR SIR.—

I have the honor to submit herewith my first report as Woman Deputy Factory Inspector, sincerely hoping that my investigations will meet your approval and that the results obtained will prove a substantial benefit to the women and children toilers of our State, firmly believing that the reforms that have and can be suggested will in the near future improve the mental and moral conditions of these less protected laboring classes to such an extent that our tax payers will feel repaid for the expense of the work.

Women and Children Employed.

I find that the factory inspection of last year shows that there are 28,618 women and 3,822 children employed in the factories of

Michigan. Many more are at work in hotels, stores, offices and at other employment and it will not be too much to estimate the total number of women and children employed in the State at considerably over 100,000. The per cent of women seeking labor outside of their home has of late years constantly increased. The tendency has been the same with children, though recently has been considerably checked by the efforts put forth to enforce the provisions of our factory inspection laws against child labor. The amendments to the law by the last legislature so that hotels and stores are brought within its provisions will aid in restricting the employment of children and the law could be still further extended with good results. . . .

THE DETROIT CANVASS.

In Detroit the places visited were 50 factories, 25 hotels, 25 laundries, 25 dry goods stores, 5 laboratories, 1 telephone exchange and the House of Correction. In all 71 orders were made. Owing to the limited time in which to make inspections no revisits to ascertain whether orders have been complied with were made. A brief abstract of work done in various institutions and industries of this city is as follows:

Canvass of Factories.
The first month was devoted entirely to factories. An active canvass was made of these industries and over 900 women and children were interviewed. At some of the factories everything was first-class and buildings new and modern throughout. The employes had rest room, dining room, sanitary lavatories and comfortable dressing room; tea and coffee furnished free and a woman to prepare it. A full hour for dinner and a half holiday on Saturdays, which affords them an opportunity for rest and recreation; and, best of all, managers who are willing to know the law and abide by it, who court investigation and are grateful for suggestions. At such places usually very little child labor was found. All had sworn statements, and while many of them looked small, just 14 years of age, they had their passports and could not be disturbed. In many of the best factories the managers will not employ children under 16 years of age, although sometimes they are deceived by the children or their parents. Close ques-

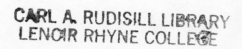

tioning, however, disclosed the falsehood that had been told and
they were promptly and willingly discharged. In these places
wages are the best, ranging from $5 to $10 per week. Piece
workers earn most money. Every move they make counts and
weary looks and pale faces tell of the continual strain put forth
to earn better pay.

In another class of factories the buildings are old, ventilation
poor, wages not so good, children at work, sanitary conditions bad
and very little regard for cleanliness. The overseers work for their
own interests, are indifferent of the conditions and means used to
crowd the work. They object to an inspection and either the
manager or someone he selects will follow the inspector, (conduct that always arouses suspicion) while investigating the premises, often making use of unbecoming language, and it is very
difficult to make them understand that their company is not desired,—in other words, to convince them that the inspector desires
to do the work without their supervision. Occasionally evidences
of immorality were found and at times it was evident that the
foremen exercised more freedom than ought to be permitted with
the girls and young ladies placed under their charge. Work stops
at 4 p. m. on Saturdays but continues until 6 o'clock on other days.

Lastly, there is another class of factories, small buildings, badly
managed, uncomfortable places without the space required by
law, everything filthy. Tobacco, cigars and candy are usually
manufactured. The manufactured articles, especially cigars, sent
out from many of these places, are often dangerous to public
health, owing to the filthy practices of, and diseases prevalent
among some of the employes. A good many small children are
employed, a considerable number of them under 14 years of age,
and the balance just within the limit. The ventilation is bad and
the very worst cases of unsanitary closets. Wages are small and
work continues full 10 hours each day and often the workwomen
are surrounded by uncleanliness and disease. It is difficult to
imagine how people can live and work exposed to such trials and
unhealthy surroundings. Here was heard many a sad story of
suffering, sorrow and hardship. At such places all was done that
could be to alleviate the sufferings of the employes. Orders were
given to clean up and improve the sanitary, and sometimes, the
moral conditions. It is observable that the poorer the surroundings

and the more unhealthy the conditions the lower the wages paid
and the greater the rebellion against reform.

Canvass of Laundries.
In the laundries are found many children. The least wages were
$3 and the best $7 per week, except forewomen, who usually
receive $10 per week. The condition of the help is much better
than that of many in other employments. They have plenty of
soap and water and are obliged to keep at least moderately clean
to retain their customers, for ill washed, smoke dried linen soon
betrays the secrets of its surroundings. The work cannot be classed
as injurious in any way to health. Monday is a comparatively free
day and nearly every day the hours are easy. The clothing need
not be expensive, but that it is neat and clean is the only requisite.
This when compared with many others, may be classed as a
desirable employment, with a chance to live, both for the em-
ploye and employers.

Canvass of Telephone Exchange.
The Telephone Exchange is in many ways a fine place. The girls
and women have a nice rest room, dining room and a motherly
matron. The working days are divided into three sections of
eight hours each, day and night, and every other Sunday included
for which they receive only $15 per month. Lunches are provided
at the company's cafe for seven cents each. For overtime they
receive 10 cents per hour. There are about 218 employed. One-
half of them board themselves. Their condition is better than the
average yet their labor is continuous and exacting and with the
low wages received it would seem to be rather a hard matter to
live with all the needs that necessarily exist to make them comfortable and present a good appearance in the public place where
they work.

Canvass of Hotels.
The hotels, many of them both large and small, are very pleasant and luxurious places for guests, but this cannot be said to apply
to the accommodations which they afford women and children in
their employ. Some of the largest are among the worst in this respect, as many as nine employes sleeping in one room and not a
very large one either. Too often the rooms given to girls and

women are the coldest in winter and the hottest in summer. Sometimes attics, sometimes basements, often four or six crowded into one small room with neither light nor air to make it wholesome, one small window or transom being the only means for ventilation and light, except the door. One of the largest and finest hotels requires its employes to give them 16 working hours per day.

Oftimes the food is so poor that to eat it is a very hard task and some claimed that they were made ill by eating, while others asserted that they felt as if they were actually starving. The chambermaids, laundresses and scrub girls earn $12 per month. Their work is very hard and as a class they have the poorest food and the least of it. Not having access to the kitchen they have to eat whatever the steward chooses to give them and that depends on his moods. In some hotels their dining room is a place which cannot be used for any other purpose—dark, filthy, and forbidding; stale meats and broken victuals from the hotel tables their food. The thought of eating under such circumstances is sickening.

The cooks and assistants in the best hotels receive $14 and $16 and even much more per month and have enough to eat and as good as the best. Your inspector took dinner in several of the hotels with the help in their dining room. It is evident that they have a hard struggle to exist.

In some instances the bell boys spend the greater part of what they earn in some nearby restaurant. There is a state of affairs in some places, where least expected, in which great reforms are necessary. In several cases a health officer was called in order to promptly abate the conditions that needed immediate attention. As a rule, the cheapest food, the poorest beds, and the hardest work with long hours, is what was found to be the lot of women and children in the hotels of Detroit.

Canvass of House of Correction.

The House of Correction is kept very clean and is well managed and the inmates look healthy. All those interviewed stated that their food was good and plentiful; that they had more to eat than formerly and that fruit and sweets have been added to their bill of fare. They were not informed that they were receiving a visit from a factory inspector, as the Warden thought that it would unsettle their minds and render them less amenable to discipline. They card buttons, bottom chairs, and put fibre in brushes. Some of them have an opportunity to earn 30 cents per week for overtime. To all appearances everything about the institution is in prime condition. One of the women said that if she was not a prisoner she would think it a fine place to work, even though she only received 50 cents per day, but that a palace would be a prison as soon as a person was compelled to remain in it against her will and was subject to daily and hourly restraint.

Canvass of Dry Goods Stores.

In these were found many children under 14 years and once the remark was made, "the younger the boy the better service he gives." They work full 10 hours each day and on Saturdays until 10 o'clock p. m. It is here that you will find the hardships. I sent many home and ordered sworn statements for many others. They are kept running from morning until night and no rest.

The wages for all classes of help are small, and the many who come from out of the city have no homes except what they make for themselves. Three and one-half to four and one-half dollars per week are the usual wages paid—$10 the highest. Only experienced clerks receive anything like living wages. It seems impossible that half of these people should have what they need to eat and how they exist is a mystery.

Most of the stores have poor sanitary conditions, and in very many cases the employes eat their lunch in the basement with nothing clean or wholesome near them. No stools to rest upon and lavatories and closets that are unfit to go into by reason of foul odors. Frequently the water tank, while it may contain ice, is so very unclean that it is far from safe to drink therefrom. I ordered many repairs and suggested many improvements, but was generally told that they would take their own time to make them.

Canvass of Chemical Laboratories.

The chemical laboratories are very fine places in which to work. They are clean and perfectly sanitary. The employes receive excellent treatment. There are rest rooms, dining rooms and free libraries, also places provided for those who are temporarily ill, and frequently a physician is furnished those who are seriously sick. Cases are known of their having paid the expenses of their employes that they might enjoy the beneficial results of other climates when needed for their recovery.

The help required for this work of necessity must be more intelligent and educated than the average. A spirit of refinement and purity born of the strict cleanliness of the places seems to pervade the atmosphere, and the busy workers apparently enjoy the many comforts provided for them.

The wages are seemingly low, ranging from $3.50 to $4.50 and $5 per week, but to the credit of the institution it can be said that no children are employed. The pill makers receive the highest wages as they work by the piece. Everybody connected with the institutions seem to be in good health and spirits.

Too much cannot be said in praise of those splendid manufactories, and Detroit may well feel proud of them, ranking as they do the largest laboratories in the world.

Detroit's Germans Lead the Antiprohibition Movement, 1887

The temperance issue was the bête noire *of nineteenth-century Detroit politics. It was a disturbing question and one of the most divisive issues in the city and helped to shape the social and ethnic composition of both political parties. Detroit's largest foreign-born and ethnic group in the last half of the nineteenth century, the Germans, played the key role in leading several personal-liberty and antiprohibition campaigns.*

This selection covers an antiprohibition rally in Detroit on 30 March 1887 that led to the defeat of a prohibition amendment in a statewide election a week later. It is from the Detroit Free Press *(31 March 1887).*

ANTI-PROHIBITION

Enthusiastic Mass Meeting at Arbeiter Hall Last Night

Speeches by Henry Kummerfeld, Prof. Hermann, Emil Pfeiffer and Councilman Look

An audience of 1,200 persons gathered in Arbeiter Hall last evening at the invitation of the Anti-Prohibition Association to hear a discussion of the negative side of the adoption of the proposed prohibitory amendment. The meeting was called to order by Henry Kapschinski, after which some thirty delegates from as many anti-prohibition societies took seats on the platform. Henry Kummerfeld, of the firm of Hertzig & Kummerfeld, was elected Chairman of the meeting and in taking the chair made a few remarks upon the history of the present movement. When the matter first came up at Lansing, the speaker said, there was already in existence an organization in favor of prohibition, but none against it. It was only of recent date that any organized movement had been placed on foot to combat this other old and well trained force. The fact, however, that only a few weeks had sufficed to place the friends of personal liberty upon a fair war-footing showed the spirit of the people in the movement when they found their rights endangered. The President concluded by announcing that six additional speakers, all gentlemen of the highest social standing had taken the field during the past week.

A German song, joined in by different German musical societies, was sung under the direction of Prof. Hermann.

The first speaker of the evening, Prof. Hermann, was then introduced. He said that, as a people, we have seen the best of our times. One of the brightest incidents in the history of the American people was the abolition of slavery. Every good citizen had come to the front in securing to the liberated colored people their rights as citizens; "and now," said the Professor, waving his hand toward S. O. Williams and Harold Ferguson, colored delegates upon the stage, "the colored people come to the front in behalf of the freedom of all men." (Applause) "We don't fight prohibition as Germans, but as citizens, voters and freemen whose liberties are threatened." One great truth had been proven by all history, the speaker said, it was impossible to make men better by preventive measures. The only betterment in the condition of any people had been brought about by moral example and education—not by legal requirements. Every man in his personality has inalienable rights which cannot be taken from him. "We need no red or blue ribbons nor pledges to show that we are men. Personal liberty is the highest of all liberty: if that be taken from us we lose all other liberties with it. It is not strange that in a republic the strangers are obliged to keep up the liberties of the citizens? It is not an evil that this matter has come up, because it brings with it the necessity for men to declare what their principles are. In the meeting at the Grand Opera House mention was made of high license in the name of the anti-prohibition principle. I declare that we have never even considered the point all we have to do at present is to fight the amendment. Therefore let none be afraid to vote against the amendment for fear of bringing about high license. Let those who are not yet certain of how they will vote look at the States where prohibition is in force. Let no saloon-keeper imagine that he is going to do business after the amendment is carried. Where will be the end, if such legislation continues? We will be relegated back to the middle ages and the days of despotism. Did not a temperance speaker say, the other evening, that we in Detroit are barbarians? Wherein lies our barbarism? We ask the liberty to eat and drink where, when and what we will. We are all in favor of closing low dives, but that is not what the temperance men want. All that we desire to do, we are willing to do openly. We don't want back doors or side doors by which to enter saloons. We are satisfied to let everybody see just what we drink. Let those temperance men practice what they preach; they are all good Christians. Jesus gave His disciples wine, but the temperance men would take it from them—and drink it themselves when nobody is around. Great things have been done in all ages, even before the American temperance men discovered that they are the saviors of the world. This agitation has no political religious or social tendency—all are united in this one great fight against our liberty."

The united singing societies again rendered a selection. . . .

Maj. Emil Pfeiffer was next introduced. He spoke in a vigorous and spirited manner and was almost constantly interrupted by applause. He said: "We have seen such dangerous clouds as prohibition before, and have beheld them without flinching. Our manhood is in question with this proposed amendment, but I hope we are men, and that we will be able to convince the opposition that we are. We do not want to be compelled to go through alleys into saloons, nor into Heaven by back ways. The danger lies in the rural districts. Let us make no mistake, for there we have to fight ignorance and bigotry. It is not many years since I was asked by a man in Van Buren County whether I was one of the Hessians who fought against the liberty of the colonies during their struggle for freedom from the tyranny of Great Britain." The speaker reviewed at some length the speech of Rev. C.I. Deyo, recently delivered in Oxford, Mich., and then said: "It is not an easy matter to move the stoical Germans to enthusiasm, but the enthusiasm displayed by this audience shows what deep interest is being taken by them in this matter. We protest against the amendment as being contrary to the Declaration of Independence." The speaker at this point wet his lips with the glass of water provided for the speakers and made a wry face. The action brought down the house. "The prohibitionists are simply trying to place a legal roof over the State of Michigan and inclose it as one vast house of correction. We must prevent this by every honorable means in our power."

Both the above speeches were in German, and when Councilman William Look, the next speaker, was introduced, he said it was a hard matter to speak in English when his heart was beating so warmly in German. Upon Monday next the people of Michigan would decide upon a very important matter. Upon that decision depends everything. It is no transitory affair but the decision then given will doubtless be for all time to come. "You will be called upon then to say whether you think yourselves men or imbeciles who require a guardian. If prohibition prevails every man who afterward partakes of a glass of beer will be a criminal in the eyes of the law. Is that the attitude you wish to occupy in the community? There is more slavery in this country to-day than there was prior to the emancipation of the colored race, and new endeavors to enslave the people are constantly being formulated and put in practice. Among them is this scheme of prohibition. The reason the Germans came to American is because the Constitution of the United States guaranteed to every man the fullest personal liberty. An article has been published in a newspaper in this city, which is an insult to the German people of the city, which states that the lives of a certain class of people will be endangered on election day if they should come east of Woodward avenue. I ask this audience if there is any truth in that statement?" Loud cries of "no, no."

"Of course there isn't. We, as Germans, came to this country for greater liberty and when we cannot concede to others what we ask for ourselves, no matter what their views may be, we will go back again. One feature more serious than all others presents itself in case prohibition is adopted. I refer to the vast amount of property which it will destroy and the vast number of men, now employed, who will have their daily bread taken from them and themselves left in idleness. Remember this when you cast your ballots next Monday."

The following resolution was unanimously adopted.

Resolved: That we repudiate and earnestly refute such imputation and slander as is thrown upon our German citizens east of Woodward avenue, as set forth in an interview in the *Evening Journal* of March 20.

Mayor Pingree Reforms Detroit, 1890–97

Hazen S. Pingree, reform mayor of Detroit 1890–97, explains some of the key measures for which he fought during his four terms in office. He pressed vigorously for low and reasonable rates for gas, light, transit, water, and taxes, which intimately affected the welfare of the vast majority of urbanites. A maverick Republican, Pingree's style was bombastic and volatile but also incredibly successful in transforming a normally Democratic Detroit into a Republican city by 1895.

Pingree's article is drawn from Outlook *(55 [6 February 1897]: 437– 42).*

The anti-monopoly measures of my administration have been supported by all classes, except what are called the best citizens. The small property-owners have supported them as zealously as the wage-earners. A great many among what are called the better classes have voted for me, but they are generally careful not to let it be known. If we had to depend upon these classes for reforms, they could never be brought about.

The conflict between the city and the street-car companies began during the great street-car strike we had here several years ago. We had at that time poor service from the street-car companies, and they were working their men from ten to fourteen hours a day. When the strike came, the officers of the company demanded that I should call out the militia. I refused to do this, and requested them to settle the dispute by arbitration. Some of them called me an Anarchist for taking this position, but public sympathy was strongly on my side, and they finally decided to accept my proposition. It then took only a day and a half to settle the whole dispute, and since then nearly everything has been settled by arbitration. In my opinion, no company ought to get a franchise unless it stipulates its readiness to submit to arbitration its disputes with its men. Both men and companies owe it to the public to keep the peace.

The public feeling against the company which this strike brought to a head made it possible to keep up a fight for a better street-car service. At first most of the aldermen seemed to be bound hand and foot to the street-car companies; but half of them are elected every year, and we tried to select men who would stand by the people, and got them, if possible, to pledge themselves. When once pledged, it was pretty hard for them to go back on their word, but of course some had their price. Not until the second year was the Board of Aldermen really out of the grip of the street-car company. All this time we were fighting the company in the courts in regard to its franchise. It was a long, bitter fight, the case being taken from court to court, and finally costing the city from $50,000 to $60,000. While this struggle was going on, with decisions sometimes in our favor and sometimes in theirs, they were trying to get a new franchise, but I kept vetoing their measures, and it was pretty hard to pass anything over my veto. I used to stir up the public by sending out notices, and the people would pack the Council chamber and fairly terrify the Aldermen who wished to go back on their campaign promises. We even told them that we had plenty of rope there and would hang them. The newspapers, with the exception of one German paper, the "Abend-Post," were on the side of the street-car companies. When they published anything from me, they had it put in such a light that it had an entirely different meaning. Once, when I issued a call for a mass-meeting to protest against a bill introduced in the Legislature to take away my appointive power, they refused to print the call, even when I offered to pay them for it. When the papers refused to publish my notices, I used to have bulletin-boards fastened with chains to four or five of the pillars about the City Hall. In this way I got a hearing.

The fight in the courts was almost as difficult to carry forward. When I got a resolution passed in the Council giving me the power to retain two lawyers outside of those already paid by the city, I picked out one prominent Democrat and one prominent Republican. These men accepted the case, but the first thing I knew the company began to bring pressure to bear upon them. The prominent Democrat, who has held a Cabinet position, took a smooth way to get out of the fight. He said that he was in National politics, and that this local struggle complicated his position. The prominent Republican did not drop out so quickly, but I found we were having a hard time to get the matter before the court. Finally I insisted that he must bring it to a head. A few mornings later I was surprised to have him come in to see me and state that he had been retained by the company and could no longer serve as our attorney. He said that he was poor and that they had offered him such an amount that he could not afford to let it go by. Of course I gave this to the papers, and you can imagine the feeling it stirred up. . . .

On the filing of the opinion of the Court of Appeals the new owners began to make overtures for peace on the basis of a thirty-year franchise and five-cent fares, but in the meantime another factor had entered into the problem. On the 20th of November, 1894, Messrs. Pack & Everett, of Cleveland, made application to the Common Council for a franchise to operate street cars on streets not, as a rule, used by the old company, and agreed to equip their system with modern appliances and sell eight tickets for a quarter, to be good from quarter before six in the morning until eight o'clock at night. When the ordinance granting this franchise was pending before the Council, the new managers of the old company exhibited the same short-sightedness as had their predecessors. They not only refused to reduce fares themselves—publicly admitting that to do so would have a bad effect upon their street-car properties in other cities—but violently opposed the granting of a franchise to the Pack-Everett syndicate. Their obstructive policy, however, went for naught, and the ordinance was adopted. The old company then announced its intention to contest in the courts the right of the new company to operate the lines, and applied for an injunction in that behalf. In this fight before the courts, however, the old company failed, and the citizens of Detroit have now access to a street-car system extending to nearly all parts of the city, with the fare during working hours practically three cents, and with universal transfers. During the last campaign there was, indeed, a practical consolidation of the new company with the old, but the combination is bound to operate the franchise of the new company upon the terms laid down in the charter. Mr. Everett, of the new company, was opposed to entering the combination. He told me when his company started that they would be satisfied if they made money in a year and a half, and afterwards admitted that they had made money almost from the start. His company at one time proposed to the Council to operate all the street-railway lines in the city at the rate of two and one-half cents per passenger, and pay the interest upon the purchase price of the street-car tracks if these tracks were condemned by the authority of the legislature and the purchase price decided by arbitrators. The fight has not ended, and may not end until the franchise of the old company expires. Fortunately, the Michigan Legislature was long ago wise enough to provide against perpetual franchises. All franchises in this State are for thirty years.

The story of our fight with the gas companies is a much shorter one. At the beginning of my administration there were three companies making gas, and the price at which they sold it was $1.50 per thousand cubic feet. Two of these companies had valid franchises, but the other company, we found after long searching, had been running under a franchise that had expired twenty years before. When we began to investigate it, they had just sold out to C. P. Huntington, of New York. We went back in the city records and found where the city's attorneys had at different times started to look into their franchise, but all of them had for some reason dropped the search. We looked everything over, and finally set a dozen men at work going through two or three carloads of old newspapers stored up in the garret. Finally a paper containing the record of this franchise was found, and it was demonstrated that the franchise had expired about twenty years before. Of course I brought this out in the papers. They had just issued $7,500,000 worth of stock, and all of it was selling at about eighty cents. It afterwards fell to fifteen cents. The company offered me $75,000 for a franchise, to be dated back two years, but I refused to give it. When Huntington found out that they had sold him something they did not own, he refused to pay, and they brought suit.

At the beginning of this contest the gas company took the position that dollar gas might be supplied in a city the size of Boston, but that in a small city like Detroit, where a smaller plant was used, and where the houses were so scattered that far longer mains had to be constructed to reach the same number of consumers, dollar gas was a visionary idea. I sent my stenographer down to Cleveland, and he brought back the official record of Cleveland's contest with the gas companies. In Ohio the City Councils have the right to regulate the price of gas, and the Cleveland Council had ordered a reduction from a dollar a thousand to sixty cents a thousand, and the gas company had gladly compromised upon an eighty-cent rate—paying five cents out of the eighty into the city treasury. The claim that gas could not be profitably furnished at a dollar fell to the ground. I tried to get the Michigan Legislature to delegate to the city of Detroit the right to regulate the rates, but the bill was fought by the corporations and defeated. Nevertheless, we were finally partially successful in our fight. The old company accepted a new franchise that reads like this: Gas for illuminating purposes, $1; when used for fuel, 80 cents.

In dealing with the electric light matter, Detroit has recently adopted the plan of municipal ownership and operation of the plant. Under this plan the cost of lighting the streets has been reduced from $11.15 to $7.20 per arc lamp. All the public buildings, school-houses, police stations, etc., are to be lighted by this plant, and in my last message as Mayor I urged upon the City Council that in the near future they should take another step forward and furnish electric lighting in the stores and homes of private citizens. If this were done, it would take electric lighting out of the luxuries of life, to be used only by the wealthy, and place it within the reach of the humblest citizens.

The water-works of Detroit have been owned by the city since 1852. No one dreams of such a thing as a return to private ownership. During my administration I have urged the adoption of the policy of furnishing free water and having the cost of the water-works, like the cost of the streets and the parks, paid for by general taxation instead of by the taxation of the homes and factories using the water. I urged this policy partly as a matter of justice to the different classes of property-owners. I called attention to the fact that there were in the city limits thousands of acres of unimproved real estate held for speculation, the value of which was being constantly enhanced by the water-rates levied upon the industrial class. In Baltimore, in Philadelphia, in Milwaukee, and in St. Paul the owners of such land are assessed for the laying of water-pipes in front of their property, just as they are assessed for improving the streets. It is simple justice that this rule should be followed, because these water facilities enhance the value of the property in the same way that good streets do. I also urged this plan as a matter of economy. At the present time the Water Board spends $150,000 annually, or one-quarter of all its expenditures, upon the salaries of officers in the collection, meter, and other departments, which could be dispensed with if water were paid for out of the general tax levy. A tax of sixty-four cents on a thousand dollars, or only a little over three dollars a year on a home assessed at $5,000, would pay all the necessary expenses of running the water-works and create a sinking-fund for the gradual redemption of outstanding bonds. Such a change seems to me to be in the line of progress as well as economy. The principle of charging more for water sufficient to wash a person all over than for the amount required to wash one's face tends to ungodliness, if cleanliness is next to godliness. I believe that Detroit would be a better city if free water were supplied in all the homes. If it is right for the city, for the sake of a better civilization, to furnish free schools, free libraries, free parks, it is right for the city to furnish free water for the promotion of cleanliness, comfort, and self-respect in the homes of its citizens. . . .

The time is coming when municipal monopolies will be owned by the people. Detroit during my administration voted by a majority of four to one in favor of public ownership of street-car tracks. If the tracks were owned by the public, it would be easy to get the service performed at competitive and reasonable prices. We must not, however, wait for public ownership before putting an end to the extortion now practiced by private monopolies. We must, under the present system, compel the corporations exercising public franchises to furnish their services at the reasonable rates contemplated in their charters. This can be done wherever the city government is intent upon accomplishing it, and the city government will be intent upon accomplishing it whenever the citizens wake up to the extent of the extortions now practiced upon them.

PART THREE

DYNAMIC DETROIT, 1900–1945

Ford's in his flivver. All's well with the world.

—Aldous Huxley, *Brave New World*

Hysteria, pandemonium reigned everywhere. The magicians of Detroit, whom Count Keyserling called *Yogis* directed their flaming eyeballs upon their new automobile models which were to bring forth rivers of gold in the coming year. Spies came and went, whispering of rival projects, of enemy motor cars painted "the colors of precious stones."

—Matthew Josephson, in *Harper's*, 30 December 1930

Introduction

The year 1900 marks a turning point in the history of Detroit and in the character of its growth. By 1900 Detroit's commercial advantage and trade preeminence had long vanished. Some of the institutions of that earlier period still prevailed. Wholesale jobbers, dry goods sellers, commission agents and brokers still lingered, and along with real estate speculators and lumber barons the sons and daughters of this merchant aristocracy formed the city's social and economic elite. They shared this distinction with some of the *nouveaux riches* such as the James McMillans with their various industrial enterprises, and rising shoe manufacturers such as Hazen S. Pingree. Yet the timber, real estate, and mercantile men were still visible socially and politically. The vast majority of the city's mayors up to 1900, for example, had been drawn from the old merchant aristocracy. That earlier Detroit had been a commercial city dominated by Yankee peddlers who sold New York custom goods and supplied the vast landed interior that embraced the midsection of the continent. The Detroit of 1900 was far more industrialized. The city's freight-car shops, stove works, and related metal crafts, including marine engineering, gave the city's industrial life a modern character. The largest single branch of industry, the car shops, employed barely seven thousand men in 1904, and that figure included several different companies and supporting concerns and comprised but 12 percent of all manufacturing employees.[1] Thus, no single industry dominated the city's manufacturing life or gave it a special character.

Under the influence of the automotive industry, Detroit grew explosively in population, exceeding even the most optimistic pre-1900 projections.[2] During the nineteenth century Detroit's population growth had been slow, incremental, and gradual. The nation's nineteenth city in population in 1860 had moved up one notch in 1870, a position which it held a decade later in 1880 when Detroit was the eighteenth most populous city. In 1890 Detroit achieved fifteenth, and in 1900 thirteenth, place. In forty years the city of the straits had gone from nineteenth to thirteenth in population. Detroit's growth rate had been unexceptional despite its location in one of the most rapidly growing areas of the nation. The twenty years of urban growth following 1900 under the aegis of the automobile would change those figures. Under the tremendous spur of the automobile industry, Detroit was propelled into becoming the foremost rank-jumping city in the nation. From thirteenth in 1900 it leaped to ninth in 1910 and then to fourth in 1920. Milwaukee's nineteenth-century twin had nearly one million people in 1920. By 1930 it appeared for a while as if the motor city might challenge Philadelphia's grip on third place, but after the gloom of the Great Depression cleared, the 1940 census revealed the high watermark of Detroit's population growth. The 1950 census registered slippage and showed that Detroit had been pushed out of fourth place by the nation's only other metropolitan rank-jumper, Los Angeles.

Geographic position, transportation advantage, or metropolitan dominance cannot explain this almost unparalleled growth of a major city located off the main East-West transportation axis. But the automobile can. By every conceivable measure the impact of the motor industry upon Detroit during the first quarter of the twentieth century was immense. Although automobile assembly began about 1900, it was in 1904 that the United States Census Bureau began to measure its growth. In that year the total number of factory employees in Detroit was 60,554, of which the automobile industry registered 2,232, or 3.8 percent. Detroit's manufacturing economy was diversified, with foundry and machine shop products, druggists' preparations, and stoves and furnaces leading the list; motor vehicles ranked only fourth in the value of products, just ahead of wholesale meat packing. By 1909 the number of manufacturing employees had doubled and those employed in automobile factories had increased a prodigious eightfold. In 1914 automobile manufacturing employees reached 40 percent of the total number of manufacturing employees, who were expanding at unprecedented rates. By a slightly different measure the Michigan State Labor Department in 1919 reported that an overwhelming 45 percent of the 308,520 industrial employees in Detroit were in automobile and automobile accessory manufacturing. The estimated value of the entire manufactured product of Detroit was then given at $1.45 billion, of which $880 million, or a spectacular 60 percent, was accounted for by motor vehicle manufacturing. From almost a zero base-line in 1900, the automobile business had soared to a multimillion-dollar category by 1920. In two decades Detroit had pushed up from sixteenth rank as an industrial center, as measured by the value of its product, to fourth place. Regardless whether one uses the United States Census or State Labor Department figures, it is clear beyond all doubt that the modern and enduring character of Detroit's twentieth-century economy was formed by 1919. Every federal and state measure since that time points to one inescapable conclusion. Detroit was and is dominated by a single industry.[3] Automobile manufacturing had transformed Detroit from a diversified trade and manufacturing economy into a one-industry town.

As the city's economy grew increasingly lopsided, the Detroit industrial area engrossed to itself an increasing share of the total national motor vehicle production. Annual model changeovers pioneered by General Motors in the mid-1920s, by raising the initial cost of entry, closed the door to new entrants in automobile manufacturing and also eliminated some small producers who lacked the sales volume to absorb restyling costs each year.[4] The depression beginning in 1929 eliminated others. Attrition generally benefited Detroit. By 1930 it was evident that no other city or industrial region in the nation would, for the immediate future, challenge Detroit's supremacy in automobile manufacturing. Detroit's control over automobile production would peak in the late 1930s, after which decentralization would slowly begin to disperse the assembly aspect of the industry and later some of the specialty manufacturing.

The coming of the automobile industry disrupted Detroit's social patterns, stretched its boundaries, crowded its housing, created new sanitary, health, and education crises, but also brought fabulous wealth to the city. A basic industry as all-pervasive as vehicle manufacturing was to Detroit affected the social and political character of the city, influenced its language and metaphors, the topics and subjects of its newspapers and magazines, and ultimately was reflected in some law enforcement practices. Detroit's suburban building boom was propelled by the automobile and expanded enormously after 1920 when automobile ownership became widespread. The city expanded in a quarter century from 28 to 139 square miles by 1925, but this immense peripheral expansion was insufficient to accommodate the dispersing population. During the 1920s, for the first time, the suburbs surrounding Detroit began to grow at a faster rate than the city. This new population mobility depended directly upon the motorcar. The automobile altered the distribution of economic power in Detroit. No longer were the merchant capitalists, lumber barons, and freight-car manufacturers the model holders of wealth. A new breed of motor moguls came to the fore after 1914, with such names as the Fords and Dodges. The civic uplifters and municipal reformers were led by Henry Leland, a motor magnate. The city's mayoralty went, in 1918, to one of the founding fathers and pioneer investors in the Ford Motor Company, James Couzens. Even law enforcement was affected by the automobile. The city became peculiarly tolerant toward reckless driving and lax in its concern for traffic safety. As the auto accident and death rate soared in 1919, Mayor

Couzens asserted, "Detroit has been liberal with the automobile. Because the automobile has made Detroit a world city, we have felt inclined toward greater leniency than we otherwise should have shown." [5]

The city underwent vast demographic changes. The new jobs in the auto factories acted as a powerful magnet to newcomers. Detroit received elements hitherto almost absent in the city. On the eve of the manufacturing "takeoff" in 1904, the foreign-born constituted about one-third of Detroit's population, among whom were 13,000 Poles, 1,300 Russians, and 904 Italians. The 1910 foreign-born population of 156,365 nearly doubled to 289,297 in 1920. The state as a whole experienced a population surge of 857,049 during the same decade, of which more than two-thirds occurred within the Detroit city limits. By 1925 the foreign-born constituted about one-half of Detroit's 1,242,044 people, with the Poles leading the list with 115,069. Italians then numbered 42,457, Russians 49,427, and from almost a zero base-line Hungarians had grown to 21,656. Whereas the city had grown by 248,305 people between 1920 and 1925, the foreign-born population had expanded by about 244,000, according to the school board enumeration. The statistics showed that between 1920 and 1925 the city's population growth can be accounted for almost completely by the foreign-born increase. The number of Polish-born alone doubled in five years.

The pressures for Americanization began earlier in Detroit than in the nation generally. The initial stimulus was the high unemployment rate during the winter of 1914–15 when it was discovered that more than 60 percent of the supplicants for work or aid at the Detroit Board of Commerce employment service were non–English speakers. English language instruction became the heart and core of the Americanization program. Motor magnates argued that the accident rates would be lowered, ethnic tensions would diminish, and industrial efficiency would increase. The Ford Motor Company's English school was concerned with more than simply imparting a new language to foreigners, however; the educational program there instructed the newcomer to "walk to the American blackboard, take a piece of American chalk, and explain how the American workman walks to his home and sits down with his American family to their good American dinner." Adopting acceptable and respectable middle-class attitudes and habits was also a vital part of the movement.[6]

While a large number of foreign-born were being attracted to rapidly industrializing Detroit, some of the more affluent native-born elements were being propelled into the outer fringe of the metropolitan area. The suburbanization of many of the wealthiest families was already in evidence during the first stages of Detroit's great automotive manufacturing "takeoff." If one examines Albert Marquis's *Book of Detroiters* for 1908 and 1914, for example, the trend is very clear. Many Detroiters classified as "millionaires" in 1902 by the *World Almanac and Book of Facts* and who resided in the city in 1908 had moved to exclusive Grosse Pointe by 1914.[7] As the car showrooms, gas stations, and store-front businesses spread up Woodward Avenue, disfiguring a fashionable residential section, the wealthy were abandoning their mansions and leaving the city. The accelerated tempo of outward movement can also be seen from Professor R. D. McKenzie's data for the 1910 to 1930 period. Using *Dau's Blue Book* and the *Detroit Social Secretary,* both compilations of the leading business, professional, and social people, McKenzie was able to demonstrate the magnitude of the flight toward the outer zones of what he called the "better elements." Of the 2,579 "substantial families" in Detroit in 1910, 52 percent lived within three miles of the downtown business section and 91 percent lived within Detroit's corporate limits. By 1930 the situation was reversed, for then fewer than 8 percent were left behind within three miles of downtown and 50 percent of the substantial families lived beyond the city limits even though these had been greatly extended in the interim.[8]

Another measure of change can be seen from the geographic distribution of *Who's Who* entrants in the Detroit region. McKenzie noted that the drop in notables in Detroit was very pronounced between 1910 and 1930 and much more rapid than that for other metropolitan centers or cities in Detroit's population class. In fact, while other metropolitan centers increased their number of *Who's Who* notables, Detroit registered a steady decline. This led McKenzie to conclude that the general pattern for highly industrialized cities was that they almost invariably had a lower proportion of notables to the total population than did metropolitan centers or

university towns. The Detroit data offered impressive support for
McKenzie's thesis. A comparison of four of the largest metropolitan
centers for 1910–30 showed a per capita increase in New York
City, Chicago, and Los Angeles averaging almost 5 percent, while
Detroit experienced a decrease of 7 percent. At that time Detroit
registered 15 notables per 100,000 population, compared to New
York City's 75, Chicago's 45 and Los Angeles' 42. Detroit was a
highly industrialized blue-collar city whose base line had been low
in 1910 and progressively sagged lower as the foreign-born and
factory workers grew in number. The comparative data also
seemed to suggest that Detroit was attracting to it a different kind
and class of population than that being drawn to Los Angeles, a
city of similar size and equally phenomenal growth rates. Detroit's
heavily foreign-born character does not explain away these dis-
parities. When McKenzie tested for this variable, he found that
the ratio of foreign-born notables to the total foreign-born population of Los Angeles was "conspicuously higher" than the ratios
for Detroit, and for that matter, even higher than the combined native-born and foreign-born ratio in Detroit.[9] Thus, the overwhelming dominance of a single heavy industry with low skills requirements had a significant and measurable impact upon Detroit's
population structure and character. Detroit was much more a
working-class city than its size would have suggested.

Negro migration to Detroit increased during the second stage
of Detroit's automobile manufacturing "takeoff" after 1915. Yet
the black migration seemed unrelated to the rapid white movement to the suburbs, which had already been in full swing before
blacks arrived in any significant numbers. What the data strongly
suggest is that the first large-scale outward flight of whites was a
phenomenon of class and not of race. Blacks constituted but a
minute fraction of the city's population in 1910 (1.2 percent), and
although rapid growth had occurred, the black population remained but a small proportion (6.5 percent) of the entire population in 1925. The social and economic conditions and age and
occupational structure of Detroit's blacks are discussed in greater
detail in one of the documents that follow. The relationship of
Negroes to labor unions appears to confirm the picture of blacks
and unions in Chicago and other large northern cities for this
period. Negroes were unwelcome in unions or at worst jim-crowed

out of them; they saw few benefits to be gained from organized labor and were viewed by whites as strikebreakers and often sympathetic to the employers' point of view.[10]

The craft unions underwent a decline with the rise of mass production industry. The great inpouring of eastern European workers, mostly with agricultural backgrounds and no union experience, and sweeping technological changes in automobile manufacturing had a debilitating effect upon the older crafts and skills. Between 1905 and 1910, during the first great spurt of manufacturing growth, the craft unions experienced difficulty in organizing, their strikes faltered and sputtered, and meanwhile the number of unorganized workers grew prodigiously. A powerful consortium of industrialists, gathered together in the Employers Association of Detroit, also won a key strike in 1907, an event that Allan Nevins called alternately the "victory for open shop," and the "Waterloo of organized labor." [11] Compounding the problem was the fact that many older skills grew obsolete with advancing manufacturing technology. In the automobile industry, which employed the vast bulk of industrial labor, jobs were broken down more and more into their component parts, the tasks separated, and the skills required for performing the task greatly simplified. By 1922 Henry Ford boasted that 85 percent of his labor force required less than two weeks of training, and of that number, 40 percent needed only one day to be broken in for factory work.[12] Even without the vigorous opposition of the employers, advancing technology would have sapped the vitality out of craft unions in Detroit. It would take thirty years after the demise of the craft unions for the rise of an alternate instrument of collective bargaining for the factory worker, the industrial union.

The automobile industry also brought to Detroit a sharply fluctuating "boom-and-bust" business cycle. Detroit began exaggerating the peaks and troughs experienced by the national economy. The short-range fluctuations were attributable to the production rhythms of an industry that shut down yearly for a model changeover that resulted in mass layoffs. The long-range undulations amplified the national highs and lows. The automobile was an expensive, durable item, and its purchase could easily be deferred for a year or two. Detroiters would discover that automobile sales were extremely sensitive to consumer attitudes and to consumer income and that slight changes in these could have serious repercussions in the salesrooms and on the assembly line. The editor of the Detroit Board of Commerce's magazine first witnessed with amazement the onset of this boom-and-bust cycle in 1915.

No such transition from extreme depression to the greatest activity ever before occurred in the history of Detroit as in the months from April to October, 1915.

In April the Board of Commerce was just closing its self-imposed task of finding work for a host of the unemployed. At the opening of the year a large proportion of the factories were running on short time, and thousands of willing and capable men were seeking work in vain. . . .

Six months later there was a striking contrast in conditions. There was an actual scarcity of various kinds of skilled labor and no surplus of common labor. Some of the factories were running overtime, more men were employed than ever before, and no one who was able and willing to work needed to be out of a job.[13]

A topic that provoked screaming headlines and almost unrivaled public attention in the 1920s was the prohibition issue. Detroit was a "wide-open booze town," and that brought big-time bootlegging, murderous gang wars, and the payoffs that corrupted the police force. Prohibition failed to dry out Detroit and probably encouraged widespread disrespect for the law. The liquor traffic was one of the key political issues in Detroit mayoralty elections for the entire decade. Candidates were expected to declare on it. The vote returns vacillated on the issue and seemed confused. About one-half of the time Detroiters seemed to be voting "dry" but drinking "wet." Every mayor during the period, regardless of the position he may have taken before the election, came down on the side of the "rule of reason" once in office. That translated into tolerance of liquor sales provided the saloon keeper ran a respectable operation and did not violate other vice laws.[14]

By the end of the decade citizens grew increasingly unhappy over lax law enforcement and the growth of gambling, the liquor business, and crime in brazen defiance of the good order of the community. A rash of underworld killings seemed to be only of casual interest to the mayor, Charles Bowles. After a particularly murderous eleven-day spree that saw ten hoodlums murdered,

Bowles remarked, "Perhaps it is just as well to let these [gang-sters] kill each other off, if they are so minded. You know the scientists employ one set of parasites to destroy another. May not that be the plan of providence in these killings among the bandits." Bowles's police commissioner made the hands-off enforcement policy plain when he added, "So long as they confine their shoot-ings to their own kind there will be no police drive or any in-crease in the squad assigned to such cases." [15]

A free hand for criminals and mounting scandals increased pressure for the mayor's head, which resulted in a recall elec-tion scheduled for 22 July 1930. The recall ended the morning after in a fiery and dramatic climax with three gunmen assassinat-ing one of Mayor Bowles's leading critics, Gerald E. Buckley, a radio announcer. The voters ousted the mayor. Bowles's recall climaxed the end of an era of rowdyism, good times, two flasks in every hip pocket, and a decade of prosperity. After 22 July 1930 savings became stretched and thin, and reserves increasingly ex-hausted, and the bite of the depression cut deeper. A new mayor and liberal reformer, Frank Murphy, came into office and com-mitted his administration to addressing Detroit's number one prob-lem, unemployment. Public attention was no longer fixed on booze, vice, and gangsters, all of which seemed to depression-ridden Detroit by late 1930 as part of a somewhat unreal and distant past.

Detroit, the "City of Tomorrow," or "Utopia on Wheels," was sadly "out of gear" by 1930. Magazine writers and the social critics seemed unable to escape motorcar metaphors, and for good reason. The extreme want and poverty in depression Detroit were in part a reflection of the extreme fluctuations in the business cycle that motor vehicle manufacturing brought to the city. From superaffluence to grim poverty, the boom-and-bust cycle tended to be exaggerated in one-industry towns. When the national econ-omy was beset by a cold, Detroit normally caught pneumonia. Auto sales sagged to new lows, and the total motor vehicle produc-tion plunged from a record-high 5.3 million units in 1929 to an abysmal 1.3 million in 1932. The number of Detroit wage earners in manufacturing fell by almost 40 percent by 1933. Automobile workers led the downward spiral with nearly one-half of them idle.[16]

Detroiters were stunned by the depression, and some of the painful adjustments by which people hoped to cope with it were recorded by Helen Hall in her article, "When Detroit's Out of Gear."

A powerful and plaintive voice for the discomfited and disinherited in the early 1930s was Father Charles E. Coughlin. His radio talks, which were aired on Detroit station WJR and the CBS network, were richly textured protests that contained pyrotechnical flashes of anger and discontent. (The spellbinder's stirring talks never read as well as they sounded.) Although the pugnacious Royal Oak, Michigan, priest was later viewed by many as a charlatan, a demagogue, and an anti-Semite, these judgments seemed less applicable to the Coughlin of the early depression. He spoke repeatedly for the remonetization of silver, for inflation, lifting interest burdens from small homeowners, and "Christianizing" the economy. He fiercely attacked the "debauchery" of international bankers, the "greed" of American capitalists, the machinations of Wall Street pirates, and also the "Red menace." He pronounced modern capitalism bankrupt and later criticized auto workers' unions with equal ferocity. The "first" New Deal won his vehement support, which he sloganized with "Roosevelt or Ruin," but then he abandoned the President late in 1935 and symbolized his departure with the slogan "Roosevelt and Ruin." [17] The cumulative effect could sometimes be confusing.

In the late 1930s his audience diminished when his talks soured into diatribes on anti-Semitism and his publication *Social Justice* turned to perverse apologetics for anti-Jewish street brawlers such as the Christian Fronters. Coughlin's moral opaqueness on the German-Jewish issue seemed strangely out of character with his championing of the sufferers of the American depression.[18]

Despite the grimness of the depression and an increasing demand for economic justice, the auto industry remained unorganized in the early thirties. Efforts to establish unions by the Industrial Workers of the World, the American Federation of Labor, and the independents had met the vigorous and fierce opposition of employers and company-controlled unions.

The year 1936 saw increasing labor unrest, and an eruption of walkouts, wildcats, and sit-downs rocked the automobile manufacturing belt whose perimeters included South Bend and Anderson in Indiana; Toledo and Cleveland in Ohio; and Midland, Flint, Saginaw, Lansing, and Detroit in Michigan, all sites of unrest. The Akron rubber workers had set off a series of spontaneous and short-run sit-downs that served to register worker discontent but only occasionally redressed serious grievances. The critical turning point for mass production labor was made close to the nerve center of the auto empire, in Detroit's satellite city, Flint.

The Flint sit-down strike at General Motors was not the first of its kind, but it was the most momentous sit-down and of great consequence. Flint, a drab GM "company town" had some 160,000 people and depended heavily upon automobile production for its livelihood. The sit-down strike began at GM on 30 December 1936 when three inspectors were demoted to the assembly line because they refused to sever their affiliations with the United Automobile Workers union, and that triggered a strike. Shortly after, at another Fisher Body plant, union stewards saw what they said was a company attempt to move out vital machinery from Flint to some other distant city where the workers were more tractable and less restive than those in Flint. The workers sat down and remained in GM's Fisher Body I and II. The fledgling union, the UAW, was without company recognition and had but a small membership and no strike victories with which to challenge the colossus of American industry, General Motors. The union's chief goal was recognition as exclusive bargaining agent, which the company countered by demanding the plants be evacuated before preliminary discussions could even be considered.[19] Thus began the siege.

The unions had generally been beaten when playing by the ground rules prescribed by the bosses. Stay-out strikes with workers shivering on cold picket lines had often been broken by scabs, police attacks, the overt use of community coercion, and the courts. It had always been an uneven struggle with the odds heavily in favor of the employers. The sit-down broke that pattern. It inaugurated a veritable revolution and gave the workers a fighting chance.

The sit-down was a new and stunning strike tactic and it aroused workers to new heights of union consciousness. No longer could the boss easily use strikebreakers, because the workers were in possession of the plant. No longer was it possible, with a show of police force, outside "muscle," and company "goons," to disperse tattered and forlorn pickets. Nor was the lockout possible. On the other hand, a decision to storm the factory and evict the sit-downers might prove difficult to carry out, for the strikers often sat in behind barricades. Furthermore, machinery and production facilities might be damaged and injuries and deaths might accompany such assaults.[20] In any event, General Motors and the police would have to assume the role of assaulters, and GM would lose the battle for public opinion if the body count included fatalities at Chevy Engine or Fisher Body. A *Fortune* magazine poll published in July suggested that bodily harm to strikers would alienate the public.

The sit-downers were led by a hardened and tough-minded cadre of organizers who knew how to capitalize on adversity. They had witnessed how the Communists had deftly turned public opinion against the Ford Motor Company in the "Hunger March Massacre." In the case of such eventuality in the GM strike at Flint, the union would stage a mass funeral with parades, public mourning, singing and marches, and a funeral cortege led by color guards with a banner reading BODY BY FISHER.[21] That kind of grim and macabre procession would damage GM irreparably in its struggle to win public opinion and legislative support for its fight to suppress the union and the strike. Fortunately, no fatalities resulted.

The revolutionary implications of the workers' taking charge of the factory seemed to be neither understood nor of interest to the majority of workers. Both the union leaders and the rank and file saw the sit-down in much more practical and tactical terms. It was a "streamlined" strike technique that enhanced the chances of the workers against what hitherto had been stupendous odds. Stopping and taking temporary possession of the means of production was not the prelude to a collectivized economy or worker ownership of the means of production. American automobile employees were militant without being revolutionary. They asserted their right, not to the factory, but to a job.

To capitalists and employers the world seemed to be turning upside down in Flint. The sit-down provoked terror, bewilderment, and confusion in the minds of management. GM had injunctions issued by the courts that were openly defied by the union. A back-to-work movement faltered and fizzled. GM unleashed a tear gas and gunfire assault that felled fourteen workers and roughed up dozens of others in open police-striker confrontations, but that also failed to do the trick. Strike resolve hardened and toughened. Finally, the company's coercive hand was held in abeyance when Michigan governor Frank Murphy sent in the National Guard and ordered them to behave in a neutral manner.

The strike dragged into a second month as GM resolutely refused to recognize the UAW as sole bargaining agent. Governor Murphy then facilitated a settlement on 11 February 1937 at a historic meeting that included John L. Lewis of the newly founded CIO (Congress of Industrial Organizations), UAW officials, and the GM hierarchy. The union won recognition as bargaining agent in the struck plants, a decision of earthshaking proportions in mass production industry. A feeble and inchoate union was the David that struck down the Goliath of industry.[22]

When GM fell, the thunder reverberated from coast to coast. After 1937 mass production industry in steel, rubber, autos, and electrical goods would never again possess the overweening and awesome power it had previously exercised over the worker. The impact of the sit-downs sent shock waves all over the nation in 1937. After GM toppled, big steel proved much easier to organize, according to John L. Lewis. One keen observer argued that the effect of the sit-down settlement was "like a huge reservoir bursting," for it seemed to "open the flood gates of organization." Workers joined the union en masse. Professor Sidney Fine's definitive study concurred in the judgment that the GM sit-down was probably the nation's "most critical labor conflict" of the 1930s. It is clear beyond any doubt that no single event in the labor history of the Detroit region or Michigan had a more profound effect upon working conditions and wages than the sit-down. It built the UAW and the CIO, the mass unions for the unskilled and semiskilled. The ripples from the sit-down would continue to be felt in our own time when civil rights workers and college-student protesters would adopt the sit-down but call it the "sit-in." [23]

As the 1930s drew to a close and World War II approached, the defense demands placed upon Detroit industry created additional jobs and finally serious labor shortages. White and black migrants responded and came in increasing numbers from the South and border states, and to a lesser extent from the Great Lakes "cutover areas" and depressed mining ranges. This caused population congestion and repeated the historic experience that occurred during World War I of ample jobs but insufficient housing.[24] The emergency defense housing that was constructed in Detroit during the early war years was insignificant in terms of need, but even some of that became the site of racial tensions. The Sojourner Truth Housing riot of 1942, which involved 200 units, was set off when whites tried to stop blacks from moving into a project designated for Negroes. Racial altercations had also occurred in some of the industrial plants between black and white workers.[25]

These events were prefatory to the bloody race riot of 1943 that took a huge toll in life and property. In the typology of American riots, the Detroit riot has been labeled the last of the large "communal," "ecological," or "contested area" riots, and the turning point after which these urban outbursts would become known as "commodity" riots, which was the prevailing type during the 1964–67 period. Detroit's classical "communal" riot of 1943 was triggered by a black-white brawl over a "contested area," Belle Isle Park, and the targets were flesh-and-blood individuals, white on black and black on white. Bloody gang forays, retaliatory attacks, beatings, shootings, and some looting took place.[26] Detroit's was one of the worst of the wartime conflagrations and was put down by federal troops. The painful story of that event is ably related in one of our documents, a report from Walter White to United States Supreme Court justice Frank Murphy.

NOTES—PART THREE

1. *Detroiter* 11 (30 October 1920).
2. All population figures are drawn from the United States Census or, where specified, the State of Michigan Census.

3. William Stocking, "The Story of Industrial Detroit," *Detroiter* 12 (22 January 1921).

4. Harold G. Vatter, "The Closure of Entry in the American Automobile Industry," *Oxford Economic Papers,* n.s. 4 (October 1952): 213–34; Bernard C. Snell, "Annual Style Change in the Automobile Industry as an Unfair Method of Competition," *Yale Law Review* 80 (January 1971): 567–613.

5. James Couzens, quoted in F. R. Johnson, "Reducing the Hazards of Peace," *Survey* 42 (12 July 1919): 566; Arch Mandel, "Detroit's Bureau of Safety Gets Results," *American City* 26 (January 1922): 37.

6. *Detroiter* 6 (24 November 1915); ibid. 11 (21 August 1920); Raymond E. Cole, "The Immigrant in Detroit" (Prepared for the Detroit Board of Commerce, May 1915), pp. 10–14, typescript in the Americanization Papers, Michigan Historical Collection, University of Michigan, Ann Arbor, Mich.

7. "American Millionaires" from *World Almanac and Book of Facts* (New York, 1902; reprinted in *New Light on the History of Great American Fortunes,* ed. Sidney Ratner [New York, 1953], p. 139). Maps, Detroit's "Substantial Families," 1890, 1900, 1930; Functional Maps of Detroit, 1890, 1900, 1910, 1920, in Federal Housing Administration file, Cartographic and Audiovisual Records Division, National Archives, Washington, D.C.

8. R. D. McKenzie, *The Metropolitan Community* (New York, 1933), p. 183; Albert N. Marquis, *The Book of Detroiters* (Chicago, 1908, 1914); *The Social Secretary* (Detroit, 1925).

9. McKenzie, pp. 122–24.

10. The Negro disposition toward the employer may have been shaped in part by the Detroit Urban League's close cooperation with large employers and the League's function as an employment bureau for Negroes in the automobile industry. John C. Dancey to Percival Dodge, 19 June 1931, Detroit Urban League Papers, Michigan Historical Collection. William M. Tuttle, Jr., *Race Riot: Chicago in the Red Summer of 1919* (New York, 1970), pp. 108–56.

11. Allan Nevins, *Ford: The Times, the Man, the Company* (New York, 1954), pp. 376–80, 512, 513.

12. Doris B. McLaughlin, *Michigan Labor: A Brief History from 1818 to the Present* (Ann Arbor, 1970), p. 99.

13. *Detroiter* 7 (17 January 1916).

14. Larry D. Englemann, "A Separate Peace: The Politics of Prohibition Enforcement in Detroit, 1920–1930," *Detroit In Perspective* 1 (Autumn 1972): 51–71.

15. Frederic L. Smith, "Detroit Apes Chicago," *Outlook and Independent* 156 (1 October 1930): 182–84; "Bootlegging and Murder in Detroit," *Literary Digest* 78 (29 September 1923): 48, 52, 53.

16. 1971 *Automobile Facts and Opinions* (Detroit, 1971), p. 3; *Detroiter* 33 (8 December 1941).

17. *Eight Lectures on Labor, Capital and Justice* (Royal Oak, Mich., 1934), pp. 34, 123–29, 132; David H. Bennett, *Demagogues in the Depression: American Radicals and the Union Party, 1932–1936* (New Brunswick, N.J., 1969), pp. 3, 4.

18. Sheldon Marcus, *Father Coughlin: The Tumultuous Life of the Priest of the Little Flower* (Boston, 1973), pp. 155–65. See also Charles J. Tull, *Father Coughlin and the New Deal* (Syracuse, 1965), and Raymond G. Swing, *Forerunners of American Fascism* (New York, 1935).

19. Mary Heaton Vorse, "Outline of Flint Pamphlet" (n.d.), pp. 1–6, typescript in Mary Vorse Papers, Archives of Labor History and Urban Affairs, Wayne State University, Detroit, Mich.

20. Joel Seidman, "The Sit-Down Strike" (n.d.), pp. 1–11, typescript in Henry Kraus Collection, Archives of Labor History and Urban Affairs, Wayne State University.

21. Mary Heaton Vorse, "New Strike Technique," undated manuscript in Vorse Papers.

22. Sidney Fine, *Sit-Down: The General Motors Strike of 1936–1937* (Ann Arbor, 1969), pp. 287–309.

23. Ibid., pp. 327, 330, 338, 339–41.

24. United States Department of Labor, "Impact of the War on the Detroit Area," Industrial Area Study no. 10 (July 1943), pp. 35, 36; "Michigan Draws Workers from All States," *Detroiter* 36 (15 January 1945).

25. Lester B. Granger to Franklin D. Roosevelt, 14 January 1942; John C. Dancey to William L. Evans, 6 March 1942, Detroit Urban League Papers.

26. Morris Janowitz, "Patterns of Collective Racial Violence," p. 321; August Meier and Elliott Rudwick, "Black Violence in the 20th Century," p. 311; both in *Violence in America: Historical and Comparative Perspectives,* eds. Hugh Graham Davis and Ted R. Gurr (Washington, D.C., 1969). Alfred McClung Lee and Norman D. Humphrey, *Race Riot* (New York, 1968), pp. xiii, 20–47.

Detroit the Dynamic, 1914

This selection requires little explanation, for it is one of the most effective and graphic expositions of the riot of sounds, the roar of machines, the smells, and the visual chaos that assaulted the senses in a first-generation motorcar factory. The excerpt is drawn from Julian Street, "Detroit the Dynamic" (Colliers, 4 July 1914, pp. 9, 10).

IN A FORD MOTOR COMPANY FACTORY

Imagine It if You Can!

Of course there was order in that place; of course there was system—relentless system—terrible "efficiency"—but to my mind, unaccustomed to such things, the whole room, with its interminable aisles, its whirling shafts and wheels, its forest of roof-supporting posts and flapping, flying, leather belting, its endless rows of writhing machinery, its shrieking, hammering, and clatter, its smell of oil, its autumn haze of smoke, its savage-looking foreign population—to my mind it expressed but one thing, and that thing was delirium.

Fancy a jungle of wheels and belts and weird iron forms—of men, machinery and movement—add to it every kind of sound you can imagine: the sound of a million squirrels chirking, a million monkeys quarreling, a million lions roaring, a million pigs dying, a million elephants smashing through a forest of sheet iron, a million boys whistling on their fingers, a million others coughing with the whooping cough, a million sinners groaning as they are dragged to hell—imagine all of this happening at the very edge of Niagara Falls, with the everlasting roar of the cataract as a perpetual background, and you may acquire a vague conception of that place.

Fancy all this riot going on at once: then imagine the effect of its suddenly ceasing. For that is what it did. The wheels slowed down and became still. The belts stopped flapping. The machines lay dead. The noise faded to a murmur: then to utter silence. Our ears rang with the quiet. The aisles all at once were full of men in overalls, each with a paper package or a box. Some of them walked swiftly toward the exits. Others settled down on piles of automobile parts, or the bases of machines to eat, like grimy soldiers on a battlefield. It was the lull of noon.

From Chaos—the Finished Car

I was glad to leave the machine shop. It dazed me. I should have liked to leave it some time before I actually did, but the agreeable young enthusiast who was conducting us delighted in explaining things—shouting the explanations in our ears. Half of them I could not hear; the other half I could not comprehend. Here and there I recognized familiar automobile parts—great heaps of them —cylinder castings, crank cases, axles. Then as things began to get a little bit coherent, along would come a train of cars hanging insanely from a single overhead rail, the man in the cab tooting his shrill whistle; whereupon I would promptly retire into mental fog once more, losing all sense of what things meant, feeling that I was not in any factory, but in a Gargantuan lunatic asylum where fifteen thousand raving, tearing maniacs had been given full authority to go ahead and do their damnedest.

Americans First: How the People of Detroit Are Making Americans of Foreigners, 1916

Detroit ranked high among the nation's most foreign-born cities in 1910, just a few percentage points below Chicago and New York City. Detroit led the way for the urban nation in inaugurating in 1915 an ambitious Americanization program that was intended to sever Old World ties and teach the immigrant the English language and American ways. Other benefits would also accrue to Detroit employers, such as improved industrial efficiency. The unfolding of that program is covered comprehensively in our selection, which is by Gregory Mason and appeared in New Outlook *(27 September 1916, pp. 193–96, 200–201).*

Every third man you meet in Detroit was born in a foreign country. And three out of every four persons there were either born abroad or born here of foreign-born parents. In short, in Detroit, only every fourth person you meet was born in this country of

American parents. Such is the make-up of the town which has
been called "the most American city in the United States."

Not for more than ten years has Detroit deserved the compli-
ment of that characterization. But the city is beginning to deserve
it again. Detroit is regaining the American spirit, which it partly
lost when the middle-sized interior town grew into the great,
bustling, cosmopolitan city.

Since returning from Europe ten months ago chance has taken
me into many of the largest American cities. Most of them have
had a flat flavor after the conscious tang of egoism which has been
sharpened by the war in the cities of Europe. The nearest approach to this vibrant pride in personal identity I have found in
Detroit. Detroit is alive and knows it. Detroit is American and
proud of it. Detroit is glad to be Detroit.

Statistics, though somewhat dry, sometimes offer the shortest
means of telling a story. In 1900 the population of Detroit was
285,000. In 1910 it was 465,766. It is now conservatively estimated at 725,000. Detroit is now treading on the heels of Cleveland for the privilege of calling itself the sixth city of the land. This
tremendous expansion has been due to the rapid growth of industry, particularly the business of making motor cars. More than
half the motor cars made in America are now made in Detroit.

The people who have been called into Detroit by this great
growth in industry are mainly foreign immigrants and their children. The colored map of the Detroit Board of Commerce showing
the population of Detroit as distributed by races and nationalities
looks like a war map of Europe. The splash of color indicating
the presence of the Slavs is the largest on the map, but other
broad smears show where live Italians, Jews, Hungarians, Ruma-
nians, Greeks, Belgians, Armenians, and other peoples.

The mills which made Detroit great in size and popular prestige
threatened to destroy its Americanism, and when business became demoralized by the outbreak of the war abroad these mills
seemed unable to maintain the level of prosperity which they
had introduced. The fall of 1914 found Detroit suffering from an
acute attack of indigestion. The city had bitten off more immigration than it could chew. Factories ran down and 80,000 men lost
their jobs. Great melancholy mobs of the jobless prowled through
the chilly streets.

Then the Detroit Board of Commerce came to the relief of the city. Under the leadership of Mr. Charles B. Warren and Mr. Byres H. Gitchell, its President and Secretary respectively, the Board organized help for the men out of work. Doctors who volunteered their services were formed into squads to provide free treatment for the sick children and wives of the unemployed, lawyers of similar altruism came forward to save penniless families from ejectment, drug-store proprietors donated medicines, and well-to-do citizens donated sacks of food, each sack sufficient to keep two people alive for three days. In the meantime the Board of Commerce tried to get work for those who had lost it. The effort was successful in the cases of those foreign laborers who could speak English, but most of the sixty thousand men who knew only the tongue of the land of their birth remained jobless. Then and there the Board of Commerce found the germ of the trouble. *They learned that most of the unemployment was due to the inability of foreign laborers to fit American jobs, which was due primarily, of course, to their inability to understand English.*

Thereupon the members of the Board of Commerce went to work to remedy the evil by striking at its root. They assisted the Board of Education in opening night schools where the foreigners might learn English. The Board of Education, by the way, had been more than anxious to do this for several years, but without the assistance of the manufacturers who employed all this foreign labor the educators were almost helpless. The leaders of the Board of Commerce got the manufacturers to help, and in the winter of 1914–15 the work of Americanizing Detroit began on a large scale. It has not ceased, until now Detroit begins to deserve, as perhaps it deserved formerly, the flattering characterization of "the most American city in the United States."

Other cities have also become aroused to the importance of being American, and have taken steps to hurry the process of digesting the foreign lumps in their midst. Rochester, New York, has been a pioneer in this direction. But at Rochester the task of making Americans from immigrants was taken up and carried through by the public schools of the city. The most interesting thing about the situation in Detroit is that this work was begun by the business men. It is true that the schools had been trying to do it before the manufacturers took hold. But until the interest of the great employers of labor was secured the efforts of the Board of Education bore little fruit. By the help of the business men the good intentions of the schoolmen have been converted into fruitful accomplishment.

Realizing the value of having the assistance of experienced advisers, the Detroit Board of Commerce invited the help of the Committee for Immigrants in America. Letters were then sent to every employer of more than one hundred laborers in Detroit, pointing out the disadvantage of having to employ men who could not speak English, asking each employer to take a census of such "dumb" workers in his factory, and requesting the direct help of the manufacturers in inducing the laborers to go to night school and learn English.

The employers, who had learned their lesson in the terrible winter of 1914–15, were not slow to respond. They met the investigators of the Board of Commerce and of the Committee for Immigrants in America, and suggested means of making it practicable for the workers in their factories to go to school. As a result of these suggestions the Board of Commerce submitted a plan to every manufacturer in Detroit who hired more than a fixed minimum of employees. In some factories the Safety First Department took the work in charge; in others control was assumed by the so-called welfare departments—which have become very popular in Detroit; in others an executive of the company made himself personally responsible.

In all factories posters were placed on bulletin boards urging the men to go to school in order to "become better citizens and get better jobs." In all factories slips bearing similar advice were inserted in pay envelopes. Every one in Detroit jumped into the campaign with enthusiasm. Saloon-keepers pasted on saloon walls the posters adjuring the alien to embrace Uncle Sam, department stores put slips of information about the night schools in the packages of every customer who looked like a foreigner, ministers preached "Americanization" in the churches of the foreign quarters, and the editors of foreign newspapers harped on the same key in editorial addresses to their people. Whenever an Italian or Polish young woman drew a book from the public library she found therein one of the ubiquitous slips telling how her friends who knew no English might learn it free.

The Board of Health, the Poor Commission, the juvenile courts, the Associated Charities, the employment bureaus, the Boy Scouts, and the Young Men's Christian Association all put their shoulders to the wheel which has been rolling Detroit out of the mire of hyphenism. Foreign consuls helped too, foreign priests caught hold, and some Greeks lent the Board of Trade some Greek type in order that their countrymen might get the helpful advice in their own language.

From August 17 to September 13, 1915, the whole city embarked on a gigantic campaign of publicity for the benefit of its adopted children from Europe and Asia. The city was bedecked with thousands of handbills. The Detroit Federation of Labor, the Brewery Workers, and the Bill Posters' Union added their approval. The Michigan Workmen's Compensation Mutual Insurance Company issued a special night school bulletin to all employers on their list throughout Michigan suggesting how the night school attendance of employees might be encouraged. This was a particularly happy move, as Mr. I. Walton Schmidt, Secretary of the Americanization Committee of the Board of Commerce, points out, because of "the immediate connection between English First and Safety First." Last, but not least, during this period Detroit's newspapers of whatever language were filled with allusions to the campaign of Americanization.

As a result of this tremendous activity the Detroit night schools opened on Monday evening, September 13, 1915, with an attendance increased over the previous record by one hundred and fifty-three per cent, and with thousands of would-be pupils turned away from school doors.

The means used by different employers in encouraging their employees to go to school varied greatly. The Saxon Motor Company made night school attendance compulsory for its non-English-speaking workmen. The Solvay Process Company offered a wage increase of two cents an hour to all employees who learned English. The Northway Motor and Manufacturing Company started a class in its own factory and announced that workers who attended neither that nor the classes in the public schools would be discharged. The Ford Motor Company, which has also had a school of its own, has rather discouraged its employees who have wanted to attend the public schools rather than the school in the Ford plant. But most concerns, like the Cadillac Company, neither organized schools of their own nor made attendance on the night schools compulsory, but encouraged this attendance in every fair way in their power.

But it remained for the Packard Motor Car Company to stir the whole industrial country with the announcement of the policy summed up in two words which to-day express the spirit of all Detroit—"Americans first."

"From and after this date," announced the Packard Company on January 31, 1916, "promotions to positions of importance in the organization of this company will be given only to those who are native born or naturalized citizens of the United States, or to those of foreign birth who have relinquished their foreign citizenship, and who have filed with our Government their first papers applying for citizenship, which application for citizenship must be diligently followed to its completion."

"Americans first." Those words are on the tongue of every Detroiter to-day. They mean, of course, not *America über Alles,* but *Put only Americans on guard.*

Instead of slackening, the efforts to eradicate hyphenism in Detroit are steadily increasing. When I stepped off the train there in the latter part of last month, there were almost no signs of the Presidential campaign which had already begun to set the rest of the country by the ears, but everywhere were evidences of this campaign of internal adjustment. "Learn English and Get Better Pay" was the advice, appropriate enough, indeed, flashed at me from a bulletin-board in the railway station and later flung at me from windows and billboards everywhere. "English-Speaking Workmen Wanted," said a sign on a building under construction. One plant, I was later told, which uses gang labor has been forced to employ Negroes because of the scarcity in Detroit of white workmen who speak English.

Detroit to-day is a wonderful spectacle of team work. There is none of the petty jealousy between different agencies working toward the same goal which usually is found in even the most praiseworthy movements engaging many men. Never have I seen a city so united for a common end, not even in the case of a city fighting a deadly epidemic. In its great desire to digest the alien ingredients which it has swallowed Detroit has achieved what Maeterlinck calls "the spirit of the hive."

Although supporters of both President Wilson and Mr. Hughes have claimed for these gentlemen the credit for the Americanizing of Detroit—as politicians claim the credit for everything from accidental prosperity to providential rain—the sober truth is that the unifying and purifying of Detroit have been accomplished by united non-partisan action, and could have been accomplished in no other way. . . .

United, non-partisan action, with nearly everybody helping from the multi-millionaire manufacturer to the humblest Hungarian ward leader, has been responsible for the great change that has come over Detroit. The shrewdness of the leaders of the movement in enlisting the aid of the chief men in the various foreign colonies, by the way, has been an important factor in the success of the work.

Detroit's Substantial Families, 1900, 1930

Figures 1 and 2 show the movement of "Substantial Families" from the inner zones of the city to the outer zones and suburbs. Substantial Families were defined by R. D. McKenzie as those names appearing in Dau's Blue Book *and its successor,* Social Secretary, *registers of the "leading business, professional, and social personages having offices in Detroit," and included 2,500 families. Those families moving beyond the city limits concentrated in two exclusive suburbs by 1930, Grosse Pointe Village (681 families) and the Bloomfield Hills–Birmingham district (206 families). Each dot on the figures does not correspond to one family but is representational. The textual information above is drawn from R. D. McKenzie,* The Metropolitan Community *(New York, 1933), pp. 183–84. The figures are from the Cartographic and Audiovisual Division, National Archives, Washington, D.C.*

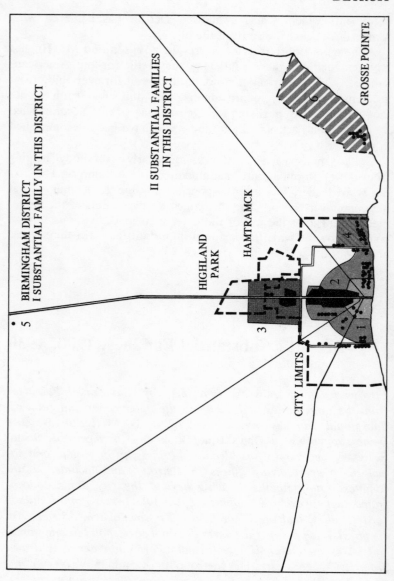

Detroit's "Substantial Families" – 1900

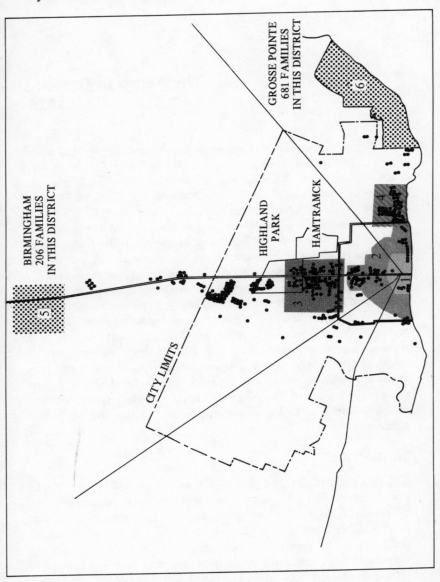

Detroit's "Substantial Families" – 1930

The Negro in Detroit, 1926

The Mayor's Interracial Committee was formed in 1926 in response to a racial altercation in which the Negro family of Dr. Ossian Sweet, while moving into a white neighborhood, became the target of an enraged white mob. The committee chaired by the Reverend Reinhold Niebuhr commissioned Forrester B. Washington of Philadelphia and Robert T. Lansdale of the University of Michigan to investigate the condition of the Negro in Detroit and to issue a report. The information on Negroes was derived largely from a survey of one thousand Negro families drawn from various sections of the black community and balanced so that the "older Negro and the recent Negro settlements received due consideration on the basis of numbers." Business, manufacturing firms, and the principal Negro employers were solicited by questionnaire, and personal interviews were conducted with employment managers of large plants, trade union leaders, Negro workmen, and the heads of public employment agencies. Our selections are drawn from two chapters of The Negro in Detroit *(Detroit Mayor's Interracial Committee, 1926, mimeograph copy in the Detroit Public Library).*

MIGRATION

The following tables give the history of the growth of the Negro population in Detroit as compared with the total population (1) by census decades, (2) by percentages of increase in numbers.

This table shows that in only two of the seven decennial periods did the growth of the Negro population by percentage surpass that of the total population growth. In the 1850–1860 period the Negro population increased 139% as compared with a total increase of 117%; in the 1910–1920 period the Negroes increased 611% to the total 113% increase. The large increase in

Table 1
Population by Census Decades

	TOTAL	NEGRO	PERCENTAGE
1850	21,019	587	2.79
1860	45,619	1,403	3.07
1870	79,577	2,235	2.81
1880	116,340	2,821	2.42
1890	205,876	3,431	1.66
1900	285,704	4,111	1.44
1910	465,766	5,741	1.23
1920	993,678	40,838	4.11

Table 2
Increase in Numbers and Per Cent

	Increase in Total No.	% Increase	Increase in No. Negroes	% Increase
1860	24,600	117%	816	139%
1870	33,958	73%	832	59%
1880	36,763	46%	586	26%
1890	89,536	76%	610	21%
1900	79,828	38%	680	19%
1910	180,062	63%	1,630	39%
1920	527,913	113%	35,097	611%

the first instance was probably due to some protection offered to Negroes by Detroit's proximity to Canada and by the general attitude taken by the city on the matter of slavery; the second great increase period was due to the need for workers in war industries and in automobile manufacturing.

Table 3 shows the per cent of Negro increase in population as compared with the per cent of white increase for various North-central cities that were attracting Negroes during the 1910–1920 period.

This table shows that of the cities listed, only Gary, Indiana surpassed Detroit in actual per cent of Negro increase.

Table 3

	NEGROES		Per cent of Negro Increase 1910–20	Per cent of White Increase 1910–20
	1910	1920		
Cincinnati, Ohio	19,639	29,636	50.9	8.0
Dayton, Ohio	4,842	9,029	86.5	28.0
Toledo, Ohio	1,877	5,690	203.1	42.5
Fort Wayne, Ind.	572	1,476	158.0	34.3
Canton, Ohio	291	1,349	363.6	71.7
Gary, Indiana	383	5,299	1,283.6	205.1
Detroit, Mich.	5,741	41,532	623.4	106.9
Chicago, Ill.	44,103	109,594	148.5	21.0

PRESENT POPULATION STATISTICS

Recent and accurate figures on the Negro population of Detroit are available through the Board of Education's Census statistics for 1925. These figures include the entire adult population as well as the child population of the city. *Of the total population of 1,242,044 the United States Colored make up the fourth largest group, 81,831. This is 6.59% of the entire population.* The Negro population is surpassed in numbers only by the United States White, 598,041 in number or 46.15% of the entire population; the Polish which constitute 9.26% of the population,— 115,069; and the Canadians,—83,685 or 6.74%. . . .

THE NEGRO IN INDUSTRY TODAY

Questionnaires were sent to most of the Detroit business establishments. With one exception exact figures were given as to the number of Negroes employed, one large manufacturing firm giving only an approximation.

Table 1
Returns from Employers' Questionnaires

Total questionnaires sent to Detroit firms	276
Total replies received	151

Total firms employing Negroes (out of 151)		120
Total number of Negroes employed		
(one approximation)	21,571	
Males	21,004	
Females	498	
Sex not given	69	

Table 2 and Table 3 show where these workers are employed.

Table 2
Processes Employing Negroes

Manufacturing and Foundry (one firm gave an approximation)	16,549
Public Service	2,745
Personal Service	893
Building Trades	675
Department Stores, etc.	295
Miscellaneous	414
TOTAL	21,571

Table 3
Firms Employing Negroes
(Listed according to number of males employed)

Name of Company	Number of Negroes Employed		Percent of Total Force
	Males	Females	
Ford Motor Co. (Approx) (Fordson)	6,000		10%
" Highland Park	4,000		10%
Dept. of Public Works	2,200		40%
Dodge Brothers	850		3.5%
Studebaker Corporation	530		10%
Packard Motor Co.	500		
U.S. Post Office	454	31	16.4%
Detroit & Clev. Nav. Co.	438		39%
Morgan & Wright	393		12%

Name of Company	Number of Negroes Employed		Percent of Total Force
	Males	Females	
Cadillac Motor Car Co.	300		5%
Mich. Copper & Brass Co.	275		30%
U.S. Aluminum Co.	230		65%
Murray Body Co.	215		4%
Midland Steel Products Co.	200		35%
Hudson Motor Car Co.	200		1.2%
Detroit Steel Products Co.	180		25%
Detroit Steel Casting Co.	179		54%
H.G. Christian Co.	179		27.8%
Whitehead & Kales Co.	175		20%
Parker-Webb Co.	172		36%
Chevrolet Motor Co.	159		3.5%
Buhl Malleable Co.	140		36%
(Name withheld)	140		14%
McCord Radiator Mfg. Co.	125		10%
Detroit Seamless Steel Tube	125		33.5%
Everett-Winters Co.	121		58.7%
Albert A. Albrect Co.	120		15%
American Radiator Co. of Michigan	118		20%
W.E. Wood	118		61%
(firm names not available;			35.9%
number employed ranges			1.4%
from 106 to 118)			14.6%
			37.5%
			18.4%
			26.6%
Tryant-Detwiler	111		43%
			36%
			57.5%
			38.4%
Riley Stokes Corp.	105		32%
Hupp Motor Car Co.	100		12%
U.S. Radiator Corp.	100		33⅓ %

(List includes only those firms employing 100 or more Negroes.)

THE NEGRO IN THE PUBLIC SERVICE

In the Public Service in and around Detroit there was 2,745 Negroes employed with a salary range of from $12,000 (paid to at least one Negro head of a department), down to $1,200 per year. There are 486 Negroes employed in the Post Office, of whom 31 are women; 28 in the County offices of whom 4 are women. The work in these departments is that of accountant, clerks, carriers, etc. and the unskilled work of janitress, window washers, etc.

In the Department of Public Works there are some 2,200 Negroes employed at an average wage of $26.40 per week, with the exception of garbage truck drivers and collectors who receive $6.50 per day, (members of Garbage Handlers Union). Most of the work in this department is unskilled labor such as street cleaning, repairing, etc.

In the Bureau of Immigration there are two Negro border patrolmen who receive $1,800 per year and one or two charwomen at 45¢ per hour.

In the Customs Service there are two Negroes employed as clerks at $2,000 a year, and one janitor at $480.

In the United States Treasury Department (custodial service) of Detroit there are 16 Negroes employed, of whom five are women, mostly in the unskilled positions.

The Public Service seems to be a place where the Negro is entrenched and making progress. This is due no doubt to the fact that these positions are based on Civil Service Examinations and naturally he cannot very well be discriminated against. Those in charge of these departments say that he makes a good employee, and gets along well.

WAGES

A conservative estimate would place the average wage at 55¢ per hour for the working group. The average monthly wage for heads of families as brought out in the 1,000 families studied was found to be $146.55, but this included professional and business men. Where the Negro can break into the skilled trades and especially if he is unionized, the Negro receives excellent wages, usually the same as whites. Little, if any, discrimination as to wages on the same job was found as shown in Table 9.

Table 9
Reported Differences in Wages on Same Job
(From Employers Schedules)

ANSWERS	ANY DIFFERENCE SHOWN?	EMPLOYING
109	No	20,568 (approx)
4	Yes	439
7	Not Given	564
120		21,571

Many employers stated accurate comparisons were difficult because Negroes and whites were not working on the same jobs. None of the Negro workers who were interviewed knew of discrimination in pay on the same job. Several of these men stated that they were not working on jobs with white men, or else that white men did not do the same kind of work. In talking with some employment managers instances were found where the job was slightly changed or the process broken up so that the Negro's work was not quite the same and for this he is at times paid less money. Some employment managers stated that Negroes were given the poorer jobs.

While little discrimination against Negroes in the matter of wages was discovered it appears that the Negro group as a whole is working on the more inferior jobs and, therefore, earning less proportionately as a group. In addition it is stated by social workers and employers that there is a marked difference in the *real* wages of the Negroes compared with the whites.

The high cost of housing for the Negro is a heavy drain upon his money wages. It was also pointed out by a Negro leader that the scale of living for a colored man is frequently higher than that of white men in a similar job because the Negro usually has to live up to a more important position in his community. The Negro workman frequently has a position of leadership in his lodge or his church to which he has to adjust his mode of living. The budgets prepared by the Visiting Housekeepers Association which are to be found in the section on Welfare throw some light on this matter.

Detroit Sets a Bad Example—
Prohibition, 1925

The dubious value of prohibition for large American industrial cities was evident in Detroit by 1925. The law was flagrantly violated, the police department was corrupted, and the courts failed to convict except for "foreigners—little fellows, suckers, . . . making booze in their kitchens." This selection by Ernest W. Mandeville, "Detroit Sets a Bad Example," is from Outlook *(139 [22 April 1925]: 612–14).*

Detroit, Michigan, is a flagrant example of a wide-open booze town. The time limits of my stay in town prevented me from visiting all of the reputed twenty thousand "blind pigs." I think I did my duty as an investigator by going to a dozen or more. Any one who would run the risks of a greater number of these places would have to be more of a hero than I am.

The "blind pig" conditions are worse in every way than in any other town I visited, and the liquor sold is of a ruinous quality. The profits here on "needle beer" are one thousand per cent. Moonshine profits are slightly over that. "Moon" (as it is called) can be bought for $2.50 a gallon and redistilled denatured alcohol for about $3 a gallon. Both of these retail in the "blind pigs" for 25 cents an ounce, which would bring in $32 a gallon. "Blind pig" owners are without scruple, and you can be sure of being served whatever will bring them in the largest profits.

These booze-selling "blind pigs" are scattered all over the town. I was in the company of men who were well informed on the question, and they pointed out several large apartment-houses which, they said, were given over almost entirely to this trade. I saw enough indications in the ones I visited to lead me to believe this statement. The Superintendent of Police has since stated publicly: "If a policeman goes into an apartment building con-

taining thirty-six apartments, he may find five or six bootlegging
places, but it would be impossible for him to stand on the sidewalk
and estimate how many there were inside. It is just as hard to estimate the number of these places in the city, but there are easily
fifteen thousand."

A request of a taxi driver, to whom I was a stranger, took me on
a tour of "blind pigs"—a tour which I gathered could last as
long as I wished it.

A good many of these places are run by women, and there
seems to be some sort of co-operation between them whereby
they summon extra women from one another to entertain their
guests. The fact is that they are centers of immorality as well as of
illicit liquor selling.

Most of the vices of Detroit are said to center around these
"blind pigs." Narcotics are said to be distributed through them,
crime plots are hatched there, and there among criminals mingle
the members of respected families. I doubt if the influence of one
class on the other, in this case, is an uplifting one.

In the downtown section every manner of store-front is used
to disguise the "blind pigs." I went to a radio sales store which
seemed well equipped and had several salesmen and clerks in
attendance. A very suave, respectable-looking gentleman nodded
recognition to my companion, and we walked through the railing
gate, back through the stockroom, into a completely furnished
barroom with easy-chairs, a white-coated bartender, and several
people sitting around nonchalantly sipping their drinks. This same
experience was repeated in a trunk store and a laundry. I was
told of an undertaker's shop which served as a "blind pig" and
stored its liquor in caskets. Lack of time prevented me from visiting it.

I did visit several saloons which were very crowded and very
reminiscent of the old-time barrooms. The only difference seemed
to be the shabbiness and temporary fixtures in contrast to the old
gilded splendor. They appeared to be selling to every one, and a
fairly constant stream of men pushed in and out for their drinks. I
noticed a very old man hobble into one saloon and put down
his quarter on the bar. The bartender drew a glass of beer and
placed it directly on top of the coin. The old man emptied the
glass and put the quarter back in his purse. My neighbor told me

that the old man was a local character whom all the bartenders served free of charge. It was always the same quarter, and always the same performance of putting it on the bar and pocketing it again.

A quite disreputable-looking "bum" told me that his tramp friends drank "canned heat," a mixture of wood alcohol and paraffin, sold in cans and used to create artificial heat. The "canned-heat drinker" buys a can, empties it into a cloth or his handkerchief, and squeezes it until the wood alcohol drains out and the paraffin is left in the cloth. Then he will mix the alcohol with ginger ale or some cheap soda pop and get a terrific "kick" from the drink.

It is hard to believe that human beings would think of doing such a thing; but they do. Just as in the navy sailors (with nothing else available) used to drink the alcohol from the shellac cans.

I talked to one saloon owner (a former army lieutenant) who complained of the high graft he had to pay. Others told me, however, that from a roving ne'er-do-well he has through bootlegging become a wealthy man. Another saloon-keeper said, "Yesterday I gave away forty-three dollars' worth of booze (wholesale prices) to a policeman."

I was told of still another saloon-keeper, that he passes in society as a gentleman, that his daughter attends a fashionable finishing school (which was named to me), that his wife drives a high-powered car and always refuses to drink at social functions.

Detroit a while ago enacted a "tip-over" order which allowed a policeman to enter a saloon or "blind pig" without a warrant and to tip over or rip out all the paraphernalia. He could use an ax on the furnishings and confiscate the liquor. (Since my trip to Detroit this "tip-over" raid order has been rescinded because the method proved a failure.)

This "tip-over" ruling put a great weapon for loot in the hands of the police and elevated the honor of the bartender. Saloon-owners had to employ bartenders whom they could trust with money payments. If the saloon was entered and about to be "tipped over," the bartender had to act quickly and supply the cash from the cash register for the raiders, if they were bribable. Therefore, on the check up of receipts with the owner, the bartender's word had to be taken for the various hundred-dollar

items missing from the cash register accounting. The bartender
also took the risk of being arrested.

A wage standard for a bartender seems to have been fixed as
follows: $75 a week and $50 extra for every time he is arrested.
If the arrest is made at a time when bail is unavailable and the
bartender has to remain in jail over Sunday, the bonus is raised to
$75.

Statistics in the Detroit Police Court for 1924 show 7,391 arrests
for violations of the Prohibition Law, but only 458 convictions.
In 1920 there were 1,952 arrests and 555 convictions.

As far as I could learn, one cannot buy liquor in the prominent
Detroit cabarets, but one sees many bringing their own liquor with
them.

Prices in Detroit average about as follows: Highballs, 50 cents;
beer, 25 cents by the glass and 50 cents by the bottle; whisky
by the quart, $8 or $9. The beer is said to be made locally and
the hard liquor to come from two sources—Canada and the eastern coast.

The province of Ontario lies just across the river from Detroit.
Though the province is dry, liquor can be manufactured and exported. At Walkerville, Ontario, there is a big distillery. An electric line carries the liquor to the river shipping points. There,
according to Detroit buyers, it is put in boats consigned, perhaps,
for Havana, Cuba. However, when the boats are not watched
they land their cargoes on both sides of the river for the bootleggers. When the patrol of the river is strict, the price of booze
goes up, but ordinarily landing is quite an easy matter.

These boats can be seen loading during the day. During the
winter, I am told, some liquor is dragged across the river on the
ice. There are many rowdy drinking dives along the water-front.

Shipments from the East come by freight disguised in many ways
—sometimes in paint cans, sometimes in piano crates, in oyster
bags, or as liquid soap. Booze has been known to have been
concealed in artificial stone shipped on open flat cars.

These car-load lots may be billed to a fictitious name and address or to some legitimate concern. This concern, perfectly innocently will refuse the car, or the railroad company will find the
car undeliverable, and it is put on a railroad siding. The bootleggers' trucks drive up at night and steal the contents.

There are many financial hazards involved in this kind of shipping. Hijackers are liable to be "tipped off" by the railroad men and then capture the booze before the bootleggers who have engineered the shipment.

In passing through Toledo I read in the papers of two city detectives and a railroad official who were arrested for robbing these liquor cars.

Rush shipments are said to come West by express.

Some of the druggists also add to the bootleg supply by selling a drink which consists of crème-de-menthe formula added to raw alcohol.

Even in such a wide-open town as Detroit I noticed the absence of drunken men on the streets. Others who spend all their days there told me that this is a true observation for all the year round, with the exception of holiday celebrations.

To supplement my own investigation, I looked up a friend who is particularly well posted both through his editorial work and through his close connection as a politician with the city administration. Inasmuch as it is his party which is in office, and inasmuch as he has no grudge, his remarks cannot be discounted as politically prejudiced. Because his reputation is of the best, because he was talking very candidly with me, and because I was able partially to check up his statements, I quote from our conversation:

"Jim C—— has cleared $7,000,000 in the booze game on the Canadian side. He is now considered a local benefactor, and generously helps any worthy project. A lot of the French-Canadians on the other side who used to make about two dollars a day are now rich, or appear to be rich with their diamonds, motors, etc.

"I know of six breweries in Detroit which are making high-powered beer, and I know that it costs each of them $500 a day for protection.

"Ten years ago a dishonest policeman was a rarity and was pointed out and 'put on the tape.' Now the honest ones are pointed out as rarities.

"The result is that the law is, I should say, ninety per cent controlled. The policeman who is a dry at heart is called down for interfering with those higher up. He is shifted around and his work made unpleasant for him.

"A good share of the policemen are Poles, and drinking liquor to them is a tradition. They can't understand why liquor should be prohibited and think of prohibition as an affront. It strikes them as a prohibition of sugar for our coffee would strike us.

"Their relationships with the bootleggers are perfectly friendly. They have to pinch two out of every five every once in a while, but they choose the ones who are the least agreeable about paying graft. The jails are full of bootleggers, but they are mostly foreigners—little fellows, suckers, who have been making booze in their kitchens.

"The booze pay-off doesn't go very high up. The Police Commissioner makes a persistent and conscientious effort to enforce the law.

"But the lower officers make a business of dealing with the bootleggers. As soon as any saloon or 'blind pig' opens the proprietor is 'propositioned,' then they 'handle him,' then everything is 'all set.' These are the terms they use.

"Seven policemen have just been dismissed for ignoring the recent mandate 'not to frequent blind pigs while on duty.' There might have been many times that number dismissed. These seven say they were framed by the rum interests, who have a grip on the police officials and wanted to get rid of them. Think of it! having to issue an order to policemen not to commit an illegal act while on duty.

"Inspectors sometimes find a plant of liquor, collect one hundred dollars apiece, and then tip off the hijackers as to the location of the liquor. Then in turn they pinch the hijackers and take half of the loot. Double-cross methods have become the reigning ethics.

"The result is that there are about eight saloons in every downtown block. William Rutledge, Superintendent of Police, says that there were 1,500 saloons in the city when prohibition went into effect, and that now there are at least 15,000 places in Detroit selling liquor.

"It has been my business to write of twenty New Year's Eves. This last one was the worst I have ever seen. Most every one who was out was putrid drunk.

"I was out driving the other day and stopped at Ann Arbor to see a little girl relative of mine who is in school there. She is only sixteen years old, and lives in one of the school rooming-houses. Even after all that I've seen here in Detroit, it shocked me to have her offer us something to drink and actually produce it. When we showed surprise, she said: 'Why, that's nothing to get shocked about. Some of the nicest boys in college here make a business of bootlegging. We have no trouble to get it from them.'

"Every other house in the outlying country districts operates a still and markets the product through our 'blind pigs.' "

A Grand Rapids newspaper man whom I ran across in Detroit said that there were no open saloons there but lots of drinking in hidden places. He said that liquor is sent from Detroit to Milwaukee, then from Milwaukee to Grand Rapids. "Gin comes this way packed as canned corn," he stated.

I called on Dr. T. R. Gruber, Superintendent of the Detroit Receiving Hospital, who said: "The proportion of alcoholics is much greater than it was before the war. The first year that prohibition went into effect it showed good results here, but now we have things worse than ever. In 1923 we had 1,533 acute alcoholics and 522 chronic alcoholics. In 1924 we had 1,548 acute and 1,014 chronic alcoholics. People are now drinking alcohol in higher concentration, because of the quickly made moonshine by amateurs. This is almost all alcohol."

My investigation in Detroit left me with the impression, Here is a city which is an example of all the evils brought about by an illegal, underground, and hypocritical liquor traffic.

While in Detroit I couldn't seem to get away from booze or booze talk. I dropped into a first-class theater for a little rest, and had no sooner sat down than I heard two young men behind me talking about their drink supply. One young man remarked to his companion: "When you make that dicker for alcohol, get a gallon a week sent up to my house. The wife and I can use at least that much, anyway."

Detroit's Murderous Election Climax, 1930

The recall of Mayor Charles Bowles and the assassination of his radio critic, Gerald E. Buckley, climaxed a decade of lawlessness, loose law enforcement, unchecked corruption, high living, and bawdy nonsense. Bowles was replaced in 1930 by Mayor Frank Murphy, whose primary concerns were unemployment and combating a grim depression. This selection is from the Literary Digest *(106 [9 August 1930]: 9, 10).*

Death was waiting for Jerry Buckley, and he was waiting for death, altho he thought it was a woman.

That is the dramatic situation pictured by the newspapers on a quiet July night in Detroit.

Little suspecting the fate lurking in that hotel lobby in the sleepy hush of the summer night, he walked to a settee and sat down, to wait comfortably.

Now he was just where they wanted him—"on the spot"—brought there by a woman's telephone call, a woman whose appointment would never be kept.

For Jerry Buckley, Detroit radio commentator, friend of the poor, idol of thousands, and hard campaigner for civic honesty, was sentenced to die. He unfurled a newspaper, an election extra, and began to read, unknowingly awaiting the arrival of the visitor who was to fill the quiet lobby with the roar of revolver shots and leave Buckley crumpled on the floor, with his bullet-riddled newspaper beside him.

Here sat Buckley, reading of the election, perusing a front page which would be recast in less than an hour to tell of his own assassination. He was well pleased with the election, for it had gone the way he had wished, the way he had fought to make it go. The result was that Mayor Charles Bowles was out, recalled from office in the special election by a majority of 30,000, after what the paper called the bitterest and most vindictive campaign this city of slashing election fights had ever seen.

Just a couple of hours before, Buckley had climaxed his own radio fight against Mayor Bowles and against crime conditions in Detroit by giving his listeners-in the final bulletin on the Mayor's defeat. It had been a hard fight. Detroit was the first large city ever to recall a mayor, and Buckley's part concededly had been an important one. The radio man might have been excused for feeling pleased with himself as he read about the vote.

Three men quietly entered the lobby, walked up to Buckley, and fired eleven revolver shots into his head and body. Then they hurried out and escaped.

Thus Detroit was plunged into a frenzy of excitement and the nation-wide interest in the city's political predicament was intensified a hundredfold.

The situation a week after the murder of Buckley in the early morning of July 23 was that the slayers were still at large, and Mayor Bowles, automatically a candidate under the law, was waiting to run again in the special election called for September 9.

Before taking up developments that followed the slaying, it may be well to acquaint the reader with the events that led to the recall of the big, placid-looking Mayor, who rode into office on a reform ticket with the backing of the Anti-Saloon League last fall. Says the Detroit correspondent of the New York *World:*

"The reasons for the Mayor's removal from office, cited on the recall petition, were as follows:

"The Mayor tolerated lawlessness by law-enforcement agencies. He destroyed efficient public service through dismissal of faithful employees. He made fifteen campaign promises and kept none of them. He withheld public records. He attempted to make the street-railway and other city employees part of a political machine. He hindered Harold H. Emmons, former Commissioner of Police, whom he himself appointed and dismissed a few weeks later, in the performance of his duties by assuming control of the Vice Squad.

"Henry Ford was among prominent Detroiters who exprest the belief that Bowles had been a good Mayor and should not be recalled."

Denying all charges, the Mayor, as we are told by the Detroit *Free Press,* summed up thus:

"While I have been in office I have served you faithfully and efficiently, and my record of accomplishments will bear me out.

"I have been independent in thought and deed, and never once have I hesitated to take the course which I thought best protected your interests, irrespective of any offense I might thereby give, either to a newspaper or to a few powerful, greedy interests which have constantly opposed me, and which now ask that I be thrown from office."

Interesting also is the information supplied by the Detroit correspondent of the New York *Times:*

"The campaign to have Mayor Bowles recalled began after his return from the Kentucky Derby last May. During his absence at the Derby, Harold H. Emmons, a prominent attorney and business man, whom the Mayor had made Police Commissioner, authorized a sweeping series of raids on race-track handbook agencies, against which a newspaper crusade had been waged for weeks. The Mayor discharged Mr. Emmons.

"Thousands of voters in the city, charging that Mayor Bowles had 'tolerated lawlessness' and 'ousted Commissioner Emmons for enforcing the law,' organized a campaign. Recall petitions were drawn up and a special election ordered.

"Despite his defeat in the election, Mayor Bowles and his supporters are confident of his reelection."

Developments followed fast after the killing of Buckley in the LaSalle Hotel, we learn from the Detroit papers, and these developments may be summarized thus:

Governor Green flew to Detroit immediately after the murder and offered the city authorities every facility of the State Police forces to break up the series of gang killings.

"The police," says *The News,* "have advanced several theories that Buckley had made gang enemies by his radio attacks on gambling, that he was an important witness of a gang slaying, and that he might have been extorting money from gamblers and bootleggers."

Adding to the uproar were two conflicting affidavits, in the first of which, given out by Police Commissioner Wilcox, a bootlegger is said to have told of lending Buckley between $3,000 and $4,000 and getting none of it back.

In the second affidavit he repudiated the first, we read, and

Buckley's brother, Paul, former assistant prosecuting attorney, bitterly attacked the Police Commissioner for his "studied and deliberate attempt to destroy the character of a dead man."

Rewards totaling $8,500 were offered for the capture of the slayers and the instigators of the murder.

The police central vice squad, established under Bowles, was broken up.

War on the underworld was launched through ax raids on blind pigs, disorderly houses, and gambling establishments.

A man who sat near the radio announcer in the hotel lobby at the time of the murder was arrested but released for lack of evidence.

A crowd estimated at 100,000 turned out for Buckley's funeral.

John Gillespie, commissioner of public works, and called Bowles's chief political adviser and financial support, resigned on July 25; but the Mayor announced he would see the fight through.

Prosecutor Chenot said he was convinced that Buckley had been put "on the spot" by the woman who telephoned him to meet her at the hotel, altho she might have been acting unwittingly.

Buckley had received threats on his life, police said, and had been carrying a gun, altho he was unarmed when attacked.

"The slaying of Gerald Buckley," comments the Detroit *News,* "is the criminal world's own comment on the see-nothing, do-nothing, leave-it-to-Providence attitude toward gamblers, racketeers, and gunmen." And *The Free Press* adds that he died "because the government of the city of Detroit failed to maintain a decent check on banditry and gunmen, but allowed them to think that the town is wide open and 'easy.' His blood cries from the ground for vengeance; and his death is a solemn warning to the municipal authorities and to the city."

In another editorial, *The Free Press* has this to say:

"The success of the recall campaign is only the first round of the struggle to restore good government to the city.

"An election, at which Mr. Bowles automatically will be a candidate, unless he decides to withdraw his name, must be held, and the outcome of this election will be quite as important as the outcome of the election of Tuesday.

"In order that it may be productive of good, there must be a candidate in the field who can inspire trust, unite sentiment, and, if elected, give Detroit what it needs in the way of reconstruction of its municipal affairs."

Another Detroit paper, *The Times,* says:

"It is unfortunate that the killing of Buckley is being attributed by some to his activities in the campaign to recall Mayor Bowles.

"The recall campaign developed into one of the most bitter political fights ever staged in Detroit. And Buckley was a leader in the fight against the Mayor.

"But the circumstances surrounding his death and events prior to it point to an entirely different solution of the crime.

"Whatever the motive behind the assassination of Buckley, whatever manner of man the trenchant radio broadcaster proves to have been, the issue remains the same.

"Is this city and this State to be ruled by the assassin or by the forces of organized government?"

Detroit: City of Tomorrow, 1929

This informed vision captures much of the essence of the Detroit of the 1920s—modernity, machinery, the hoopla of motor magnates, and "dynamite" selling by the leader of the sales "shock troops." Matthew Josephson's "Detroit: City of Tomorrow," is one of the best impressionistic pieces written about Detroit during the last dazzle of the prosperity decade. It is excerpted from Outlook *(151 [13 February 1929]: 243–46, 275, 278).*

No sooner had I arrived in the mass production city than I learned some highly significant news: the local museum possessed one of the four original versions of Rodin's "The Thinker"! Now, musing before this gloomy and somewhat bilious man of stone I wondered seriously if he were not the only being in Detroit who was thus engaged in meditation.

Surely Detroit was not "thinking" in the old-fashioned sense; there was none of your peripatetic or seated philosophy. Thought had somehow been circumvented; something that was automatic, something that ran by an internal combustion engine had taken its place. In fact a new word was needed to express the trance, the fearful concentration with which all men awaited the approaching Automobile Show.

And if our naked and lugubrious friend, "The Thinker," could have arisen to stroll down Woodward Avenue, to mingle with the Christmas throngs in Grand Circus Park, he would have witnessed an astounding and, for him, indefinable spectacle.

Hysteria, pandemonium reigned everywhere. The magicians of Detroit, whom Count Keyserling called *Yogis,* directed their flaming eyeballs upon their new automobile models which were to bring forth rivers of gold in the coming year. Spies came and went, whispering of rival projects, of enemy motor cars painted "the colors of precious stones."

No one thought of the human body, or the body politic. All minds were bent wholeheartedly upon the new Fisher or Chrysler bodies. The surrounding ether vibrated with anticipations, as General Motors' President broadcast to hypnotized millions: "1929 Will Be the Biggest Automobile Year in History."

Henry Ford, the genius, the oracle, intoned vatic words that bore the stamp of his originality:

"No American Boy Ever Became a Success by Saving Money."

And so the jostling, the gaily suffocating mass now surged forward as one man to buy everything on the shelves of the great chain stores. Stop saving. Trust in the organism. Have a full Christmas stocking stuffed with six-cylinder cars! In a common burst of enthusiasm, in a splendid, patriotic response to the call of the radio, the press, the bill-boards, all the people flung out last year's furniture, refrigerators, fur coats, electric irons, and purchased new ones. As all records for consumption and ejection were broken the mass production plants geared themselves up to a new speed . . .

Nowhere in the world may the trend of the new industrial cycle be perceived more clearly than in Detroit. In this sense it is the most modern city in the world, the city of tomorrow.

There is no past, there is no history. Neither traditions nor the accumulated handiwork of man's leisure time or deeply reflective moods obtrude upon the eye. There is primarily the wealth of mechanism and "turnover." One day, thousands and thousands of human beings turned themselves over and found that they were in the huge metropolis of Detroit.

The city boasts a romantic colonial history, under three flags. But all the important historical facts—so few in themselves—are economic. In 1829 wooden stockades still protect the citizenry from Indians; 1840, and the Erie Canal is opened; 1860, lo, the railroad comes; 1890, and Henry Ford completes his first version of the horseless carriage. Detroit had only 200,000 inhabitants; but *der Tag* had come. An economic empire began which produced here, in two generations, a concentration camp of a million and a half souls. Out of an interlude of frantic, highfevered growth, giant industries arose, directed by men of genius who revolutionized the economy of Steam Power. . . .

All of the industrial leaders whom I saw voiced their optimism and their intense satisfaction over the present state. Nowhere in the world or in human history were great masses of human beings lifted to such a scale of well-being and mechanical comfort. And by the same token, one could have answered that nowhere in the world did men seem so *automatised,* submissive and monotonous. . . .

The stunning noise and the heat continued to oppress me. The workingmen were all powerfully built; they were absorbed in the common rhythm and arduous effort of the job. Here was a magnificent African, fully six and a half feet tall, laboring before a furnace of hell. Beside him was an Italian. . . .

In the meantime an element of waste was at work night and day to nullify the advances and economics made in manufacturing technique: the rising cost of selling gave automobile chieftains white hair and sleepless nights. Super-salesmanship, nation-wide advertising, show-rooms, potted plants, drinks for buyers, all of this added to overhead as attempts were made to keep up with the enlarged capacity of the factory. Mass production meant mass sales; and mass sales, the passionate effort to get the last inch, the last ten per cent of purchasing power in a given territory, were becoming incalculably expensive.

Nothing more could be done in the way of reducing labor costs.

I was told that the average labor on a $3,000 car amounted to $180; that a certain widely used accessory netted the manufacturer a profit at $5.00 and retailed at from $17.50 to $25.00.

The larger companies have therefore been uniting in "mergers" chiefly to cut down sales costs. In 1928 Chrysler and Dodge, Studebaker and Pierce-Arrow, Huppmobile and Chandler, consolidated forces. Twenty years ago there were nearly 350 companies; now there are about 70, and of these only a dozen made all but a tiny fraction of the cars.

"Agreements" came into being. The Society of Automotive Engineers organized forces for a wide standardization of parts and materials. New devices and inventions, unless revolutionary, were to be made available to all simultaneously. So much for Mr. Hoover's "rugged individualism in business."

Just as the automobile is the golden calf, the favorite sculpture of America's multitude, so it is the key industry. Its discoveries and policies are symptomatic of all the other industries which long to emulate its advances.

The procession of gigantic mergers typical of the Machine Age is now openly tolerated by the whole nation. The unspoken policy of Mr. Coolidge and Mr. Hoover hastened the process. An enlightened capitalism sets the labor standard at the highest in the world and the masses remain tranquil, accepting the great economies and universal luxuries of the new system, and even participating in profits by buying stocks. It is idle to talk of individualism! No mechanical unit geared for national sales can be run by Jeffersonian principles.

The defenders of the new "benevolent oligarchy" always speak in the same tones of optimism.

". . . Never in the history of the world have such great numbers of men been so prosperous and physically contented. Is not that alone an enormous advance? And the automobile! Think of what conveniences it has brought to millions of farmers; the tractors, the 'buses . . . We live at a new speed; we have extended our faculties, our enjoyments. You and I are infinitely superior in our way of life to our fathers . . ."

It was an official of the General Motors Corporation speaking.

What he said, had been said to me everywhere in the industrial Middle-West; and it was literally true. But the optimism was dangerous; and likewise the blindness to much social disarrangement, to the effects on the human fibre of the leveling and regimenting processes which sucked all people into the great capital (or collectivistic, if you will) combines, which imposed nationally the common salesman psychology, the spirit of the flunky and the "yes-man."

We were standing by a window in the great stone castle of the General Motors company. Before our eyes there was a scene of the unspeakable ugliness and chaos. There were mills in the midsts of the city, belching thick smoke, high office-buildings side by side with wooden frame residences, grimy garages and desolate parking-spaces for automobiles. Finally our eyes fell upon a small and hideous wooden cottage with drawn blinds, just across the street.

"It's a 'blind pig,' " said the official. "Close enough! Yes, this is a terrible city. I wouldn't have my son grow up in the smoke and filth here. We live away out in the country. I have a garden . . ."

In the period of transition between individualistic competition and "benevolent oligarchy" there are terrible, silent upheavals or dislocations; individual fortunes change hands; whole masses are thrown out of work, and left to their own devices; whole industries, regions of the country are depressed; small capital weeps and cowers as it goes to the wall.

Out of curiosity I visited also the office of a small automobile manufacturer who was reputed to be having difficulties, harassed as he was by gigantic competitors. The head of the plant seemed to be in a state bordering on hysteria during my visit.

To my questions he replied in tones of the greatest anxiety: "I cannot say anything. Whatever I said might be misinterpreted or misunderstood."

Despite rigorous efforts toward manufacturing economies, ferocious sales-campaigns, "prize contests" between crews, a deluge of propaganda and advertising, business was declining. All the officers of the company, otherwise amiable and prepossessing men, looked sick-eyed.

From his office window the Manager and Vice-President of this company pointed to a Bridge-of-Sighs affair, an enclosed trestle that ran from the building we were in to an adjoining plant. Over this bridge the finished machines were run on a conveyor belt to the other building to be packed and shipped away automatically.

As each unit moved into its place, a machine, like a turnstile in the subway, clicked off a number which showed the hourly and daily production instantaneously, in the central office!

I marveled greatly at this instrument. By such a medium in a National Central Office, a benevolent dictator could determine just how many automobiles or vacuum cleaners should be made, and when to slow up output, or when to increase it; how to have enough and not too much; how to divert energy and capital from one industry into another, from one region to another. Some day, the fearful economic and social dislocations (which went on even during prosperity) would be avoided . . .

There was also a map of the United States with great black and red spots on it. The red showed areas of low sales-pressure. I took it that the manager would thereupon send a crew of fiery men, hell-bent, hammer and tongs, to work up the red area until it was black. What, I thought, if the same enthusiasm, the same constructive passions could be diverted to other channels? There would be a map with red spots to show where there was dirt, poverty, illiteracy. And the great Manager from his Central Office could send a mighty band of super-salesmen to "clean up" this area, to give it prosperity, beautiful public buildings, gardens and pools!

The incredibly flat plains of Michigan and Ohio were given to a wintry desolation as the Broadway limited fled from them at sixty an hour.

To New York! *À Berlin! Nach Paris!* Always, the soul strained after the Capital. The confusion of races was no different in the island city which destiny for a time had made the spiritual concentration camp of the nation. Much of the population was "hand-picked," originating from all the forty-eight states, and arrived in the capital after the most painful sacrifices. Graceful illusions persisted that made life tolerable. The colorful activities of theatres on Broadway, of musicians, painters, university and literary circles, permitted one to forget the flaming forges, the mines, railroad yards, motor factories of which the country was actually composed. Ideas existed for their own sake, at least to a minority class, truly disinherited but stubbornly believing that it summed up the human aspirations of a whole people.

In the great common meeting ground of the club car the Super-Salesman made overtures, offered the convivial bottle, and then confidences to a fellow traveler who, he persisted in believing, was also a fellow-salesman.

He spoke in the very accents (upon my honor) of Sinclair Lewis's "Babbitt." He wore horn-rimmed glasses which disguised his nearly expressionless face. Let us call my composite American only Smith; he was tremendously symptomatic! His features, his intonation were anonymous; save for his yellow complexion, his pale, blue eyes, and an edge of hysteria in his voice, which frightened me.

"I have a growing business, a fine income, a beautiful home with the finest books in it. Yes, only the best: Elbert Hubbard, Robert Louis Stevenson, and Lud—Ludwig . . . And I have an eight-cylinder coupe, and, let me tell *you,* a wonderful wife . . . Finest little woman in the world—and yet, and yet . . ."

Here his voice grew husky and broke in a stagy sob: "I don' know what's the matter with me. Something's wrong, something's just wrong with me, somewhere, I guess. I can't seem to get back into my stride.

"Just come back from ninety days in a sanitarium out in Wisconsin. Cost $165 a week. Company's been wonderful to me. Here's a letter the President sent me. Finest fellow in the world, biggest-hearted man you ever saw. Yes, sir, wants me to take six months off in Bermuda, forget all about business, and on the company's time!

"Nerves! A nervous break-down they tell me," went on Smith woefully. "And I can't get my mind off business! I've been ringing door-bells for eleven years, and let me tell you I'm proud of it. The American woman is the shrewdest little buyer in the world. And when I come *with my hat in my hand,* recommending our high-pressure suction vacuum cleaner, and get a hard look, I don't mind. Something's been wrong, worries her. Her husband might have said a cross word. . . ."

The earnest Mr. Smith was a Division Manager for a Detroit Company, covering three States from his Milwaukee headquarters, and employing three hundred and fifty salesmen, whom he alternately lashed, or patted on the back, individually. Every Monday morning he made a speech. He raved.

"I give 'em DYNAMITE," he told me. "I never let up. I give 'em dynamite, after breakfast every day. I never stop."

He held contests, awarded airplanes as prizes, maneuvered his little army and reported regularly to Detroit. He had been a favorite leader of shock-troops, up from the ranks, when his nervous breakdown had come.

"All of a sudden," he related, "on a rainy night, I was driving like hell, trying to forget everything, trying to get away. All of a sudden my legs went dead on me, my hands too. I saw another car crossing. I skidded and crashed. Nothing *bad*. Only afterward I couldn't sign any checks, or letters. My secretary (that's my wife) had to sign for me. Rest didn't help. One night I fainted at our National Dealers' Convention . . ."

Since boyhood, Smith, it appears, had never played, never really amused himself. Perhaps, as I suggested to him, he had used up twenty years worth of nervous energy in ten. When he was a boy on the farm in "Missourah" he used to play the fiddle. Perhaps it would have been better for him to have remained a musician rather than work up to dynamite-selling at $16,500 a year.

"But I just *love* to sell vacuum cleaners!" (*sic*)

"The American woman is the shrewdest little buyer in the world. Dust is the greatest agent of disease, is it not? I come to give away free a government pamphlet recommending our high-pressure vacuum cleaner . . ."

At this point the whole club car arose in revolt. No one else had been able to hear himself think. As for the government recommending *his* vacuum cleaner, Tommy-rot, said a Detroit lawyer. That would be "restraint of trade." Tut-tut, said a Detroit advertising agent; the company's advertising was full of holes and buncombe. Smith rose to the defense of his Company hysterically. But he was cried down by the whole smoking car, who, now thoroughly aroused, championed the great Rival Company, rejected the idea that dust was an evil, and called for a return to the days of wool carpets, old-fashioned upholstery, and no dynamite!

The conversation became general. It was at a fairly high level for a smoker. I am by no means exaggerating when I say that the skeptical and destructive ideas of H. L. Mencken seemed to have gained a wide hearing among the Rotarians of the land. One by one these men, flunkies, "yes-men," and salesmen, gloated and joyed in revealing the deceptions, exaggerations and "bunk" which their own companies broadcast. Smith would periodically interrupt, crying that he had "rung door-bells for eleven years, and was proud of it," only to be shouted down by the whole indignant, sardonic smoking-room again and again.

When Detroit's Out of Work, 1930

This document is a poignant and moving firsthand account of the struggle the unemployed faced in depression Detroit. With no re-serves to tide them over, thousands stood in relief lines, went on welfare, and alternately spent weeks, and sometimes even months, searching for nonexistent jobs. The frustration prompted one job seeker to complain: "Only God knows and sometimes I think even God don't know much about hunting a job." This selec-tion by a social worker, Helen Hall, "When Detroit's Out of Gear," appeared in the Survey *(64 [1 April 1930]: 9–14, 54).*

I have never confronted such misery as on the zero day of my arrival in Detroit. It was still dark at 7:30 when our train pulled in and I had forgotten how cold cold could be until I stepped out onto the station platform that January morning. After breakfast at Franklin Street Settlement, we set out for the Department of Public Welfare. There we came upon muffled men and women at the entrance. They crowded the lower corridors and we had to push by. They were on the stairs and filled the upper halls, standing, waiting their turn. I wanted to look at them and see what type of men and women they really were, but I was ashamed to look. I felt suddenly conscious of the fur lining of my coat and the good breakfast I had eaten. Perhaps it was the bitter cold I had come in from and they had come in from that gave me the impression that they were congealed into one disconsolate lump.

When I came out two hours later the same lines were there, literally the same lines for I recognized a red knitted cap on one of the men—such a sad little man and his cap wasn't much nearer the window. And inside they were working fast and steadily and it seemed to me with great kindliness. In December alone the de-

partment had disbursed nearly half a million dollars in public relief. Two-thirds of the families had been driven to apply because of the unemployment of the breadwinner. In January the
figure was to rise to $650,000. . . .

When I came to visit the homes of some of these men and
women I could gauge something of the struggle that so often had
gone on before they had come to the welfare stations. Asking for
help, even if the cause for it lies far outside our own control,
means a serious breakdown in family pride and self-confidence,
a self-confidence which seldom blossoms again with the same
sturdiness. As one woman said to me, "My husband hated to go
stand in those lines, but I drove him to it. We couldn't see the children starve. He don't seem to mind it so much now!"

The Onottos were living on potatoes and pancakes when the
father finally asked for help. He had been out since October from
the Michigan Steel Corporation. Before Wesley Rollins finally ap-
pealed, he had carried his family for five and a half months, in
spite of the serious illness of one of the children. He is a Nova
Scotian, thirty-two years old and for four years had worked at
Murray Body.

Susie Lock was in the line because her husband had deserted
her and her two small children. Matthew had worked at the Timken
Axle Works for the first four years after he and Susie were married.
Then he changed to the Cadillac Motors where they were paying
more per hour. But his department so often didn't work the full
nine hours a day and with time out each year for inventory, they
weren't able to save enough to tide them over this last three and a
half month's idleness. She was still bewildered by what had happened when I saw her in their neat flat in the rear of a two family
house. Her story as she told it:

> I said to him, "You must be lazy or you'd have gotten a job!" I
> don't know what ever made me say it, but he'd been gone so long
> that day I thought surely he'd got something. And he just gets up
> and says, "All right, if you feel that way about it, I'll go to Chicago
> and look for a job!" And then he gets right out. You see he knows
> a guy who's got an old Ford and him and three others have gone
> off in it. But it's an open car and it's so cold and that was Tuesday
> and I ain't heard. And I wish I'd never said it.

The age factor may have entered somewhat into Henry Nelson's problem. He seemed anxious to sit down when we came in and steadied himself by the furniture, but I didn't know then that he was weak for lack of food. When the department had come in on the case he had had little or nothing to eat for three days. He was fifty-two, a bad age, practically hopeless for a job when young men couldn't get work, and he was aware of it; for he was an old Detroiter, had worked for Ford, Graham-Paige, and Fisher Body, and knew the ropes. But he had kept on trying because he had the "missus to look after." There were two sons and a married daughter. Both sons and the son-in-law had been out of work for three months. Four men workless and wage-less in one family!

The lines at the city welfare stations are not the only ones. More of the automobile workers were to be found among the men and women shuffling dejectedly at the public and private employment offices, and again all of them at one time or another in those lines which run into the thousands before the gate of any of the large plants which are hiring help, and in lesser numbers, before the door of any plant whether it is hiring or not.

For the men who are laid off feel that they still belong. They go back and back. Detroit is spread out. Even in normal times workmen sometimes travel two hours to work and two hours back. But when work is hard to get, they may spend the night in line waiting to be let in through the gates to the employment offices in the morning. In freezing weather they build fires to warm themselves, and what with the wet and the strain, there are occasional fracases to get up front and a rush when opening time comes. Joe Smith told me he was put through the line so fast at Hudson Motors that he had time to tell of only one thing that he could do. So as he had worked in four different departments, he changed hats and coats with his friends and went through the line four times.

John Rogers made comment on the search for employment: "Only God knows and sometimes I think even God don't know much about hunting a job." He has had varied experience with automobile factories—Dodge, Chrysler, and Briggs Manufacturing Company—and with the ups and downs of prosperity. In 1928, the year after their child was born, he worked steadily, making an average of thirty dollars a week. "We lived that year," Mrs. Rogers said to her Franklin Street neighbor. "We went on the boat and I

went to the library and got books. We furnished our rooms, too."
She looked about the rooms with pride. "We didn't spend our money
foolish. But then came the black year." The black year was 1929.
John worked from January to July last year and during that time
he earned $644.06. In April he saw signs of a lay-off and Mrs.
Rogers started in to earn. In the summer months several families
for whom she worked went away and she averaged only about
two days a week. They managed out of that and out of the little
they had saved.

Ralph Benda, ten years in the automobile industry. Forty-one
years old. His earnings for 1927 were $621.77, for 1928, $708.50
and for 1929, $903.

Benjamin Desuka; at Dodge Brothers for nine years. His yearly
income for 1929 was $934.50. He is 33, his wife 30, and they have
five small children.

William Powers, 30, two years at the Chevrolet. $1,043.52
earned in 1929. He has seven small children under eleven years of
age.

Stanley Kopper, two years with L. A. Young; income for 1929,
$702. He is 38 and they have three small children.

John Wilson; earnings for 1927, $346; for 1928, $438, and for
1929, $513.52. This man, laid off by Chrysler after steady em-
ployment, has been off and on with both Dodge and Murray
Body since. He is 40 and his wife 37. Eight children.

These men are all in the highest wage-earning period of their
lives and are equal to sticking to a job and willing to work. Yet
they were not able to average enough in a year to support their
families in spite of a daily wage which has rung around the world.

Take Frank Rogers, who ran a press for the Kelsey Wheel for
twelve years, starting at 20¢ an hour and getting 65¢ when he was
laid off last June. He is a big red-cheeked man of about fifty who,
as he said, always paid the bills on the first of the month, and
moved to his present house because there was a bath in it. When
he was let go the plant was working two or three days a week. He
found it a discouraging struggle to be out of work eight months
and was now beginning to get in debt, but because he had always
been so steady before, people were willing to trust him a bit
longer. He goes in and asks where there is no help wanted. Once
he got a job when the sign was down. He said he knows it is dis-

couraging for a firm to see men hanging around, but he goes back every Monday morning to Kelsey's. All they say is, "Keep in touch with us."

The part-time work bears harder if anything on women wage-earners. Lucy Lawler is a widow with three children. She was thirty-two her last birthday. She assembles small parts at the Hudson Motors and in a busy season with steady work, gets $28 a week. She was laid off in August and up to January had had nothing since but one day and sometimes one hour a week. One week she was notified to come in. She reported for several days and finally was put to work for half an hour. Her pay for that week was 28¢ and her carfare 60¢. . . .

Anthony Lombardo was still out of work when I called at his home. He came from Italy to America twenty years ago and to Detroit in 1923. The day he arrived he found a job at Ford's, taking it over from a man who quit because he had found lifting girders too hard. He said:

> He was the big man with the long neck. Now me, I'm broad and short and it's not so hard for me to stoop down. In Bridgeport where I was the fireman in a hospital for seven years when I putta da coal on the fire sometimes I standa and sometimes I stoop; but when I do this job I never get a look up. I worka six years with this job, but all that time eight months is the longest I ever go steady in one year. For more than one year I only work two or three days a week. Everybody say here, "Why don't you save when you work?" But how can you save when you no work steady? If I could get $5 a day all year, I could put this little pieca for the rent, this pieca for the coal, this pieca for the electric and then maybe I can putta this away for to save and know where I go. But now you work, you make something, you stop. You spend what you got save. You getta the debts. Then you get a job. You pay the debts. You save a little. You stop. And now I stop too long this time.

*   *   *   *   *

Perhaps three hundred years from now, or a hundred, or fifty—or less if you are hopeful—some sculptor will fashion a knot of men standing in our employment lines of today as hostages of the modern industrial center, so that all men may see their personal tragedies as well as the civic drama of it. And the citizens of Detroit may set the statue up in a public square as symbol of their deliverance from a great threat to the life of the people.

Father Charles E. Coughlin Speaks, 1934

Father Charles E. Coughlin's Sunday radio talks departed from usual pastoral mold and addressed themselves directly to the material needs and spiritual hurts that millions suffered during the depression. Controversial, bombastic, and mellifluent, the Royal Oak, Michigan, priest deftly intermingled biblical allusions and democratic symbols and built up a radio audience numbering in the millions. Although he later broke with President Roosevelt in 1936, Coughlin fervently supported FDR and the first New Deal, as he did in this radio talk, which was delivered on 11 March 1934 over Detroit radio station WJR. The talk is from Eight Lectures on Labor, Capital and Justice *(Royal Oak, Mich., 1934, pp. 100–114). Reprinted by permission of The Reverend Charles E. Coughlin.*

It is absurd to imagine that the habits of the industrialist and the philosophy of the financialist can be destroyed within a month or a year or a lifetime.

The struggle for physical freedom endured almost eighteen hundred years. Agrarian liberty or the right to own your own home or farm was won only after a contest which lasted more than one thousand years—from the Magna Charta to Queen Victoria. The struggle to destroy political bondage lasted not only throughout the centuries of pagan history. Today there are many battlefronts upon which it is still being waged. And last and most important economic liberty, which for more than seven years it has been my privilege to proclaim, cannot be acquired in its completeness in a day, or in the life of one Administration.

The physical, the agrarian, the political liberties which we possess are most imperfect in themselves as they exist today. What

advantage or thrill exists for the derelict scavenger—an innocent victim of the financial and industrial systems of today—as he
gathers the crumbs of existence which fall from the tables of the
rich—what matters whether or not he possesses a physical liberty
when his hands are bound by the manacles of forced idleness;
when his poor hovel of a home is overburdened with taxation or
subject to confiscation and when his vote must be cast year after
year to perpetuate his bondage?

Liberty as we have experienced it—save the god-given liberty of
conscience—is a cheap coin to trade even for the exactitudes of
Communism or the fetters of Fascism if these systems of economics
supply heat and shelter and a chance to live.

Without economic liberty—and by that I mean freedom from
the slavery of fear; from the tyranny which scientifically deprives
one of the necessities of life—without that economic liberty, little
else matters. . . .

I might add, that no one can eat, can live, can establish a home,
can dare procreate children. Instead, to satisfy the greed of modern capitalism and to uphold the system which protects it your
machinery rusts, your body deteriorates and your just complaints
are labeled *"radical"* by the prostituted panderers of purchased
propaganda.

In this contest upon which depends the outcome of civilization
the voice of Catholicism shall not be silent. We not only condemn
the credit system and, therefore, the modern financial system
which disgraces our nation and disgraces us who pretend to the
name of Christianity. We stand opposed today and forevermore, if
necessary, to the *"whole economic side of modern life which has
become hard, cruel and relentless to a ghastly degree."*

Those are the words of Pius XI who continues by stating that:
*"The desire for profits has been followed by the unbridled ambi-
tion for domination . . . Furthermore business affairs have become
scandalously mixed up with the duties and offices of the civil
authority . . . and the state has become a slave bound over to the
service of human passion and greed."*

There are several obvious thoughts associated with these
statements.

The first point, my friends, that is obvious in our present economic life is that a few men—not many—not 10-thousand out of

our 123-million citizens—have chained and shackled us to the whipping post of poverty. A handful of pagan minded profiteers have scourged your bodies with want in the midst of plenty and seared your souls with the hot iron of deceit until you believe that starvation, slave wages, slum dwellings, nakedness, the fear of tomorrow and the bitter cup of unemployment are the threads, as it were, out of which the fabric of life is spun upon the loom of their diabolical tyranny.

And the second point that is obvious not only to the mind of Pius XI but also to the observation of any high school boy is that while these few men protest against Government entering into business or into finance, they themselves have forced their way into Government until they have controlled it.

Your Mellons and your Morgans; your Baruchs and your Bailies! Your Treasury Department needlessly attempting to balance a budget; hopelessly trying to borrow itself out of debt; and erroneously refinancing the bloody war bonds to perpetuate a taxation in favor of the few—bloody Liberty Bonds better called "slave bonds" which you and your children are expected to honor for the privilege of having made a shambles out of France and a shame out of civilization.

It was not bad enough to refinance them. It was worse in its effect upon the country last week to bungle the refinancing and to show that the Treasury economic advisory giants were out of touch with market conditions to such an extent as to add to the burden of the taxpayer a stupid overcharge of interest of $4,600,000 by issuing the bonds at ¼ of 1 per cent at excess interest.

What is a little matter of $4,600,000 to the taxpayers especially if it goes into the vaults of the bankers?

If the Catholic Church through its official voice speaks of the *"irresistible power exercised by those who hold and control money,"* the complaint is justified and verified when you read the American *"Who's Who"* and discover *"What's What."* This is the third obvious point well recognized by the American public.

As a rule, the ordinary person knows as little about money as he does of the secret workings of the roulette wheel. He does know that it is owned and controlled and concentrated in the hands of a few. He does know that the only reason why factories are inoperative, why wheat is burned, why economic desolation reigns supreme is because there is scarcity of money—a man-made, bookkeeping scarcity so that the debts contracted yesterday will be twice as hard to pay tomorrow; so that the money-lenders and changers can profit and the non-money-changers can suffer. . . .

Bankers' imagination!

Did they ever visualize that they put Christ on a hospital cot? Did they ever think as they passed through the slums that they multiplied the cave of Bethlehem ten million times? Did they ever conceive as they stand at a death-bed often made by their own thoughtlessness that they have treated the brothers of Christ as Iscariot treated our Elder Brother; that they have erected ten million crucifixes which point to the throne of God because credit is controlled and because wealth is concentrated in the hands of a few?

Imagination! Not even the conscience of a Christian!

I again say: *"It is either Roosevelt or Ruin!"* . . .

The new system must be programmed on the policy of plenty for all. This can be done by driving from the Temple the money-changers who have usurped both the pulpit of doctrine and the altar of sacrifice—the altar whose stones are dripping with the blood of human beings.

Our blessed Lord has expressed it all in one concise sentence: *"You cannot serve God and Mammon."* This is exactly what we have been trying to do. We have put money on the throne of God —and there it reigns—mysterious, supreme, constantly clamoring for fresh victims.

Before we logically dare hope to see human rights supersede financial rights, both our currency and our credit must be nationalized. This is our ultimate goal.

I wonder how many of you ladies and gentlemen will join in this crusade? . . .

But let us become more specific, as we concentrate on the immediate things already accomplished and about to be accomplished before this final victory will be gained.

First of all, we were thrilled with President Roosevelt's public pronouncement last Monday. He assured us that there was no returning to the moorings of the old system from which we have definitely cut loose. He was forceful in stating that the basic principles of the NRA are here to remain. Wages must be raised. Working hours must be shortened. . . .

Henceforth it is the duty of every American citizen to support the NRA in its program for shorter hours, higher wages and the God-given right for the laboring man to organize. There is, too, the corresponding duty on the part of the Government to enable the manufacturer to acquire credit money without which he cannot conduct his business.

To enforce one duty without the other is to invite industrial chaos.

The General Motors Sit-down Strike and the Formation of Mass Unions, 1937

The key sit-down strike that helped to bring about the formation of unions in mass production industry was that which occurred in the auto plants of Detroit's satellite city, Flint. Mary Heaton Vorse, a labor writer, covered the GM work stoppage in February 1937, and even though her observations were written at a time when the outcome was uncertain, she correctly foresaw the potential and profound impacts of this daring and innovative strike technique. Vorse's assessment exists in manuscript form in the Mary Heaton Vorse Papers (Box 109) at the Archives of Labor History and Urban Affairs at Wayne State University. The three letters from sit-downers were drawn from the Henry Kraus Papers, also at the Archives of Labor History and Urban Affairs, Wayne State University, Detroit, Michigan. All are reprinted by permission.

When they tie the can to a union man,
　Sit down! Sit down!
When they give him the sack, they'll take him back,
　Sit down! Sit down!

Chorus
Sit down, just take a seat,
Sit down, and rest your feet,
Sit down, you've got 'em beat.
    Sit down! Sit down! [1]

The city of Flint is today an armed camp. More than 4,000
National Guards are here, including cavalry and machine gun
corp. A night visit to the big Chevrolet plant and Fisher Body #2
reminds one of an American sector in war time France. A military
pass is required to go through the lines, the visitor is challenged
every few feet. The soldiers are huddled in the snow around a
fire in front of Chevrolet #4; on the other side of the six foot fence,
topped with barbed wire, are the Union pickets.

"You boys got plenty of wood for your fire?" a striker calls,
"Just sing out if you need more and we'll pass some through."

"Thanks, we're expecting more soon."

No hard feelings between the boys in overalls and the boys in
uniform. Why should there be? Almost all of the rank and file of
the guardsmen have been automobile workers at one time or another. They mutter among themselves that they are not going to
do any dirty work should they be ordered to clear the factories of
sit-down strikers.

On both sides of the dark street which is punctuated with red
fires, windows of idle factories shine with green lights. In Fisher
Body #2 the strikers are singing "Hold The Fort." It is after
midnight but both sides are alert.

The sprawling city of Flint, which has 130,000 inhabitants
and no distinguishing feature or beauty, is owned body and soul
by General Motors.

Today it is the core of the automobile strike. A strike, which in
its far reaching implications, is perhaps the most important that
this century has seen in America.

At this present moment there are strikes in twenty cities. Because of body and part shortages, it has closed or curtailed production in more than fifty General Motors units and thrown out of

---

1. Lyrics and music by Maurice Sugar, attorney for the United Automobile Workers of America.

work 150,000 employees. It has practically stopped General Motors from making passenger cars. The January program called for the completion of 130,000 cars, only 53,180 have been assembled, according to General Motors figures.

Like ninety per cent of the strikes in this country the most important question involved is that of Union recognition. The employers in the key industries have yet to recognize the principle of collective bargaining. In America many lives are lost annually and millions of dollars of both the workers and employers because management still refuses to bargain with the representative of its workers.

The refusal to recognize the union is a "matter of principle" among anti-union employers like General Motors. They will spend millions in the employment of thugs and spies from strike breaking detective agencies. Vigilante committees are organized and paid for by the company, the law of the land is defied and the entreaties of the Secretary of Labor to enter into conference are ignored.

So the power of all non-union forces is massed against the auto workers.

So if this strike is even partially won the mass industries of steel, rubber, electrical workers, etc. will be organized for the first time.

The winning of the strike, moreover, will make the Committee of Industrial Organization which is headed by John L. Lewis, the dominant factor in the American labor movement. The ten unions forming it have been suspended by its parent organization the American Federation of Labor.

The C.I.O. had formed the Steel Workers Organizing Committee, the S.W.O.C., and was rapidly pushing organizations in steel. An organizational drive of a lesser nature was also begun in automobiles. Before the automobile drive was well under way a sit-down strike occurred in Fisher Body #2 in Flint late in December, shortly followed by Fisher Body #1. The strike movement flung itself across the country like a prairie fire. Soon General Motors was tied up by the sit-downs, by walk-outs and shut down, forced through the lack of necessary parts and bodies.

The principle strike demands are: Union recognition, the United Auto Workers to be sole bargaining agent for the workers, control of the speed up, a thirty hour week, seniority rights, higher wages.

The sit-down is a new feature in strike strategy in America. The revolutionary implications of men holding the possession of a factory is not understood by the majority of the workers. It must be remembered that the American worker is often militant and revolutionary in his action without having the least revolutionary philosophy. The sit-down strikers in the automobile industry have no idea of "capturing the industry." They merely consider the sit-down a new and potent strike tactic, as modern as the streamlined cars which they build.

Entry into the sit-down Fisher Body plant is a formal affair. The reporter first receives credentials from the Union and only reporters who belong to the Newspaper Guild are allowed to enter the plant. A picket hut labeled "Information" has been built just outside the long, yellow building, here credentials are carefully checked. To enter the visitor climbs through a window, around which there always crowds women and children waiting to see their husbands and fathers. The credentials are again examined at the window and a thrice time after you enter.

An orderly little world has been set up within the automobile fortress. As we went in men were playing ping-pong. The long line of cars on the conveyor belt seemed like crouching elephants. Comfortable beds had been made out of seat springs and cushions. We passed a man who was sleeping profoundly, a magazine thrown by his side, the name of the magazine was "Terror."

Scrupulous order is kept, the automobiles under construction are without a scratch. No liquor is allowed inside. Very swiftly classes were set up, the plant has been transformed into an educational institution. Labor History, Economics, Public Speaking is taught, skits are performed by the workers using strike episodes as subjects, a band has been improvised and meetings are held every day in the plant frequently addressed by out of town visitors. Ellen Wilkinson, M.P. recently spoke to the sitters in Fisher Body #1 and #2.

In January the negotiations for strike settlement were deadlocked. General Motors refused the request of Secretary of Labor Perkins for a further conference. Tenseness mounted in Flint.

Pressure for more action came from the rank and file. This pressure became insistent when Union organizers cars were wrecked by vigilantes and workers were dismissed from the Chevrolet factory for Union activities.

It was decided to tie up the Chevrolet plant at exactly the same time when the injunction hearing against the sit-down strikers was going on in the Court House. A neat bit of strategy was employed. Plant #4 where the motors are made is the heart of Chevrolet, tie up plant #4 and you tie up production. This was the strikers objective.

A disturbance was started in a distant department—plant #9, which diverted the company police. to this point. The crowd gathered outside just as the night shift went on. The sound car, whose voice is at once intimate and remote, urged workers to strike. All at once pandemonium broke loose. Workers marched through the plant calling for a sit-down, the company police attacked them. Behind the windows struggling shapes were seen, a window was broken and mens bloody faces appeared at the window.

Cries went up, "They are beating our boys to death."

Tear gas was thrown.

The women of the Emergency Brigade went into action, crying: "They're gasing our boys we've got to give them air."

They crossed the street and broke windows. Wounded men were brought out of the plant, seventeen were hurt.

In the meantime the real sit-down was going on in distant plant #4. The sound truck ordered the picketing crowd to go there. The women of the Emergency Brigade rested a moment and wiped the tear gas from their eyes.

The Emergency Brigade is a new feature in this strike and it is spreading rapidly among the automobile workers wives in many automobile towns. It was formed after the women had routed the police in what is now known as the battle of "Bull's Run." This first riot occurred sometime ago when the police tried to keep the women from taking food into the sit-downers in Fisher #2.

The womens Auxiliary decided to form an emergency unit to be ready at all times to defend the Union. They wear red tams and arm bands with E.B. in white. A group of them is on guard in the Union hall and in the food kitchen day and night, ready to spring into action at a moment's notice.

They had soon recovered from the tear gas and marched to

Chevrolet #4. The plant lies in a little hollow. With their red tams on and their flag going before they marched down the hill singing "Hold The Fort." They swept past the police reserves which had just arrived and holding hands they backed up across the plant gate singing, "We Shall Not Be Moved." The sound car entoned: "Everything is quiet. The sit-down is accomplished. We suggest that you barricade your doors against tear gas. Barricade your tunnel between #2 and #4. Everything is quiet. Protection squadron! Guard your sound car, guard your sound car!"

A compact line of several hundred paraded in front of the factory. They carried wooden staves in their hands, a protection man circled the sound car. Salamanders were improvised from oil drums and stood blazing in the center of the crowd. There was no disturbance, these demonstrations all occurred in an orderly fashion. There was no street fighting or rioting, nor did the police make any effort to disperse the crowd which gradually drifted away.

The Sheriff and the Mayor clamored for troops and the cordon of guards was swung around the plant by half past ten that night.

When next day the injunction was granted the zero hour for enforcing the evacuation of the plant was half past three on February 3. An enormous picket line was formed in front of the big yellow brick plant of Fisher Body #1. This plant is situated on the main thoroughfare leading into town, all day automobile workers from Detroit, Toledo, Lansing and other cities had been arriving. These flying picket squadrons are a recent development in strike strategy making it possible to concentrate large numbers of pickets at any point necessary. There must have been 10,000 people before the quarter mile long yellow plant. A great loop was formed and they marched around six abreast, singing. Everyone carried staves, the crowd was bright with banners and with the womens' red and green tams.

It was Womans' Day and the Flint Emergency Brigade had been joined by the newly formed Emergency Brigade from Detroit wearing green tams, there were also women from Toledo, Lansing and other cities all marching in the picket line. Not a policeman appeared, traffic was regulated by the pickets.

The windows of the plant were filled with bearded faces. There are the men who swore not to shave till the strikers won. They gave their yell.

"No shaves till victory."

The crowd cheered and shouted. It was a surprisingly good-natured and well behaved crowd. Yet it had a terrifying latent power. While the mass meeting was being held that evening, word came to Union headquarters that hundreds of armed vigilantes were assembling and that they had been armed with the consent of the Chief of Police, but over the protests of the Sheriff.

Violence trembled on the edge of a knife. The tenseness was somewhat relieved by a midnight agreement between the city authorities and the union leaders. The union agreed to avoid congregating in great numbers and to put down their wooden staffs and clubs, the city authorities promised to demobilize the vigilantes who were assembling to attack the strikers with guns. The next day however, a citizens army was recruited.

At this writing the negotiations for settlement which were resumed after the sit-down in Chevrolet, are deadlocked. The Citizens Army wait in their homes for a call to action, the strikers crowd their headquarters in the Pengelly Bldg., the town of Flint is so nervy that people jump at the sound of a siren. General Motors still holds out against Union recognition.

"They won't settle till someone is killed," people prophesy.

THREE LETTERS FROM GENERAL MOTORS SIT-DOWNERS

(Edwin C.)
Feb. 3, 1937

Dear Liz & All

We are all OK and well and having a swell time. The National Guard Captain just came through the plant to see if we were all OK. They are shure using us fine. We are holding the fort strong and when it is all over it only means one thing and that is victory. They sent us cots & blankets & we have a food store almost as big as Hamadys. I dont know how long we will be here but I know we will never give up. We have the key plant of the G.M. and the eyes of the whole world are looking at us and we shure appreciate the cooperation and support we are getting from the outside. A report just came over the radio that told us that any medical attention eather we or the Fisher body neaded would be ready at all times. You see the boys at Fisher did not leave at 3 P.M. We can watch there plant from here. There are plenty of Artitelary all around us so the G.M. stools and hired thugs dont worry us. We shure done a thing that G.M. said never could be done when we took posession of Plant 4. drop me a line and if you can get $1.00 send it along. send my union reciept.

> My address is Edwin C.
> United Automobile Workers of America
> 318 Pengelly Building
> % of Chevorlet Plant #4

Dear Emma

I am very soory I annot keep my date with you thursday, But I am in the Chevrolet Fact No 4 on a sit down strike with about 2000 other men and I like it here. All we have to do is Sit! Eat! Sleep! Wash dishes! and Guard! I guess you will have to find a temporary boyfriend because I am staying till we win! Frank is here too. Hoping this letter finds you in the best of health.

> Your   ?????
> Tony K.

Dear Margarett

We are having a hell off a good time in Plant 4 and we are here to stay till hell frezes over if we have to i have to good faith in the CIO to let you be without coal or food go down to the Hall when the coal gets low tell Mary the same if they say anything about the car let me now at once fore i would hate to lose it dont let Roy drive the car all over. Take your letter to the Hall Adress i to Plant 4 Chev write as soon as you get this   I will say good by

> Earnest P.
> Plant 4 Cheve

the oil is low in the car so be carefull of it
P.S. Say Mag tell Mary everything here is OK and I intend to stay if it takes till Christmas if she wants anything let me know though the hall.

What Caused the Detroit Riot of 1943?

In the typology of urban unrest, the Detroit race riot of 1943 was the last of the large "communal," "ecological," or "contested area" riots and a turning point after which urban outbursts would become known as "commodity" riots, the prevailing type during the 1960s. The causes of the Detroit riot, one of the worst wartime conflagrations, are ably canvassed by Walter White in this preliminary report, which was sent to Frank Murphy, justice of the United States Supreme Court, in whose papers the report is found, at the Michigan Historical Collection, University of Michigan. Reprinted by permission of the National Association for the Advancement of Colored People.

In 1916 there were 8,000 Negroes in Detroit's population of 536,650. In 1925 the number of Negroes in Detroit had been multiplied almost by ten to a total of 85,000. In 1940, the total had jumped to 149,119. In June, 1943, between 190,000 and 200,000 lived in the Motor City. According to the Detroit Bureau of Governmental Research Negroes constituted 9.2% of the total population of the 2,015,623 persons who lived in Detroit July 1, 1942.

According to the War Manpower Commission, approximately 500,000 in-migrants moved to Detroit between June, 1940, and June, 1943. Because of discrimination against employment of Negroes in industry, the overwhelming majority—between 40,000 and 50,000—of the approximately 50,000 Negroes who went to Detroit in this three-year period moved there during the fifteen months prior to the race riot of June, 1943. According to Governor Harry S. Kelly, of Michigan, a total of 345,000 persons moved into Detroit during that same fifteen-month period. . . .

According to the Research and Analysis Department of the UAW-CIO, the United States Employment Service, the Detroit Bureau of Governmental Research, and the Detroit branch of the

National Association for the Advancement of Colored People, the
overwhelming majority of the 250,000 to 300,000 white in-migrants to Detroit during the year immediately preceding the race
riot came from the South. There was no surplus labor in nearby industrial centers like Chicago, Pittsburgh, Cleveland, Toledo, Akron,
and Kansas City. Recruiting, therefore, was concentrated in the
Deep South with the result that the already high percentage of
Detroiters with Southern background was enormously increased.
Here and there among these Southern whites were members of the
UAW-CIO and other labor unions, churchmen and others who
sloughed off whatever racial prejudices they had brought with
them from the South. But the overwhelming majority retained and
even increased their hostility to Negroes. . . . During July, 1941,
there had been an epidemic of riots allegedly by Polish youths
which had terrorized colored residents in Detroit, Hamtramck,
and other sections in and about Detroit. Homes of Negroes on
Horton, Chippewa, West Grant Boulevard and other streets close
to but outside of the so-called Negro areas were attacked by mobs
with no police interference. . . .

The desperate scarcity of housing for whites, however, limited
Negroes in finding places to live outside of the Negro areas. The
Detroit newspapers have contained for months many advertise-
ments offering rewards for housing of any nature or quality for
whites. Meanwhile but little public housing was created to meet
the tragic need for housing of both whites and Negroes in Detroit.
Even this was characterized by shameful vacillation and weakness
in Washington which only added fuel to the flames of racial tension
in Detroit. The notorious riots revolving about the question of who
should occupy the Sojourner Truth Housing Project in February,
1942, are an example of this. When Negroes pleaded for decent
housing, a section of 200 units was separated from a larger housing project and assigned to Negroes. It was named after the famous
Negro woman abolitionist, Sojourner Truth. Pressure of real estate
interests in Detroit who had consistently fought public housing,
and agitation by Polish youth led by Father Dzuik, and other
priests, and by other agencies such as the Ku Klux Klan, and the
National Workers' League, caused the National Housing Administration to yield and to announce that Negroes would not be permitted to occupy the Sojourner Truth Houses. . . .

Equally contributory to the explosion which was to come has been the attitude of the Detroit Real Estate Association. Mention has already been made of the opposition of the real estate interests to public housing in Detroit. Their contention was that such housing as Detroit needed should be created by private interests. But by the time private interests were ready to begin erection of homes and apartments for the greatly augmented population of wartime Detroit, priorities on building materials were put into effect. Meantime, every train, bus, or other public conveyance entering Detroit disgorged an ever increasing torrent of men, women, and children demanding places to live while they earned the war wages Detroit factories were paying. Overcrowding, lack of sanitation, a mounting disease rate resulting in absenteeism and a severe tax on the hospital and clinical facilities of Detroit were bad enough among whites. Among Negroes it resulted in a scandalous condition. The pot of frustration and discrimination boiled more and more furiously. Resentment among Negroes mounted higher and higher, even as they bought war bonds and sent their sons off to fight for the preservation of democracy. Each day brought example after example of the widening margin between the war aims of the United States and the extent to which the Negro Detroiter was permitted to participate with his fellow white American in the sharing of benefits as well as the burdens of the struggle, *JOBS*. Early in June, 1943, 25,000 employees of the Packard Plant, which was making Rolls-Royce engines for American bombers and marine engines for the famous PT boats, ceased work in protest against the upgrading of three Negroes. Subsequent investigation indicated that only a relatively small percentage of the Packard workers actually wanted to go on strike. The UAW-CIO bitterly fought the strike. But a handful of agitators charged by R. J. Thomas, president of the UAW-CIO, with being members of the Ku Klux Klan, had whipped up sentiment particularly among the Southern whites employed by Packard against the promotion of Negro workers. During the short-lived strike, a thick Southern voice outside the plant harangued a crowd shouting, "I'd rather see Hitler and Hirohito win than work beside a nigger on the assembly line." The strike was broken by the resolute attitude of the union and of Col. George E. Strong of the United States Aircraft Procurement Division, who refused to yield to the demand that the three Negroes be down-graded. Certain officials of the Packard Company were clearly responsible in part for the strike. . . .

Detroit Labor Unions and the Negro

One of the most extraordinary phenomena of the riot was the fact that while mobs attacked Negro victims outside some of the industrial plants of Detroit, there was not only no physical clash inside any plant in Detroit but not as far as could be learned even any verbal clash between white and Negro workers. This can be attributed to two factors: first, a firm stand against discrimination and segregation of Negro workers by the UAW-CIO, particularly since the Ford strike of 1941. The second factor is that when the military took over, the armed guards in the plants were ordered by the Army to maintain order at all costs and to prevent any outbreak within the plants. There is possibly a third factor, namely, that on Monday, June 21st, and to a lesser extent on succeeding days, Negroes were unable to get to the plants because of attacks upon them when they sought to return to work by roving mobs chiefly composed of boys between the ages of 17 and 25. . . .

Law Enforcement Agencies

Politically minded public officials have winked at the activities of agencies like the Klan, the Black Legion, the National Workers' League, the followers of Father Coughlin and other similar groups. During the 30's especially when there was keen competition for jobs because of the depression, Southern whites sought and secured jobs on the police force of Detroit and in the courts. There was a period of years when cold-blooded killings of Negroes by policemen were a constant source of bitterness among Negroes. Eventually, protest by such organizations as the Detroit branch of the NAACP, and other Negro and interracial groups led to a diminution and eventually a practical cessation of such killings. But a residue of distrust of the police remained. When the riot of June, 1943, broke forth, this suspicion of the police by Negroes was more than justified when 29 of the 35 killed were Negroes shot by police and a number of them shot in the back. The justification usually given by the police was "looting." There is no question that shameful and inexcusable looting of stores operated by whites in the East Side Negro area, particularly on Hastings and John R. Streets was perpetrated by Negroes. Part of this looting was for the sake of the loot. But part was due to bitter frenzy which had been too long bottled up in Negroes, and which was a form of vengeance both against the prejudice in Detroit from which Negroes had suffered, and against the looting of Negro homes and businesses ten days before in the Beaumont, Tex., riot of June 15–16, 1943.

Samuel Leiberman of the East Side Merchants Association reports that white policemen joined Negroes in the looting of stores on the East Side. In one instance a policeman carried two twenty-five-pound cans of lard from a store and locked it in the back of the police patrol car to be transported, apparently, to his home. There also is evidence that at least one of the 17 Negroes hot [*sic*] for "looting" was not looting, nor was there any evidence to substantiate such a charge.

The wilful inefficiency of the Detroit police in its handling of the riot is one of the most disgraceful episodes in American history. When the riot broke out on Sunday night, June 20, following a dispute between a white and Negro motorist on the Belle Isle Bridge, an efficient police force armed with night sticks and fire hoses could have broken up the rioting on Woodward Avenue and broken the back of the insurrection, had the police been determined to do so. Instead, the police did little or nothing, though there were a few individual instances of courage by policemen which are commendable.

More typical, however, was the following episode: An official of the Detroit educational system was riding Monday afternoon, June 21st, on a Woodward Avenue car. According to his statement, an inspector of police boarded the car with eight patrolmen. He announced that a mob was headed in that direction and that he and the patrolmen would take charge of and protect any Negroes on the car who wished such protection. Four of the eight Negroes accepted the offer. The other four chose to remain on the car. They crouched on the floor of the car and were concealed by the skirts of sympathetic white women. These four got to their destinations safely. But the four who had entrusted themselves to the police were either taken from the police by the mob and beaten unmercifully, or were turned over to the mob by the police.

After Federal troops had restored a semblance of order to Detroit, Police Commissioner John W. Witherspoon sought to shift the blame for the total failure of the Detroit Police Department to the Federal government for not sending troops sooner to police Detroit. Commissioner Witherspoon alleged that he had not been given information by the Federal authorities that a Presidential proclamation was necessary before Federal troops could be brought in. He sought also to prove that the police had been blameless. But this assertion was negated by photographs taken by the Detroit *Free Press* and other newspapers. Most revelatory of these is one taken on Woodward Avenue during the day of June 21st. An elderly Negro's arms are pinioned by two policemen while two mounted police sit astride their horses immediately behind. In the meantime, a white rioter strikes the helpless Negro full in the face with no indication on the part of any of the four policemen of any effort to protect the Negro.

The Detroit *Free Press* also took photographs of the same man in four separate acts of mob violence. As this report is written, this easily identified rioter is unarrested. Two other photographs show another white man engaged in two separate acts of violence against Negroes. In one of them he is about to strike a fleeing Negro with an iron bar. It is stated that this man was arrested but released almost immediately "for lack of evidence."

The faces of between 800 and 1,000 white rioters engaged in assaulting, killing, kicking or otherwise violating the law against the persons of Negroes, or engaged in wilful destruction of property such as the overturning and burning of the automobiles of Negroes are clearly identifiable. But as of the date of the writing of this report, few if any, of them have been even arrested.

The anti-Negro motivation of the Detroit police department is further illustrated by these facts and figures. It has already been pointed out that the Negro population of Detroit at the time of the riot was 200,000 or less, out of a total population of more than 2,000,000. The inevitable riot was the product of anti-Negro forces which had been allowed to operate without check or hindrances by the police over a period of many years. But 29 of the 35 persons who died during the riot were Negroes. An overwhelming majority of the more than 600 injured were Negroes. But of the 1832 persons arrested for rioting, more than 85% were Negroes. And this in the face of the indisputable fact that the aggressors over a period of years were not Negroes but whites.

Commissioner Witherspoon along with Attorney General

Herbert J. Rushton, State Police Commissioner Oscar C. Olander, and Wayne County Prosecutor William E. Dowling were appointed by Governor Harry S. Kelly to investigate the riot. But a few days later, the investigating committee reported that there was no necessity of a Grand Jury investigation. . . .

Statement and Recommendations to the Mayor's Committee
We commend the Mayor for his appointment of a Commission to study racial problems, and urge that the Commission begin work immediately. That there immediately be provided:

1. Such assistance as the commission might need by way of research.

2. Funds for its work be provided through the Mayor or through the Common Council.

3. Agencies of propaganda, education, and other media be immediately placed at the disposal of the Commission.

4. Executive assistance and proper personnel.

5. Power of subpoena and access to all necessary records.

Police Department
We recommend an immediate grand jury investigation of the Police Department to determine its failure during the past crisis; that all persons within the department found to have affiliations or sympathy with the Ku Klux Klan, National Workers' League, or any other such organization, especially those that are guilty of non-feasance, mis-feasance, or mal-feasance while on duty, be dismissed.

For a long time we have recognized, and on numerous occasions pointed out, the inadequate number of colored policemen; that Negroes have confidence and faith in their officers and respect them.

We recommend that the number of Negro officers be increased from 43 to 350; that there be immediate promotions of Negro officers. . . .

Housing
Now is the time to reconsider living together. The riot has proven that segregation whether voluntary or involuntary, produces separateness and friction. On the other hand where people were living together in the City of Detroit, there was no friction.

We reiterate our position that public housing should be for all people regardless of race, creed, or color. We urge that the Detroit Housing Commission rescind its policy of not disturbing "neighborhood patterns", and open war housing projects to workers who qualify. We urge that additional housing be considered and built immediately; that a request be made to the President of the United States and such other Federal officials to grant priorities on building materials as a war measure to provide adequate housing. We contend that housing for war workers is as necessary to the war effort as camps for the armed forces.

Labor

Because a large number of workers will be affected by events of the past few days, the rank and file of labor must make some plans for adjustment.

We recommend:

1. That inter-racial commissions be set up in all locals in which a mixed labor force is employed.

2. That inter-racial committees of international unions be activated where they are already in existence by launching a program of education and adjustment to problems of racial differences.

3. That there be a coordinated inter-racial labor commission composed of representatives of labor organizations, the AFL, CIO, and independent unions. Such commission representatives are to be appointed by heads of respective organizations, and these in turn correlated by program and activity with plant committees.

4. That trade unions in cooperation with management immediately develop a sound, intelligent, and over-all program, for the complete integration of workers of minority groups into industry.

Reparations

We urge that the City Government immediately take steps to make reparations for the loss of life, limb, and property in Detroit.

We also urge that an inter-racial committee be set up by the Mayor to receive and adjust claims.

PART FOUR

DETROIT, MATURITY
AND _____?
1945–

At Dodge Main, there's a young black work-force being supervised by reactionary Polacks. Like, you've got a 63-year-old Pole bossing 25-year-old jitterbugs.

—Young, white, radical
auto worker quoted
in *Dissent,* January 1970

The term 'Property Values' to many is merely a euphemism for racism and it has undoubtedly served as that. Yet for Poles of Detroit it is also a code phrase which expresses many barely understood, rarely articulated feelings. It is no accident that 70–80% of them own their own homes. They brought with them from the villages of the Polish Plain not only the land hunger of peasants . . . but also the pre-capitalist notion that land is the most important component of status. . . . Self esteem and personal identity are still strongly associated with land ownership.

—T. Radzialowski
"The View from a Polish Ghetto," 1974

Will the last person leaving Detroit please turn out the lights.

—Bumper sticker in Detroit, 1975

Introduction

As World War II was winding down, social planners and thinkers grew increasingly fearful that the postwar period might repeat that after World War I, when a sharp recession shook the economy. Very little solid preparation for such contingencies occurred, for events soon overran planning. The war ended with suddenness in 1945, but instead of recession a pent-up demand for consumer goods took up the slack. The simple replacement need for automobiles was estimated at nine million units by *Fortune* magazine in 1944, which surpassed even the banner prewar production years. Autos, which had not been on the civilian market in any quantity since 1941, were in heavy demand, and Detroit went about rapidly reconverting and retooling from military vehicles to manufacturing passenger cars.

The unions, although on firmer footing in 1945 than in 1940, were still uncertain how the automobile industry would regard them once the pacifying hand of federal controls lifted. Ford, the last of the big holdouts, fell to union organizers in 1941, but no one was certain that the company's tough union-busting attitude would not reassert itself after the war. Spokesmen for Chrysler also made ominous sounds and the corporation's chief economist warned, "If you believe in economic freedom and competition, then you will be opposed to collective bargaining . . . and we should look forward to the time when all federal labor laws will be repealed." Furthermore, the UAW's hard-won seniority system seemed to be in some danger when management spoke airily of firing older workers and replacing them with returning veterans and servicemen. The mettle of labor would be tested in a series of protracted and bitter postwar strikes, from which the UAW emerged strengthened. The postwar period was also a time of testing the depths of each other's convictions, not only at the bargaining table, but also in other areas of public life such as politics.[1]

The influence of the Detroit area upon state politics was tremendous. The automobile manufacturing magnates and auto unions would by the late 1940s come to dominate both major political parties. Although never absent, the automobile management moved in to control the state Republican party about 1940 and developed what became known as the Summerfield Plan. Its originator, Arthur Summerfield, was a Flint Chevrolet dealer who later became President Eisenhower's postmaster general. The Plan, according to a United States Senate investigation in 1948, linked the automobile industry to the Republican party and installed in power the management side of the industry. The financing of party campaigns was systematically organized in the state's eighty-three counties, and the majority of finance managers were connected to the auto business. Contributions were solicited from car dealers on the basis of the number of vehicles sold, the number of employees, and the total annual volume of business. The Michigan Automobile Dealers' Association was an active participant in the plan and arranged a special directors' meeting in 1946 to facilitate fund-raising. Ostensibly, all contributions had come from the private personal funds of dealers, but a federal grand jury in 1948 found much evidence of corporate contributions and indicted twenty dealers for violations of the Federal Corrupt Practices Act.[2] Nevertheless, Ford and GM executives remained large contributors. The automobile industry was by 1948 the dominant force in the Republican party. Later when a squabble rose between the two titans (Ford and GM) over responsibility for the 1954 off-year election disaster, disgruntled GM executives turned a deaf ear to the party's pleas for help. As one observer explained: "The GM executives are simply hardheaded and successful businessmen who are willing to support and reward effective men in politics, just as they reward competent men in business. If they see failure in business performance, they make a change. The same in politics."[3] The estrangement was short-lived. GM returned to the fold to share in the direction of the state's GOP.

Similarly, the Detroit UAW with their Political Action Committee achieved equal influence, not only in the metropolitan-area Democratic party, but also in the state organization. In 1948 the union fathered a new political force by fusing the state's liberal–New Deal remnants to a solid UAW core and forming a liberal-labor coalition in which the UAW was the controlling partner. Spoilsmen and patronage seekers were no longer at home in the Democratic party. Issue orientation replaced job orientation. Health, welfare, and labor measures became the goals of the party, and progressive welfare programs were advanced with unprecedented vigor. Wage workers and low-income people were galvanized to political action. In 1959, when Republican obstructionism in the state's upper house cut off federal benefits to unemployed UAW workers and others, Walter Reuther reminded workers that "there is a direct and inescapable relationship between the bread box and the ballot box. . . . The best way to be sure your ice box will be filled with good food is to see that the ballot box is filled with good votes on election day." [4]

Under UAW sponsorship the Democratic party was transformed into a progressive-minded, militantly liberal, and successful political organization. The UAW provided money for campaigns, doorbell ringers, poll watchers, and challengers, gave the use of its publications and radio outlets, and mounted massive voter registration and education efforts. The results were impressive: between 1948 and 1962 the Democrats elected governors for seven consecutive terms and in 1962 and 1964 won all statewide administrative elections below governor. The liberal-labor influence in the Democratic party was a progressive influence in modernizing the state's health, welfare, and workmen's-compensation programs and moving the state ahead vigorously in providing public parks and recreation areas for workers and citizens.

Labor's phenomenal successes at the top of the ticket in winning statewide office was mocked by repeated failures in Detroit mayoralty races. From 1937 through the 1960s the UAW was unable to elect a solely labor-supported candidate as mayor, despite Democratic majorities in the 70 percent range for national and state elections. The UAW experienced only moderate success in the at-large city council elections. Detroit's nonpartisan charter seemed to rebound to the favor of conservative candidates. Nonpartisanship prevented labor from exploiting the natural party affinities of Detroit voters. On those occasions when labor's endorsements were advertised blatantly and candidates were labeled prolabor, the press and citizens' good-government groups deftly turned the election into a defense of the nonpartisan charter and unbossed candidate, and arraigned labor for injecting class conflict into the political process. Such tactics, even in normally Democratic Detroit, worked against the UAW, as the record shows. In four elections—1937, 1943, 1945, and 1949—organized labor pulled out all stops and financed a massive effort to elect a labor mayor, but was repulsed all four times. Suffering both defeats and the sting of public criticism over UAW-controlled candidates, labor drew back in the 1950s and lowered its interventionist posture in Detroit mayoralty races. Ironically, even when labor became circumspect, it made mistakes. In 1961 labor joined a broad conservative consensus including the news media and citizens' groups in supporting the reelection of Mayor Louis Miriani, a conservative, law-and-order figure. The incumbent lost to a relatively unknown outsider and liberal, Jerome Cavanagh, who had the backing of liberals, Negroes, and many UAW members. The UAW officialdom again had supported a loser in Detroit.[5]

Labor's stunning victories in statewide races were often frustrated by a Republican-controlled state legislature. The upper house was a bastion of obstructionism where big business and conservative farm interests prevailed. They thwarted the Democrats and "gleefully wrecked liberal programs" advocated by Governor G. Mennen ("Soapy") Williams. This was possible during the 1950s because of Michigan's serious malapportionment which gave sparsely populated rural districts overwhelming influence in the senate. Even with statewide majorities, Democrats could not carry more than one-third of the upper house. Democratic strength lay almost entirely in the Detroit urban area along with the mining counties of the Upper Peninsula, both sections where union politics were important.

The deadlock between a Democratic governor and a Republican legislature finally resulted in the fiscal crisis of 1959. When faced with the need for additional revenue, the governor insisted upon personal, graduated income tax and a corporation profits tax, which the Republicans saw as the "device of the devil," or worse yet, a product of the feverish brain of Walter Reuther, the left-wing ideologue who headed the UAW. The GOP called for a flat-rate sales tax to be placed primarily upon consumers. A deadlock resulted in insufficient revenue to pay state employees in 1959, an event that became known across the nation as the "payless payday." This "fiscal mess" caused needless embarrassment to the state, damaged the Democratic party, and weakened labor's political influence. So heated were political passions in 1959 and so determined were old-time Republicans to score against their seemingly invincible antagonist, the six-term governor Williams, that they were willing to plunge the state into temporary bankruptcy. Williams and the Democrats were equally intransigent. The "fiscal fiasco" damaged Williams's political reputation irreparably and knocked him out of contention for high national office.[6] The financial crisis also seemed to climax more than a decade of successful issue-oriented politicking by the Democratic party. Williams's Democratic successor would win only one term, to be defeated by a new Republican leader from the automobile industry, the former president of American Motors Company and a political moderate, George Romney.

Smarting over the program setbacks suffered from a malapportioned legislature, August Scholle, president of the AFL–CIO Committee on Political Education (COPE), picked up the apportionment issue in 1959 and fought it vigorously through the state courts on the "one man, one vote" principle, reaping the benefits of the United States Supreme Court's landmark reapportionment decision, *Baker* v. *Carr,* 1962.[7]

The impact of the Detroit-based automobile industry upon city and state politics was an event of unprecedented proportions. It shaped and guided the character of politics in the entire state, and although it did not result in any vast political realignment, it did fundamentally transform the character of both political parties from an old-fashioned concern over jobs and patronage to an ideologically based, issue-oriented, programmatic politics as defined by big business (auto industry) and big labor (auto unions). Labor and management entered state and city politics, not for the traditional rewards, but to control, shape, and influence the state's social and economic policy.[8]

The all-encompassing nature of the automobile also had a serious and lasting effect upon the industrial structure of Detroit and the state. Detroit had been presented with opportunities at key points of its development to diversify its industrial base, but had failed to do so. Airplane production during the 1920s had made a healthy start with a few small manufacturers, and also one major motor company, but had not survived the Great Depression. World War II brought the return of aircraft manufacturing to Detroit with mass-produced bombers, but when the war ended, airplane manufacturing fell by the wayside. The Willow Run bomber plant was given over to the manufacture of the new Kaiser–Frazer automobile. The pent-up domestic demand for passenger automobiles proved irresistible to business in 1946, and Detroit returned to its old mainstay of mass-producing motor vehicles.[9]

By the late 1950s the negative effects of this singular preoccupation became evident. Detroit's share of defense contracts fell precipitously after the Korean War. Modern technology and modern war changed the character of defense procurement from wheeled vehicles to electronics, computers, and missiles. Detroit was caught unprepared to share in this massive cold-war defense spending. Many of the new industries and technologies derived sustenance in the early-growth stages from extensive research activities, an area where the automobile industry had seldom led and never pioneered. The industry had become muscle-bound with assembly lines and obsessed with model changeovers and retooling, calibrating production to sales, and the cosmetics of restyling. The industry's attitude toward research in general was perhaps captured by a General Motors president's remark that "basic research is when you do not know what you are doing." One banker wryly summarized research and development work in Michigan, saying, "In Michigan development is what goes on next year's car; research is what goes on the year after's model." There was no escaping the fact that the auto industry in Detroit "had let the space age pass her by."[10]

A view of Detroit from aggregate statistics, graphs, and tables provides the reader with an important road map. Patterns of the past, long-range trends, and future projections can often be discerned from such data. A practitioner of that art and a leading urban economist, Professor Wilbur R. Thompson, sees a rosy future for Detroit. His observation is based upon an interpretation that shows that Detroit is tending—slowly, but nonetheless tending—to become more of a metropolis and less of an "automobile city." The statistics that show a modest relative decline in automotive employment's ratio to all other employment and some increase, as well as anticipated increase, in service-sector employment are cited to support this view. In short, Detroit's behavior, as shown by aggregate data, seems to be slowly reorienting itself toward norms that describe other large metropolitan centers in the nation.[11] Unlike the sudden onset and almost explosive impact the early auto industry had upon Detroit, this diversification of a one-industry town toward a more balanced business structure moves at a glacial speed at the very best. Whether change can occur in time and whether it would beneficially affect a currently troubled Detroit remains to be seen.

"Distress city" has replaced "dynamic Detroit," as early-twentieth-century boosters were fond of calling it. The motor kingdom has indeed fallen upon hard days. Detroit during the 1970s has been suffering from inadequate school financing, increasing segregation, and the accelerated outward migration of business and industry. The job center of the Detroit area has shifted to the north and west and is now located somewhere in a broad belt from Mount Clemens to Flint. The downtown central business district continues to shrink, boxed in by moatlike expressways and much vacant space and empty lots.[12] Race relations since the 1967 riot have remained at a flash point, with many brutish and nasty altercations between blacks and whites.

Inner-city criminal activity has also redefined the geography of human movement. A description by a knowledgeable observer at Detroit's Wayne State University captures some of the constraints under which inner-city travelers labor.

In many instances, the pattern of spatial behavior imposed by a busy daily schedule is strengthened by a fear of the inner city. Student surveys and informal conversations reveal that members of the Wayne community limit their inner city travel to "necessary trips" along "safe" routes. Many avoid remaining on or returning to campus after dark for this reason. Well-lit, sunken and fenced expressways are preferred to surface streets with their slower speeds and intersection stops. Women take escorts to parking lots after dark and keep their car windows up and doors locked while driving in the city. There is evidence that this fear and its accompanying precautions have risen since the Detroit riots of 1967, which were centered on 12th Street, less than a mile from the campus. Very high crime rates in this part of the city do little to allay fears in the Wayne community.[13]

Detroit's problems are not unique. It is just that the urban malaise in Detroit seems exaggerated beyond that suffered by other metropolitan centers.

In one respect, volatility seems very much in character with Detroit. Economically the city continues to live by the roller-coaster ups and downs that the auto industry brought into the metropolitan business cycle. University of Michigan's Dean William Haber labeled it as a "feast or famine" economy. Production peaks such as the Korean War buildup in 1953 and big sales years for cars such as 1955 and 1965 can escalate wages and income upward, fill normally vacant housing, and attract to the city new workers who are often unemployable under more normal production conditions. Down years such as 1958, 1961, and 1970 result in incredibly high unemployment figures that often dwarf national percentages. The 1958 recession, relatively mild at the national level with 6.8 percent unemployment, was devastating in Detroit, where 15.1 percent of the labor force was out of work. On the other hand, the Korean War buildup of 1953 shot employment records to such dizzy heights that Dean Haber referred to this abnormally high percentage of the state's population at work as "over-employment." During the 1955 buying spree the industry reached a high watermark in employment. The absolute loss of automotive manufacturing jobs can be measured from that benchmark.[14] In short, during boom years in the nation Detroit has for the last half century led the pack, and during recessions it has also led on the way down. The city has in the past and continues to the present to exaggerate national business cycles.

A major shift in the character of defense spending away from wheeled vehicles also injured recovery in Detroit's automotive manufacturing belt during the late 1950s. Detroit still continued its traditional manufacturing of surface transport, and no appreciable changes occurred during the 1960s. These factors along with some decentralization of the auto industry and the installation of labor-saving machinery, known as automation, seem to have overtaxed Detroit's capacity to spring back from adversity. Motor vehicle manufacturing employment in big car-producing years such as 1968, 1969, and 1971 never approached the heights of the 1950s. Moreover, it was only because of a net loss from out-migration—more people leaving the state than coming in—

that Detroit's early 1960s unemployment problems were kept
within limit. One scholar has called these collective developments
an "economic change of life." [15] No longer is the auto capital
referred to as "dynamic Detroit."

In one of those morning-after-the-nightmare-before scenes,
Detroit Mayor Jerome Cavanagh was interviewed by a national
press panel in 1967. Billed as the golden boy of American mayors,
Cavanagh had earned the reputation of having a Midas touch
with Washington. He inaugurated a well-financed antipoverty program, did his utmost to catch Detroit up to the urban renewal
efforts of other cities, and presumably enlisted solid Negro support
behind him. During the urban riots that began in 1964 and 1965,
Detroiters were afflicted by the mistaken notion that "it couldn't
happen here." Cavanagh's interview of 30 July 1967 unmistakably
registers shock over the fact that Detroit had experienced the worst
riot as of that date, and as later evidence would show, the worst
riot of the decade. Even a clear thinker like Cavanagh could only
suggest that urban problems would be solved by more of the same
types of programs that were then being carried out. Later in 1968
the mayor would argue for a formal acceptance of the international reparations principle whereby reparations would be paid
to blacks for past sins committed by whites—only the reparations
would flow mostly to cities like Detroit in distress.[16] Cavanagh's
dismay and puzzlement were characteristic of mainstream liberalism. Dozens of knowledgeable liberals, urbanites, and planners
were thunderstruck with shock when they heard of the rioting
and burning in Detroit. High hourly wage scales and strong representation in the auto plants and the unions by blacks were not
sufficient to check the firestorm that swept American cities. Like
so many rough bumps of the 1960s, the riots seemed to drain
off vitality that Detroit could not spare.

B. J. Widick's article is a somber appraisal of post-riot Detroit,
tension-ridden and full of frictions. Widick and Thompson seem
almost to be writing about different cities. In part they are. Thompson's canvass is the entire metropolitan area, which embraces not
only the troubled central city but its affluent suburbs and satellite
motor producers (and it includes those affluent whites who have
fled the inner city). Widick's subject is the volatile inner city and
the economic mainstay of the Detroit metropolitan area, the auto

factory. It is difficult to perceive from Widick's data the favorable climate for invention and innovation that Thompson says is necessary if Detroit is to progress. A downward shift in educational attainments, for example, is not a favorable omen. Even Walter Reuther's dream of a raceless, class-conscious working force seems mocked by the day-to-day realities of the assembly line. Race, it seems, is now at the center of the majority of work conflicts and encounters. As one commentator saw it: "At Dodge Main, there's a young black work-force being supervised by reactionary Polacks. Like you've got a 63-year-old Pole bossing 25-year-old jitterbugs." [17] These are not the qualities that Thompson has in mind or that are likely to facilitate the realization of Thompson's dynamic, innovative, entrepreneurial Detroit. On the other hand, perhaps inner-city frictions have little bearing upon those variables that make for innovation and entrepreneurship. New York City, for example, is just as beset by ethnic and racial conflict, but continues to sponsor advance in many areas of American life. In any event, Thompson's Detroit is a statistical abstraction and perhaps operates quite independently from the abrasive flesh-and-blood encounters of the Detroit assembly line. Whether Thompson or Widick has divined correctly the Detroit metropolitan area's future remains to be seen.

One aspect of Detroit's future unfolded in a pyrrhic community struggle. Hardly had the wounds and abrasions of the 1967 riot begun to heal than the school busing issue fell with full force on Detroit. Again the question of race was the central issue, rubbing raw the wounds of past discontents and focusing the city's attention on new areas of harsh conflict.

A school desegregation case was begun in 1970 by the Detroit National Association for the Advancement of Colored People, and a district court found that Detroit had maintained attendance zones and fostered transportation and construction policies that resulted in racially "identifiable" or segregated schools within the city of Detroit. In July 1972 the district court, on the advice of a special panel, ordered the Detroit Board of Education to purchase or lease 295 buses and to prepare to transport inner-city black pupils to white suburban schools and white suburban students to Detroit's black schools. The district court reasoned that a "Detroit-only" desegregation plan was futile because the "target population" was 65 percent black and only 35 percent white, a racial balance that would not, in the judge's view, enable the city to achieve meaningful integration. Furthermore, the court accepted the argument that busing in Detroit only would trigger a "white flight" and drive the remaining white, school-age population beyond the city limits, thereby creating a "racially identifiable," or nearly all-black, school system. Hence, the cross-district or city-suburban busing solution. In 1973 a court of appeals upheld the district court in its metropolitan-wide busing plan. The issue became the object of rancorous public debate in the metropolitan area for months. The case was sent to the United States Supreme Court, and on 25 July 1974 a five-to-four decision reversed both lower courts and ruled invalid the city-suburban busing plan. The decision ordered the case returned to the district court for settlement on a "Detroit-only" basis. The essence of Chief Justice Warren Burger's majority opinion is found in one of our documents.

The minority problem can no longer be dichotomized as black and white only, for the resurgence of ethnicity has complicated immensely the implementation of national policies predicated on the simple assumption that America is composed of Negroes and Caucasians. The same reasoning that leads blacks and federal bureaucrats to claim that unequal results in getting society's choicest jobs is conclusive evidence (at least conclusive enough to base policies on) of race discrimination is now being extrapolated and extended by ethnic groups to explain their own success and failure rates. Increasingly, urban whites have begun to view themselves by discrete and specific tribal units and by national identities. The rebirth of ethnicity, although initially triggered by the Negro revolution, has proceeded beyond a defensive role and spawned a renaissance of its own, particularly among descendants of southern and eastern Europeans. Goaded by slurs from white liberals and black-power advocates on their unenlightened blue-collar, political views and Slavic origins, Poles especially have vigorously asserted their displeasure and also their own ethnicity. Annoyed and even outraged by what they perceive as the slings and arrows of nasty and venomous criticism, Poles have struck back stridently, as one of our documents shows.

Detroit may be the canary in the mineshaft, a gloomy portent of the effects yet to be felt by other cities. Detroit is clearly the most energy-vulnerable big city in the nation. Not only is it an energy consumer, as are all cities, but additionally Detroit is the nerve center that directs the manufacturing of the nation's biggest petroleum consumers, motor vehicles. A decision by a half-dozen unknown sheikhs to embargo oil shipments in October 1973 sent Detroit into an economic tailspin and threatened to pull the entire economy down into a cataclysmic crash. Detroit's initial response was palsied and shaky, but finally settled on manufacturing a smaller luxury-loaded automobile with only modest improvements in gas mileage but a massive increase in prices. The second phase of the response was to ask for federal help in the form of waiving environmental improvements and safety requirements or postponing their implementation into the distant future. The industry promised in exchange to undergo a major retooling and to produce a car with 40 percent better gas mileage. Whether the industry is simply whistling in the dark and promising sweet nothings remains to be seen. Thinking small and producing a lean, light-footed, and close-to-the-bone gas miser is not the style that Detroit is accustomed to manufacturing in. A half-century romance with the fetish of big cars and rapid design change was pioneered by GM and codified into practice by its titan Alfred Sloan with his remark "The laws of Paris dressmakers have come to be a factor in the automobile industry." That is not the kind of climate that creates broad-based research and development and technologies ready to respond with inventions and innovation to crises. Only in the cosmetics of design, heightened rates of mass production, and salesmanship has Detroit excelled since World War II. How an industry that grew up in the fat years of cheap raw materials and cheap gas will adjust to a world of scarcity economics, high prices, and oil shortfalls is the challenge of the next decade. On the outcome rests the future of Detroit, for its prosperity is inextricably linked to the automobile industry, as it has been since 1919.

NOTES—PART FOUR

1. "Needed: Nine Million New Cars," *Fortune* 30 (July 1944): 163; Irving Richter, "Detroit Plans for Chaos," *Nation* 160 (30 June 1945): 719.

2. U.S. Congress, Senate, Committee on Rules and Administration, *Report of the Subcommittee on Privileges and Elections, Hook against Ferguson,* report no. 801, 81st Cong., 1st sess. (Washington, D.C.: Government Printing Office, 1949) pp. 5–7; Stephen B. and Vera H. Sarasohn, *Political Party Patterns in Michigan* (Detroit, 1957), pp. 33–38.

3. Duncan Norton-Taylor, "What's Wrong with Michigan?" *Fortune* 52 (December 1956): 143.

4. Reuther quoted in *Business Week,* 17 October 1959, p. 156; John H. Fenton, *Midwest Politics* (New York, 1966), p. 16; "Labor in Michigan Politics," *Newsweek,* 25 October 1948, pp. 37–38.

5. See typescript "History of the Work of the Political Action Committee in the Detroit Municipal Elections, 1937," in the Henry Kraus Papers, and assessment of "Mayoralty Race, October 25, 1943," in Detroit Commission on Community Relations Papers, both in Archives of Labor History and Urban Affairs, Wayne State University, Detroit, Mich.; J. David Greenstone, *Labor in American Politics* (New York, 1969), pp. 110, 112, 120–24.

6. H. H. Martin, "Michigan: The Problem State," *Saturday Evening Post,* 25 February 1961, pp. 13, 14, 86.

7. "Bigger Voice for Big Cities," *Newsweek,* 9 April 1962, pp. 20–33; Doris B. McLaughlin, *Michigan Labor: A Brief History from 1818 to the Present* (Ann Arbor, 1970), pp. 140–42.

8. Greenstone, *Labor in American Politics,* p. 110; James M. Hare, *With Malice towards None: The Musings of a Retired Politician* (East Lansing, 1972), pp. 13, 14, 17, 174; Carolyn Stieber, *The Politics of Change in Michigan* (East Lansing, 1970) pp. 7, 8, 11, 12.

9. "Detroit Is Logical Aircraft Center," *Detroiter* 19 (24 October 1927); "Adventures of Henry and Joe in Autoland," *Fortune* 33 (March 1946): 96.

10. Eric F. Goldman, "Good-By to the Fifties—And Good Riddance," *Harper's* 220 (January 1960): 28; "Businessmen Ponder What Ails Michigan," *Business Week,* 3 November 1962, p. 88; "Michigan: The Problem State," p. 86. See also Lawrence J. White, *The Automobile Industry since 1945* (Cambridge, 1971), pp. 258–59, 274, 275.

11. See Wilbur Thompson document that follows.

12. *New York Times,* 12 November 1972; Susan McBee, "Detroit, Problem Town U.S.A. Grows Older, Poorer, Tougher," *Boston Globe,* 4 March 1973; Constantinos A. Doxiadis, *Emergence and Growth of an Urban Region: The Developing Detroit Area* (Detroit, 1970), III, 149.

13. Judith S. Humphrey, "Wayne State University and the Inner City,"

in *Metropolitan America: Geographic Perspectives and Teaching Strategies,*
ed. Robert D. Schwartz et al. (Oak Park, Ill., 1972), p. 105.

14. William Haber, Eugene C. McKean, and Harold C. Taylor, *The
Michigan Economy: Its Potentials and Its Problems* (Kalamazoo, Mich.:
E. W. Upjohn Institute for Employment Research, 1959), pp. 3–25, 45, 56–
58, 62.

15. Ibid., pp. 46, 65; William Haber, W. Allen Spivey, and Martin R.
Warshaw, *Michigan in the 1970's: An Economic Forecast* (Michigan Business Studies, Ann Arbor, 1965), pp. 2, 3. For automobile production figures
see *Detroit Area Economic Fact Book* (Detroit Area Economic Forum,
May 1971), p. 11.

16. Richard Strichartz, *Mayor's Development Team Report to Mayor
Jerome P. Cavanagh* (City of Detroit, October 1967), pp. 10, 201–3.

17. Thomas R. Brooks, "Workers, Black and White," *Dissent* 17 (January–February 1970): 16. See also "Negro Militants Scored by U.A.W.,"
New York Times, 13 March 1969.

The Automobile Industry
Takes Over Both Political Parties

*This document focuses on a short-term conflict by the two princi-
pal automobile interests in the state's Republican party and shows
the dominant role of big business (automobile management) and
big labor (auto workers' union) in both political parties. The
selection is excerpted from Duncan Norton-Taylor, "What's Wrong
with Michigan?" Fortune (52 [December 1956]: 142–45, 190,
195–96, 198, 201).*

Nowhere are the political choices faced by Republican businessmen more sharply defined than in the state of Michigan. Nowhere
in the U.S. is a business community under more intense political
attack. The Michigan situation has its ironic aspects. The community's great $4.5-billion auto industry makes and sells a prod-
uct that every American loves; the industry's 400,000 workers
are among the highest paid in the world; and all in all, U.S.
capitalism seems to stand out in its finest colors and in its greatest
genius in the manufacturing area around Detroit. And yet it is in
this area that those preeminent exponents of capitalism, the Re-

publicans, have been exposed to a potent and acid attack from a combination of Democrats and C.I.O. labor. And from this encounter with one of the greatest concentrations of labor power in the U.S., the Republican party has emerged so scarred as to be no longer recognizable as the party that it once was. In a letter to businessmen, the G.O.P. State Finance Committee announced what everyone in Michigan has come to realize—that organized labor "is rapidly taking over the state."

Calamity has overtaken the Michigan G.O.P. only within the past two years. Up until 1930, Republicans were so entrenched that Michigan could hardly be called a two-party state. Even during the Democratic Thirties and Forties, Michigan Republicanism remained a formidable force. Though Roosevelt carried Michigan in all but one of his campaigns (1940, when he lost by less than 7,000 votes), the state consistently sent to Congress more than twice as many Republicans as Democrats. Republicans lost only one U.S. senatorial race (to Prentiss Brown in 1936). Republicans generally dominated the state Senate and House of Representatives. The Democrats won the governorship five times, the Republicans six times; in 1952 the Republicans lost the governorship again but on the surface they still appeared to be in good shape. Only two years later Republicans were being swept out of their old strongholds in the state offices. Even before President Eisenhower's heart attack, the Michigan G.O.P. was facing the 1956 election in the worst condition in all its history and in the worst condition of any G.O.P. organization in any key state. Since Eisenhower's illness the situation has not improved.

The extent of the Michigan G.O.P.'s deterioration is even more serious than the loss of political offices indicates. The party's leaders have produced no effective program for winning future campaigns. Republican backers are fighting among themselves. Mutual political interests are being overlooked in feuds involving not only the politicians but the businessmen who might be expected to stay out of such internecine scraps.

Meanwhile the House Burns Up

General Motors and Ford have carried their business animosities into the political back lots. How G.M. and Ford became embroiled in this fashion is partly explained by a Michigan G.O.P. worker who prefers to keep his name out of it:

"Ford is moving heaven and earth to place Ford cars first in the hearts and minds of the public. G.M. is mad at Ford. It is mad about Ford's giving in on the supplemental unemployment benefit deal. For years G.M. officials have been supporters of the Republican party, and had a lot more political consciousness than Ford. But within recent years Ford had taken a greater interest in state affairs. So now this business jealousy has extended over into politics. They just don't like each other. If one was for God, the other would be for the Devil. But the thing that amazes me is the way they will go on fighting when the house is on fire, and it's certainly on fire now."

Ford is supporting the state G.O.P., and the men who are now running it. These men were mostly Citizens for Eisenhower zealots before the Republican convention of 1952, and are sometimes described as Young Turks. Henry Ford II and other Ford Executives have come to the party's aid with their pocketbooks. (Henry, Benson, and William Ford each contributed $3,000 this year.) But G.M. President Harlow Curtice, though he was an early Eisenhower man, supports a faction that would like to see the state machine's present leadership ousted. So far as the record shows, Curtice and other G.M. executives who were willing Republican contributors in the past are now contributing nothing. There are indications that G.M. suppliers, aware of Curtice's disgruntlement, are also turning a cold shoulder to the party's pleas for help.

G.M. officials will not discuss their attitude, but one well-informed politician describes it thus: No personalities are involved. The G.M. executives are simply hardheaded and successful businessmen who are willing to support and reward effective men in politics, just as they reward competent men in business. If they see a failure in business performance, they make a change. The same in politics. They are convinced the present G.O.P. leadership is failing and they want a change. At any rate, they are not going to continue to give the present leadership their financial support. . . .

The Man from Flint
The story of how the Republicans came to their present pass revolves principally around two earnest and politically dedicated men—one of them, Arthur Summerfield, Postmaster General of

the U.S., and a veteran of Michigan politics; the other, John Feikens, a solemn young lawyer from Grand Rapids, now chairman of the state G.O.P., who became preoccupied with politics three years ago.

In 1940, Wendell Willkie made a campaign stop in Flint. Michigan labor was in a defiant and triumphant mood. Flint had been the scene of the 1937 sitdown strike that ended in G.M.'s recognition of the infant U.A.W. as a bargaining agent. The day before Willkie's arrival in Flint, when he was in Pontiac, Mrs. Willkie was spattered by an egg.

Arthur Summerfield, who was then a highly successful Chevrolet dealer, took his wife to the Flint rally to hear Willkie speak. The crowd was sullen and jeering and at one point drowned out the Republican candidate with auto horns. Summerfield marched directly from the rally to the Flint City Club and ate lunch with a number of other businessmen who, like Summerfield, had previously taken only the faintest interest in politics. Among the other lunchers was Harlow Curtice, Summerfield's close friend and neighbor in Flint who at that time was head of the Buick Division.

Summerfield easily recalls his sense of outrage, "I thought, when a candidate for the presidency of the U.S. gets that kind of treatment, it's time everyone takes an active interest. I said to the men at the lunch, 'This is our community and government and country. Let's talk about doing something about this.'" From the Flint City Club the little band of wrathful businessmen marched forth to effect a new order, a few of them to become very durable Republican workers indeed, most of them (it must be admitted) simply temporarily upset about the catcalling and the eggs.

Summerfield was one of the durables. He was instrumental in setting up a Republican Finance Committee that went about the systematic collection of political funds. Some aging G.O.P. leaders were subsequently upended by Summerfield and the other crusaders, and a drive was begun to broaden and fortify the whole Republican front. Summerfield, in the van of all this, in the end became leader (he abhors the word "boss") of the Michigan G.O.P.

In that year of Summerfield's entrance into active politics, the Republican party had managed to hold most of its positions. Democratic State Highway Commissioner Murray Van Wagoner won the governorship in 1940—with the help of Roosevelt and an effective personal machine that Van Wagoner had built while officiating over a $57-million WPA highway program. But he was the last Democrat to win it for some time. The reinvigorated Republicans recaptured the office in 1942, and held it in 1944 and in 1946. . . .

The Man from Grand Rapids

John Feikens, who had set up a law office in Detroit, thought the party had "kissed off labor in 1946," and that it suffered from "inaction and reaction." Feikens was then thirty-three, brought up in the Dutch community around Grand Rapids, a man with an inherited Dutch stubbornness, somewhat humorless, intense, and now, like Arthur Summerfield back in 1940, inspired by a cause. Feikens' cause was the promising figure of General Dwight Eisenhower, and in this he was joined by a number of other young Republicans. Among those early joiners of Feikens' Citizens for Eisenhower was Thomas Reid, Director of a newly formed civic-affairs department at Ford Motor Co. Henry Ford II hovered in the background.

Feikens and friends rode splendidly along on the Eisenhower wave, but their activities also stirred up some resentments. There were, to be sure, among the older Republicans a number of men, including Harlow Curtice, who were also for Eisenhower, and who had no reason yet to feel any pique at Feikens. But there was also, in 1952, a very vociferous Old Guard, which included Homer Ferguson and which backed the presidential candidacy of Robert Taft. And this wide difference of devotions threw the Michigan camp, amateurs and professionals, into a preconvention scuffle.

Summerfield himself remained ostensibly neutral throughout, resisting pressure from Feikens' side to push the Michigan delegation over to Eisenhower; and declining to join his old friend Ferguson on the side of Taft. Summerfield was criticized by the Eisenhower zealots for trying to walk, as they described it, a political tightrope. Summerfield claims that his whole aim was to keep the Eisenhower-Taft contest from blowing the Michigan delegation apart, and the fact was that the delegation did get through the convention without any rending explosion. Michigan's delegates voted as they separately saw fit, thirty-five for Ike, eleven for Taft; Summerfield finally cast his own vote for Eisenhower.

In the Republican triumph in November there were rewards for all. Congressman Charles Potter, an Eisenhower supporter, was elected to the U.S. Senate. Summerfield himself, after serving as the G.O.P. national chairman, was taken into the Eisenhower Cabinet.[1] And in February 1953, Charles King, who had been chairman of the Taft state organization performed the rite of nominating young Feikens to be the party's new state chairman, an office to which Feikens was duly elected by the confident young state delegates who had ridden the Eisenhower wave. That spring, with its stresses deep but not showing, the G.O.P. seemed once again to present a smooth and polished face. It was then just a year and a few months before the G.O.P.'s crack-up.

The Statistics of Defeat

The 1954 business "recession" hit Detroit and environs hard. Chrysler was shut down for model changes just before the November elections, and in Michigan some 300,000 people were out of work. Also, Eisenhower was not on the G.O.P. ticket that year. These were factors in the Republican defeat. In any case, in the two years since Eisenhower's triumph a spectacular shift in Michigan's voting had taken place . . . Senator Potter had ridden in in 1952 with a plurality over the incumbent Moody of 45,000. In 1954, the Democratic candidate for the Senate, Pat McNamara, an ex-pipefitter and a political unknown, beat the incumbent Homer Ferguson by a plurality of 39,000.

It was the landslide after a steady erosion that had been taking place since 1946. Only by virtue of Michigan's districting and the rural Republican majorities outside the heavily populated southeast were the Republicans able to hold a slim majority in the State House of Representatives. The Democrats picked up two congressional seats that had been Republican for some twenty years, and in the total vote in the congressional elections, a Republican

---

1. Michigan got more than its share of presidential appointments; e.g., Detroit banker Joseph Dodge became Director of the Budget, G.M. President Charles Wilson, Secretary of Defense. Neither had been particularly active in Michigan Republican affairs.

plurality in 1952 of 143,000 was transformed in 1954 into a Democratic plurality of 72,000. Democratic Governor Soapy Williams got himself re-elected to his fourth term, and carried in with him a majority of Democrats to state administrative offices.

The "Progressive Force"
To a certain extent, the Republicans had knocked themselves out. But of course this was not the whole story. Arrayed against the G.O.P. was an enterprising political force that had been alert to any advantage that might present itself.

The enemy of Michigan Republicanism is frequently described as a coalition of liberal Democrats and organized labor. This was the way it started out, some eight years ago, when a group of liberal Democrats got together with representatives of the U.A.W.-C.I.O. to ponder how they might seize control from the Democratic party's old-line bosses. The Democrats also had their Old Guard, among them the bosses of the Teamsters Union. The stated aim of the liberal coalition was to "remold the party into a progressive force."

The initial strategy was to infiltrate the party, seize precinct offices from unwary old-line bosses, move hence to the state conventions, and gradually install coalition men in key party and state offices. The focus of the campaign was Wayne County, which has 37 per cent of Michigan's population, polls more than two-thirds of the state's total Democratic vote, and contains around 375,000 of the 400,000 members of the Michigan U.A.W.

The campaign was carried out under the guidance of a handful of Democratic liberals, the U.A.W.'s Walter Reuther, and August Scholle, a hard-bitten veteran of labor's ideological feuds and the director of the Michigan branch of the C.I.O.'s Political Action Committee, the instrument with which the C.I.O. conducts its political campaigns. Their operations met with some resistance from the Democratic Old Guard, but in the end were spectacularly successful. In some districts Democrats had been simply losing offices by default, by not even putting up candidates. Soapy Williams, who had won his first term more by virtue of G.O.P. Governor Sigler's mistakes than through any previous record or any regular Democratic support, was at that time, in

1950, a kind of wandering politician in search of a party, hoping to be re-elected. The labor group took him under their wing and Williams won again.

The C.I.O. had learned one lesson from Ohio's 1950 senatorial campaign, when organized labor's widely ballyhooed assault on Taft backfired badly and inspired Republicans in record numbers to turn out and vote. In Michigan the C.I.O. stepped very softly, keeping itself at least half hidden behind the new liberal Democratic front. But there was no question of the C.I.O.'s key role in Democratic affairs, and there is no question now that it dominates the party. Eight of the fifty-one Democrats now sitting in the Michigan House, C.I.O.-P.A.C.'s Scholle points out, came directly from organized labor's ranks, and the other Democratic representatives and the eleven Democratic state senators vote with almost unbroken regularity for the "progressive" legislation (more unemployment compensation, higher minimum wages, corporation profits tax, etc.) that emanates in a steady stream from Governor Williams' office. Much of this legislation is the work of Paul Weber, the Governor's press secretary, a founder of the Detroit Association of Catholic Trade Unionists and later executive secretary of the Detroit Newspaper Guild.

A majority of Republican legislators have voted against such legislation with almost the same degree of regularity with which Democrats vote for it. Many Republicans have automatically opposed anything the Governor has recommended, despite the fact that some measures (e.g., a fair-employment-practices bill, a mental-hospital bill) were designed to take care of improvements badly needed in the state. This behavior of the Republicans has been a matter of not too secret delight to Gus Scholle, who, while confiding that there may be a half-dozen "decent guys" among the Republicans, happily labels the rest of them "a passel of the most reactionary blank-blanks I ever saw in my life."

Michigan labor's political apparatus has had its inner stresses, but at critical junctures it presented a united front. It could send thousands of men and women out ringing doorbells and drumming up Democratic votes. It could vote a 15-cent per member contribution from the Wayne County C.I.O. locals and raise a $46,000 political fund for the 1955 spring elections. It could draw on U.A.W.'s treasury. . . . For allegedly putting union funds at the disposal of C.I.O.-P.A.C. and individual Democratic candidates, U.A.W. is now under indictment on a violation of the Federal Corrupt Practices Act. Labor leaders argue that the law is unconstitutional.

The Incessant Voice
Labor's propaganda machine, moreover, made itself felt far beyond the bounds of the state. Before the 1954 elections it distributed copies of the October *United Automobile Worker* in eighteen key states attacking the record of the Republican party all the way from Hoover to Eisenhower. Sample gibes: "This Is Prosperity? 5,000,000 Unemployed!" " 'Dynamic' Doodling: There is no sound government plan afoot for doing something sure, sensible and determined to lift our economy out of its rut and to put it back on the high road of full employment and a steadily expanding rate of national output."

Today the machine's propaganda is incessant. In addition to the *United Automobile Worker* and the weekly C.I.O. *News,* the labor group publishes a monthly magazine, *Ammunition,* loaded with such clear and simple statements as "Republican Bosses in Michigan are fighting U.A.W.-C.I.O. because union political action has meant corporations are paying a fairer share of taxes." Organized labor finances two daily news broadcasts and a weekly TV program carefully slanted along the union line and delivered in a confident tone by one Guy Nunn.

And Governor Williams trots tirelessly around the state, speaking at union meetings, P.T.A. meetings, civic groups. Soapy floats around so much, in fact, beaming, shaking hands, and vowing to drag the Republican party into the twentieth century, that Feikens is continually getting frantic calls from G.O.P. county chairmen, demanding Republican speakers, reporting that Williams has been in the area "four times in the last two weeks." Actually Soapy might have been there once. "They were just seeing a mirage," says Feikens sadly. . . .

No High Ground Left
The effectiveness of the labor group on the one hand, the uncertainty of Michigan businessmen about their political responsi-

bilities on the other, the lack of Republican leadership, the intra-party feuding, the battle behind the fence between Ford and G.M., have all contributed to the fall of the Michigan G.O.P. . . .

Michigan Republicans are indeed beginning to realize that continued factional fighting can bring final disaster to the party. The state itself is undergoing tremendous change. Industrialism has been expanding right across the state, and as industrialism marches into Michigan's small towns, organized labor marches right in behind it. Furthermore, Michigan's traditionally Republican farmers are unhappy with their economic lot, and "safe" G.O.P. territory out-state is gradually being washed away. For the Michigan G.O.P. there is practically no high ground left.

Who Believes in Capitalism?

But there is one other, basic factor in the fall of the G.O.P. "Business," as Feikens says, "has got to be willing to accept responsibility for solving the problems that free enterprise creates. Labor in this state has been drifting further and further from the Republican party because workers are not convinced that the supporters of free enterprise are for them." But beyond that, large segments of labor are being persuaded by their leaders that the whole philosophy of capitalism, at least as Republicans define it, is contrary to their best interests.

Michigan's Republican businessmen have shown little talent for dealing with this aspect of the problem. For some years they obstinately fought the growing power of organized workers by cracking heads. They saw their power begin to dissolve in the revolution of the New Deal, and they turned finally from cracking heads to making concessions, which culminated in last summer's supplemental unemployment-benefit contract, signed by Ford and then, of necessity, by G.M. The new policy kept the peace. But it obviously failed to bring about any sympathy on the part of labor with the G.O.P.'s political views. Organized labor still stood adamantly opposed to Republican capitalism—in which Michigan's businessmen themselves have given only half-hearted support.

Detroit and Michigan
Fail to Diversify:
Autos As Usual

Automobiles not only dominated Detroit's economic life but, as this selection shows, were a major force in shaping the character of the state's industry. The influence of motor vehicle manufacturing did not stop at the plant gate but spread to Michigan's colleges and the business community in general. This document is from "Businessmen Ponder What Ails Michigan," Business Week, (3 November 1962, pp. 89, 90).

Michigan, along with the rest of the U.S. midcentral region —normally prosperous as the mass production heartland of the country—has a gnawing worry that even a boom year in autos can't cure: It's not getting its share of the lucrative research and development business that has sprung up in the past five years, particularly in the space field. This question is agitating businessmen throughout the Midwest. Many fear that the prosperity of mass production may not last, and—for a new growth stimulus— turn to new fields of technology, such as electronics, computers, space technology, solid state physics, and bionics. Last week, in meetings at Racine, Wis., Chicago, Cleveland, and the University of Michigan, they debated how to bring to their states profitable R&D work in these fields.

SPACEBID. For Michigan and its businessmen, the worry goes deepest; the auto state already needs R&D work not merely to spark growth but to solve existing economic ills.

Employment in autos, steel, and machine tools, the state's traditional strongholds, has been shrinking steadily. In the past two years, the Michigan Employment Security Commission reports, employment has dropped 76,000, and another 60,000 workers have left the state for lack of available jobs.

So Michigan, like other areas and cities, such as Boston [*BW* Oct.6'62, p111], turns toward space. At the state's first space research conference at the University of Michigan last week, with Vice-Pres. Thomas Morrow of Chrysler Corp. as chairman, businessmen and university executives tried to sell federal procurement officials on the virtues of Michigan schools as research centers.

WHAT'S WRONG? But some businessmen questioned whether such meetings are the answer—whether they do not shun the real causes of Michigan's deficiencies. As to what these real causes are, the businessmen—in a revealing symptom of the state's ailments —refuse to speak their mind publicly, fearing sharp criticism by state officials, union leaders, or other businessmen.

In businessmen's inner circles, however, they raise these points:

NEARSIGHTEDNESS ON COLLEGE CAMPUSES IN THE STATE. A college professor points out that most Michigan schools have not emphasized the sophisticated fields that pay off with big R&D contracts. He says: "Our curricula and research follow local industry's heavy reliance on manufacturing, particularly in transportation. Then, too, Michigan college administrators have not encouraged faculty members to consult for industry the way Eastern colleges do."

RELUCTANCE OF INDUSTRY TO DIVERSIFY. Auto executives, for example, remind you that their business is building better cars. A Detroit management consultant points out that auto companies have moved to new fields—but reluctantly, and not always successfully.

Chrysler seems back in the missile and space business—but mostly out of Michigan—after a boom and then a slump. Ford has had as many disappointments as successes with its Aeronutronic Div., which a Ford executive says failed in its plan to become a big computer supplier. With its purchase of Philco, Ford has a second chance at R&D—but, again, outside Michigan and the Midwest. General Motors, says the consultant, has done only enough sophisticated R&D work in space to head off criticism of it as a social laggard.

As for auto suppliers, a banker complains that some tool and die shops in the Detroit area "shut up shop rather than seeking out new fields" when auto business declined.

LACKADAISICAL BUSINESS LEADERS. The same management consultant declares that civic leaders lend only lip service to activities for bringing more R&D companies to the state. Contrasting Detroit with San Francisco, he says: "In Detroit, the Chamber of Commerce is dead. And our retailers say . . . : 'We're making enough money, so why worry.' "

STIFLING EFFECT OF LABOR UNIONS. Almost since the days of the sit-down strikes, Michigan has been known as a labor state—"rightly or wrongly," says a businessman. "Somehow," says another executive, "we have to stop the harsh, almost psychotic criticism of businessmen and business that flows from some Michigan labor leaders and the union papers and TV shows."

"They preach class hatred; that's the only way to describe it," adds a third. "A scientist would be crazy to start a company in that kind of atmosphere. . . ."

INCENTIVES. A lot of people in Michigan have taken up the cudgel against profits, a line of attack popular with leaders of some United Auto Workers locals. Henry Ford II, one of the few Michigan businessmen willing to speak out in public, told the Michigan Chamber of Commerce last month that such prejudices make it difficult for business to function. A businessman who applauded his speech commented: "This attitude about profits discourages the bright young scientist who starts an R&D company to make his fortune."

MIRED STATE FINANCES. Almost everybody in the state is still embarrassed by the notorious 1958 cash crisis, when the state could not meet some bills. After that, "it's a wonder anybody would even consider the state," says one manufacturer.

Since then, there has been a continuous battle between a Democratic governor and a Republican-controlled legislature, and the state's fiscal structure is a hot issue in the current gubernatorial election.

SENSITIVITY TO CRITICISM. Both state officials and business boosters have been hypersensitive to criticism of the state. When a business consultant in Massachusetts, Stephen P. Sobotka, sent proofs of his study, Profile of Michigan, soon to be published—discussing labor unrest and monopoly, industry's need of diversification, and overhauling of higher education—Michigan officials and University of Michigan economists alike labeled it "just another smear of the state."

FIGHTING HISTORY. On top of all this, Michigan has to fight history, both its own and that of R&D. Historically, the great research centers have grown in the East and West.

Almost everybody agrees that Michigan businessmen are too close to industries that live on high volume—"where you tool up and then crank out parts in huge volumes," as a banker puts it. An executive quips: "In Michigan, development is what goes on next year's car; research is what goes on the year after's model."

Detroit Riot, 1967

The Detroit riot, 23–30 July 1967, was not a classic race riot, in that it did not involve interracial mob fighting but rather saw Negroes attack the symbols of white power and white-owned property. Nonetheless, forty-three died, seven hundred were known to be injured, thousands arrested, and property damage totaled $50 million in what was the worst civil disorder of the 1960s. Jerome P. Cavanagh, who was mayor of Detroit from 1961 to 1969, was interviewed on the closing day of the riot by a panel from "Meet the Press: America's Press Conference of the Air" (National Broadcasting Company, 30 July 1967, Washington, D.C.).

MR. NEWMAN: Our guest today on MEET THE PRESS is the Mayor of Detroit, Jerome P. Cavanagh, whose city has just experienced the worst racial violence in modern history. Mayor Cavanagh, elected in 1961, is one of the nation's leading spokesmen on urban affairs and is the only Mayor to have served simultaneously as President of both the United States Conference of Mayors and the National League of Cities.

We will have the first questions now from Mr. Bill Matney of NBC News.

MR. MATNEY: Mr. Cavanagh, President Johnson has asked this question, and people across the nation are asking this question:

Why? Why Detroit? You have had seven days to study this situation. Do you have any answers now?

MAYOR CAVANAGH: Mr. Matney, I think that really it is sort of a geographic happenstance that this broke out in Detroit. By that I mean that it is a national malady—that which occurred in Detroit—and could just as easily have happened in any major American city or any other city even smaller than Detroit, anyplace in the United States.

That may sound sort of defensive, but really it isn't. I think Detroit by anyone's standards had done at least all the textbook things in relation to dealing with some of these urban problems, and still it broke out. So it indicates to me that it was more than just a local problem. There were all sorts of reasons. We could sit here all afternoon probably and talk about them. Basically we were confronted with thousands of people that felt alienated from our society, that proposed to take the law into their own hands and violate that law, that weren't bound by any of the precepts that you and I understand, which constitute regular law and order in this country.

MR. MATNEY: Of all the big city Mayors, your ties in communication with the Negro community were considered just about as good as anybody could get, and yet this happened. What broke down? What went wrong?

MAYOR CAVANAGH: I think the ties which the city government had and still has certainly with much of the Negro community, the vast percentage of the members of the Negro community in this city, are still good. But still there are people in this as well as every city in the country that are outside of our society—not just the white society, but the society in which most of the Negroes and most of the whites belong. And, given the slightest provocation—in many instances even no provocation is needed —the law is taken into their own hands. You can characterize it as protest or you can characterize it as resentment. They have been popularly fashioned as the "have-nots." I think all of those things are probably apt characterizations, and certainly I don't know of any government in America, local government, state government or national government, or any institution for that matter, that is communicating in any way or carrying on any kind of a dialogue with the so-called have-nots.

MR. MATNEY: Let's get a bit more specific, Mr. Cavanagh, there has been strong criticism and a great deal of it is coming from the Negro community, that the riot could have been avoided had your police department moved in early Sunday morning and squashed the thing—when the atmosphere was pretty much fun and games, and people were standing around laughing and so forth.

MAYOR CAVANAGH: I know that there is a great deal of criticism both here and around the country. I really don't lend any substance to it, and I will tell you why. I don't think it deserves any substance. The tactics which were used this year by our police department last Sunday morning were the same tactics that were used by our police department a year ago in this community when we had a potential riot. We had some very serious incidents with which I am sure you are familiar out on the east side. Our police department moved with speed, but restraint, and with what we thought was reason and order, and this series of incidents didn't balloon into a riot. Everyone around the country credited the moderation or the restraint or the order which the police department exercised that morning. The same tactics were used last Sunday. It is not and has not been our position in this city, nor has it been really in most of the major cities, I think, the position, to move in bristling with a lot of hardware and weaponry when you have mobs out on the street, because it has been proven time and time again that generally this just incites people into further violence and further rioting.

Frankly, what happened was the fact that our police department, when it moved in—and incidentally Sunday morning in any big city is almost like Pearl Harbor on Sunday morning, at least like it was back in 1941. We are at our weakest; there are fewer men on the streets at that period of time. When our police department moved in, the crowd just overwhelmed them. We were attempting to protect firemen when they were fighting fires, and our primary concern at that point—and these were field decisions which were made, by the way. There was no order which came down from on high, from me or from the Commissioner of Police:

"Do not shoot." At no time during the week did I issue any order of that kind or any other kind in relation to police procedure to the police department, but the police department has been instructed in this city over the years by its professional police leaders that they are to use such force as they deem necessary and as the circumstances deem necessary. If they can apprehend a criminal without the use of force, then that is what they should attempt to do. It was their judgment out on the street that morning that these rioters and looters were just going to overwhelm them if they shot into the crowd, so they refrained initially from shooting in many instances.

[announcement]

MR. HAYDEN: Mr. Mayor, going back to the subject that Bill Matney raised about action at the time the riot started, one of the ranking officers in the field was an Inspector Paul Donnelly, who yesterday retired from the department—this had already been arranged. He was in charge of two squads of commandoes who were at 14th and Euclid Street, kept there idle, then finally moved farther away to the Tenth Precinct station because they were attracting crowds. On the eve of his retirement, without naming anybody, he said the politicians held the police back from effective control and said specifically, "If we had been permitted to go after the looters and troublemakers on 12th right from the start, we might have stopped it."

What about it; do you agree with the Inspector?

MAYOR CAVANAGH: No, I certainly do not agree with the Inspector. I don't know of any politicians downtown or anyplace else that gave any kind of instructions to our police officers, especially in those early morning hours about which you are speaking, in relation to their conduct. As a matter of fact, Inspector Donnelly, when he was questioned by our Police Commissioner about that specific reference, which he made in your newspaper, indicated he wasn't talking about the politicians in Detroit. He was talking about politicians sort of as a euphemism, I suppose, for people who have handcuffed police officers generally speaking. He was one of the commanders out there, and we had given the field commanders—as they always do in situations like that certainly—broad authority to use whatever force, whatever tactics, whatever means are necessary to contain the situation or deal with it as they see best.

I wasn't then nor all during that day, for that matter, familiar with the exact tactics that were being used in the field because these are police matters, professional police matters. It has always been my policy in the five years which I have served as Mayor to allow the professionals in the police agencies or any others of those agencies to do those things, particularly in times of stress, which they knew better than anyone else.

MR. HAYDEN: Mr. Mayor, in retrospect, now that it is over and not knowing why it started here, if it starts next Sunday again, would we be doing things differently right at the start?

MAYOR CAVANAGH: I think in all candor that I would have to say to you that the role of the police officer and the definition of his authority and his authority to act out on that street should be more clearly defined. We assumed that it was clearly defined in the minds of the men, in the minds of certainly their sergeants and their lieutenants and their inspectors. I think it was, generally speaking, but obviously in the minds of some, as evidenced by the remark made by Inspector Donnelly and evidenced by remarks made by other police officers, they were, if not unsure, at least a little dubious at times about exactly what role they should be taking and what role they should be playing.

I talked to a number of police officers, and if I might just quickly bring my answer to a conclusion on that one, that were out on the scene that morning. One, a patrolman, very interestingly told me just the other day—he said he was one of a squad guarding a fire company that was fighting a fire early on 12th Street, early that Sunday morning, and the mob was all around them, looting down the street. The sergeant in command of that squad ordered them not to fire at those looters, many of the looters being mothers and fathers with seven- and eight-year-old children, walking along in, as Mr. Matney said, sort of a carnival-like spirit, garnering up groceries and shoes and things like that. They said their primary function at that point was to guard the firemen, to guard the lives of the firemen, guard the lives of the people out in the neighborhood. This policeman said to me—he is a veteran police officer and no particular friend of mine, I had never met him before—he said as far as he was concerned, had any man in the squadron fired at that crowd, that whole squad of police officers probably would have been wiped out by that mob, and certainly he agreed with that field decision which was made at that point. . . .

MR. JOHNSON: When you say there is a madness in the country and you refer to the billions of dollars for defense, are you alluding there also to the war in Vietnam which many critics this week —Senator Fulbright among them—linked, again, as a direct relationship between the urban violence and our commitment overseas?

MAYOR CAVANAGH: All I know is that I have yet really to convince myself in my own mind that—what will it profit this country if we, say, put our man on the moon by 1970, and at the same time you can't walk down Woodward Avenue in this city without some fear of violence or fear as to your own safety and security?

And we may be able to pacify every village in Vietnam, over a period of years, but what good does it do if we can't pacify the American cities. And the American cities aren't pacified, there is no question about it.

What I am saying, really, Mr. Johnson, is that our priorities in this country are all out of balance. There is no question about it. I am not too sure what we have to do to change those priorities, but maybe Detroit was a watershed this week in American history, and it might well be that out of the ashes of this city comes the national resolve to do far more than anything we have done in the past. Because what we have done has been proven to be not only inadequate, but certainly I think we have to take some whole new directions and new looks in this country at our dealings with the urban affairs.

MR. STEELE: Mr. Mayor, you have already said that the rioters were somehow outside of society. Do you really believe that increased federal funds, say, for education and housing and other city problems would have made any difference in those riots of this summer, not only in Detroit but elsewhere as well; would they have been avoided? Is it a matter of money, in other words?

MAYOR CAVANAGH: I think much of the answer does boil down to money. I know that may sound like a very simple response to a very difficult question, but there is no doubt about it. Expectations have been built up not by just federal officials but local officials about what those programs, those federal city programs would do, and then when the programs are cut back and sniped at, really, they only nibble at the real periphery of the problem. They never really get at the heart of it.

What we have to do in this country—and long ago we declared a commitment to do it, but we have never really done it—and that is, provide full employment in this country. And the government, I think, the United States Government, should be the employer of the last resort—that if, through the public or private sectors, it is impossible to obtain employment, the United States Government should guarantee the opportunity for employment, maybe not guarantee a job but at least the opportunity for a job.

This isn't a new concept. I think President Roosevelt back in 1944 first suggested it. But we need jobs, and certainly we need a far greater involvement on the part of the private sector. There are a lot of government people in this country, both federal, state and local, that like to talk about the need to involve the private sector, and yet government as yet in this country has not defined very clearly, if at all, the areas into which the private sector should be moving. . . .

MR. MATNEY: Mr. Cavanagh, you have said this rioting was not racial in the traditional confrontation of white and black, such as occurred here in 1943. But nevertheless it was racial—you and I both know this——

MAYOR CAVANAGH: I won't dispute it.

MR. MATNEY: —in the sense there was almost pinpoint accuracy in the fire bombing throughout this city. It is very obvious that the vengeance and the wrath was directed at the white businessman. In walking the streets of the riot area, I have been told time and time again that "Whitey, don't come back. We don't want you in here."

If this is true and if this is widespread, then what about your plans for the redevelopment of this city? What sort of voice do you plan to give these people in the ghetto who are being so vocal about this?

MAYOR CAVANAGH: Let me first preface my answer by saying that the usual and the classic kind of race riots that we have been led to believe exist in this country, the white mob against the Negro mob, did not happen in this city, as you know. But I agree with you, and let's be frank about it, that underneath the surface, this in fact was a race riot and a race revolution. It did involve the race, the races, particularly the Negro race.

It is our plan to involve as best we can—and we are making every effort just in the last week or so, to involve some kind of participation, as full as we can get it, from the residents of the neighborhoods involved. We have been trying to do this in the poverty program; we have been trying to do it in some of the other programs. We haven't succeeded completely, but we have succeeded to a better degree than a lot of people would give us credit for.

Let me just say in relation to the poverty program—I am sure all of you gentlemen would be interested in this—we have done some fast analysis—of the 5,000 young people who are in your neighborhood Youth Corps and other youth programs connected with the poverty program here, only three of those 5,000 were involved in any kind of illegal activity. I'd hesitate to contemplate how many more people would have been involved in this riot this week had we not had a poverty program.

MR. NEWMAN: Less than four minutes, gentlemen.

MR. HAYDEN: Mr. Mayor, do I understand you to say that this is going to keep up—I mean for you as the Mayor of the fifth biggest city—to say that this is going to keep up until Congress passes legislation and gets these long-range programs into effect and builds housing and gets job equality and education, all of which is a matter of years?

MAYOR CAVANAGH: It shouldn't be a matter of years, and I don't think that we can wait . . . because until we get at these root causes and until we start to provide things like that great American Pat Moynihan has suggested, I think, a children's allowance—he makes the point that we are the only industrial democracy in the world that doesn't have a children or a family allowance, and yet we seem to be the only industrial democracy that every summer has race riots in all of our cities—until we start to do these things, provide some guarantee of money or income for all of our people in this country, and until the Congress begins to realistically deal with the problems of the cities, we are going to have not just a continuation, but I'd say—and it is terrible to contemplate—we are going to have some things far, far worse. It may well be that Washington, D. C.—and I hate to think of this, and I would pray that it would never happen, but if what happened in Detroit this week happened in Washington, D. C., this might lift the veil off the eyes of the Members of Congress.

Black City: Black Unions?

B. J. Widick outlines some of the larger contours of a city in "painful transition," and he also pinpoints through human interest vignettes how race has become, more than class, the cutting edge of social division in Detroit. This selection appeared in Dissent *(Winter 1972, pp. 138–45), and was adapted from Widick's book* Detroit: City of Race and Class Violence *(Chicago, 1972). Reprinted by permission of the author.*

Detroit in the 1970s is startlingly different from the factory complex associated with the auto industry, the UAW, and Walter Reuther. Auto workers no longer rush to and from huge industrial plants on the east and west sides. Now the major traffic flows are of white suburbanites driving into the downtown commercial center and inching their way out before darkness. The new buildings downtown stick out like shining thumbs amid parking lots, expressways, and vacant land—less than 30 percent of downtown Detroit is used for commercial and industrial purposes. Within the city limits, there are large blots of wasteland.

All the auto companies have decentralized production, partly into the vast metropolitan area surrounding the city—an area in which almost half of Michigan's 8 million people live—and partly by developing plants in other states. Meanwhile, the deterioration of the city is visible everywhere.

For every new business moving into Detroit, two move out. There are over 7,000 vacant storefronts in the city. Thousands of small stores, with their steel fronts, look like tiny military posts under siege. The *Detroit News* building, downtown, is surrounded by a brick wall, reminiscent of a medieval fortress. These are signs of the changes making Detroit into a black city, surrounded by a white-dominated suburban ring like a noose around the city's neck.

The city lacks a rapid-transit system to facilitate spending from suburbanite consumers. Public sensitivity to race tension and a much publicized "high crime rate" keep buyers away. Even during the day the city seldom looks busy. Downtown shoppers are mostly black. At night, only a few whites can be seen in the downtown theaters. Restaurants do a minimum of business at night; many are quietly folding, as are the night clubs.

The city continues to shrink both physically and in population. There has been a net loss in total dwelling supply each year since 1960, when 553,000 units were available. In 1970 there were only 530,770. The Department of Planning and Building Studies of the Detroit Board of Education explains:

> The net loss is the result of demolitions for both public and private purposes. In the public sector there have been 5,000 units removed for freeway construction, 9,700 units for urban renewal programs, 3,300 for school sites, and 1,000 for recreation and other public uses. In the private sector there has been clearance for gasoline stations, parking lots, and some demolitions with no other objective than reducing value for tax assessment purposes.

A decline in population has offset the decline in dwelling units. Detroit in 1970 was still the fifth largest city in America, though its population of 1,492,507 showed a drop of 190,000 from the 1960 figure. Meanwhile, in the same period the population in the wider metropolitan area of Detroit grew from 3.7 million to 4.2 million.

Even more important is the change in social composition. Another 345,000 whites fled to the suburbs in the 1960–70 decade, causing a 29.2 percent decrease in the white population. Blacks now constitute 43.7 percent of the city's population and are on the way to becoming a clear majority. The city is also left with more than a normal share of old, very young, and poor blacks and whites. Since there is little middle- or lower-income housing in downtown Detroit, and upper-income housing is at a premium, the trend toward suburban living continues unchecked. A survey of the number of blacks living outside the city limits shows an all-white pattern in major suburbs scarcely duplicated anywhere in the United States. Warren, Michigan, has doubled its population to 180,000 in the past decade; it has all of five black families. Dearborn, with over 100,000 people, lists one black family. Grosse Pointe has two, Harpers Woods one, Hazel Park one, Birmingham five.

Anxieties permeate the life of Detroit. An astonishing number of citizens have armed themselves, in fear and rage, both black and white. Detroiters possess over 500,000 hand guns, more than 400,000 of them unregistered. The city seldom has a moment of respite from racial incidents. In spring 1971, R. Wiley Brownlee, principal of the Willow Run high school, was tarred and feathered by masked men because he was considered an integrationist. In the fall of 1970 there was a shoot-out between black militants and the police, in which a patrolman was killed. Only the brave intervention of a black woman leader, Nadine Brown, who arranged for a peaceful surrender, kept the city from exploding again.

To the whites, the police appear incompetent to handle major troubles. For the black community, there is the legacy of the Algiers Motel killing of three young blacks. No police were convicted in that incident, although two brilliant studies and newspaper accounts exposed the truth. The full horror was revealed in Van Gorden Sauter's and Burleigh Hines's book, *Nightmare in Detroit:*

> The events of the next hour left a stain on the Detroit police department that will not be erased for decades. Pollard, Cooper, and Temple—unarmed and outnumbered—were shotgunned to death. Each was shot more than once at a range of fifteen feet or less by twelve-gauge double 0 buckshot. Temple and Pollard were apparently shot while lying or kneeling.

Community passions ran high in 1969 when a policeman was killed and another wounded near the New Bethel Baptist Church and police poured gunfire into the church where 143 men, women, and children were meeting. Mass arrests, recriminations, and mutual antagonism between the black community and the police dominated the city for weeks on end. For one year, while Patrick Murphy acted as police commissioner, he provided the city with a breather because of his effective control of the police, but then he returned to Manhattan. Meanwhile, another police scandal broke: Inspector Alex Wierzbicki, 3 lieutenants, and 12 policemen were indicted in April 1971 on graft charges, confirming what most blacks think about white policemen. . . .

On three different visits and through intensive interviewing, including a return to the plant where I spent 15 years as a plant worker and UAW official, I learned that both within the plants and in the city, the big concern was not class strife but hard drugs and race.

The execution of seven young men and women in June 1971, part of a bloody war between two black gangs seeking to monopolize the profitable heroin trade, dramatized the city's overall drug problem. Between 25 and 50 persons had already been killed, gangland style, in this dispute. But until the *New York Times* reported the concern of auto management over the use of hard drugs in the auto plants, little attention was given to this problem.

The *Times* report was published about a week after I visited an auto plant, talking to plant and local union officials, and to one of the UAW staff members who functions as a "troubleshooter." Sam Bellomo, vice-president of Chrysler Local 7—he's been elected to office either in the plant or the large local for almost 30 years—described the situation this way:

> Boredom on the job? The speedup? That's routine. What the workers fear most is the drug addict in the plant. They worry about safety of operations, and they dread knowing that pushers operate in the plants, and their victims work there. Drugs are not confined to any one people. It's the young mainly, both black and white. They don't give a damn about anything.

I checked this with other officials whom I have known for years. They confirm what Bellomo says. Nor could this be attributed to the returning Vietnam veterans, my friends insisted; there weren't that many of them. It was more of a general problem. At a pay rate

of $35 a day, an assembly-line worker is far more likely to have
the "loot" to buy expensive fixes than is the welfare client. Hard
drugs have found a new marketplace, the auto shop, and a new
victim, the young worker. The drug scene is so frightening that it
is one reason many local union officials, men still in the shops, feel
a need to carry guns.

The other obsession has to do with race relations. A decade ago
this plant, like many others, had a mixture of workers: about 20
percent black, the rest Polish, Italian, and Southern white. Winning
a local union election usually meant getting together the right
coalition with each ethnic group represented. It was basically an
integrative concept. This has changed drastically. Now 65 percent
of the membership is black, and only the skilled trades remain a
white work force. In the plant we were told by white workers,
"They have taken over. You do your work, keep your mouth
shut and get the hell out when the whistle blows." At best, the black
and white workers tolerate each other in the plants. The UAW of
class solidarity, as it was once supposed to exist and in part did, is
no longer much in evidence. Jesse Cundiff, a local union president for three terms before becoming a staff man, says:

> Among skilled workers and the oldtimers, the ethnic groups, noth-
> ing has changed. They are still anti-. They hate the colored man's
> guts but can't do anything about it. As for the blacks, they are
> aggressive and taking over wherever and whenever they can—in
> many cases long overdue, after all they have had to suffer.

Politics in local union elections generally follows this pattern.
Where the blacks are a majority, they take the big spots and give a
white a token job. Men like Sam Bellomo are now the exception;
he's executive vice-president in a local where all other officers, including the president, William Gilbert, are black. An indication of
how black leadership keeps developing through union politics and
bargaining—ten years ago Gilbert was going to union classes to become a better chief steward. Now he teaches at the Wayne State
labor college, besides being president of this large local. Another
young steward ten years ago was Quintan McCrae. He used to represent the janitors. When I talked to him in June 1971, he had just
finished five local negotiations with Chrysler. How many dozens
of such young leaders have been developed in the UAW no one

can say. But they are there, and more are coming up all the time.

Where whites are a majority, they keep as much control as possible and have a token black officer. It works strictly as a power relationship based primarily on race—and with little love lost. Election contests are intense. Each year, as the composition of the plants changes, the blacks gain more and more power on the local union levels—and now have a real base in the international union. Eleven local presidents in the Detroit area now are black.

Between the high quit rate among young workers—over 30 percent annually despite the recession—and the new industry policy of hiring blacks, there are now over 250,000 black workers in the auto plants: at GM about 25 percent, at Ford 35 percent, and at Chrysler about 25 percent. In many Detroit plants the blacks are either a majority or about to be, and this has vast significance for the future of black unionism.

Symptomatic of these trends is the impact on management. We asked what happened to a former secretary of Local 7, one of the first blacks elected to that position. It turns out that he is now an assistant labor-relations director for the company. What about the most popular black steward the Local ever had, a self-educated man with a white constituency? Now superintendent of the night shift! There are black foremen throughout the plant, yet it is only ten years ago that the issue of having one black foreman was raised with the corporation. Those were the days when management didn't believe a black man could fill any supervisory position. They have learned better.

For both blacks and whites, this shift in power is a painful process. Violent incidents exacerbate the tensions. A major topic of conversation in the auto plants last June was the acquittal of a black worker who killed a white foreman, a black foreman, and a white skilled worker in the Chrysler Eldon Avenue plant last year—hence, as the men feel, another reason for carrying guns in the shops.

This case attracted much attention, for the black worker was a veteran, James Johnson, Jr., and his attorneys were Kenneth Cockrel of the League of Revolutionary Black Workers, and Justin Ravitz. They claimed that Johnson was temporarily insane—and a jury of eight blacks and four whites agreed. The lawyers argued that he suffered severe mental illness resulting from his days as a sharecropper in Mississippi, and that unsafe working conditions coupled with harsh treatment by Chrysler foremen drove Johnson to a point where he could not control his impulse to kill. Transferred from his job over his protest, Johnson went home, got his carbine, and returned to the plant on a rampage of killing.

The extent to which these events affect in-plant attitudes, and inner-union relationships was illustrated by the election at the Eldon plant in May 1971. A *Detroit Free Press* article described the situation:

A candidate supported by black militant auto workers was narrowly defeated Friday in a runoff election for president of UAW Local 961 at the troubled Chrysler Corp. Eldon Ave. gear and axle plant. Jordon Sims, fired by Chrysler May 1, 1970, for allegedly provoking a wildcat strike, was defeated by Frank McKinnon, chief steward on the third shift, by a vote of 1,178 to 1,142. Sims planned to protest the vote and appeal the election results because, he said, armed private guards patrolled the union hall corridors and intimidated voters. Sims also said about 250 votes were invalidated and he was unable to get from election authorities an adequate explanation for the invalidation.

Local 961 represents 4,000 production workers at the plant, scene of a triple slaying last summer. The plant has also been plagued by wildcat strikes, demonstrations and other violence.

McKinnon, who is white, and Sims, who is black, were pitted in the runoff after leading four candidates in a hotly contested previous contest earlier this month. Sims, whose opponents identified him with militants, led the four candidates in the first round of balloting. He had 806 votes to 739 for McKinnon. Elroy Richardson, the incumbent president, finished third and was eliminated from the runoff. McKinnon and Sims became runoff candidates because neither had a majority as required by union bylaws.

Sims has denied he is a member of any radical group. But Richardson said Sims was endorsed in leaflets distributed by the Eldon Revolutionary Union Movement (ELRUM), an affiliate of the militant League of Revolutionary Black Workers.

The armed guards were hired by the incumbent president Elroy

Richardson. He defended the decision saying that it assured a fair election. He said the guards prevented "extremists and outsiders from disrupting the election process."

Like it or not, in Detroit color-consciousness has come to prevail over class-consciousness, and for this a major cause has been the growth of the black-power movement. Forty years of strikes have failed to make Detroit workers class-conscious; at best, they are union-conscious, and even this loyalty is being strained by the rise of black unionism.

The growing black working class of Detroit had in 1971 an annual income of $7,500 per person, providing a socioeconomic base unlike any in the nation. Since many of these workers have to drive out into the suburbs to the new plants and return to the city at night, they have a daily reminder of the restrictions placed on them in metropolitan Detroit.

This concentration of blacks has made the UAW a vanguard in the rise of black unionism. Among the black officials are Nelson "Jack" Edwards, an international vice-president; Marcellius Ivory, a Detroit regional director; and 11 local presidents in the Detroit area. Not to mention the hundreds of black local union officers, shop committeemen, and stewards. Unlike most other unions, the UAW has caucuses, and an influential one is the ad hoc black caucus, chaired by Robert "Buddy" Battle III, with over 100 members, all of them local union leaders, who used to meet periodically with Walter Reuther and now have a similar relationship with Leonard Woodcock. Battle is also executive vice-president of Ford Local 600, and president of the Trade Union Leadership Council he formed with Horace Sheffield, which led the struggle to get black men elected to top positions in the UAW. Many of these men constitute a new generation of ambitious unionists who have no more in common with, say, the building trades workers than early CIO militants with the fogies of AFL craft unions.

Almost half of Detroit's unionized schoolteachers are black; other city unions have a similar composition. Symbolic of the new relationship was the election of Tom Turner, a black steelworker, to the presidency of the AFL-CIO council. Detroit in the 1970s may well be for this kind of unionism what the city was for the CIO in the 1930s: a major forerunner and an example for other black unionists, still chafing under white paternalism. For while there are more than 2.5 million black workers in the AFL-CIO, they are somewhat less than adequately represented in most AFL-CIO unions, to say nothing of the AFL-CIO top leadership.

The expansion of black economic power suggests that new kinds of struggle, with the city as base, are more likely to occur in the near future than are the primitive battles of Detroit's past. But many obstacles remain to both black aspirations and social peace.

Henry Ford II recently announced that he had approved the construction of a $750 million housing-commercial project in all-white Dearborn. The drain from Detroit is obvious. Even if some token integration were to occur, what remains of the white middle class in Detroit will have another place to run to. Max Fisher, the oil millionaire, is also spending millions in new housing in the suburbs, beyond the reach of the blacks. Still, it is too soon to accept former Mayor Jerome P. Cavanagh's projection of Detroit's place in the future: "Detroit's twin cities—Nagasaki and Pompey."

Nor should it be assumed that the city of Detroit is similar to Newark or Chicago. Economically, Newark is far weaker than Detroit. Detroit blue-collar wages make Newark pay scales seem feeble. The unions and the blacks within them are a powerful socioeconomic force. A black mayor in Detroit, with all his handicaps, would have an economic base impossible to achieve in Newark, where Mayor Kenneth Gibson is at the financial mercy of the state and federal governments.

Detroit offers notable possibilities for blacks. It could become a black metropolis with a strong middle class, a stronger working class, and a generation of young leaders bursting out in every institution. Precisely these factors make unlikely any real revolutionary crisis, the kind loudly proclaimed by both the black and white Left.

The sitdowns in the 1930s turned out to be a demand for a voice and a share in the system rather than a prelude to revolution—as antagonists feared and some proponents hoped. Very probably, black radicalism in the '70s will turn out to have played a similar role. Only when radicals work within the framework of viable institutions—unions, parties, community groups—can they maintain any social roots, and thereby have some impact on events.

For most blacks in Detroit, the industrial and public-sector unions and the political process offer an effective vehicle for protest, power, and progress. At times, angry voices from the Left spur the leaders of these organizations and unions to greater effort. What is unmistakable, affecting all aspects of city life, is the trend toward blacks coming to have a major stake in Detroit.

Many setbacks lie ahead; Detroit may explode again. The national economic and political climate always affects the city deeply. Certainly, the police, the firemen, the building trades, and other white-dominated and white-based organizations may be expected to continue resisting black power—I use the phrase to describe a visible reality, not an ideological slogan. But essentially this resistance is a rear-guard action.

The most severe strains are likely to continue in the plants, the unions, and political and social institutions where the blacks have had the biggest impact. Only recently a black caucus was formed in the Michigan Democratic party—a sign of power and independence. In the UAW, it is only a matter of time before all four regional directors in Detroit are black. This trend poses an acute challenge to white politicians and white unionists. The challenge is to form a coalition of *equals*—an integrated coalition, otherwise the current rise of separatism may turn out to be more than the detour we hope it is on the road toward an integrated society. A society of fear and racial clashes cannot be reformed by the tepid measures so often prescribed in the past for Detroit. The blacks have too much power to accept "tokenism" a moment longer.

The Future of the
Detroit Metropolitan Area

A leading urban economist, Wilbur R. Thompson, presents in this article his important "ratchet" concept of urban growth and uses an "export model" to show that Detroit's heavy dependency upon automobile manufacturing is slowly shrinking in the face of new and hopeful diversification. This selection is by Wilbur R.

Thompson, "The Future of the Detroit Metropolitan Area," in
Michigan in the 1970's, *edited by William Haber, W. Allen Spivey,
and Martin Warshaw, Ann Arbor: Bureau of Business Research,
Graduate School of Business Administration, University of Michigan, 1965, pp. 203–240. Copyright by the University of Michigan
and reprinted with permission.*

The Role of Exports in Urban Growth *

The economy of an urban area can be analyzed and an attempt
made to tell its fortune in a number of different ways. Although
urban-regional economic analysis is a relatively new art, it has
already become traditional to depict the community as a small nation engaged in foreign trade. In this figurative view the outside
world begins at the outer edges of the nearby hinterland, which
the city serves as a trade and service center, and extends to distant
cities in the nation and overseas—wherever sectors of the local
economy trade their manufactured goods. The urban area becomes, above all, a local labor market, a primary unit of employment and income generation. The locality is buffeted by changes
in demand for its "export" products and in the "derived demand"
for local labor, changes that originate outside the local economy
and over which it has little or no control. Even those workers employed by local business that sells largely or entirely to local households depend on "foreign" demand, since the customers for such
business are, in the last analysis, employees of the local export industries. Or, viewed from a slightly different angle, the community
can buy from outsiders—food, clothing, gasoline, and other necessities—only by selling to outsiders, in other words, exporting.

The literature of urban-regional growth, largely written by such
non-economists as economic geographers, economic historians,
and city or regional planners, characteristically projects the future
size and shape of the whole urban economy from the anticipated
size and shape of its export sector. The format is simple and direct.
The export base of most urban economies is dominated by a relatively small number of manufacturing activities; therefore, one
simply estimates the number of export manufacturing workers that

* The terms "Detroit area" or "Detroit metropolitan area," as used
throughout this chapter, refer to the Detroit Standard Metropolitan Statistical Area (S.M.S.A.), consisting of Macomb, Oakland, and Wayne counties.

would be employed locally at the target date and then adds the number of local service employees needed to accommodate the export industry workers and their families (and, of course, to serve each others' families). Finally, if the projected total number of export and service industry workers is multiplied by the average number of dependents per worker, the future total population of the area falls neatly into place.

Following this logic, we could proceed here by analyzing the growth prospects of the automobile industry. Such an analysis would, of course, concern itself both with the output and employment trends for the industry as a whole and with these trends in the Detroit area's share of that industry. The effort would, in fact, consist essentially of coming up with the likely national employment in automobile production in the target year and the likely local employment share. The product of the two quantities is the projected local export base. All that would be left, then, would be to link export employment to total employment and the latter to total population, through the estimated future labor force participation rate.

Certainly this would be the best way to predict the future of a small urban economy, but there are a number of reasons why a simple export base projection is not entirely appropriate for judging the economic prospects of the Detroit area. First, the leading industry here is a mature one; moreover, it has recently been decentralizing. A moderately optimistic projection of employment for the local automobile industry would show it remaining constant during the next two decades. To predict a constant local export base (and thereby a constant total size) would contradict the clear trend toward concentration of an ever larger share of the national population in the very large metropolitan areas, the class into which the Detroit area falls. This is not to say that the automobile industry will not continue to be the principal employer in the area for decades to come, only that it will probably not provide the significant *marginal changes* that will be the key to local development.

Second, the golden age of manufacturing seems to have run its course in the sense that the *share* of manufacturing in total employment has begun what threatens to be a long-term decline. True, manufacturing will probably not experience as precipitous a decline in its share of employment as that which characterized agriculture during the past century. The income elasticity of demand for manufactured goods is generally much greater than for foods and fibers, and this condition ensures a growth in per capita consumption of manufactured goods which will take much of the bite out of the rapidly increasing productivity per worker. The situation is therefore unlike that of farming, where labor displacement has made a severe impact. Still, manufacturing in general and production employment in particular would not seem to hold the key to the pattern of employment growth in the age of automation, especially in an already overspecialized manufacturing economy such as that of Detroit.

Third, for reasons developed at some length in the pages to follow, the large metropolitan area seems to have a life of its own, and its growth pattern is far more subtle and complex than can be explained simply by magnifying the growth pattern of its principal export industries. A second broad approach, then, would be to see the Detroit area as a potential metropolis and, by observing the trends in economic structure and performance of the other major metropolitan areas of the nation, to seek some regularities in the behavior of these very large urban economies to which this local economy might tend to conform. This latter approach will be stressed in this paper, although the intention is not to deny in any way that Detroit is both a metropolis—potentially, at least—*and* an automobile city. Because a full understanding of Detroit would patently call for a study of the automobile industry in depth, and because that ambitious work is beyond this brief effort, the choice was made to turn instead to a less appreciated local growth dynamic—the growth momentum of the large metropolis. . . .

The Growth Pattern of a Metropolis

We turn now to view the Detroit area economy not on the basis of its export industries but rather as a metropolis whose growth may be to some extent independent of export industries. A strong case can be made, in fact, for choosing a hybrid economic-demographic approach in the case of very large urban areas. While a small urban area may rise and fall with the fortunes of its principal export industries, urban areas having, say, a population of a half-million and over ordinarily achieve considerable stability (through industrial diversification) and thereby acquire considerable holding power. For any city there seems to be some critical size. Short of this point, continuing growth is not inevitable, and even the city's very existence is not assured. Beyond that particular size, however, although the rate of growth may slacken at times even to zero, absolute contraction is highly unlikely. Some process or mechanism, like a ratchet, seems to come into being, locking in past growth and preventing contraction. . . .

Detroit as an Industrial Entrepreneur
The long-run prospect is for new products to emanate from this industrial environment as it grows richer. One should, in fact, recognize that as a city grows larger its role changes from producer to creator. Rather than simply disgorging volumes of standardized products (*à la* Flint), Detroit has been and must continue to be the center of automotive technology and design. But Detroit must become something more than just a center of automotive technology; it must emulate New York and Boston and Chicago by finding its very reason for being in invention and innovation that strike out in many and diverse directions. The economic history of New York is instructive at this point and indicates an important moral for the Detroit area economy and its leaders.

> The New York metropolitan area grew by incubating new functions, nurturing them and finally spinning them off to other sections of the country, all the while regenerating this cycle. The flour mills, foundries, meat-packing, textiles and tanneries of the post-Civil War period drifted away from New York, their place taken by less transport-sensitive products—garments, cigars, and office work. Currently, New York is losing the manufacturing end of many of its most traditional specialties, as garment sewing slips away to low-wage Eastern Pennsylvania leaving only the selling function behind, and as printing splits away from immobile publishing. But New York's growth never seems to falter as the new growth industries are much more than proportionately regenerated in its rich industrial culture.

Because it is almost inevitable that a substantial amount of decentralization will occur with the maturing of the local growth industries, the big city in particular should spend less time worrying about losing a share of some existing industry and more time working to cultivate new replacement industries. The city that aspires to be a true metropolis should pattern its actions on the executive image, delegating tasks readily as they become routine and keeping itself free to take on the new and sophisticated work in which it has a comparative advantage over smaller places. In taking this direction the big city often has no choice, for the smaller community offers lower costs of production for routine operations and will often maneuver desperately to underbid for the work that its survival demands; tax concessions, rent-free plants, low-interest loans, and the like are lures used mainly by small urban areas. The small, isolated manufacturing town is much less able than its larger counterpart to compete in research and development work or even in manufacturing operations in the early stages of the "learning curve."

The very large metropolitan areas of the country do, in fact, show some evidence of resembling each other in the business of inventing and innovating. The estimated number of scientists and engineers per thousand manufacturing workers and per thousand total employees for nine metropolitan areas was computed and expressed as a percentage of the 9-area average. (It is not obvious whether manufacturing employment or total employment is the appropriate deflator. Is research and development generated largely from manufacturing activity, or is it rather a function of total activity?) In either case, a clear tendency toward convergence is exhibited, as shown in . . . Table VI-5. The coefficient of variation of the nine index numbers decreased by about one-third between 1945 and 1955, in both the manufacturing and total employment forms. The tentative conclusion is that research and development work—industrial entrepreneurship in its highest and most dynamic expression—must be assumed as a *routine* function by the aspiring metropolis.

To the extent, moreover, that the critical urban problem of the day is to find ways to provide full employment, industrial entrepreneurship has much more to recommend it than straight production work. The sophisticated job of creating more and more new products and processes is almost sure to use more labor than the routine work of running standard manufacturing operations, especially in this age of automation. Technical discussion, experimentation, setting up pilot plants, and other such work is the big city's forte. Much of this is professional service work rather than manufacturing activity as we have known it in the past, however the Bureau of the Census may classify it. This is especially true of contract research in university laboratories, proliferating market survey activities, consulting, patenting, financing, and so forth. A true metropolis must be fully as much a center of business and technical services as of consumer and personal-family services.

Detroit as a Major Professional and Personal Service Center
The coming diversification of the Detroit area economy will probably be accomplished through a broadening and deepening of the service industry even more than through vertical integration of the automobile industry. This seems to follow from both the nation-wide trend toward an expanded service sector share and the fact that Detroit is relatively underdeveloped in this area of activity.

One can adduce a number of reasons why a substantial expansion of the service sector is in the offing. First, many services, though not all, are income elastic—they are "luxury goods"—and so the demand for them will rise more than would be proportionate to our increasing per capita income. Examples are: financial counseling, psychiatric treatment, restaurant services, and theatre performances. Second, we should expect an increasingly affluent society to demand not only much more of *almost all* kinds of professional services but more of *many* kinds of personal services; moreover, rapid employment growth in these directions can also be expected because services are, on the whole, less subject to automation. Even if we should come to employ machines in medical diagnosis and to automate insurance offices from top to bottom, some services are extremely resistant to automation whereas almost no manufacturing is.

Third, we may find that, as a direct by-product of the process of automation in manufacturing, new service work is created. The need for much more intensive and personal treatment of the displaced factory worker, through vocational testing, psychological analysis, counseling, retraining, relocation, and so forth, could become one of the principal sources of new jobs in the next decade. (There is hardly need to mention other social services related to child care and such kinds of social pathology as alcoholism, crime,

Table VI-5

Number of Scientists and Engineers in Eleven Selected Industries in Nine Metropolitan Areas—1945, 1950, 1955

Metropolitan Area	Number of Scientists and Engineers			Index of Number Per Thousand Manufacturing Employees *			Index of Number Per Thousand Total Employees *		
	1945	1950	1955	1945	1950	1955	1945	1950	1955
Boston	778	1,135	3,544	53.9	65.8	120.3	55.5	51.9	95.1
Chicago	3,403	4,483	7,191	74.3	74.5	70.3	77.5	79.5	76.6
Cleveland	1,345	1,875	2,897	103.5	135.7	91.1	122.0	127.6	114.8
Detroit	2,190	2,762	4,891	81.2	75.3	74.5	102.1	97.1	100.8
Los Angeles	1,494	3,124	9,159	85.9	103.4	128.9	54.2	77.4	110.4
New York	12,074	14,325	22,582	155.9	136.0	119.4	167.4	182.8	153.2
Philadelphia	3,134	3,531	5,909	121.6	104.5	103.0	124.2	102.9	99.5
Pittsburgh	1,541	2,146	2,943	94.2	101.3	83.4	126.7	110.9	93.2
San Francisco	1,025	1,434	2,111	129.5	133.1	109.0	69.5	69.5	56.6
Standard deviation of number per thousand				1.43	1.44	2.03	0.856	0.871	0.967
Arithmetic mean of number per thousand				4.84	6.20	10.14	2.36	2.39	3.85
Coefficient of variation				0.295	0.233	0.200	0.363	0.364	0.251

* 15-area average = 100.

Source: Derived from George Perazich, "Growth of Scientific Research in Selected Industries, 1945–1960," Contract Research Report of Galaxy, Inc., to the National Science Foundation, Oct. 14, 1957, table VI, p. 36. (Mimeographed.)

and delinquency.) And these new "personnel" jobs could prove to be ones we desperately need: semiprofessional work suited to the abilities and training of the deluge of C^+ to B^- students due to pour out of our expanded colleges in a few years. We may expect continued rapid growth in the local public sectors and in the private, nonprofit sectors of our economy, especially in the many social service sectors (e.g., social case work).

Fourth, a growing and diversifying Detroit area economy will almost certainly exercise increasing influence over its hinterland—the rest of Michigan, excepting perhaps the southwestern corner of the state which is economically oriented to Chicago. Now that Detroit has reaped the easy harvest of a wealthy and expansive automobile industry, it will become necessary and profitable to go back and glean the fields for unexploited opportunities in service industries. And more than casual evidence does exist that Detroit is growing up and blossoming out in finance, education, and wholesale trade. Witness the new buildings downtown, Wayne State University's growing graduate programs, and the proposed new Detroit merchandise mart.

Objection has been raised to so rosy a view of Detroit's potential as a service center for an extended region. Some observers doubt that Detroit can reach a point where it will not only fill more of its own service needs but even begin to export a significant amount of service. The counterargument is advanced that Detroit's position on a peninsula, constrained by the existence of Chicago to the west and Cleveland to the east, so constricts its potential service market that major status as a metropolis, a "mother city," is not a real developmental choice for this area. One needs only to peruse a set of maps, however, to appreciate that Detroit's near monopoly of Michigan provides fully as rich a hinterland as Boston's *share* of New England, Cleveland's *share* of Ohio (some portion of which goes to Pittsburgh and Cincinnati), Milwaukee's sparsely populated Wisconsin hinterland (for whose trade Milwaukee competes with Chicago), or Philadelphia's cramped market wedged between New York and Baltimore-Washington.

Moreover, with the continued drift to the large metropolitan areas, each metropolitan area becomes increasingly its own region. That is, the next couple of decades will probably see the Detroit area pulling its hinterland customers right into its immediate environs, or expanding to absorb its satellites like Ann Arbor at least as much as it reaches out to provide them with services where they are. In sum, the Detroit economy has already amassed a more or less captive market of over 4 million people, whose per capita income is above the average and larger than that of all but four other metropolitan areas. And, for reasons argued in the first section of this paper, this area is likely to keep all or most of its natural increase. This prospect alone ensures substantial growth and further economic development, at not much below the national average rate, in all but the most adverse circumstances. . . .

Re-counting Our Mixed Blessings

The economic implications of the coming transition of the Detroit area from a brash and dynamic industrial center to a full-blown metropolis are implicit throughout this paper. But a recapitulation here will make the major points more explicit.

As the Detroit area matures, its many growth and income characteristics will approach those of the average metropolis and the nation. The movement of more and more of our population to these giant urban areas will create a situation where the major metropolises almost are the nation. The "nationalization" of the performance characteristics of the Detroit area economy will not be an unmixed blessing. True, greater cyclical stability will be achieved as the area comes to depend less on motor vehicles and more on metropolitan services. But this area's per capita income, now above average, will probably exhibit a *relative* drop because it will rise less rapidly than that of other urban areas. Again, Detroit as the biggest factory town on earth has enjoyed a relatively low level of income inequality. The narrow range of occupations and the egalitarian influence of trade unions have combined to produce this effect. Now with the ascendancy of finance, entertainment, and various professional services, Detroit will assemble more and more of the very rich and very poor—corporate lawyers as well as messenger "boys." This means that the talented will find more opportunity, although the implications with respect to the unprepared are less favorable to general welfare.

The local growth rate, much faster than the nation's up to 1955 or so, has slowed and will probably approach the national rate of change. In population terms, the Detroit area growth rate will probably approach the local rate of natural increase, roughly that of other large metropolitan areas and ultimately that of the nation at large, as the nonmetropolitan areas are drained to minimum populations. But then slow, steady growth in population probably presents the optimum conditions under which to plan and develop an efficient and pleasant urban area.

All in all, I foresee a Detroit area large enough to offer the advantages which ensure its competitive position. As a metropolis it will therefore share, if no longer exceed, the general nationwide level of well-being and will grow steadily and exhibit greater cyclical stability. This rather rosy picture is dimmed a bit by the further expectation that a growing income inequality will demand of local leaders the closest attention and greatest skill. In common with all metropolitan areas, the Detroit area must, then, address itself to the growing problem of welfare and the development of human resources. "Detroiters" will have the money; they must also have the will.

To Bus or Not to Bus: The United States Supreme Court Orders a "Detroit-Only" Solution, 25 July 1974

The United States Supreme Court's five-to-four ruling on 25 July 1974 against a metropolitan-area busing solution for curing Detroit's school segregation problems was the first clear decision on the very controversial issue of city-suburban busing of schoolchildren. Chief Justice Warren Burger delivered the Court's opinion, which found no substantial evidence that actions (interdistrict violations) of suburban schools had directly contributed to the segregation of Detroit's city schools. Justice Burger's opinion is drawn from "William G. Milliken, Governor of Michigan, et al., Petitioners, v. Ronald Bradley and Richard Bradley, by Their Mother and Next Friend, Verda Bradley, et al." ("Slip Opinion," circulated, August 1974, Washington, D.C.).

Chief Justice Burger delivered the opinion of the court in which Justices Stewart, Blackmun, Powell and Rehnquist joined. . . .

Ever since *Brown* v. *Board of Education,* 347 U. S. 483 (1954), judicial consideration of school desegregation cases has begun with the standard that:

> "[I]n the field of public education the doctrine of 'separate but equal' has no place. Separate educational facilities are inherently unequal." 347 U.S., at 495.

This has been reaffirmed time and again as the meaning of the Constitution and the controlling rule of law.

The target of the *Brown* holding was clear and forthright: the elimination of state mandated or deliberately maintained dual school systems with certain schools for Negro pupils and others for White pupils. This duality and racial segregation was held to violate the Constitution in the cases subsequent to 1954, including particularly *Green* v. *County School Board of New Kent County,* 391 U. S. 430 (1968); . . .

III

We recognize that six-volume record presently under consideration contains language and some specific incidental findings thought by the District Court to afford a basis for inter-district relief. However, these comparatively isolated findings and brief comments concern only one possible inter-district violation and are found in the context of a proceeding that, as the District Court conceded, included no proofs of segregation practiced by any of the 85 suburban school districts surrounding Detroit. The Court of Appeals, for example, relied on five factors which, it held, amounted to unconstitutional state action with respect to the violations found in the Detroit system:

(1) It held the State derivatively responsible for the Detroit Board's violations on the theory that actions of Detroit as a political subdivision of the State were attributable to the State. Accepting, *arguendo,* the correctness of this finding of State responsibility for the segregated conditions within the city of Detroit, it does not follow that an inter-district remedy is constitutionally justified or required. With a single exception, discussed later, there has been

no showing that either the State or any of the 85 outlying districts engaged in activity that had a cross-district effect. The boundaries of the Detroit School District, which are coterminous with the boundaries of the city of Detroit, were established over a century ago by neutral legislation when the city was incorporated; there is no evidence in the record, nor is there any suggestion by the respondents, that either the original boundaries of the Detroit School District, or any other school district in Michigan, were established for the purpose of creating, maintaining or perpetuating segregation of races. There is no claim and there is no evidence hinting that petitioners and their predecessors, or the 40-odd other school districts in the tricounty area—but outside the District Court's "desegregation area"—have ever maintained or operated anything but unitary school systems. Unitary school systems have been required for more than a century by the Michigan Constitution as implemented by state law. Where the schools of only one district have been affected, there is no constitutional power in the courts to decree relief balancing the racial composition of that district's schools with those of the surrounding districts.

(2) There was evidence introduced at trial that, during the late 1950's, Carver School District, a predominantly Negro suburban district, contracted to have Negro high school students sent to a predominantly Negro school in Detroit. At the time, Carver was an independent school district that had no high school because, according to the trial evidence, "Carver District . . . did not have a place for adequate high school facilities." Pet. App., at 138a. Accordingly, arrangements were made with Northern High School in the abutting Detroit School District so that the Carver high school students could obtain a secondary school education. In 1960 the Oak Park School District, a predominantly White suburban district, annexed the predominantly Negro Carver School District, through the initiative of local officials. *Ibid.* There is, of course, no claim that the 1960 annexation had segregatory purpose or result or that Oak Park now maintains a dual system.

According to the Court of Appeals, the arrangement during the late 1950's which allowed Carver students to be educated within the Detroit District was dependent upon the "tacit or express" approval of the State Board of Education and was the result of the refusal of the White suburban districts to accept the Carver students. Although there is nothing in the record supporting the Court of Appeal's supposition that suburban White schools refused to accept the Carver students, it appears that this situation, whether with or without the State's consent, may have had a segregatory effect on the school populations of the two districts involved. However, since "the nature of the violation determines the scope of the remedy," 402 U. S., at 15–16, this isolated instance affecting two of the school districts would not justify the broad metropolitan-wide remedy contemplated by the District Court and approved by the Court of Appeals, particularly since it embraced potentially 52 districts having no responsibility for the arrangement and involved 503,000 pupils in addition to Detroit's 276,000 students.

(3) The Court of Appeals cited the enactment of state legislation (Act 48) which had the effect of rescinding Detroit's voluntary desegregation plan (the April 7 Plan). That plan, however, affected only 12 or 21 Detroit high schools and had no causal connection with the distribution of pupils by race between Detroit and the other school districts within the tri-county area.

(4) The court relied on the State's authority to supervise school site selection and to approve building construction as a basis for holding the State responsible for the segregative results of the school construction program in Detroit. Specifically, the Court of Appeals asserted that during the period between 1949 and 1962 the State Board of Education exercised general authority as overseer of site acquisitions by local boards for new school construction, and suggested that this State approved school construction "fostered segregation throughout the Detroit Metropolitan area." Pet. App., at 157a. This brief comment, however, is not supported by the evidence taken at trial since that evidence was specifically limited to proof that school site acquisition and school construction within the city of Detroit produced *de jure* segregation *within* the city itself. Pet. App., at 144a–151a. Thus, there was no evidence suggesting that the State's activities with respect to either school construction or site acquisition within Detroit affected the racial composition of the school population outside Detroit or, conversely, that the State's school construction and site acquisition activities within the outlying districts affected the racial composition of the schools within Detroit.

(5) The Court of Appeals also relied upon the District Court's finding that:

> "This and other financial limitations, such as those on bonding and the working of the state aid formula whereby suburban districts were able to make far larger per pupil expenditures despite less tax effect, have created and perpetuated systematic educational inequalities." Pet. App., at 152a.

However, neither the Court of Appeals nor the District Court offered any indication in the record or in their opinions as to how, if at all, the availability of state financed aid for some Michigan students outside Detroit but not within Detroit, might have affected the racial character of any of the State's school districts. Furthermore, as the respondents recognize, the application of our recent ruling in *San Antonio Independent School District* v. *Rodriguez,* 411 U. S. 1, to this state education financing system is questionable, and this issue was not addressed by either the Court of Appeals or the District Court. This, again, underscores the crucial fact that the theory upon which the case proceeded related solely to the establishment of Detroit city violations as a basis for desegregating Detroit schools and that, at the time of trial, neither the parties nor the trial judge were concerned with a foundation for inter-district relief.

IV

Petitioners have urged that they were denied due process by the manner in which the District Court limited their participation after intervention was allowed thus precluding adequate opportunity to present evidence that they had committed no acts having a segregative effect in Detroit. In light of our holding that absent an inter-district violation there is no basis for an inter-district remedy, we need not reach these claims. It is clear, however, that the District Court, with the approval of the Court of Appeals, has provided an inter-district remedy in the face of a record which shows no constitutional violations that would call for equitable relief except within the city of Detroit. In these circumstances there was no occasion for the parties to address, or for the District Court to consider whether there were racially discriminatory acts for which any of the 53 outlying districts were responsible and which had direct and significant segregative effect on schools of more than one district.

We conclude that the relief ordered by the District Court and affirmed by the Court of Appeals was based upon an erroneous standard and was unsupported by record evidence that acts of the outlying districts affected the discrimination found to exist in the schools of Detroit. Accordingly, the judgment of the Court of Appeals is reversed and the case is remanded for further proceedings consistent with this opinion leading to prompt formulation of a decree directed to eliminating the segregation found to exist in Detroit city schools, a remedy which has been delayed since 1970.

Reversed and remanded.

Ethnicity in Detroit

This document deals with the phenomenal resurgence of ethnicity and illustrates how ethnic spokesmen are pressing the claims of pluralism. The author, an academic of Polish extraction, sympathetically sketches the history of Detroit's Polish community and perceptively assays many of the grievances common to inner-city ethnics. This selection is from Thaddeus Radzialowski, "The View from a Polish Ghetto" (Ethnicity 1 [July 1974]: 125–26, 141–50). Reprinted by permission of the author and Academic Press, Inc.

Along a short stretch of Canfield Street on Detroit's near east side, in the heart of the Black ghetto, stand three majestic Catholic Churches—*Sweetest Heart of Mary, St. Albertus,* and *St. Josephat.* Amid an alien population they stand as lonely symbols of the deep, other-worldly faith and worldly pride, bordering on arrogance, of the Polish immigrants who built them. Like the medieval men they were in essence, the Poles adorned their communities with soaring Gothic churches of a kind that few peasant villages in

Poland had ever known. They were status symbols of a country people who could now build their monuments bigger than those in the towns of the old country. Building funds for the churches were produced only at the cost of heroic and sometimes brutal sacrifices. During the depression of the 1890's, the parishioners of *Sweetest Heart* mortgaged their homes to buy back their church at the court auction at which the church and its properties were being sold to satisfy creditors. The Canfield churches stood as visible daily reminders that God had come with the immigrants on their long journey and that perhaps the voyage had been worth it. They were stone and mortar roots which bound them to the soil of the new world.

The churches of Canfield Street are still alive as Polish parishes. A few parishioners remain in the area, but the overwhelming majority of the 350–400 families that support each parish live in distant suburbs. They drive in each Sunday to attend Mass and many continue to bus their children in daily to attend the parochial schools. Few peoples have ever had as great sense of place and of history as have the Poles and because of it they are determined to hang onto their beloved churches, in spite of the universal claims of Roman Catholicism and in spite of the best laid plans of John Cardinal Dearden, the Archbishop of Detroit. These are the Mother Churches. Even Poles who grew up elsewhere find part of their identity in them. The Parishioners still point out with pride the significance of each part of their church and environs:

Father Dabrowski used to come across this street every day to say Mass.

This is where Archbishop Cieplak stayed when he visited Detroit.

General Haller stood right on that spot when he spoke to the people.

For the priests, parishioners, and many other Poles in Detroit, opening the doors of these churches to the Blacks would be an enormity comparable to turning Westminster Abbey into a West Indian mission parish. . . .

The disintegration of the Polish ghetto in Detroit began in the late 40's as the result of many converging factors. The most important of these was the end of World War II and the return of the first American-born generation to seek jobs, wives, and homes.

They came back full of American patriotism and experienced in the ways of the world outside the home neighborhood. Increasing affluence and the introduction of television widened the crack in the wall and undermined the old life style. Polish language and culture had been eliminated in most parish schools. The Poles of Detroit began to learn—many reluctantly, some with gusto—to be Americans. But it was a confusing, secular world with no clear directions. The old neighborhood had been isolated and poor but it had also been protective and nurturing. It seemed to many that they had given up certainty for uncertainty, a hard and clear notion of who they were for the vague identity of an "American." The opening of the ghetto brought a deep anxiety which was compounded by the upheavals in the Catholic Church. *Aggiornamento* appeared to many Poles as a betrayal. The last bastion of truth, the rock on which they had based so much of their identity, had begun to change. By the mid-sixties there was for many, little left to hang on to. The Polish working people of Detroit—especially the women—probably spent more sleepless nights worrying about whether such things as their beloved rosary, from which they had extracted so much solace in the past, would be snatched from them by the hurried and often intolerant reformers than they did about Law and Order and Crime in the Streets. As difficult as it might be for secular liberals or radicals to imagine, such religious concerns struck very deeply into the private lives of the people. It may make little difference, for example, even to most American Catholics, whether one kneels or stands to receive communion, but to many of the older people in the ghetto, standing has a symbolic significance which clashes violently with the old religious *Weltanschauung*.

Student radicals and Black Militants tended to merge in many minds with the Church reformers as further proof of a disrupted world. The so-called "Backlash" of the 1960's was as much of a protest against the traumatic breakup and secularization of the ghetto compounded and accelerated by Church reform as it was a reaction to Black militance.

In 1968, when John Cardinal Dearden gave 1.5 million dollars of the Archdiocesan Development Fund—collected from all the parishes in the Archdiocese—for use in the Black Ghetto, there was the expected strong reaction from the Polish neighborhoods of

Detroit. What was surprising about the reaction was that the Cardinal's action was deemed a deliberate attack on the Polish community. The "Irish" were the villains to many. "They never liked us," said a middle-aged woman the day after the announcement. "They gave our money away out of spite." An usher at a Polish parish had a slightly different version, "They knew we needed that money for our schools," he said. "They gave it to the colored just so we couldn't use it."

The Catholic Church has been for the Poles a ruthless and efficient agency for centralization and Americanization. The largely Irish and German hierarchy imposed on its Slavic adherents—whom it regarded as barbaric and only a step removed from paganism—a quasi-puritan American orthodoxy that derived from both the Irish Church and the Protestant milieu of the United States. Because of the necessity of presenting a united front to a hostile Protestant majority, Church officials tried to make the immigrant over into an "American" Catholic and to force him into centralized organization forms he neither understood or wanted. It is a measure of the intensity of this pressure that many devout Poles were forced into schism. Rather than submit to the anti-Polish policies of their Bishops and surrender control and ownership of their parishes, Poles in Chicago and Scranton, Pennsylvania broke off from the church in the late 1890's under circumstances similar to the Kolasinski episode in Detroit a decade earlier. These scattered dissidents came together to form the Polish National Catholic Church. In the first decade of the twentieth century, Detroit became one of the centers of the movement. Still the only permanent schism from American Catholicism, the P. N. C. C. with about 300,000 members at present, stands as a reminder of the importance of community control of basic institutions for Poles.

The majority of Poles has continued to support the Catholic Church in the Archdiocese of Detroit in spite of continued neglect and even hostility by the Chancery. There have been only two Polish auxiliary Bishops in the first hundred years. The Seminary of Saints Cyril and Methodius at Orchard Lake, just north of Detroit, the country's only Polish seminary was established to train priests for ministry in Polish parishes in Detroit and elsewhere. It has been purposely by-passed for years in the attempt to destroy the unique Polish character of these parishes. Polish candidates for the priesthood in all major dioceses of the U.S. are forbidden to study at Sts. Cyril and Methodius. It can hardly be argued that the Detroit diocesan seminary, St. John's, prepares its candidates for the priesthood better since not only does Sts. Cyril and Methodius have a more distinguished faculty, but it is well known in Detroit that the Cardinal often turns to its theologians for an opinion on a theological question rather than to his own faculty at St. John's. The position of Poles in the American Catholic Church generally is no better than it is in Detroit. Although they comprise at least 20% of the national membership, they hold few leadership positions. Less than 2% of the entries in the 1970–1971 American Catholic *Who's Who* are Polish.

Poles have not fared much better in the secular world outside their community. *Who's Who in American Politics, 1967–68* lists about 82 Poles out 12,500 entries or about 0.6%. The world of industry and finance has been even less congenial to the Poles according to *World Who's Who in Finance and Industry,* wherein only 0.3% of the some 27,000 entries are Polish. Although evidence drawn from *Who's Who* may have a distorting effect, even a cursory examination of industry, labor, government, education, and the Catholic Church shows that Polish representation in leadership positions is grossly out of line with the percentage of Poles in the general population (6–8%) illustrating that a decided pattern of discrimination exists. Impelled partially by choice and partially by necessity ambitious Poles sought status, recognition and satisfaction within their community in the traditional roles of lawyers, doctors, pharmacists, undertakers, and priests. The so-called "Polish Bar" made up of graduates of the city law schools whose practice is confined to a largely Polish clientele is still very much a reality in Detroit. Most of its members know quite well how remote are the possibilities of entering the executive ranks of the prestigious downtown law firms. Until World War II the only significant avenue for advancement for talented women with a desire for education and social mobility lay through the teaching and nursing orders of Polish sisterhoods.

The mood in the Polish community today is mixed. On the one hand, one senses a great physic weariness—the weariness of the survivor—and a desire to be left alone. On the other, there is anger and confusion; the feeling that someone is changing the rules on them. They have paid a high psychological price to become American. It now seems to them that the establishment and its children are changing the definition of what a "good American" is. They have discovered that they are as much the object of ridicule as "Americans" as they were when they were foreigners. While the plans to improve the lot of the Negro has been long on rhetoric and very short indeed on action, the Poles have, as have other ethnic groups, taken the propaganda at face value. After a heavy admission fee, they have been enrolled in American society and allowed to approach the stairway of success only to find, in their view, that someone is letting the Blacks in by a side door and threatening to turn the stairway into an escalator for them. The reaction has in some cases bordered on paranoia. The Blacks are seen merely as the latest and most potent weapon of the "rich people" or the "English" to keep them in their place because they are Poles, because they are workers, or both; since the two identities are often fused. The emotion that results borders on nationalist reaction and class hate.

The generation that came to maturity during World War II and led the exodus out of the ghetto toward the promised land of assimilation is the most troubled. As part of the capitalistic ethic they accepted (along with the implicit idea of their own culture's inferiority) the idea, so convenient for maintaining social peace, that everyone has the same chance for success and that success or failure is solely determined by native ability and effort. The implications of this idea for ethnic Americans were different than for most other citizens. They had consciously jettisoned their old culture and accepted American identity, espoused all the more fervently as they realized that it did not fill the void. To quiet the nagging doubts about the wisdom of their choice and silence the inner voice which told them they were imposters who were always in danger of exposure and rejection, they entered the race for success as a test of Americanism. Failure was un-American. This generation broadcast its successes, and there were many, and refused to admit its failures. The Black Power movement in America changed all that. It attacked the thesis that anyone can succeed if only he tries, and stressed that the failure of the Negro to make it was the result of a pervasive racial prejudice. This attack called into question their new faith, and forced them to take a second look at their own situation. The evidence that their own people also had not made it loomed up before them. If they accepted this evidence, and many did not, they were left with the cruel choice of rejecting their new belief in the American way or admitting that by their own standards they came from a people who were not worthy to be Americans. There is still much of the psychology of the outsider with its accompanying fear of rejection in the Polish-American mind. A young Polish professional man who learned that the author intended to publish the information from *Who's Who* regarding the sparcity of Poles in high places in our society, was profoundly disturbed "But *they* might think that we are asking for something," he said in an anxious voice.

To assert that Poles have suffered as heavily from discrimination as Blacks is obviously absurd. However, their past and present experiences have done severe damage. These experiences have engendered sullen withdrawal from an unfriendly environment. "Poles are such a lively and argumentative people and yet I've noticed they have nothing to say when there are outsiders present," observed a Polish-born sociologist recently. Or as a priest noticed about the leaders of the community, "They are leaders in their own community but more or less self conscious when they get outside their own group."

Too many Poles incorporated elements of the stereotyped immigrant—a retardate with a strong back and an unpronounceable name—into their self-image with unfortunate results. "A Polack is a dummy who takes orders from the priests, the foremen, and the bosses and doesn't cause any trouble. He works his ass off for nothing and gets dumped on by everyone," reflected a middle-aged worker bitterly. An elementary school teacher reported that on meeting her pupils for the first time, she asked a child, whom she discovered subsequently was one of her brightest students, what was her nationality. The girl answered very defensively: "I'm Polish, but I'm not stupid." As it often happens, it is always jarring to hear a Pole declare himself "just a dumb Polack" to a new acquaintance or mumble his name self-consciously and wait for a crack and a laugh. Parents from most mixed population areas in the city and suburbs have complained that their children have come home in tears because of the "Polack" jokes told by their school fellows or even more disturbing, that they acquiesced in these and played the buffoon.

The "Polack" joke, in fact, is unhistorical. It contains little or no reference to recognizable Polish traits or national experiences even in distorted form. The frequent mention of cowardice, for example, is utterly antithetical to the historical record of the Poles. Possibly they are in part the old "nigger," "dumb immigrant," and "kike" jokes redirected at what appears these days to be a safer target. Most of these jokes are cruel attacks on the life style of the workers. In addition to slandering the Poles, therefore, such jokes are a savage mockery of the white working class of which Poles form a recognizable segment. They are a weapon in the American class war. Many people who tell "Polack" jokes are ironically, those who consider themselves friends of the oppressed and warm supporters of Black Americans or who at the very least, are too sophisticated to tell "nigger," or "kike," jokes in public. Even many well meaning people do not realize the full implication of these jokes. A kindly and liberal college professor explained to the author on one occasion the basic difference between "Polack" jokes and "nigger" jokes. The former were "harmless and amusing" because they were not "ill-intentioned" whereas the latter were "truly vicious."

The awakening of Black pride and the intense interest in Black history has led to a reawakening in the Polish community. The Polish Seminary and College at Orchard Lake acknowledged with thanks that debt to "our Black Brothers" in a full page ad in the *Michigan Catholic* in 1970. The Poles and other ethnic groups have begun to realize that they rate even less space in the history books than the Negro and their own heritage and culture is also ignored.

About five years ago in a number of Detroit areas, a renewal of interest in things Polish sprang up spontaneously. The study of the Polish language and culture was reinstituted in some parochial schools. Sunday afternoon travelogues on Poland were begun. Folk dancers performed in suburban school auditoriums and thousands attended. Traditional observances such as the Strawberry Festival at the beginning of May were revived in some parishes with great success. Attendance at a Moniuszko Concert held at St. Stanislaus, a large inner city church, far exceeded the expectations of its organizers and hundreds were turned away after the church was filled beyond official capacity. At the end of August, 1970, a Polish festival held in downtown Detroit drew a large crowd of 125,000 people; the same festival drew an incredible 200,000 people in 1971 and an even more astounding crowd estimated at 300,000 in 1972.

The Polish revival was strengthened, at least among the young, by the cultural upsurge in Poland which brought a number of writers, artists, stage and film directors, and musicians to international prominence in the 60's. If Mickiewicz, Chopin, Paderewski, Modzejewska, Kransinski, or Reymont had no particular relevance to the younger generation, they could identify proudly with Kosinski, Penderecki, Grotowski, Polanski, Hlasko, Skrowaczewski; or if one had a New Left leaning, with Leszek Kolakowski. It became respectable to be a Pole in the late 60's.

A new mood of militance accompanied the cultural revival and a willingness to engage in public demonstration. A silly and offensive article by an unidentified author entitled "A Survivor's Account of a Polish Wedding" in the *Detroit Free Press* Sunday magazine section brought three days of demonstrations by several thousand Poles in November, 1970. The paper finally agreed to a public apology and a series of articles on Polish history and culture. The attempt by the Detroit Archdiocese to close three self-supporting Polish elementary schools in the inner city brought demonstrations and picket lines at the Chancery office in March of 1971. The arguments used by the protestors in this case are interesting. Arguing that these schools and churches have been built at great sacrifice, are presently viable, and meet all other criteria set by the Archdiocesan Officials themselves, they asserted that the move was arbitrary, undemocratic, and in violation of the rights of the people of the parishes. They denounced the closing as a move designed to end the integration of the neighborhood by driving the Poles out. Reportedly, in at least one case it was clearly an attempt by Chancery bureaucrats together with a small number of Blacks in the Vicarate to seize the Polish parish. The community's pressure and its willingness to continue to bear the heavy costs caused the Chancery to rescind the order in April in two of the three cases.

Poles are presently demanding from the Archdiocese of Detroit the right to educate priests at Saints Cyril and Methodius Seminary at Orchard Lake, the reestablishment of Polish language and cultural traditions in diocesan schools, establishment of a provicarate for Polish Laity (evidently one was offered unofficially to the Blacks who constitute only a tiny minority of Catholics in Detroit), and a Bishop of Polish ancestry who would be representative of the Polish-American community. The Poles of Detroit have not been so militant since they drove Bishop Borgess from his residence almost ninety years ago.

It is difficult to predict what lasting effects the cultural revival and the new mood of militance will have. The leadership for this grass roots movement has come from a variety of individuals and some of the older community organizations; most notably the Polish-American Congress. However, not all of the community intelligentsia has identified with the new movement. The cultural revival, taking place in a community unified for the moment by external threat, has raised implicitly the question of what it means to be a Pole in America. The struggle to build a community, the fight for Polish independence, the hunger and poverty of the Depression, World War II, and the Cold War battle against Communism served to keep that question from being clearly posed. The intelligentsia, with a few exceptions, has not attempted to explore the meaning of the American experience nor to interpret it for the people. Perhaps the task of preserving the native heritage for a large group of poor and unschooled immigrants together with its deep involvement in the monumental struggles of Poland in this century, prevented it from focusing on any other goals.

The revival in the Polish community must come to grips with the problem of defining the relationship of the Polish-American to Poland now that the Cold War thaw, with all of its profound psychological consequences, is finally having an impact. The future of the community and its place in American life demand something beyond the preservation of past tradition and continued importations from abroad, however emotionally satisfying it may be to draw further on the intellectual and cultural capital of Poland. The first real beginnings of what could be a rich and genuine Polish-American culture coming out of a union of old Polish tradition and modern creativity with American culture, appear to be emerging in a number of areas of the United States, among them Detroit. If Polish-American culture is to become something other than the partial adaptation of a deteriorating East European village culture to an American working class life style (as opposed to the high Polish culture of the intelligentsia) the Poles in America must come to grips with their history over the last one hundred years. Until the American experience is chronicled, interpreted and understood in terms of both Polish and American history a creative fusion of Polish and American Culture will only remain a promise. This is the task for the seventies.

The most pressing problem that has to be faced in the 1970's is that of Black–Polish relations. To a large extent these relations are determined by forces that are at the moment beyond the control of both communities. As automation squeezes off access to upward mobility, the present arrangement and distribution of rewards in society are forcing both groups to compete for an increasingly smaller piece of the pie. It is also in the interest of other groups higher up the social ladder to keep the two peoples divided so as to provide themselves with pawns in the game of urban politics. These pawns can be controlled and manipulated to advantage by inducing them to compete for "official" acknowledgement and support. This is also true of Church politics. There are cases wherein "English" parishes have had their potential Black members reassigned to Polish parishes, thus killing two birds with one stone. In spite of the obstacles, an alliance between the Negro and the Polish communities is not impossible. It must be based on simple self-interest in the many areas which are of vital concern to both groups, housing, wages, urban blight and pollution, social security, reasonably priced medical care, a draft that draws their sons in far greater numbers than the sons of the well-to-do, and social justice in general. The many legitimate conflicts of interest between Poles and Negroes could be defused and put into perspective if each understood better the experiences and aspirations of the other. Tolerance, basic civility, and mutual respect should be the goals, leaving the love and guilt to the suburban liberals. An interesting experiment in this direction is Father Daniel Bogusz's Black–Polish Alliance. The Alliance has no political purpose at the moment and Father Bogusz disclaims any for the future. Its sole purpose is to promote better group and inter-personal relations between Poles and Blacks in the city. It is doubtful that a group with such limited purposes can provide the basis for any real alliance with the aim of political and social action but it may be an important first step.

The Energy Crisis and Detroit

This document deals with the auto industry's response to the energy crisis and high gasoline costs. Although Detroit automotive wizard Charles Kettering warned a half century ago of the dangers of designing overweight, gas-guzzling cars, "Boss Ket" was ignored until recently. The Arab oil embargo of 1973 prodded the auto industry into trying to reconcile high-volume car production with low energy consumption, and it is upon a satisfactory resolution of these conflicting pressures that Detroit's future economic health rests. The article was written by Agis Salpukas and is from The New York Times (2 February 1975), © 1975 by The New York Times Company. Reprinted by permission.

DETROIT—In the fall of 1925, Charles Kettering, one of the great pioneering engineers of the auto industry, delivered a prophetic paper to a meeting of the American Chemical Society in New York City. The paper was called "Motor Design and Fuel Economy."

Mr. Kettering's major points: petroleum is a finite resource; supplies could some day run short, posing a catastrophe for the auto industry. The catastrophe could be averted "if motor car fuel economy can be materially increased."

Mr. Kettering then outlined the design of a hypothetical car which would yield maximum gas mileage. It would be small, light, streamlined. It would have a high-compression engine, an ignition system whose spark would always be properly adjusted for speed and load, a four-speed transmission with a system providing for the disengagement of all other gears at fast speed except the high gear, which would only be engaged when the car was riding on a level road. All these innovations were possible in 1925.

The auto industry has waited some five decades to implement Mr. Kettering's prophetic conception. Why did it take so long?

Mr. Kettering even had the answer for that back in 1925. While his hypothetical car would have good gas mileage, he said that the public probably would not buy it. It would not produce fast acceleration in high gear. It would not climb hills well. It would lack "that reserve power so much desired by the motoring public."

For the next 50 years, American auto makers paid little attention to the matter of fuel economy. Gas was cheap, supplies steady, and new oil fields were being discovered virtually every year. The efficiency of all cars on the road slipped from an average of 15.3 miles a gallon in 1940 to 13.75 miles a gallon in 1975.

This was due to a number of meshing priorities—governmental, corporate and private. The Federal highway system was under construction. The buying public wanted bigger cars, more power, higher speed, more room and comfort, and a smooth ride. Detroit wanted bigger sales and larger profits.

The consumption of petroleum products by cars in America has tripled since 1950. Two major reasons have been the enormous growth in the number of cars on American roads, and the increase in the number of miles driven.

How Many, and How Far

In 1950, Americans owned some 40 million cars. Today, there are 105 million, or about 1.4 cars per family. In the same period, the number of total miles driven went up by 170 per cent. It is clear that the factor of efficiency in cutting national fuel consumption does not stand in isolation. It is also linked to the number of cars Americans continue to buy, and how far they will drive them.

There is another factor as well—the imposition by government of antipollution and safety standards. The necessary accessories, including auto-emission devices, have added more weight and further reduced gas-burning efficiency.

By way of example, one can see the effect of all this on a Ford Galaxie 500. In 1965, the Galaxie had a small engine, and weighed 3,543 pounds. It averaged 15 miles per gallon. But by 1973, the same car weighed 4,300 pounds, and had acquired a bigger, heavier engine to propel the extra weight, including such options as air conditioning. In eight years, it had gained 757 pounds, about 300 of which were due to new equipment installed to meet Federal standards. The Galaxie's fuel-burning efficiency dropped 21 per cent to 11.8 miles per gallon.

The same trend was true of most cars. One fact, however, helped keep the over-all national consumption of fuel somewhat in hand—the trend to smaller cars. The fuel economy of the compacts helped offset the reduced efficiency of the larger cars.

The Arab oil boycott tipped the balance, and President Ford's intention of reducing American dependence on foreign oil has now put the auto industry on notice. It has agreed to improve fuel economy by 40 per cent within five years. Each company has said that it probably can meet the President's goal, provided that Congress agrees to a five-year moratorium in imposing tighter air pollution and safety standards.

To get there, the industry will not have to develop any basic new technology. It will do what could have been done in Mr. Kettering's day. Here are the basic steps:

WEIGHT REDUCTION. General Motors, for example, plans to reduce the weight of its cars by an average of 500 to 1000 pounds by 1978.

The changes are relatively simple. Most cars will be reduced in body size so that future standard models will be roughly the size of today's intermediates. The body will be designed so that it rides closer to the chassis, saving space and material.

The bodies will also be streamlined, using such configurations as sloping hoods to cut down on air resistance at high speeds, and thus save fuel. Two examples currently on the road are the Saab and the Volkswagen Beetle. Since the cars will also weigh less, smaller engines can be used, further reducing weight. Also, smaller engines burn gasoline more efficiently.

AXLE RATIOS. They will be reduced, which means that less energy will be needed to keep the car moving, particularly at cruising speeds of 50 to 60 miles an hour. But this will also mean reduced acceleration.

TRANSMISSIONS. They will be tightened up. Instead of changing smoothly from gear to gear, as in the past, future automatic transmissions will produce a slight jerk as they shift. But they will also deliver better fuel economy because they will transfer power more efficiently from engine to wheels.

A recent study by the Department of Transportation and the

Environmental Protection Agency, on which the President based his five-year efficiency goal, concluded that these technological changes, including installation of smaller engines, would produce a 43 per cent improvement in auto efficiency.

An even more dramatic improvement in overall national fuel consumption would be achieved if the auto-buying public continues to switch to smaller cars at the rate of the past five years.

This is the present mix of models on the road: large cars, 27 per cent; intermediate size, 45 per cent; small size, 28 per cent. Based on current projections, the mix by 1980 would be: large cars, 10 per cent; intermediate size, 50 per cent; small size, 40 per cent.

Maintaining Standards

No major shifts away from conventional engines to diesels, Wankels, or the stratified charge engine are anticipated before 1980, although some manufacturers may try them out in small numbers in the American market to test consumer reaction before then.

Can the auto makers earn enough from smaller, more efficient cars to stay in business? The answer is yes. During the rapid shift to smaller cars brought about by the energy crisis, the four American auto makers raised prices on the compacts by an average of 15 per cent, in order to preserve their profitability, while raising big-car prices by only about 10 per cent.

Though the industry will reduce the size of its larger cars in the coming years, it is not expected to reduce current prices. Detroit will, in effect, deliver less car for roughly the same amount of money.

Reaching the goal of a 40 per cent increase in auto efficiency in the next five years, while not a matter of new technology, is one of consumer adjustments to the new national priorities.

As Ernest R. Starkman, General Motors' Vice President for Environmental Affairs, put it at a recent scientific meeting: "We hope the American public will drive the car that goes from zero to 60 in 18 seconds rather than 12 seconds, because that's where we are going."

APPENDIX

TABLES

POPULATION OF DETROIT

Year	Size (sq. miles)	City Population	Percent Population Change	SMSA [1] Population	Urban Population Rank
1830	2.56	2,222			53
1850	5.85	21,019	845.9		23
1860	12.75	45,619	117.		18
1870	12.75	79,577	74.4		17
1880	16.09	116,340	46.1		17
1890	22.19	205,876	76.9		14
1900	28.35	285,704	38.7		13
1910	40.79	465,766	63.		9
1920	79.62	993,675	113.3		4
1930	139.6	1,568,662	57.8		4
1940	139.6	1,623,452	3.5	2,377,329	4
1950	139.6	1,849,568	13.9	3,016,197	5
1960	139.6	1,670,144	−10.2	3,764,131	5
1970	139.6	1,511,482	− 9.5	4,199,923	5

SOURCE: U.S. Bureau of the Census.

1. Standard Metropolitan Statistical Area.

PRINCIPAL FOREIGN-BORN POPULATION OF DETROIT

Country of Origin	1850	1880	1910	1920	1940	1960 ᵃ	1970
United Kingdom							33,033
England	1,245	4,200	9,202	17,195	21,049	23,479	
Scotland	474	1,783	3,320	6,933	17,061	18,132	
Poland		1,771	35,745 ᵇ	56,624	52,235	49,993	33,705
Germany	2,851	23,769	30,908	30,238	23,785	25,942	19,968
Ireland	3,289	6,775	5,584	7,004	6,791	6,626	3,301
Canada		10,754	42,814	59,702	74,137	94,027	67,766
French			4,166	3,678			
Russia		77	6,842	29,931	20,252	19,435	13,330
Italy	4	127	5,724	16,205	26,277	30,794	27,048
Hungary		64	5,935	13,564	11,382	10,790	6,784
Yugoslavia				3,702	6,278	8,570	8,457
Austria	7	557	3,984	10,674	7,992	6,725	5,245
Mexico						3,565	4,031
Belgium		240	2,237	6,219	6,890	6,840	
Total foreign-born in Detroit ᶜ	9,927	45,645	157,532	290,884	320,664	364,575	294,369
Percentage of Detroit population foreign-born	47.2	39.2	33.8	29.08	19.75	21.8	19.47

SOURCE: U.S. Bureau of the Census.

ᵃ All 1960 figures are for foreign-born in the Detroit Standard Metropolitan Statistical Area.

ᵇ Persons reported in 1910 as having Polish mother tongue but born in Austria, Germany, or Russia have been deducted from the respective countries and combined with Polish-born.

NEGRO POPULATION OF DETROIT

Year	Size (sq. miles)	Total Population	Negro Population	Percent Negro
1830	2.56	2,222	126	NA
1850	5.85	21,019	587	2.9
1860	12.75	45,619	1,402	3.1
1870	12.75	79,577	2,235	2.8
1880	16.09	116,340	2,921	2.4
1890	22.19	205,876	3,431	1.7
1900	28.35	285,704	4,111	1.4
1910	40.79	465,766	5,741	1.2
1920	79.62	993,675	40,838	4.1
1930	139.6	1,568,662	120,066	7.7
1940	139.6	1,623,452	149,119	9.2
1950	139.6	1,849,568	300,506	16.2
1960	139.6	1,670,144	482,229	28.9
1970	139.6	1,511,482	660,428	44.5

SOURCES: U.S. Census Bureau; Urban League, *Profile of the Detroit Negro 1959–67;* D. Katzman, *Before the Ghetto* (Urbana, Ill., 1973).

AGE AND SEX DISTRIBUTION OF DETROIT AND DETROIT SMSA

	1870 (City)		1920 (City)		1970 (SMSA)	
Total population	79,603	100	993,678	100	4,199,931	100
Male	39,437	49.5	540,248	54.5	2,047,548	48.8
Female	40,166	50.4	453,430	45.6	2,152,383	51.2
Age						
Under 5	9,069	11.4	134,385	11.3	378,586	9
5 to 19	28,711	36	336,564	33.8	1,285,811	30.6
20 to 64	39,038[a]	49	519,432	52.2	2,195,131	52.2
65 and over	2,785[a]	3.5	24,708	2.5	340,369	8.1

SOURCE: U.S. Census Bureau.

[a] The 1870 census age intervals are 20 to 59, and 60 and over.

INDEX OF RESIDENTIAL SEGREGATION FOR
A SELECTED LIST OF LARGEST U.S. CITIES, 1940–70

City	"How Many Non-Whites Would Have to Move?" [1]			
	1940 %	1950 %	1960 %	1970 %
Baltimore	90.1	91.3	89.6	88.3
Boston	86.3	86.5	83.9	79.9
Chicago	95.0	92.1	92.6	88.8
Cleveland	92.0	91.5	91.3	89.0
Detroit	89.9	88.8	84.5	80.9
Houston	84.5	91.5	93.7	90.0
Los Angeles	84.2	84.6	81.8	78.6
New York	86.8	87.3	79.3	73.0
Philadelphia	88.0	89.0	87.1	83.2
Pittsburgh	82.0	84.0	84.6	83.9
St. Louis	92.6	92.9	90.5	89.3
San Francisco	82.9	79.8	69.3	55.5

SOURCE: Karl E. and Alma F. Taeuber, *Negroes in Cities* (New York, 1969); and for 1970 see Annemette Sorensen, Karl E. Taeuber, and Leslie J. Hollingsworth, Jr., *Institute for Research on Poverty Discussion Papers: Studies in Racial Segregation,* no. 1 (Madison, Wis., 1974).

1. "How Many *Non-Whites* Would Have to Move?" shows the percentage of non-white households that would have to move in order to achieve a random distribution of whites and non-whites throughout the city.--ED.

HOUSING IN DETROIT

	1940	Percent	1950	Percent	1960	Percent	1970	Percent
Total dwellings	441,454		522,430		553,198		529,185	
Total occupied	425,547	100	512,414	100	514,846	100	497,753	100
Owner occupied	226,949	37.8	276,313	53.9	299,507	58.2	298,624	60
Tenant occupied	258,614	58.6	236,101	46.1	215,339	41.8	199,129	40
Persons per room,								
1.01 or more	15,296ᵃ	3.6	51,787	10.1	45,126	8.8	36,542	7.5
Needing major repairs								
or no private bath	61,592	14.9	30,152	5.8	15,050ᵇ	2.7	14,547ᵇ	2.4

SOURCE: U.S. Census Bureau, Census of Housing.

ᵃ 1.51 or more per room.
ᵇ Lacking some or all plumbing facilities.

DETROIT METROPOLITAN AREA (WAYNE COUNTY) VOTE BY PARTY AND PARTY PLURALITY

Year	President	Governor	Year	President	Governor
1854		D 527	1916	R 9,121	R 27,438
1856	D 527	D 881	1918		R 8,647
1858		D 1,002	1920	R 168,709	R 155,442
1860	R 624	R 353	1922		R 53,283
1862		D 1,567	1924	R 244,836	R 263,908
1864	D 724	D 1,739	1926		R 11,323
1866		D 1,245	1928	R 265,852	R 105,194
1868	D 1,067	D 1,020	1930		D 19,614
1870		D 630	1932	D 98,008	D 132,802
1872	R 2,897	R 3,531	1934		D 25,588
1874		D 980	1936	D 213,323	D 119,427
1876	D 2,496	D 3,328	1938		D 92,127
1878		D 630	1940	D 175,029	D 217,785
1880	R 1,093	D 3,299	1942		D 89,878
1882		*F 493	1944	D 238,400	D 138,120
1884	D 3,615	F 3,685	1946		R 44,482
1886		F 2,657	1948	D 167,881	D 237,027
1888	D 4,660	F 9,751	1950		D 167,524
1890		D 5,837	1952	D 165,865	D 277,244
1892	D 1,219	D 2,819	1954		D 303,014
1894		R 8,624	1956	D 182,835	D 382,527
1896	R 10,169	R 19,107	1958		D 280,811
1898		R 8,416	1960	D 378,842	D 332,655
1900	R 10,334	R 180	1962		D 216,682
1902		D 10,633	1964	D 570,773	D 103,579
1904	R 28,845	D 6,171	1966		D 10,993
1906		R 9,961	1968	D 383,591	
1908	R 25,452	R 4,742	1970		D 103,038
1910		R 6,511	1972	D 79,036	
1912	P 8,081	D 4,832	1974		D 114,567
1914		D 22,799			

SOURCE: *Michigan Manuals;* J. P. White, *Michigan Votes, 1928–1956.*

* F designates fusion of Democrats with Greenbacks, Labor, and other groups.

MANUFACTURING IN DETROIT AND DETROIT SMSA, 1859–1970

Year	No. of Estab- lishments	No. of Wage Earners	Total Wages	Value Added by Manufacturing
1859	368	3,710	$ 1,080,095	$ 2,755,308
1879		16,110	6,306,000	
1889		38,281	18,911,000	
1904	1,363	48,879	22,786,576	61,966,689
1909	2,036	81,011	43,007,000	122,721,000
1919	2,176	167,016	245,434,000	578,607,000
1921	1,684	95,376	150,619,761	315,367,137
1923	1,686	170,960	282,672,478	
1929	2,418	221,588	386,692,131	942,693,593
1933	1,732	126,557	134,994,653	331,776,367
1937	2,078	235,341	380,167,464	944,753,534
			(millions)	(millions)
1939	2,684	372,900	655.1	1,087.6
1947	4,761	557,200	1,852.3	2,912.7
1954	6,159	589,900	3,113.8	4,713.2
1958	6,604	467,400	2,972.1	4,312.4
1963	7,023	493,900	3,847.2	6,690.4
1970	NA	537,200	5,658.3	8,673.1

SOURCE: U.S. Census Bureau, Survey of Manufactures.

NOTE: Figures from 1879 through 1937 apply to the city of Detroit, and from 1939 through 1970 to Detroit SMSA; 1859 applies to Detroit and Wayne County.

PRINCIPAL INDUSTRIES OF DETROIT, 1860

	Value Products
Copper Smelting	$1,500,000
Lumber Sawed	619,049
Machinery—Steam Engines, etc.	608,478
Iron—Bar and Railroad	585,000
Leather	380,225
Flour and Meal	313,837
Liquors, Malt	262,163
Iron, Pig	145,000
Furs	143,000
Soaps and Candles	137,915
Printing—Newspaper and Job	136,400
Boots and Shoes	131,852
Sash, Doors, and Blinds	126,929
Bread and Crackers	99,200

PRINCIPAL INDUSTRIES OF DETROIT, 1904

	Value Products
Foundry and Machine Shop Products	$8,306,184
Druggist Preparations	8,305,935
Stoves and Furnaces	5,564,609
Motor Vehicles	5,382,212
Meat Packing—Wholesale	4,748,343
Tobacco—Cigars and Cigarettes	3,933,225
Tobacco—Chewing and Smoking	3,793,591
Malt Liquors	3,271,962
Varnishes	3,078,339
Flour and Grist Mill Products	3,034,388
Clothing—Men's	2,957,095
Bread and Other Bakery Products	2,932,462
Brass Castings, etc.	2,721,613
Furniture	2,624,404
Printing and Publishing—Newspaper and Periodical	2,537,068
Iron and Steel, etc.	2,362,114

SOURCE: U.S. Census of Manufactures.

NOTE: The 1860 table includes Wayne county and the 1939 table is for the Detroit Industrial Area which includes Wayne, Oakland, and Washtenaw counties.

PRINCIPAL INDUSTRIES OF DETROIT, 1939

	Value of Products
Motor Vehicles, Parts, Accessories	$1,658,794,884
Meat Packing, Wholesale	41,409,199
Bread and Bakery Products	35,968,892
Machine Tool Accessories	34,660,133
Paints and Varnishes	27,934,823
Machine Shop Products (n.e.c.) [1]	26,360,511
Newspapers—Printing and Publishing	23,555,670
Malt Liquors	20,088,244
Oven Coke and By-products	18,964,326
Wirework (n.e.c.)	18,080,368
Steel Works and Rolling Mills [2]	99,939,525
Chemicals (n.e.c.) [2]	59,518,193
Refrigerators, Air Conditioning [2]	51,805,725
Drugs and Medicines [2]	49,953,160
Petroleum Refining [2]	37,226,330

SOURCES: U.S. Census of Manufactures.

NOTE: Detroit industrial area included Wayne, Oakland, and Washtenaw counties.

1. N.e.c.—not elsewhere classified.
2. For Michigan. Data on these important local industries not available for Detroit area.

EMPLOYMENT BY INDUSTRY IN 1940 IN SELECTED CITIES

City	Manufacturing	Trade	Service [1]	Public Utilities	Construction	Government	Finance, Insurance, and Real Estate	Miscellaneous [2]
Detroit	47.2%	18.7%	15.5%	5.8%	3.9%	3.1%	3.7%	2.1%
Cleveland	40.5	20.6	17.5	8.2	4.0	3.4	3.4	2.3
Milwaukee	38.5	21.4	17.4	8.1	4.2	3.9	4.2	2.3
Philadelphia	35.3	21.5	19.2	7.3	4.8	4.4	4.4	3.4
Buffalo	34.7	21.5	18.9	10.7	3.6	4.2	3.4	3.0
Chicago	34.1	23.0	17.8	10.0	3.9	3.5	5.4	2.3
St. Louis	33.1	22.5	20.2	9.2	4.3	3.5	4.7	2.5
Baltimore	31.6	20.3	20.6	10.0	4.8	5.1	4.4	3.2
Pittsburgh	26.9	24.2	21.9	9.7	5.1	4.5	4.9	2.8
New York	26.3	21.9	21.7	8.8	4.6	4.5	7.9	4.3
Boston	22.0	25.3	23.6	9.2	4.5	6.3	5.4	3.7
Los Angeles	18.2	25.4	23.5	7.6	5.7	4.5	6.4	8.7
Houston	18.6	24.0	26.9	11.5	6.8	2.2	4.8	5.2
San Francisco	16.6	25.3	22.3	11.4	5.1	7.1	7.8	4.4
Washington	7.2	17.0	26.5	6.9	6.4	29.0	4.7	2.3
Urban U.S.	29.2%	21.4%	21.6%	8.7%	4.8%	4.7%	4.6%	5.0%

SOURCE: U.S. Census of Manufactures.

1. Includes business and repair services, personal and professional services.
2. Includes agriculture, forestry, fishery, mining, amusement, recreation, and those industries whose employment was not reported.

EMPLOYMENT BY INDUSTRY IN 1970 IN SELECTED SMSAs

City	Total (add 000)	Manufac- turing	Wholesale and Retail Trade	Services	Transpor- tation and Public Utilities	Contract Con- struction	Finance, Insurance, and Real Estate	Govern- ment
Detroit	1,483	37.6%	19.9%	14.8%	5.3%	3.5%	4.6%	14.3%
Boston	1,291	21.5	22.7	24.9	5.9	4.0	7.3	13.7
Chicago	2,981	31.4	22.5	16.9	6.9	4.0	6.1	12.1
Cleveland	859	34.5	21.4	16.2	6.0	4.1	4.9	12.8
Houston	770	19.2	24.5	18.2	8.3	8.9	5.4	11.8
Los Angeles	2,897	28.2	22.3	18.9	6.0	3.8	5.9	14.5
New York	4,861	20.9	20.9	20.5	7.8	3.5	10.6	15.8
Philadelphia	1,796	30.5	20.5	17.7	5.8	4.8	5.7	14.8
Pittsburgh	875	31.8	20.3	18.3	6.8	4.9	4.3	12.6
St. Louis	913	30.5	21.3	16.8	7.5	4.5	5.2	13.9
San Francisco- Oakland	1,264	16.1	21.3	17.8	10.6	4.8	7.8	21.5

SOURCE: *Statistical Abstract of the U.S., 1971.*

THE BAROMETER OF DETROIT'S ECONOMIC HEALTH

Motor Vehicle Factory Sales from U.S. Plants for Selected Years

Year	Passenger Cars Number	Value (add 000)
1900	4,192	$ 4,899
1905	24,250	38,670
1910	181,000	215,340
1915	895,930	575,978
1920	1,905,560	1,809,171
1921	1,468,067	1,038,191
1925	3,735,171	2,458,370
1929	4,455,178	2,790,614
1930	2,787,456	1,644,083
1932	1,103,557	616,860
1935	3,273,874	1,707,836
1940	3,717,385	2,370,654
1946	2,148,699	1,979,781
1950	6,665,863	8,468,137
1955	7,920,186	12,452,871
1958	4,257,812	8,010,366
1960	6,674,796	12,164,234
1961	5,542,707	10,285,777
1965	9,305,561	18,380,036
1970	6,546,817	14,630,217
1973	9,657,647	26,350,000
1974	7,340,373	21,800,000
1975	6,725,680	

MAPS AND FIGURES

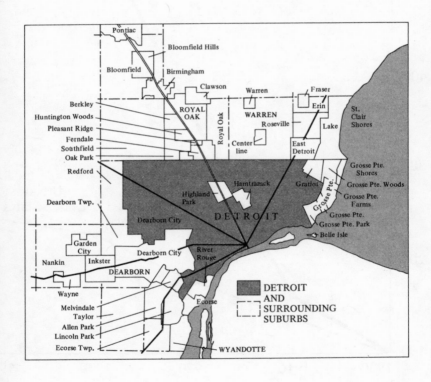

Pontiac
Bloomfield Hills
Bloomfield
Birmingham
Clawson
Warren
Fraser
Berkley
ROYAL OAK
Erin
Huntington Woods
WARREN
St. Clair Shores
Pleasant Ridge
Royal Oak
Roseville
Lake
Ferndale
Southfield
Center line
Oak Park
East Detroit
Redford
Grosse Pte. Shores
Dearborn Twp.
Hamtramck
Gratiot
Grosse Pte. Woods
Highland Park
Grosse Pte.
Grosse Pte. Farms
DETROIT
Dearborn City
Grosse Pte.
Grosse Pte. Park
Garden City
River Rouge
Belle Isle
Nankin
Inkster
Dearborn City
DEARBORN
Wayne
Ecorse
DETROIT AND SURROUNDING SUBURBS
Melvindale
Taylor
Allen Park
Lincoln Park
Ecorse Twp.
WYANDOTTE

DETROIT AND SURROUNDING SUBURBS

SOURCE: U.S. Bureau of Labor Statistics.

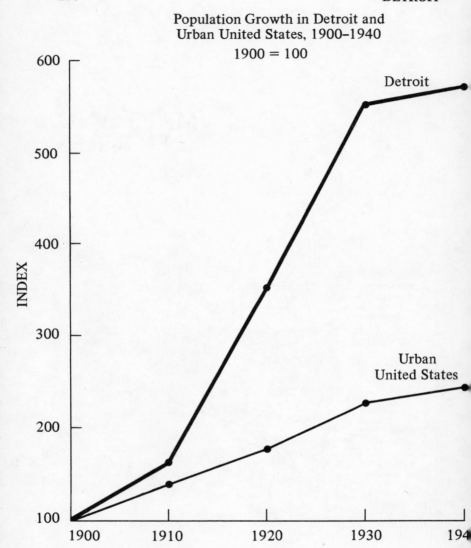

Population Growth in Detroit and
Urban United States, 1900–1940
1900 = 100

**POPULATION GROWTH IN DETROIT AND
URBAN UNITED STATES, 1900–1940**

SOURCE: United States Department of Labor Bureau of Labor Statistics.

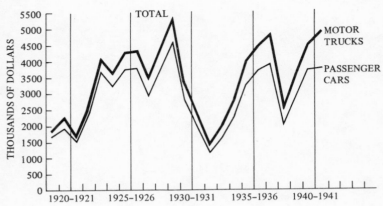

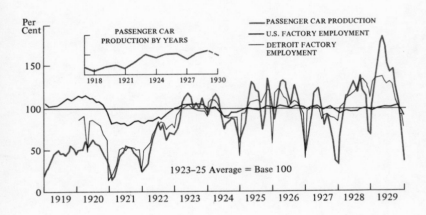

THE DETROIT BUSINESS CYCLE
MOTOR VEHICLE SALES IN THE UNITED STATES AND
DETROIT FACTORY EMPLOYMENT

NOTE: The Detroit business cycle was subjected to long-range fluctuations that lifted the city to the peaks of prosperity and then dumped it into the valley of despair, as figure 1 shows. Even the short-range, year-long employment picture was one of violent ups and downs due to model change-overs, which Figure 2 illustrates.

INDEX

ABOUT THE EDITOR

Melvin G. Holli is a member of the history faculty at the University of Illinois at Chicago Circle. He received his B.A. at Northern Michigan University, Marquette, and both his M.A. and his Ph.D. at the University of Michigan, Ann Arbor.